WHEATON PUBLIC LIBRARY

3 5143 00749234 8

W9-AZH-232

355.009 BAT

Battlefield : decisive
conflicts in history

WITHDRAWN

JUN   2008

Wheaton Public Library

225 N. Cross

Wheaton, Illinois 60187

(630) 668-1374

Battlefield

Battlefield

DECISIVE CONFLICTS IN HISTORY

Edited by Richard Holmes
and Martin Marix Evans

OXFORD

UNIVERSITY PRESS

OXFORD
UNIVERSITY PRESS

Great Clarendon Street, Oxford OX2 6DP

Oxford University Press is a department of the University of Oxford.
It furthers the University's objective of excellence in research, scholarship,
and education by publishing worldwide in

Oxford New York

Auckland Cape Town Dar es Salaam Hong Kong Karachi
Kuala Lumpur Madrid Melbourne Mexico City Nairobi
New Delhi Shanghai Taipei Toronto

With offices in

Argentina Austria Brazil Chile Czech Republic France Greece
Guatemala Hungary Italy Japan Poland Portugal Singapore
South Korea Switzerland Thailand Turkey Ukraine Vietnam

Oxford is a registered trade mark of Oxford University Press
in the UK and in certain other countries

Published in the United States
by Oxford University Press Inc., New York

© Oxford University Press 2006

The moral rights of the authors have been asserted
Database right Oxford University Press (maker)

First published 2006

All rights reserved. No part of this publication may be reproduced,
stored in a retrieval system, or transmitted, in any form or by any means,
without the prior permission in writing of Oxford University Press,
or as expressly permitted by law, or under terms agreed with the appropriate
reprographics rights organization. Enquiries concerning reproduction
outside the scope of the above should be sent to the Rights Department,
Oxford University Press, at the address above

You must not circulate this book in any other binding or cover
and you must impose the same condition on any acquirer

British Library Cataloguing in Publication Data
Data available

Library of Congress Cataloging in Publication Data
Data available

Typeset by Alliance Interactive Technology
Printed in Great Britain
on acid-free paper by
Biddles Ltd
King's Lynn

ISBN 0-19-280653-X   978-0-19-280653-6

3 5 7 9 10 8 6 4 2

Contents

Preface

This book originated in *The Oxford Companion to Military History*, of which I was general editor. With the help of Martin Marix Evans, who bore the considerable burden of the process, I captured the battle entries from the *Companion*, revised them where required to reflect recent scholarship (there have, for instance, been two good books on Agincourt alone in the past eighteen months, and the Zulu War of 1879 generates such a spate of new books that it is hard to keep abreast of them) and to remove slips which had infiltrated in their exasperating way into the original version. I have also tweaked the balance inherited from the *Companion*, whose main emphasis was with events in Europe and North America in the last three centuries. For instance, as Hew Strachan has recently emphasized, the battle of Sarikamish, where the Russians defeated the Turks in a bitter and wide-ranging action in the winter of 1914/15, had enormous strategic repercussions. I was wrong not to ensure that it appeared in the *Companion* and have remedied the omission here.

Although I said a good deal about the American Civil War, I said too little about the Americas more generally, and I am not sure that I did justice to the 'storm from the east', those successive waves of horse-using peoples from the steppe whose impact, like that of a pile-driver striking earth, sent shock-waves rippling out in many directions. There are also more minor adjustments. My Huguenot forebears would be gratified to see the major battles of the French Wars of Religion included, and the 1814 battle of Leipzig now enjoys the same word-space as the 1812 battle of Borodino.

I was, however, anxious not to make this book either too inclusive or too exclusive: I did not want to produce another dictionary of battles on the one hand or a summary of a dozen decisive clashes on the other. Winston Churchill called battles 'punctuation marks in history', and they are usually a great deal more than specifically military events. They reflect political, social, and economic developments, and it is impossible to separate them from the technology that created the weapons used in them, the tactics employed by the men who fought them, or the strategic framework into which they fitted. The dictionary of battles may produce a ready reference for professional historians or military enthusiasts, but it is usually contextually weak, and lumps together the battles of Caporetto, Capua, and Carberry Hill by accident of alphabetical propinquity.

I am also suspicious of attempts to isolate a limited number of decisive battles and to write only about them. Some battles were obviously decisive. Hanoverian victory at Culloden in 1746 dashed hopes of a Stuart restoration; allied triumph at Waterloo in 1815 wrote finis to the Napoleonic empire; and after Kursk in 1943 there was to be no stopping the Red Army. In other cases the decision was only temporary. Austerlitz in 1805 bought Napoleon less than a decade's supremacy; the stunning achievements of blitzkrieg in 1939–41 did not win World War II for the Germans, and more recently there is room to doubt whether the coalition's defeat of the Iraqi armed forces and its capture of Baghdad were decisive in the way that victorious generals hoped.

Yet often a battle's long-term consequences were dependent on its strategic context. We cannot logically review the Somme in 1916 without also considering Verdun, for the German offensive there forced the British to attack on the Somme sooner than they might have wished. And although the Somme was not immediately decisive, its battlefield was, as one German officer admitted 'the muddy grave of the German field army', and it saw the British army take the crucial steps which were to make it an effective mass army for the first time in its history. Demographic or social historians might wish to extend the battle's impact well beyond World War I, and indeed, as Gary Sheffield has observed, the battle is 'indelibly branded on the British psyche as a disaster' in a way which, perhaps, tells us as much about national perceptions as it does about history.

So, although this is a book whose prime concern is with events on the battlefield, I have tried to put battles into this all-important context, first by grouping them into chapters, sometimes regional and sometimes chronological, and then by prefacing each chapter with an introduction which sets out the main issues (battles that fall outside these groupings are included at an appropriate point and are separated off by narrow borders). I make no attempt to be comprehensive, and there will be times when my judgement on an action's worthiness for inclusion, or on battles' relative importance, may not accord with a reader's. When I compiled the original *Companion* I expressed my real gratitude to the many scholars whose work had made it possible. The present book is no less dependent on their labours, and I hope that they will agree that my application of the editorial pen (and occasional wielding of the editorial scissors) has done them no injustice.

RICHARD HOLMES

Ropley
February 2006

1 The Ancient World

The military history of the ancient world covers a huge span, from the battle of Megiddo (c.1476 BC), the first about which we can write with even a degree of confidence, to the swamping of Roman infantry by mounted warriors at Adrianople in AD 378. It is scarcely less wide in its geographical spread, from the sands of Egypt to the forests of Germany, and from Spain to north India. Within this long timescale and against this varied backdrop empires waxed and waned, great cities rose and fell, and powerful pulses impelled whole peoples into conflict.

There are recognizable currents within this broad and complex torrent. The first is that the essential ingredients of tactics, the art of fighting battles and engagements, became established very early on. Even before men used lethal tools to kill one another, they employed both weapons designed for direct impact, and the more distant effect of projectiles, in the chase. Animals were killed at close quarters with clubs and stabbing-spears, or brought down by the arrow, slingshot, or throwing-spear. Until our own times tactics have centred upon this relationship between what later generations would call shock and fire. In 2004 in Iraq (its context doubly poignant, for this was once Mesopotamia) some British soldiers fought with bayonet and rifle butt, a grim illustration of the fact that even in an age when fire seems wholly dominant, shock still raises its ancient head.

It is difficult to be sure precisely when the weapons and techniques of the hunt were used in raids and ambushes against other humans, but the process was certainly under way by 8000 BC. There were to be significant technical improvements across the age, foreshadowing the intimate relationship between weapons and tactics throughout history. Around 2000 BC stone weapons, remarkably sharp, but often fragile and always the result of a long and painstaking production process, were being replaced by bronze. Although some small items, including spear-tips, were fashioned from iron recovered from meteorites as early as 4000 BC, it was not until 1200 BC that iron was widely used in the Middle East, and it took some time to replace bronze. Tactics always embodied an unstable relationship between fire and shock, and also evolved to reflect changes in technology. This was to become an enduring feature of military history, and it still presents thinkers and practitioners alike with the most intractable of problems.

It is tempting to regard the whole age as part of what the military theorist Major General J. F. C. Fuller was to call 'the infantry cycle'. The *Cambridge Illustrated History of Warfare* takes a similar line, describing it as 'the age of massed infantry'. It is true that some of the most remarkable warriors of the period were infantrymen, and the Greek hoplite, the Macedonian phalangist, the Roman legionary have all left enduring marks on history, not least because many early armies identified structures—eight to ten men in primary groups, a hundred in the next group up, and so on—which strike a chord with man's basic relationships, and have been regularly imitated ever since. But it is scarcely less true that, very early on, warfare was a matter of the combination of the various combat arms, and over-reliance on a particular technique (or on its practitioners) eventually led to disaster.

Infantry did indeed develop to a remarkable degree. Intensive arable agriculture in Egypt and Mesopotamia, itself the product of improving agronomic techniques, saw the rise of cities like Babylon, Lagash, Sumer, and Ur. The bulk of the soldiers raised by these states fought on foot: in the second millennium BC an Assyrian force was said to number 100,000 men, of whom 1,500 were cavalry and 20,000 archers. Foot soldiers of specific types, like spearmen, archers, or slingers, were armed and equipped alike, and went into battle in massed formations, subject to a recognizable hierarchy and disciplinary code. Without these it was impossible for men to use their weapons effectively in tightly packed phalanxes in which mishandled blades or points might as easily hurt friend as foe, and through which the contagion of panic or disorder might so easily spread.

The Greek city states, which coalesced in the eighth and seventh centuries BC, represented a very different form of social organization from the monarchical regimes which had characterized Egypt and Mesopotamia. Efficient, family-run farms generated food surpluses, and there was neither need nor appetite for state bureaucracies or rigid central control. The hoplite (named for his shield, the *hoplon*), the bronze-clad foot soldier of classical Greece, was voter, farmer, and warrior too, generally reluctant to embark upon risky or expansionist military ventures, but both obliged and prepared to fight shoulder to shoulder with his fellow citizens in the sweaty, stamping mass of the phalanx, where a single clash usually decided the campaign. The hoplite could be a formidable opponent, as Plutarch's description of the Spartan phalanx suggests: 'It was a sight at once awesome and terrifying, as they marched in step to the pipe, leaving no gap in their line of battle and cheerfully advancing into danger.'

The Macedonian phalanx came later. It relied on deep ranks of sturdy peasant infantrymen, less heavily armoured than the hoplite, and plying spears up to 4 m (13 feet) long, and was not simply a formidable tactical tool. In the hands of monarchs bent on conquest, it was an imperial instrument too, and formed the basis for the extraordinary achievements of Alexander the Great. Lastly, the Roman legion was different yet again. At the peak of its development it combined both the missile effect of the javelin (*pilum*) and the shock of an armoured soldier charging in to close quarters to ply his short sword. The Greek or Macedonian phalanx had always required flat, open ground for successful deployment, and formations of heavy infantry were traditionally vulnerable to light, elusive, missile-armed skirmishers unless their own light troops could keep them at bay. And the pike, formidable though it was, brought vulnerabilities of its own. When legion met phalanx the result was bloody murder, for once Roman swordsmen had got inside the reach of the pike as the battles Cynoscephalae and Pydna showed.

Various sorts of light troops developed alongside heavy infantry. Often these were provided by subject or allied peoples, or by citizens too poor to afford full armour, and their military utility and social status alike were often seen in an unflattering light. Some Greek city states brought with them to the battlefield what Victor Davis Hanson has called 'the unarmoured poor', and native-born peltasts (who carried a lighter shield than the bronze *hoplon*) were increasingly supplemented by mercenaries, like Thracian peltasts who could hurl missiles into the enemy phalanx and scamper off before retribution reached them. The Macedonians used Agrianian and Thracian javelin men as well as Cretan archers, and the Romans too found light infantry, archers, and slingers from amongst their subject peoples.

Yet if the period witnessed the dominance of infantry, it also saw the development of chariots, cavalry, engineers, and even artillery, so that (with the obvious exception of air power) all the thematic ingredients of a modern combined arms battle were present long before the age of Alexander. When horses were first broken to human service, they were used to pull chariots, which were developed in Bronze Age cultures across and beyond the area. The *Standard of Ur* (*c*.2500 BC) shows primitive four-wheeled vehicles drawn by four wild asses and carrying spearmen. From perhaps 1700 BC lighter two-wheeled chariots with a pair of horses enabled the Hyksos to overrun Egypt, and the chariot soon became a characteristic weapon of war across the Middle East. The cost of chariots and their horses, and the skills required not simply to drive them but to use bow and spear from such an unstable platform, were such that skilled warriors who fought from chariots became a 'chariot aristocracy' distinct from the peasant infantry whose great phalanxes provided the pivots about which chariots manoeuvred.

In common with other high-cost and high-value weapons systems across history, chariots remained in use long after their real utility had passed, and Zela (47 BC) was the last time they were employed on a significant scale. By then horses able to carry a man had been bred, broken, and trained, and cavalry made their first appearance on the stage of war between the twelfth and eighth centuries BC. It was long to be axiomatic that steady infantry, drawn up on suitable ground, had little to fear from cavalry. The Greek mercenary commander and writer Xenophon mocked that 'only the weakest in strength and the least eager for glory' mounted horses, and in his experience 'no one has ever lost his life in battle from the bite or kick of a horse'. In part these comments reflected the Greek farmer's traditional resentment of mounted aristocrats and their hungry horses, for in fact the Persians already fielded very effective armoured cavalry, and Xenophon's employer, Cyrus the Younger, was killed in a cavalry engagement at Cunaxa (401 BC). The decisive blows on Alexander's battlefield were usually struck by the Companion Cavalry, led with near-suicidal courage by the king himself. An early example of what cavalry who had mastered the bow could do to even the best foot soldiers was graphically provided when the triumvir Crassus was routed at Carrhae (53 BC), where Parthian horse archers did appalling damage to legionary infantry.

It was already evident that cavalry fell into two broad types, heavy horsemen, who sought to break their opponents by shock action on the battlefield, and light horsemen, whose principal weapon was the bow. The latter came increasingly from peripatetic horse-using societies sweeping out of the steppes of central Asia, sometimes because they had been displaced by even more ferocious adversaries, for whom the horse was a quintessential part of life and not simply an instrument of war. The Huns, it was said, ate, drank, defecated, and even gave judgement from the saddle.

The collision between the storm from the east and settled folk in cities was already a major factor when the period ended, and it was to be no less marked in late antiquity and the early middle ages. The defence of settlements was scarcely less old than warfare itself, and we know that the town of Çatal Huyuk in central Turkey was fortified well before 6500 BC. During the second millennium BC the cities of Mesopotamia were protected by curtain walls, ditches, projecting towers, and elaborate gateways, and the attack and defence of fortifications was central to warfare in the region. The bas-reliefs which give us such a penetrating insight into Assyrian warfare show engineers at work undermining fortress walls, creating a cavity beneath the foundations, which was then propped up with timber, to be fired at the appropriate moment. Covered battering rams assailed gates and walls, and infantry used scaling ladders to climb ramparts.

If battles in open field were often bloody, especially if they involved a clash between enemies who were culturally dissimilar, sieges were sometimes even more lethal. Attackers might promise lenient terms for a speedy capitulation, and, conversely, a protracted defence in which the besieger lost men, resources, and time would cost the defender dear if the fortress fell. The Roman historian Tacitus, for instance, recommended the alternate use of frightfulness and clemency to break an opponent's will. In around 1100 BC the Assyrian king Tiglath-Pileser gleefully announced his destruction of Hunusa:

Their fighting men I cast down in the midst of the hills, like a gust of wind. I cut off their heads like lambs; their blood I caused to flow in the valleys and on the high places of the mountains ... That city I captured, their gods I carried away. I brought out their goods and their possessions, and I burned the city with fire. The three great walls of their city which were strongly built of burnt brick, and the whole of the city I laid waste, I destroyed, I turned into heaps and ruins and I sowed crops thereon.

On a much smaller scale, when the timber-faced rampart on the hill-fort at Hambledon Hill in Dorset was fired by its attackers it collapsed, burying many of the defenders beneath it. In the debris archaeologists found the skeleton of a man holding a small child in his arms: he had been killed by a stone-tipped arrow. And when, in AD 491, the Saxon king Ælle besieged and took Anderida, the old Roman fort at Pevensey, then held by the Britons, he killed every man, woman, and child in the place. The Romans would have called it *vastatio*.

If the Romans were adept at destruction, they were no less masters of field engineering. Marching forts of a standard pattern were thrown up when a legion halted for the night, and larger and more lavish structures were built to defend key terrain or mark out frontiers. Enemy strongholds were surrounded by lines of circumvallation: Caesar's siege of Alesia in 52 BC had two lines, one to keep the defenders in and the other to keep a relieving force out. The Romans bridged great rivers, and knitted together their empire with a network of roads, and the Persian royal road connected Susa, at the head of the Gulf, with Sardis, near the coast of Asia Minor, sweeping across 2,400 km (1,500 miles) of wild country.

The first artillery used mechanical principles. The Roman ballista was essentially a giant crossbow, and soon such weapons were given added power by the use of twisted animal sinews or human hair to hold the two arms of the bow. The Greek *lithobolos* (stone-caster) looked much the same, but instead of a large metal-topped bolt it threw stones out to perhaps 275 m (900 feet). The Roman *onager* (named after the wild ass because both had a nasty kick) was a single-arm catapult, its arm held in twisted sinew, and not long after the fifth century BC the traction artillery piece, the trebuchet, was also being used. This consisted of a long beam, mounted on a fulcrum close to one end, to which a heavy weight was attached. The long end of the beam was hauled downwards, and a stone or other suitable missile (sometimes a plague-ridden corpse) was fitted in its sling. When the long end of the beam, held downwards against the tug of the counterweight, was released, the chosen missile flew off through the air. Modern tests suggest that the only real limitation to the missile that can be hurled by a trebuchet is the weapon's size: replica weapons had little difficulty in flinging a grand piano 180 m (600 feet). Weapons like this were most useful in siege warfare, but we know that the Romans and Greeks used ballistae in open field: Alexander's Hellenistic successors were fond of little weapons called 'scorpions'.

Long before the birth of Christ all the weapons which were to characterize war until the invention of gunpowder had already been invented. The unstable balance between shock and projectile weapons was a feature of tactics, and technological development could give one side or the other a decisive lead. Disciplined armies, whose structures were firmly rooted in man's psychology and the practicalities of command with the living voice, already contained arms of service which foreshadowed future structures. And although there were times when a common culture might mitigate war's horror, there were also times when frightfulness was employed as a matter of policy, and when the terrors of the siege pointed the way ahead to the aerial bombardments of the twentieth century.

ANCIENT EGYPT

The military history of ancient Egypt spanned three millennia, embracing the Stone, Bronze, and Iron Ages. One thing that did not change was the economic and strategic situation of the Egyptian civilization: its wealth was based upon the annual inundation of the Nile flood plain, which was only open to land invasion through narrow points of access. These are the Fourth Cataract in the south, halfway between modern Khartoum and the Egyptian border at Wadi Halfa, and the Gaza Strip, between the Mediterranean Sea and the Gulf of Suez, in the east.

Under the Old Kingdom (2686–2160 BC) there existed a system for recruiting a militia from the *nomes* (tribes) and there were officials responsible for training and for logistics, which already displayed a high level of organization. During this period the troops were entirely infantry.

During the Middle Kingdom (2133–1786 BC) columns of heavy spearmen were supported by archers, perhaps split 50 : 50. Soon after 1700 BC, there took place an invasion that brought about a military revolution. The Hyksos (the name means 'desert princes') brought with them a vastly superior technology, comprising bronze weapons and armour, the composite bow, and the chariot. The Egyptians soon adapted these innovations and within little more than a century they had expelled the intruders and established the New Kingdom (1567–1085 BC), during which they grew to their greatest power. Chariots became heavier (with six-spoked wheels instead of four) as the crews were armoured. The composite bow was the primary weapon for charioteers, and it was as a bow-wielding charioteer that the pharaoh was increasingly depicted.

The Battle of Megiddo (c.1476 BC)
In around 1476 BC Egyptian pharaoh Thotmes (Thutmosis) III led perhaps 10,000 men in a rapid march against rebel Palestinian chieftains, approaching by an unexpected route. They had sent outposts to hold the Megiddo pass, but this covering force which was easily scattered, leaving the king of Kadesh to face the pharaoh on the Megiddo plain. Thotmes' army advanced in a concave formation, its southern wing enveloping the rebels while the northern wing drove in between them and the town of Megiddo itself. The Egyptians used surprise, shock action by means of their massive chariot corps and the firepower of their archers, cut communications, and enveloped their enemy. The booty won was said to include over 2,000 horses. The siege of the city took another seven months, but with its fall Thotmes was able to establish his authority as far as the Euphrates.

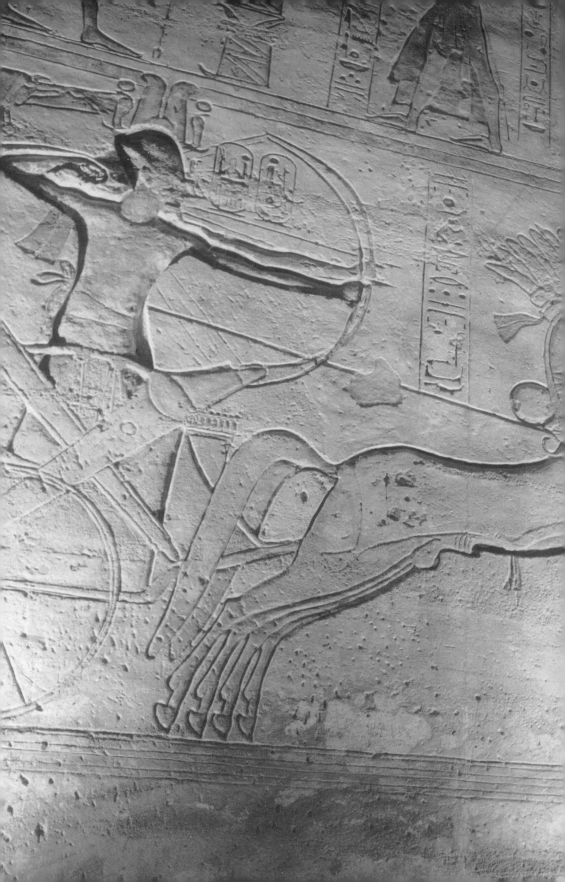

The Battle of Kadesh (1300 BC)

The Egyptian success at Megiddo brought them into conflict with the equally expansionist Hittite empire, and it was in the same region, outside the strategically important city of Kadesh on the river Orontes, in the Bekaa valley of northern Lebanon, that Ramesses II, pharaoh of Egypt (1304–1237 BC), fought the Hittites of King Muwattallish (1315–1296). The conquest of the state of Mitanni in the late fourteenth century by the Hittites had created a crucial border zone between their empire and the Egyptians. Ramesses led four divisions north, each of 500 chariots and 5,000 men, against 15,000 Hittites. His vanguard division, Amun, was already encamped north-west of Kadesh when the pharaoh arrived. The Hittites had planned an ambush which caught their enemy by surprise. From its camp on the far side of the Orontes river, and using a wood as cover, the Hittite chariot force, recorded as 2,500 strong, swung south and got in behind the advancing Egyptians. Fording the river, still undetected, it fell upon the following Egyptian division, Re, and destroyed it. Ramesses then counter-attacked with the support of the Ne'arim force which had come up from the west, and drove it off. Neither side's infantry took part, perhaps because they could not get across the river. Ramesses claimed the victory from this drawn fight which is commemorated in temple reliefs at Thebes.

THE GRAECO-PERSIAN WARS

The Greeks first came into conflict with the Persians in Asia Minor, as a result of the conquest of Lydia by Cyrus the Great, probably in 546 BC. In the early years of the fifth century BC there was a rebellion against the Persians. Five land battles are recorded, but almost no details have survived. The decisive Persian victory was at sea and they went on to conquer Thrace and to bring even Macedonia under their control. Two mainland cities, Athens and Eretria, had helped the Asiatic Greeks in the early stages of their rebellion, and this led, in 490, to the first Persian attack on Greece proper.

The Battle of Marathon (490 BC)

The Persians, led by Datis and Artaphernes, came by sea and had possibly 25,000 troops, including cavalry. The Athenians and their Plataean allies had perhaps 10,000 men. Though one of the ten Athenian generals, Miltiades, was later given much of the credit, the titular Greek commander was Callimachus, the polemarch (war-leader). The Athenians blocked the route to Athens from the landing beach at Marathon and sent to Sparta for reinforcements. Their messenger, Phidippides, ran the 240 km (150 miles) in two days. Before the Spartans arrived it seems that the Persians began to move on Athens, and the Greeks encamped near the southern exit from the plain were forced to fight. Thinning their centre to cover the longer Persian line, but leaving their wings strong, the Greeks

---

The light chariots with which the Hyksos invaded Egypt after 1700 BC were adopted by the Egyptians themselves and used en masse at Megiddo. Their success was celebrated in tomb carvings such as this one at Abu Simbel.

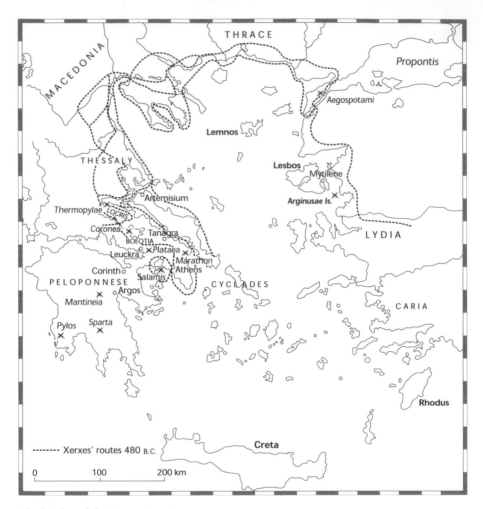

The battles of the Graeco-Persian wars

advanced. They probably broke into a jogtrot when they came within bowshot. On each wing, the Persians were routed, and their flight may have carried away their cavalry, which apparently played no part in the struggle. In the centre, the Persians forced the Greeks back, but were then probably taken in both flanks when the victorious Greek wings wheeled inwards. It is said that 6,400 Persians were killed for only 192 Athenians.

Ten years later, in 480, the Persians were back, this time overland by way of Thrace and Macedonia, and led by King Xerxes in person. His army was perhaps 50,000–100,000 strong, and his navy may have contained over 1,000 warships. Resistance in Greece centred on Sparta and its Peloponnesian allies, but Athens also joined the alliance. It was decided to hold Thermopylae, while stationing a fleet at Artemisium, some 65 km (40 miles) to the east, on the north coast of Euboea.

The Battle of Thermopylae (480 BC)

In antiquity the pass of Thermopylae ran between Mount Kallidromon and the sea, which has now receded. Here a force of perhaps some 6,000 Greeks, under Leonidas, one of the kings of Sparta, held off the army of Xerxes for three days, until a local offered to guide the Persians to their rear by a mountain track. Informed of this by deserters and scouts the Greeks divided, probably under orders, some withdrawing and the Spartans, Thespians, and Thebans remaining to act as a rearguard. The Thebans possibly surrendered at the very end, but the rest were annihilated.

Most of central Greece now more or less willingly went over to the enemy, but the people of Thespiae and Plataea in Boeotia took refuge in the Peloponnese, and now, if not before, Attica, too, was evacuated. The Greek fleet took station at Salamis, and it was here that the first decisive encounter of the war took place.

The Battle of Salamis (480 BC)

Following three days of skirmishing off Artemisium, the Greek fleet fell back to the island of Salamis, and it was here, in the narrow channel between the modern Ambelákia on Salamis and Pérama on the coast of Attica, that the reckoning with Xerxes' navy took place. It is possible that the Persian fleet was induced to move into the channel, at night, by a message from the Athenian commander Themistocles, but in any case the Greeks were informed by a deserter and were ready at dawn. It is unclear exactly what happened. Even numbers are uncertain, though the Greeks appear to have had 300–400 ships and the Persians rather more. Persian morale may have been low both after a night at the oar and because they had thought the Greeks would not fight. It seems probable that the Greeks initially outnumbered the leading or right-wing Persian squadrons, and were able to cut them off and drive them ashore before turning on the left wing and driving it out to sea. All that we know for sure is that the Persian fleet, having yielded the advantage of their numerical superiority and manoeuvrability by being lured into restricted waters, was defeated. The survivors withdrew to Asia Minor.

Salamis certainly did not end the war. The Persian army still remained undefeated, and Xerxes probably left the bulk of his army behind, under his cousin Mardonius. Wintering in Thessaly, Mardonius tried to woo Athens to his side, and when this failed, marched south again in late spring, perhaps with as many as 25,000 infantry and 10,000 cavalry as well as 13,000 infantry of his allies, notably Thebes. This compelled the re-evacuation of Attica. In the end the Spartans realized that their defences across the Isthmus would not save them if the Athenian navy passed under Persian control, and mobilized their army. Mardonius fell back to Boeotia, and it was here, some 50 km (30 miles) north-west of Athens, that the final encounter took place, probably in August.

The Battle of Plataea (479 BC)

Plataea (Plataia) was fought about 8 km (5 miles) east of the ancient town, near the modern Erythrai. The Greeks, under the Spartan regent Pausanias, had the largest hoplite force ever assembled, over 38,000 strong, and maybe even more lightly armed troops. After defeating the Persian cavalry at the foot of Cithaeron, the Greeks moved down to a position along the river Asopos. Here, however, they were increasingly harassed by Persian mounted archers, and eventually attempted to withdraw at night. But this led to the army dividing, with the centre back near Plataea, the Spartans on the right, the Athenians on the left. Mardonius, perhaps as he had intended, had got his enemy on the run, and should have been content with a moral victory which might have caused the disintegration of the fragile Greek alliance. But whether because he lost control of overenthusiastic men or because he saw a chance to annihilate the Spartans, who, being on higher ground, were all the enemy he had in view, he made the mistake of engaging the hoplites in hand-to-hand battle and his, lighter, infantry was routed. Meanwhile, the Athenians managed successfully to fight off the Boeotians on the Persian side. The battle ended Persian ambitions in Greece, but it was left to Alexander the Great to bring the long-running conflict to a close.

THE PELOPONNESIAN WAR (431–404 BC)

The first Peloponnesian War, between Sparta and Athens and their allies, lasted from about 460 to 446 BC. It began because of Athenian aggression and ended after a Peloponnesian army invaded Attica. Although it withdrew after ravaging the plain of Eleusis, Athens had had enough and a thirty-year peace was concluded.

In the spring of 431, this peace was broken by a Theban attack on Athens's ally, Plataea, and 80 days later by a Peloponnesian invasion of Attica. Now able to invade Attica through the Megarid, Sparta did so five times down to 425. At first, on Pericles' advice, the Athenians took refuge inside the walls surrounding the city and the Peiraeus, and responded to the Spartan ravaging merely by minor cavalry operations, raids on the Peloponnese, and biennial invasions of the Megarid. But after Pericles' death in 429, Athens adopted a more daring strategy, establishing bases on the Peloponnesian coast, notably at Pylos in Messenia.

The Battle of Pylos (425 BC)

Pylos was the headland at the north-west corner of Navarino Bay in the south-west of the Peloponnese seized by the Athenian Demosthenes in 425. Sparta recalled its army from Attica, but failed to take the position by a land and sea assault. Worse still, 420 hoplites placed on Sphacteria, the island south of Pylos, in order to deny it to the enemy, were trapped when Athenian ships arrived in force and defeated the Spartan fleet in the bay. When negotiations failed, the Spartans kept their men supplied by boat and swimmer, until Demosthenes was joined by specialized light troops brought by the Athenian demagogue Cleon. Demosthenes then landed on the island in overwhelming strength, with 800 hoplites and the rest divided into easily controllable groups of about 200. The guards at the southern tip of the island were taken by surprise and annihilated, and when the main body of Spartans tried to close on the Athenian hoplites, they were deluged with missiles by the light troops. Eventually they retired to the north end of the island, but were compelled to surrender when an enterprising Messenian climbed the supposedly inaccessible cliffs behind them.

Athens also countered Peloponnesian operations in Acarnania, and twice attempted to knock Boeotia out of the war by over-elaborate, two-pronged invasions, the second of which was at Delium, probably in November 424 BC.

The Battle of Delium (424 BC)

In the battle of Delium (also Delion, now Dhilesi) an Athenian army of 7,000 hoplites, under Hippocrates, had crossed the border into Boeotia and fortified a temple to Delian Apollo on the coast opposite Euboea. After leaving a cavalry garrison, the retreating Athenians were caught just inside Athenian territory by a Boeotian army under Pagondas. The Boeotians also had 7,000 hoplites, 1,000 cavalry, and large numbers of light troops, although these appear to have played no part in the battle. When the hoplites closed, the Boeotian left was defeated. But on the right the Thebans, massed 25 deep, were steadily pushing back the eight-deep Athenians when two squadrons of Boeotian cavalry, sent by Pagondas to support his reeling left, suddenly appeared from behind a ridge. Thinking that their appearance heralded the approach of another army, the Athenian right broke and fled. The left soon followed. Although night cut short the pursuit, the Athenian losses of nearly 1,000 hoplites killed (14 per cent of those engaged), including Hippocrates, were proportionately the worst ever suffered by a hoplite army.

The death in battle of the Spartan leader Brasidas and of the Athenian demagogue Cleon in 422 led to the conclusion of peace. It was unsatisfactory to many of Sparta's allies, and this and the ending of a peace between Sparta and Argos was exploited by the Athenian Alcibiades to create an anti-Spartan coalition in the Peloponnese.

The Battle of Mantineia (418 BC)

The battle of Mantineia was fought near the city of Mantineia in central Peloponnese between a largely Spartan and Tegeate army, and a combined army consisting largely of Mantineians, Argives, and Athenians. Having the larger army, the Spartan king Agis II attempted to cover the enemy overlap on his left by shifting his left wing outwards and plugging the resultant gap with units from his right. But his orders were disobeyed and the enemy right exploited the gap to defeat his left. On the centre and right, however, the Spartans carried the day, and wheeled left past the retreating Athenians and the gap left by the flight of most of the Argives, to take the enemy right in its shieldless flank as it streamed back across the battlefield. The victory restored Spartan morale and reinforced its control in the Peloponnese.

With Sparta's position in the Peloponnese once more secure, Alcibiades turned elsewhere for a field in which to exercise his talents, and, principally at his urging, in 415 Athens sent an expedition to Sicily, with himself as one of its three commanders. The expedition became bogged down in a siege of Syracuse and ended in disaster in 413.

The Siege of Syracuse (416–413 BC)

Syracuse was the principal city of the rich grain-producing area of Sicily, but it appears that it was an unhealthy spot: the siege was all but decided by the outbreak of an epidemic. The Athenian expedition to seize Syracuse was under the command of Nicias, whom the Athenian historian Thucydides represents as both unwilling and incompetent. He also records that Nicias' force was '100 triremes and 5,000 hoplites', with archers and Cretan slingers in proportion. The Athenians cut off Syracuse with two forts, and began a twin circumvallation, but left their northern walls incomplete, which was to prove disastrous. After two attempts to build counter-walls were defeated, the Syracusans appealed for Spartan help, which was refused. But Gylippus, a Spartan general, managed to raise 3,000 men for an independent relief effort and he landed and captured the unfinished northern fortifications, and built a wall from there to the city. Nicias changed the axis of his attack to the south and built three more forts, but an outbreak of disease forced him to give up the struggle. Since Gylippus had blockaded the harbour where the Athenian fleet lay, the Athenians attempted to escape overland, but were run down by Syracusan light troops and forced to surrender. This was Athens's greatest reverse and a turning point in the war. Whether it would have succeeded if Alcibiades had remained in command is doubtful, but in any case he was recalled early to answer charges of sacrilege, and rather than risk condemnation fled to Sparta.

Meanwhile mainland Greece had once more slipped into war. The Spartans were encouraged to try to match Athens at sea, while Athens's allies in the Aegean were in revolt and the king of Persia supported Sparta. Moreover, Athens was rent with internal disputes, with the democracy overthrown in 411 and then restored a year later. This brought about the return of Alcibiades, who, after success in the north, including the recovery of Byzantium in 408, returned triumphantly to Athens in 407, and was soon given supreme command of the Athenian navy on the west coast of Asia Minor.

But the new Spartan commander in the area, Lysander, won a minor victory at Notium while Alcibiades was absent. Furious, the Athenians sacked Alcibiades, who fled to Thrace. When Lysander in turn was superseded, the new Spartan commander, having succeeded in bottling up the Athenian fleet in the harbour of Mytilene, was then himself defeated off the Arginusae in 406.

The Battle of Arginusae (406 BC)

The battle of Arginusae was named after small islands (now Garipadasi and Kalemadasi) between Lesbos and the mainland. The Spartan commander, Kallikratidas, had to leave 50 triremes to cover Athenian ships blockaded in Mytilene, and so had only 120 to face about 155, but had the advantage of trained crews, whereas the Athenians, commanded by eight of their generals, had only a scratch fleet. This explains their unusual double line abeam, intended to prevent the enemy from breaking the line. Possibly, too, to prevent their being outflanked by the enemy's single line abeam, the Athenians kept wider gaps than usual between the ships of their front line, with the ships of their second line covering the gaps. Few details of the fighting survive, but Kallikratidas was killed, and the Spartans lost over 70 ships as against 25. The Athenian victory was marred by the failure to rescue survivors from their wrecked ships, allegedly owing to bad weather. This resulted in the subsequent trial and execution of six of the eight commanders who had won what was then the greatest naval battle between Greeks.

The Persians and Sparta's allies in western Asia Minor then demanded Lysander's reinstatement, and it was he who won the decisive battle at Aegospotami in 405.

The Battle of Aegospotami (405 BC)

The name Aegospotami (Aigospotamoi) means 'Goat's Rivers' (probably the modern Büyükdere), and it was the scene of the final battle of the Peloponnesian War. The Spartan fleet of perhaps 200 triremes under Lysander had a secure base in Lampsakos (Lampsacus, Lapseki) opposite, but the 180 Athenian ships under various commanders had to make do with an open beach, probably adequately watered but with food having to be brought from Sestos, 19 km (12 miles) to the south-west. The Athenians had to recover control of the sea lanes to the Black Sea, whence came Athens's essential grain supplies, and dared not risk the exhausting row against the current from Sestos. What actually happened is controversial. The historian Xenophon has Lysander ignore the Athenian challenge for four days, carefully noting how they dispersed after delivering it, and on the fifth, at a signal from his scout-ships, fall upon a scattered enemy. Diodoros, on the other hand, has him attack 30 ships apparently sailing off to Sestos for supplies and pursue them back to Aegospotami. However, both are agreed that he achieved complete surprise, with many Athenian ships being partly or completely unmanned, and that very few escaped.

Athens held out to the spring of 404, but, now blockaded by both land and sea, was eventually compelled to surrender. The Spartan policy of winning the war at sea brought them success.

The Battle of Cunaxa (401 BC)

The battle of Cunaxa was the decisive encounter in the contest between the rebel Cyrus the Younger (424–401 BC) and his brother Artaxerxes II for the rule of Persia. It is the only major land battle between Plataea and Granicus about which detailed (partly eyewitness) information survives, and took place on the Euphrates in northern Babylonia. Cyrus' Greek mercenaries, the 'gallant 10,000', chased their adversaries from the field but had no influence upon the crucial episode: a cavalry encounter in which Cyrus wounded the king but was himself killed. The armies' relative size, the role of Cyrus' barbarian levies, and other aspects of the battle remain unclear. The Greek mercenaries, however, were left isolated in hostile territory and, according to their leader Xenophon in his work *Anabasis*, it was his skill that brought them safely to the Black Sea.

THE GREEK CITY-STATE WARS (395–362 BC)

Defeat of Athens in the Peloponnesian wars ended the artificial order imposed on a normally fragmented Greece by the great alliances headed by Athens and Sparta. Fear of Sparta was essentially the cause of the Corinthian war (395–386 BC), in which her former allies, Thebes and Corinth, made common cause with Athens and Sparta's inveterate rival in the Peloponnese, Argos. In attempting to coerce Thebes before the rest joined in, Lysander was killed at Haliartus, in 395, but in 394 Sparta crushed coalition forces at the battle of Nemea, north of Argos.

The Battle of Nemea (394 BC)

Though called after the river Nemea, the battle was probably fought near Rachiani (Longopotamos) to the east. Here, perhaps some 24,000 Boeotians, Corinthians, Argives, Euboeans, and Athenians faced between 18,000 and 19,000 Spartans and their allies, in possibly the greatest hoplite battle ever fought. In the advance, both sides edged to the right, as had occurred at Mantineia in 418. Perhaps on this occasion it was not just because, as the historian Thucydides says, hoplites tended to seek the protection of their right-hand neighbour's shield, but in a deliberate attempt to outflank the enemy. As a result, both armies were defeated on the left, but whereas the Boeotians and their allies streamed off in disorderly pursuit, the Spartans, as usual under perfect control, fell upon the shieldless enemy right as it tried to retreat. According to Xenophon only eight Spartans fell, but this may have just been the full citizens of Sparta itself. The writer Diodorus, however, gives the losses among the Spartans and their allies as 1,100, as against 2,800 on the other side.

The Battle of Koroneia (394 BC)

The narrow neck between the foothills of Helicon to the south and Lake Copais to the north, on the road from the north-west towards Athens, could be blocked at Koroneia (Coronea). Here King Agesilaos of Sparta, with Xenophon, returning from Asia Minor to face a growing crisis in Greece, now in his service, found his way barred by a combined army of Boeotians and their allies. As so often happened in hoplite battles, both sides won on their right, but when Agesilaos was informed that the Thebans who had formed the enemy right were now in his rear, he countermarched his phalanx, and met them head on as they tried to march south to rejoin their defeated allies on the slopes of Helicon. Eventually the Thebans broke through, albeit with considerable losses. Strategically the battle represented a victory for Sparta, but the breaking of a Spartan phalanx by Thebans was ominous for the future.

The war on land now became increasingly desultory, fought largely in and around Corinthian territory—hence its name. In the end, it was won and lost at sea. When a Spartan fleet, with Persian help, again cut Athens's supply line through the Hellespont, the anti-Spartan coalition collapsed. But then all began to go wrong for Sparta. In the winter of 379/8 Thebes was liberated by patriotic exiles, and Athens invited the Aegean states to join it in a new confederacy, to which Thebes also adhered. The 370s were a decade of almost continuous warfare.

The Battle of Leuctra (371 BC)

The culmination of the war took place near a small hamlet in central Greece in 371 BC where the Theban general Epaminondas and his Boeotian confederates crushed the

---

Citizens who could not maintain horses, but could afford to equip themselves, served as hoplites. The core of the infantry, they were slow and heavy in attack, but could withstand the assaults of archers or cavalry. This one, from a painting, is called Megakles the Fair.

Spartan army. The battle marked a dramatic end to three centuries of Spartan infantry superiority and prompted four subsequent Theban invasions of the Peloponnese itself. Ancient sources disagree over what led to this astounding victory, but modern scholars emphasize Epaminondas' mass column, 50 shields deep, on the Theban left wing that ploughed through the Spartan elite right, killing their king and leaving nearly a thousand of his men dead on the battlefield. The usual pattern of success on the right had been broken.

Thebes overstretched itself in turn by seeking to dominate both Thessaly in the north and the Peloponnese in the south. Eventually it found itself facing a coalition of Sparta and its erstwhile friends, including Athens, Corinth, and even some of the Arcadian states.

The Battle of Mantineia (362 BC)

The second of the three important battles that took place at the same site in central Peloponnese was fought between a Boeotian, Euboean, Thessalian, and Arcadian army, commanded by the Theban general Epaminondas, against a combination of Mantineians, Spartans, Eleans, and Athenians. Epaminondas massed his left as he had done at Leuctra, 50 shields deep, but it was a charge by cavalry, mixed with light infantry which had been trained to run into battle with cavalry, that broke the enemy right. A decisive victory was prevented by the death of Epaminondas himself, and although Thebes remained the greatest military power in Greece for a number of years, its hegemony was effectively ended.

THE CAMPAIGNS OF ALEXANDER THE GREAT

Alexander the Great (336–323 BC), son of Philip II and king of Macedon, was the greatest commander of the ancient world. In 340 he briefly served as regent and in 338 accompanied his father in battle against the combined armies of Athens and Thebes, the two most powerful Greek cities.

The Battle of Chaeronea (338 BC)

Chaeronea, a small Boeotian city located 50 km (30 miles) north of Thebes, commanded the Cephissus valley, an important north–south route through central Greece, and provided a suitable position to block forces advancing south from Thermopylae. The Athenians and Thebans confronted Philip's Macedonians here, with the Athenians occupying the left wing and the Thebans the right. Details of the hard-fought battle are uncertain, but Philip probably enticed the Athenians out of line by a feigned retreat and then launched his cavalry, commanded by Alexander, into the resulting gap. The Athenians suffered 1,000 casualties, the Thebans more; Athenian prisoners were released without payment, whereas Thebes had to ransom its men. Victory ended Greek resistance to Philip, who now organized most Greek cities into the League of Corinth, a device to ensure Macedonian control and to promote a Greek crusade against Persia.

Philip was assassinated in 336 and Alexander, the only serious candidate to succeed him, at once consolidated his hold with characteristic energy. In 335 he marched north to impose his authority over Balkan neighbours, and Thebes rebelled during his absence. Alexander's speed of movement disconcerted his opponents; the Macedonians captured the city after fierce resistance and everything, except for temples and the house of the poet Pindar, was razed; survivors were sold into slavery. This severe treatment, which Alexander made his Greek allies confirm, cowed potential opponents like Athens.

Alexander was now ready for the campaign against Persia which Philip had planned. In 334 he crossed the Hellespont with somewhat over 40,000 infantry and 5,000 cavalry; the crack troops were Macedonian, though there were also important units of Thessalian cavalry, and archers and javelin men from Crete and Thrace. He met the local Persians at the Granicus.

The Battle of the Granicus (334 BC)

Alexander, having visited Troy, marched east towards the provincial capital, Dascyleium, and reached the river Granicus (modern Kocabas). The Persian governors had assembled local Persian troops and a substantial contingent of Greek mercenaries. The Persians planned to hold the east bank of the Granicus; this is normally a small stream flowing in a broad bed between steep 2-m (6.5-foot) banks, but was probably in spate and so a more formidable obstacle. Alexander, arriving on the west bank in late afternoon, was urged by Parmenio to find an alternative crossing. Most authorities agree that he rejected this advice and led his cavalry diagonally across the stream; he was nearly killed in a confused skirmish on the east bank as the Macedonians struggled out, but once the crossing point was secured the scratch Persian army crumbled. The Greek mercenaries were surrounded and either slaughtered or consigned to the Macedonian mines.

This victory allowed Alexander to dominate western Asia Minor, where the Greek cities welcomed their self-proclaimed liberator with mixed enthusiasm. Alexander was now embarrassed by Persian supremacy at sea, but the balance shifted when the dynamic Memnon of Rhodes died and Darius recalled the Greek mercenaries to bolster his land army. In 333 Alexander rapidly traversed central Asia Minor but was then detained in Cilicia by serious illness.

The Battle of Issus (November 333 BC)

Alexander's first encounter with the Persian king Darius took place on the narrow coastal plain between the Mediterranean and Amanus mountains, just north of modern Iskenderum (south-east Turkey), which is named after him. Darius had mobilized a large army and advanced to Damascus, where he was reinforced by Greek mercenaries previously attached to his navy. He then moved north-west through the Amanus Gates (Bahçe Pass) into Cilicia. Simultaneously, Alexander marched south-east across the Syrian Gates (Belen Pass) and only at the summit of the pass did he discover that the Persians were now behind him. He at once hurried back to confront Darius, who deployed defensively on the north bank of the small Pinarus stream (probably the modern Payas). Alexander strengthened his left wing on the Mediterranean shore, where Parmenio confronted the bulk of the Persian cavalry, while he put his Companion Cavalry on the right. While his outnumbered phalanx struggled in the centre, Alexander thrust in around the main battle and forced

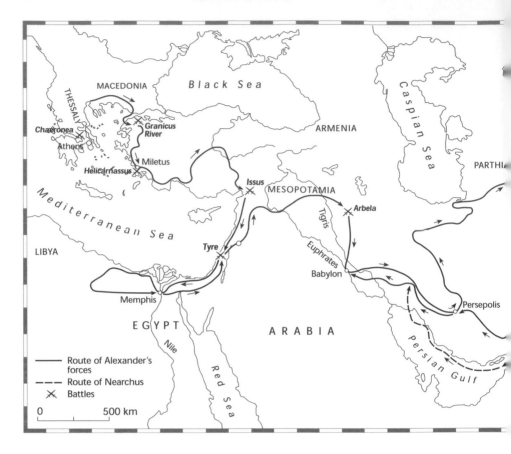

Darius to flee, whereupon his army disintegrated, leaving only the Greek mercenaries to
die fighting.

This success left the whole of the Levant open to Alexander and 332 was spent securing
the cities of Phoenicia. In 331 he turned east for the decisive confrontation with Darius at
Arbela.

The Battle of Arbela (Gaugamela) (331 BC)

Gaugamela, located west of the Tigris about 80 km (50 miles) from modern Erbil
(Arbela), was the site of Alexander's third victory over the Persians. Following defeat at
Issus, Darius had assembled a massive army from his eastern provinces, especially heavy
cavalry: 200,000 infantry and 45,000 cavalry are the lowest of various grossly exaggerated
figures. Alexander disposed his 40,000 infantry and 7,000 cavalry to offset this numerical
difference: his shock troops, primarily Macedonians, occupied the front line (phalanx in
the centre, cavalry on the wings), while his Greek allies and mercenaries constituted a
second line which could face about to form a square if the Persians threatened to encircle.
Alexander advanced obliquely, threatening to drag the Persians off the terrain prepared

The campaigns of Alexander the Great

for an attack by scythe-chariots; a Persian outflanking move on the right failed, their chariots were neutralized by Thracian javelin men, and Alexander then charged with the cavalry on the right wing, broke the Persian centre, and again forced Darius to flee. On the Macedonian left Parmenio endured a fierce assault, which was only terminated when Alexander was recalled from pursuing Darius.

Before winter Alexander forced his way across the Zagros range to reach the upland capital of Persepolis. In spring 330 Alexander left Persepolis, after burning the palace— symbolic revenge for the Persian destruction of the Athenian Acropolis in 480—closely pursuing the fleeing Darius, who was deserted and killed by his entourage. In 326 Alexander advanced into India, again with a tenuous claim to reassert Persian control, with support from the ruler of Taxila.

The Battle of the Hydaspes (326 BC)

King Porus, ruler of the territory between the Jhelum and Chenab, deployed his army, which included numerous elephants, to thwart Alexander's crossing of the river Hydaspes (modern Jhelum), which was swollen by melting snows. For once Alexander was superior

in numbers and, by splitting his army, feinting upstream and downstream, and exploiting the cover of various islands, he managed to transport part of it across the river during a tempestuous night. Porus at once sent his son to confront him but the Indian cavalry and chariots were brushed aside and Alexander marched downstream to take on the king. Porus relied on his elephants to disrupt the Macedonian cavalry and terrify the infantry, but Alexander already had experience of dealing with them and was able to force them back into the Indian ranks. Porus' army was encircled and massacred, although Alexander's historians preferred to depict a more epic encounter with Porus holding out bravely on the royal elephant. Alexander's beloved horse Bucephalus died of wounds after the battle.

At the Hyphasis (Beas) the long-suffering troops eventually mutinied and Alexander was forced to abandon plans to reach the ocean via the Ganges. Reluctantly he turned back to the Persian heartland, where his plans for future campaigns were frustrated by his death at Babylon in June 323.

The Battle of Ipsos (301 BC)

The battle of Ipsos was the largest of Alexander's successors' wars: the protagonists were all his former commanders. On one side Antigonus the One-Eyed and his son Demetrius deployed 70,000 infantry, 10,000 horse, and 75 elephants; on the other Ptolemy and Seleucus had 64,000 infantry, 10,500 horse, between 400 and 480 elephants, and 120 chariots. The armies drew up conventionally: in the centre a phalanx of pike-armed heavy infantry flanked on both sides by cavalry. Demetrius opened the battle with a furious cavalry attack on the Antigonid right which swept away the opposing horse; unfortunately he lost control of his men who hurtled off in pursuit. Seleucus in the meantime deployed a chain of elephants, which may have been held in reserve for such a contingency, between the exposed left flank of the allied phalanx and Demetrius' victorious cavalry. Horses were notoriously frightened of elephants and, after rallying, Demetrius' command was unable to approach the centre of the battlefield and influence events there. Seleucus harassed the Antigonid phalanx, possibly with horse archers, and in time large numbers defected. Finally, Antigonus was killed by a javelin and his army collapsed. The battle's outcome was decisive, with Seleucus becoming leader of Syria and Mesopotamia, and Ptolemy king of Egypt.

THE PUNIC WARS

Three wars between Rome and Carthage (264–241, 218–201, 149–146 BC) decided the struggle for mastery of the Mediterranean world. Before the first war, Rome was still a purely Italian power, not even in control of northern Italy; after the last, its writ ran from the Levant to Spain and from the Alps to Tunisia.

Spearmen of Darius's army, the Medes, in rounded helmets, and Persians, wearing square-topped head-dress, from a bas-relief at Persepolis.

The first war, sparked by an incident involving Messina in Sicily, became essentially a conflict between Rome and Carthage for control of the island. Mostly fought out in and around Sicily, apart from a brief Roman foray to Africa, it was the largest naval war in ancient history. Beginning with Mylae (modern Milazzo) in 260, which saw the first use of the *corvus* (the grappling plank for holding an enemy ship and boarding it), Rome won a series of victories—Sulci (258), Tyndaris (257), and Ecnomus.

The Battle of Ecnomus (256 BC)

Taking its name from a hill above modern Licata, the battle of Ecnomus was the greatest naval battle of the first Punic War. The historian Polybius records that the Romans had 330 warships, carrying nearly 139,000 men, the Carthaginians 350, carrying 147,000. The Roman fleet, heading west on its way to Africa, was in a triangle, with two squadrons in line ahead echeloned outwards, a third forming the base towing horse transports, and a fourth covering the rear. The Carthaginian centre, in line abeam, feigned withdrawal to disrupt the Roman formation, while their left along the shore and their right out to sea reached around to attack the Roman rear. Thus, possibly as planned, the battle dissolved into three separate engagements. But the Carthaginian ships still had no answer to the *corvus*, and when their centre was defeated and fled, one of the two leading Roman squadrons returned to help the fourth drive off the Carthaginian right, then both went to help the third, now backed up against the shore by the Carthaginian left. Carthaginian losses were 64 ships captured and 24 sunk, the Roman 24 ships sunk.

In 249 Carthage won its sole naval victory.

The Battle of Drepana (249 BC)

The Roman commander, the consul Publius Claudius Pulcher, with a fleet of probably 123 warships, attempted to surprise the Carthaginians, under Adherbal, in the harbour of Drepana (now Trápani) in north-western Sicily. But Adherbal, who probably had a few more ships, managed to get to sea in time and, by swinging round the islands at the harbour mouth, got to seaward of the enemy, where his ships had room to manoeuvre. In the ensuing battle Roman marines still proved superior whenever it came to boarding, but lacking the *corvus* and outmatched in seamanship, their ships were unable to turn fast enough either to prevent themselves being rammed in the side or stern or to do the same to the enemy. In the end, the consul, who was on the left of his line, managed to escape with the nearest 30 ships, but the remaining 93 were captured. Although the contest was on a smaller scale than other naval battles in the war, Roman losses were proportionately the highest suffered by either side.

The Battle of the Aegates Islands (241 BC)

The battle of the Aegates Islands (modern Isole Egadi) was the last battle of the first Punic War, fought on 10 March 241 BC between a Carthaginian fleet of about 250 quinqueremes commanded by Hanno, and 200 Roman quinqueremes commanded by the consul Caius Lutatius Catulus and the *praetor urbanus* Quintus Valerius Falto. Although it had more warships, the Carthaginian fleet had been hastily raised, may have been undermanned, and was hampered by the supplies for the army in Sicily it was either escorting or carrying. Its intention was to land these supplies and only to fight when it had taken on board some veteran soldiers from Hamilcar's army. The Roman ships, on the other hand, had been modelled on a particularly fast captured vessel, and were manned by the best crews available. The stormy conditions thus favoured the Romans, and they won decisively, disabling or capturing about 120 Carthaginian vessels, for the loss of perhaps only about 30. Only the fact that the wind shifted to the east, enabling the remnant of the Carthaginian fleet to hoist sails and flee, saved it from complete destruction. Carthage was obliged to make peace, outstripped in both resources and staying power.

The second war may have been deliberately engineered by Hamilcar and his son Hannibal as a war of revenge. Hannibal, who had succeeded to Hamilcar's command in Spain eight years after the latter's death, may also have inherited his father's belief that Rome could only be defeated in Italy. At all events, when warned by Rome not to attack Saguntum in the autumn of 220, Hannibal showed no hesitation. He took it in 219, and then seized the initiative by his audacious march to Italy and a series of devastating victories.

The Battle of the Trebbia (218 BC)

By sending his Numidian cavalry to harass the Roman camp on the right bank of the river Trebbia, which flows into the Po at Piacenza, Hannibal provoked the Roman commander Sempronius Longus into crossing to his side. The Romans had some 36,000 foot in the usual triple line, with skirmishers in front, and 4,000 cavalry on the wings. Hannibal had 20,000 African, Spanish, and Celtic infantry in a single line behind a screen of 8,000 skirmishers, with elephants in front of the wings, Celts in the centre, and his 10,000 horsemen equally divided on either flank. His cavalry easily routed their Roman counterparts and then fell on the flanks of the Roman infantry in cooperation with the skirmishers, who had fallen back through the main infantry line. Assailed in front and flank, the Roman infantry wings began to crumble and fled when Hannibal's brother Mago, and 2,000 men who had been placed in ambush to one side of their line of advance, fell on their rear. But in the centre, 10,000 Roman infantry managed to break through Hannibal's Celts and eventually made their way to safety at Placentia (now Piacenza).

The Battle of Lake Trasimene (217 BC)

The battle of Lake Trasimene, fought on 21 June, was an ambush on a huge scale. Hannibal, with about 60,000 men, trailed his coat before the consul Flaminius, at Cortona, halfway between Florence and Rome, before disappearing into the narrow passage north of Lake Trasimene. Flaminius, probably with about 25,000 men, followed and was caught between the hills and the lake, either between Pieve Confini and Passignano or between the latter and Magione. Some 6,000 Romans in the van managed to escape, only to be rounded up later, but the rest, including Flaminius, were destroyed.

The Battle of Cannae (now Canne della Battaglia) (216 BC)

Hannibal's most famous victory was the origin of the tactic 'double envelopment'. The battle took its name from a small town on the right bank of the Aufidus (now Ofanto, south of Foggia) and was almost certainly fought on the same side of the river and down-stream from the town, with Hannibal's army facing north-east towards the sea. Hannibal deployed his 40,000 infantry with alternate companies of Celts and Spaniards in the centre and Africans on the wings; beyond the Africans he placed his cavalry, Spaniards and Celts to the left by the river and Numidians on the right, open flank. The Romans formed in their usual three lines of infantry, with citizen cavalry on the right and allied horse on the left. Hannibal bowed out his centre to tempt the Romans to attack it, while the cavalry on his left swept the Roman citizen cavalry from the field, then rode around the Roman infantry to help the Numidians rout the allied cavalry. Meanwhile the Roman infantry pushed back the Celts and Spaniards in Hannibal's centre, bunching inwards away from the Africans who were thus able to take them in flank. The encirclement was complete when the Spanish and Celtic cavalry, leaving the Numidians to pursue the routed allied horse, took the Roman infantry in the rear. The result was a massacre without parallel in the history of western warfare, with the Roman army suffering worse casualties (allegedly 48,200 killed) even than the British army on the first day of the Somme; in addition, some 19,300 were taken prisoner. Cannae was for long an ideal of all commanders, and has a resonance far beyond its own age.

After Cannae, Rome returned to the strategy, first introduced by Fabius Maximus, of refusing to fight Hannibal in the field while aggressively defending strategic bases and retaking places when he was elsewhere. The turning point came in 212–211 when first Syracuse and then Capua fell.

The Siege of Syracuse (213–210 BC)

Syracuse was held by the mercenary Hippocrates for the Carthaginians. In 213 Marcellus, a renowned soldier but with only three legions at his disposal, began a siege. He directed his main attack on the northern 'Little Harbour', deploying 60 quinqueremes for a naval assault. Pairs of galleys were lashed together to carry a sliding assault ladder called a *sambuca* (harp) invented by Heracleides of Taras. But the city was defended by Archimedes, a greater inventor, whose 'burning glasses' and other counter-engines destroyed the attackers' siege engines. Hearing the news of a Carthaginian relief force under Himilco, Hippocrates slipped out of the city to join him, but he was surprised by Marcellus and his forces dispersed. The following year Marcellus exploited the fact that the defenders were drunkenly celebrating the feast of Artemis to seize a gate and the dominant Epipolae plateau. A Carthaginian relief force was defeated in two assaults and then fell victim to disease, and Syracuse surrendered

In the summer of 204, Publius Cornelius Scipio (Africanus) invaded Africa but it was a year before he broke out of his beachhead to win the battle of the Great Plains, and to bring direct pressure on Carthage by occupying Tunis, while his lieutenants overran Numidia (Algeria). Carthage now sued for peace, but negotiations broke down. Military operations were resumed by Scipio with great vigour, and eventually Hannibal was compelled by the clamours of his fellow countrymen to confront his rival inadequately prepared.

The Battle of Zama (202 BC)

Though usually called 'Zama', the final battle of the second Punic War was actually fought near a place of uncertain whereabouts called 'Margaron' or 'Naraggara'. Hannibal probably had 36,000 infantry, deployed in three lines, like the Romans, mercenaries first, Carthaginian levies next, veterans in the rear, 2,000 cavalry on either wing, with 80 elephants in front of the infantry. Scipio, now allied with the Numidians who had once given Hannibal the advantage in cavalry, probably had 29,000 infantry and about 6,000 cavalry, the latter on the wings, the infantry drawn up with the maniples one behind the other, leaving 'corridors' to accommodate the elephants. In the event, some of these were frightened out to the wings, helping Scipio's cavalry to sweep their counterparts from the field; others did cause some casualties among the infantry but they were mostly ineffective. The infantry then closed and after the Romans had broken the first two Carthaginian lines, Scipio redeployed his second and third lines on either wing of the first and closed with Hannibal's veterans, who were also probably now flanked by the remnants of their first two lines. The struggle ended when the Roman cavalry returned and fell on Hannibal's rear. Hannibal then insisted that peace be made.

In 150, Rome was presented with a fresh excuse to declare war when a Carthaginian army invaded Numidia in defiance of the treaty with Rome. Command was finally given to Scipio Aemilianus who took the city in 146, razed it to the ground, sowed salt in the ruins, and sold the inhabitants into slavery.

The Battle of Sellasia (222 BC)

At Sellasia, north of Sparta, a Macedonian-led coalition army under Antigonus Doson defeated a Spartan army under their king, Cleomenes III. The battlefield was dominated by two hills, separated by the Oenus stream, which were occupied by 20,000 Spartan infantry, predominantly pike armed. Cleomenes further strengthened his position by erecting a palisade in front of his right. Antigonus had 28,000 infantry, of which approximately 13,000 were pike-armed hoplites, and 1,200 cavalry. He attacked on his right with missile-armed light troops and Illyrians supported by heavy infantry, who crashed into the Spartan left and forced it downhill. A flanking attack on Antigonus' troops by Spartan light infantry stationed in the Oenus valley was thwarted by an aggressive cavalry attack led by the Achaean general Philopoemen. As the Spartan left advanced it became disorganized by the rough terrain and was defeated. Watching these events unfold, Cleomenes decided that he had to abandon his defensive position and attack if he was to save the day, but his troops were defeated after becoming disordered by their advance down the broken hillside into an especially deep Macedonian phalanx.

The Battle of Raphia (217 BC)

Antiochus III the Great became king of Syria in 223 BC and, after securing his power at home, turned his attention to his neighbours. At Raphia (modern Rafa), on the shores of the Mediterranean south-west of Gaza, Antiochus led his Seleucid army of 62,000 infantry, 6,000 cavalry, and 102 Indian elephants against a force, led by Ptolemy IV, of 70,000 infantry, 5,000 cavalry, and 73 African forest elephants. Both armies deployed in typical fashion with pike-armed infantry in the centre and cavalry with elephants on the flanks. The Seleucids echeloned their right wing forward to gain tactical advantage. The battle opened with a fight between the elephants, the Seleucids coming off the better due to the greater size and ferocity of their beasts. This was swiftly followed by cavalry actions on both wings, each army's right being victorious and pursuing the enemy from the field. The decisive clash came in the centre. The Ptolemaic army was victorious due to the personal leadership of Ptolemy IV and the greater size of its phalanx which used Egyptians to supplement the Macedonian settlers who traditionally wielded the pike, or *sarissa*, in Hellenistic battles. Antiochus, who had ridden from the field with his victorious cavalry, returned just in time to see his infantry collapse. He subsequently concentrated on a massive campaign (212–206 BC) to the east, rivalling the achievements of Alexander the Great.

MACEDONIAN WARS

The Battle of Cynoscephalae (197 BC)

The battle of Cynoscephalae was the Roman victory which concluded the second Macedonian war against Philip V, and demonstrated the superiority of the more flexible Roman legion over the Hellenistic phalanx. The Macedonian army consisted of 16,000 pikemen, 5,500 other infantry, and 2,000 cavalry. The Roman army was about the same size, but had more cavalry, including a highly effective contingent from their Aetolian allies. The battle began accidentally when the armies met on the march at the pass of Cynoscephalae. Both Philip and the Roman commander, Titus Quinctius Flamininus, deployed by wheeling their marching columns to the right, the front of the column forming the right flank. The Romans were formed in their customary three lines, the Macedonians in a single phalanx. Both sides' right wings attacked and routed the enemy left, which had had less time to prepare for battle. A Roman tribune gathered twenty maniples from the rear lines of the Roman right wing and led them in an attack on the Macedonian right flank. With no reserves to counter this, and with his men at a fatal disadvantage once the legionaries were inside their reach, Philip was beaten, losing 8,000 dead and 5,000 prisoners against a Roman loss of 700.

The Battle of Pydna (168 BC)

The outcome of the third Macedonian War (171–168 BC) was determined by a battle in which the Romans led by L. Aemilius Paulus inflicted a crushing defeat on the Macedonians of King Perseus south-west of modern Thessaloniki. Neither side had planned to fight on that day, but a bickering between their outposts escalated as more and more supports were committed, until both armies were drawn in. After a series of running fights between detachments, each side managed to form a battle line. The Macedonian pike phalanx had, as a result of its hasty advance, fallen into disorder, breaking up into its constituent units. The Roman legions encouraged far greater initiative in their junior officers, the centurions, in charge of each maniple. The centurions began to infiltrate the Macedonian phalanx with small groups of men, isolating sections of it and attacking the

The Antonine Column in Rome (c.180) shows soldiers taking part in a ritual around a funeral pyre. By this time a round or oval shield was in use, but body armour was similar to that used in previous centuries.

pikemen in the flank. The Macedonians were encumbered by their long pikes, and had no reserves to confront these breakthroughs. In only an hour the phalanx collapsed and was cut to pieces. The Romans claimed that they killed 20,000 Macedonians and captured 11,000, for the loss of only 100 dead and a greater number of wounded.

The Battle of Magnesia (189 BC)

King Antiochus III of Syria mounted an expedition to Greece which was defeated at Thermopylae in 191. In 190 a Roman army of some 30,000 men under Lucius Cornelius Scipio, accompanied by his brother, Scipio Africanus, crossed the Dardanelles and advanced to meet Antiochus' army of 60,000 infantry and 12,000 cavalry, with scythe-chariots and 54 elephants, near Magnesia (south-east of modern Izmir). After eleven days of skirmishing and manoeuvre, in which the Romans gradually moved closer to the Seleucid camp, Antiochus was forced to fight. He posted his phalanx in the centre with elephants in the gaps between its units. After the battle had opened with an ineffective charge by the chariots, the main lines clashed. Antiochus, leading his cavalry on the right, achieved a breakthrough, but was repulsed by the troops left to guard the Roman camp, supported by a tactical reserve. Elsewhere the Romans had pushed back the Seleucids and soon their entire army was in flight. The Romans claimed to have killed 53,000 of their enemy, and captured 1,400 with fifteen elephants, losing only about 350 themselves.

ROMAN CIVIL WARS (49–30 BC)

The foundation for civil war was laid with the formation of the unofficial first Triumvirate in 60 BC, in which Julius Caesar, Pompey the Great, and Crassus agreed to pool wealth and influence to dominate politics for their own ends. Julius extended the provinces of Gaul, Pompey and Crassus controlled domestic politics in Rome, and had their own armies in Spain and Syria respectively. Crassus, keen to acquire military glory to balance that of his colleagues, went east and invaded the Parthian empire.

The Battle of Carrhae (53 BC)

In the battle of Carrhae the Parthians encountered a Roman army for the first time. The battle itself was indecisive, the Roman legionaries and Parthian horse archers and armoured troops proving unable to damage each other seriously, but a detachment led by Crassus' son Publius was lured away from the main body and annihilated. Crassus' nerve broke and he ordered a night retreat which the Parthians were swift to exploit. Crassus and perhaps 20,000 men were killed, 10,000 were captured, and the legions' eagles were taken.

Pompey, now allied with the republican faction in Rome, threatened Caesar with prosecution, and his former colleague effectively declared war by crossing the river Rubicon, the boundary between his province of Gaul and Italy proper, in January 49. Pompey fled to Greece and, after dealing with the fugitive's forces in Spain, Caesar followed in January 48 BC.

The Battle of Pharsalus (48 BC)

At Pharsalus (near modern Fársala) in northern Greece, Pompey fielded 45,000 infantry and 7,000 cavalry against Julius' 22,000 and 1,000, and massed his horse on the left, intending to sweep around the enemy flank. Julius stripped one cohort from the third line of each of his legions and concealed them behind his right flank as a fourth line. Pompey's cavalry crashed through Julius' outnumbered horse, but was then stopped in its tracks by this reserve force. In the centre Julius' veteran infantry prevailed and killed thousands for the loss of only 230 of their own.

Pompey fled to Egypt where he was murdered. Caesar then defeated the new alliance against him, but his triumph endured less than a year; he was assassinated on 15 March 44.

Caesar's death initiated a fresh phase of civil war to determine who should be emperor which brought Caesar's nephew Octavian into a Second Triumvirate with Lepidus and Mark Antony, the losers of Mutina (Modena). While Lepidus held Rome, the others invaded northern Greece in pursuit of Brutus and Cassius who were commanding republican forces in the east. In 42 BC, they, too, crossed to northern Greece to confront the Triumvirate's army.

The Battles of Philippi (42 BC)

The armies met east of Philippi, in Macedonia, and the first battle took place in early October. Brutus on the republican right defeated Octavian and captured his camp. Octavian himself was ill and escaped by hiding in nearby marshland. On the republican left Antony personally took the camp of Cassius who, unaware of Brutus' victory, committed suicide. After three weeks of inactivity, with both sides suffering supply problems, Brutus decided to fight again on 23 October. This time he was routed with heavy loss. He and other republican leaders committed suicide, though some surrendered or escaped, and their army went over to the triumvirs. By 34 the situation had simplified into a clear west/east divide, with Octavian in a strong position in Italy and Sicily while Antony and his mistress Cleopatra were in declining command of the east. In 31 Octavian declared war on Cleopatra.

The Battle of Actium (31 BC)

The decisive battle was fought on 2 September. It took its name from the promontory south of the entrance to the Gulf of Arabracia (Amvrakia, north of the isle of Levkás). Antony, his forces eroded by enemy action and the desertion of some of his Roman supporters because of his relationship with Cleopatra, decided to break out by sea. He had about 230 ships of various sizes, while Octavian had 400, many of them smaller. Octavian's admiral Agrippa probably tried to draw Antony's fleet out to sea, where his more numerous and manoeuvrable ships would have an advantage, while Antony, bent chiefly on escape, had to wait for the sea breeze to veer north so that he could clear Leucas (Levkás). When battle was joined, Agrippa's left tried to outflank Antony's right, which, in covering the enemy's move, parted company from its centre. Cleopatra and about 60 ships which had remained behind the line of battle then managed to escape through the gap, possibly as planned, and Antony joined her with about twenty more. His left either refused to fight or was forced back into the gulf, where it surrendered or was burnt by incendiary missiles.

The lovers were pursued to Egypt where they committed suicide in 30 BC. Three years later Octavian became Augustus, basing his lasting power on the standing, professional Roman army created by his adoptive father.

2 Medieval Europe

History cannot be divided comfortably into time periods, and in a military sense the line between antiquity and the Middle Ages is a jagged one. The defeat of the Byzantine emperor Valens by the Goths at Adrianople in 378 is often regarded as one of history's decisive battles. But while the power of the western Roman empire had evaporated, that of the eastern empire, based on Constantinople, was to survive, albeit in an state of gradual and interrupted diminution, until Constantinople was at last stormed by the Ottoman Turks in 1453.

Throughout the period Europe faced the risk of invasion, and this helped shape not simply its military history but its social structure too. The first tide of Islamic expansionism surged along the coast of North Africa, up into Spain, and thence into France, whence it was repulsed by Charles Martel at Tours in 733 or 744. Another wave boiled down onto Europe from the north. In 793 a group of seaborne raiders, known as Vikings, sacked Lindisfarne monastery, off the north-west coast of England, beginning two and a half centuries of turmoil as Vikings attacked the British Isles and tracts of Europe, moving up rivers and commandeering horses to strike inland, pushing deep into Russia and down into the Mediterranean. At first they launched brief but bloody attacks, but in 864–5 a Viking force overwintered in England, and from then on they often established permanent settlements.

There was also repeated pressure from the east, whence a sequence of steppe nomads surged over the principalities of what was to become Russia, to batter the borders of western Europe. The fall of Constantinople and the subsequent Turkish advance through the Balkans posed yet another threat. Louis II of Hungary was catastrophically defeated at Mohacs in 1526, and it was not until the repulse of the Turks from Vienna in 1683 that the danger had at last passed.

European response to the threat of invasion by both land and sea was less cohesive than historians once suggested. We would now shy away from the term 'feudal system' to talk more broadly about feudalism, with its many local variations, and would be cautious about the word 'knight', using wider terms like armoured horseman. But for all this we can still see clear trends. The battle of Hastings (1066) did not mark the end of the 'infantry cycle' which, some would argue, had characterized warfare in the ancient world, and the beginning of the 'cavalry cycle' which would last until the development of gunpowder weapons. There was in fact a good deal of similarity between the men who stabbed and hacked at one another that short October day. The Saxon English were of continental stock and had themselves displaced native Britons, while the Normans were of Viking origin (they were known as *Normanii*, northmen, by the French). Although the Saxons fought on foot that day and were eventually swamped by repeated cavalry charges, we now know that they sometimes fought on horseback. Conversely, long after Hastings Norman knights might dismount to fight on foot. At the battle of the Standard (1138) they stood alongside north-country levies, formed in the old shield wall of their forefathers, and broke the wild rush of King David's Scots. And at Agincourt (1315) most French horsemen dismounted for their long plod across October mud into the arrow-storm.

Yet the trend is clear. The armoured horseman was becoming the dominant military instrument across the whole of Europe, and often beyond it. The Byzantine princess Anna Comnena affirmed that a charging Frank would bore his way through the very walls of Babylon. The process was gradual. In Europe, as Frankish power declined so local magnates, whose fortified castles became a feature of the age, gathered horsemen about them to enforce their newly acquired rights. These warriors (*milites* in Latin) rose from being servants of the nobility to become a minor aristocracy in their own right. The word sergeant, now used to denote a senior non-commissioned officer, then referred to an armoured soldier who fell below a knight in status, and his title stemmed from the Latin *serviens*, or servant. Not all armoured horsemen were knights, though the practical difference between an individual actually holding the order of knighthood and a man at arms who trotted alongside him might be very small.

Armoured horsemen were expensive to create and maintain. They required the latest armour, which became progressively more costly as the long mail shirt or hauberk of the eleventh and twelfth centuries was replaced by plate armour. They also needed a warhorse (destrier) which could sustain the weight of man and armour, remain steady in the press of battle, and perhaps use its own hooves and teeth to assist its master. The horseman and his steed were useless without training and practice, and the custom of allocating a knight land (fief) enabled him not only to bear the cost of horses and armour but to devote himself to a martial lifestyle. This soon acquired overtones which went beyond the narrowly military. The world chivalry stems from the French for horseman, and the notion of knighthood came to embody ideals of Christianity, romance, and courtly love.

There were wide variations in local practice as far as both the allocation of fiefs and the responsibilities arising from their tenure were concerned. Post-Conquest England, where the new monarch ruled the land by right of conquest and distributed it to his followers as he chose, saw a form of feudalism more sharply defined than that which existed in most other areas. Tenants in chief, who held their land from the king, were required to produce a specified number of knights when required to do so, and they allocated 'knight's fees' to enable knights to maintain themselves.

Even in England the process rarely operated as logically as its design suggested. There were 5,000 knight's fees by 1166, but probably nothing like this number were ever summoned, and the largest feudal force called out by Edward I, in 1277, constituted 228 knights and 294 sergeants. Scutage, a tax whose name was based on *scutum*, the Latin for shield, enabled knights to pay up to avoid military service, and this often suited the crown, which was able to devote the money to other things, including the payment of soldiers whose terms of service were far less restrictive than the old obligations of knight-service. When the young Henry V raised troops for the Agincourt campaign he did so by contracting with men who agreed to provide a specified number of soldiers—knights, men at arms, and archers. However, although this was not a feudal summons (the last with genuine military intent had been issued in 1327, and subsequent issues were more concerned with raising cash) Henry expected all noblemen to serve unless they had a good reason for not doing so, and the men who provided contingents doubtless used old networks of loyalty and obligation to encourage enlistment.

The tactical essence of the armoured horseman was the mounted charge, in which he galloped forward, lance couched under his arm, striking down opponents by shock action at its most direct, and then laying about him with sword, battleaxe, or mace. When delivered across suitable terrain against an opponent who stood to fight the knightly

charge could be shattering, and even in adversity the knight could be a formidable opponent. When Saladin beat King Guy of Jerusalem at Hattin in 1187 his son remembered how,
even though the crusaders' position was hopeless, Saladin tugged his beard in desperation
as Guy's knights bravely surged forward to counter-attack, and did not relax until he
heard that the king's tent had at last been struck down and the day was his.

Sir Charles Oman, to whose work students of my generation were so grateful, is dismis-
sive of the military art of the era. 'Arrogance and stupidity combined to give a certain def-
inite colour to the proceedings of the average feudal host,' he wrote. 'When the enemy
came into sight, nothing could restrain the western knights; the shield was shifted into
position, the spur touched the charger, and the mailclad line thundered on, regardless of
what might be before it.' Modern scholarship has changed our view. Vegetius' De Re
Militari was widely read by medieval commanders, and campaigns were often planned in
a very modern sense, with regard for both economic and diplomatic considerations; and
the chevauchée, a destructive march through enemy territory, had as its object the weak-
ening of an opponent by the avoidance of battle and strongholds.

There were indeed times when poor reconnaissance or overconfidence cost knights
dear. Robert of Artois's men became literally bogged down at Courtrai in 1302, and at
El Mansura in 1250 the crusaders charged as soon as the enemy presented himself, to be
swallowed up in street-fighting for which they were wholly unsuited. But at Dorylaum
(1079) Raymond of Toulouse hammered victory out of defeat by charging his hitherto-
victorious opponents, and at Arsuf (1191) Richard I of England beat the able Saladin by a
well-executed charge, which fell narrowly short of being wholly conclusive.

The military orders, monastic orders of knights dedicated to defending Christendom,
were active not only in the Middle East, but also in Spain, eastern Europe and briefly in
France and Italy too. They were militarily formidable: the orders of the Temple and the
Hospital between them could field 6,000 knights and a large number of foot, and the
Teutonic knights established their own state in Prussia. However, their confidence and
self-regard often encouraged rashness, and their obdurate views made them disinclined
to accept local live-and-let-live arrangements which other Christians were often happy to
tolerate. One of the greatest crusader defeats, at Harbiya in 1244, arose when the
Templars pressed for an all-out attack, which failed with catastrophic results.

Changes in western techniques during the Crusades illustrates that the process of
tactical development was at work throughout the period, and that although the knight
remained supreme—his status as much social and political as it was military—by the
fourteenth century familiar trends were asserting themselves. The crossbow had been
known to the ancients and was used in Europe from the late tenth century, but although
it was powerful and accurate its complexity and slow rate of fire limited its value. The precise origins of the longbow remain disputed, but it was developed as a result of Edward I's
Welsh and Scottish wars. Archers could operate in terrain which was unsuitable for
knights, and though, like the knight, they required long training, they were cheaper and
easier to recruit. If deployed in the open without natural or artificial cover (Henry's
archers protected themselves with sharpened stakes at Agincourt) they might be ridden
down by cavalry. However, if combined with dismounted men at arms and backed by
mounted knights they could bring together the best qualities of fire and shock. In the
Middle East they were successfully employed to screen squadrons of knights by keeping
horse archers out of range.

Although much of the infantry of the age was of poor quality, with peasants snatched

from the plough to follow their lords, or sleek burghers turning out nervously in city militias, medieval foot soldiers were by no means universally contemptible. Robert of Artois's
men discovered this when robust Flemish infantry, their favoured weapon a spiked club
known, in a jest which must have sounded wry indeed, as a *goedendag* (Good Morning!),
fell on them at Courtrai.

The Swiss, much of their native terrain unsuited for cavalry operations, produced
some of the best infantry of the age. They moved in great columns with pikemen to the
front and flanks, and burly hillmen with axes ('Lucerne hammers') and double-handed
broadswords in the centre spilling out to wreak havoc once the pikemen were locked in
contact. The Swiss won battles like Morgarten (1315) and Sempach (1386) and left
Charles the Bold of Burgundy cloven to the teeth at Nancy (1477). Swiss tactics eventually
foundered in the face of firearms and pikes combined. When they sought to storm the
fortified camp of La Bicocca in 1522 the Swiss left 3,000 dead in the last ditch to block
their assault. Their imitators the German *Landsknechte* were scarcely less formidable.
Both Swiss and Germans played a prominent part in the mercenary armies of the late
middle ages and early modern period. For centuries monarchs muttered: 'Where are my
Switzers?' when trouble was brewing, and in the doublets and hose of the pope's Swiss
guard we see the last shadow of a force that once made feudal Europe shudder.

Fortification was already a response to invasion when the period began. Stone Age folk
had sheltered in hill-forts, and the Anglo-Saxons and the Danes built *burhs* (from which
the word borough derives) or fortified townships. These early fortifications first used
earth ditches and banks and wooden palisades, but in the tenth century stone was replacing wood across Western Europe. Geoffrey Greymantle, count of Anjou, began work
on a huge quadrangular tower at Loches. His son Fulk Nerra not only completed it in
about 1030, but went on build stone castles, carefully sited so as to dominate the route
and waterways through the Angevin heartland. One of the notable features of the Norman
Conquest was the new order's ability to nail down its authority with the stone castles
which still form a distinctive part of the landscape. The science of fortification blossomed
across the period. Edward I's great castles in Wales (like Aberystwyth, Beaumaris, Carna-
rvon, and Harlech) built towards the end of the thirteenth century, and the later crusader
castles in the Middle East, like Crak des Chevaliers (described by T. E. Lawrence as
'perhaps the most wholly admirable castle in the world'), Marqab, and Athlit, built at
much the same time, stand at the very apogee of the castle-builder's art.

The importance of the castle, especially as a power base for those 'over-mighty
subjects' who played such notable roles in European history, meant that the attack and
defence of fortresses loomed large across the period. Almost all the techniques of medieval
siegecraft had been borrowed from the ancient world. Mangonels and trebuchets hurled
stones, massive crossbows shot javelins to pick off sentries or notables, battering rams
assailed gates, siege towers and scaling ladders helped infantry assault walls, and miners
burrowed beneath fortifications. However, a resolute and well-provisioned garrison in a
stout castle could defy the might of a kingdom. In 1224 William de Breauté held Bedford
castle, on behalf of his brother Fawkes, against Henry III. The whole of the king's military
might was bent against Bedford, with siege engines carted from Lincoln and Oxford, rope
from London, Cambridge, and Southampton, and miners from Hereford and the Forest
of Dean. Even so it took eight weeks to take the place.

Although gunpowder was known to the Chinese and in the Muslim world, it was not
until the thirteenth century that it was used in Europe, and even then its effect was slow

to develop. Early handguns were inaccurate, short ranged, and slow to load, and primitive cannon were scarcely better. The earliest illustration of a European cannon, in the 1327 de Milemete manuscript, shows a bulbous gun firing an arrow. Some believe that the English used cannon at Crécy (1346) but it is impossible to be certain. However, over the next century 'villainous saltpetre' steadily gained ground. In part this was because it was far easier to train a handgunner than an archer, a crucial point, for in terms of range, firepower, and accuracy the musket would not outshoot the longbow till the mid-nineteenth century. In part it was easier to cast a gun than to combine the artisan skills of the bowyer, arrowsmith, and fletcher, and in part it was natural for monarchs, anxious to forge centralized states, to demonstrate that they commanded the very latest technology.

But in one sense gunpowder was indeed decisive. High stone walls built to resist siege engines fared ill against great guns firing cannon balls at their base. Constantinople had resisted several previous sieges before the Turks sat down before it in 1453. This time, however, they had huge bombards, built by the Hungarian gunfounder Urban, and these duly breached the walls, enabling the Turks to storm the city. There was no sudden or identifiable end to the middle ages, but in a military sense the period closed amidst the bad-egg stink of black powder.

THE LATE ROMAN EMPIRE

Rome's first emperor, Augustus, feared that the rich province of Gaul was vulnerable to German attack from across the Rhine and determined upon the Elbe and Danube as the empire's northern boundaries. He sent his able son Tiberius to campaign in the region in AD 4–5, and in AD 6 the responsibility for consolidating his work fell to the legate Publius Quinctilius Varus.

The Battle of the Teutoburger Wald (AD 9)

The disastrous encounter for the Romans known as the battle of the Teutoburger Wald, the forest in which the ancient historians said it took place, occurred, according to modern archaeological research, in a different location.

Varus was in command of five legions and German auxiliary forces. Prominent among his auxiliary commanders was Arminius, a chief of the Cherusci tribe. In AD 9 Varus was conducting operations with three legions in central Germany, east of the Weser near modern Minden. Arminius had planned a rebellion, and, although warned of this, Varus still trusted him. Setting out to return to winter quarters, the Romans, 12,000–15,000 strong, with many dependants, had to march between the mountainous and heavily wooded Wiehengebirge and the Great Bog to the north, a route that narrowed, like a funnel, to a pass through the hills. Arminius and his following deserted, and the Romans became subject to guerrilla attacks. Varus continued the march despite the problems his unwieldy column was experiencing in the terrain. The attacks grew more severe, and, although we cannot be certain of the details, at the Hill of Kalkriese the Germans erected a serpentine, temporary wall. From this shelter they tormented the Romans with arrows and javelins, forcing their enemies to attempt an assault. At least one section of the wall collapsed, burying Roman soldiers beneath the rubble, and the assault was a bloody failure. Fighting ranged over a vast area, but in the end the soldiers and all their families were massacred and Varus committed suicide.

Tiberius stabilized the military situation and in AD 13 his younger brother Germanicus led an expedition to the Elbe again. He found the site, still strewn with remains, and had the bones buried; some graves have recently been discovered and excavated.

The Goths were a Germanic people whose origins lay along the lower Vistula (modern Poland). Their southerly migration brought them into contact with the Roman empire in the 3rd century AD. In 376 the Goths were dislodged from Dacia (modern Romania) by nomad Huns, bringing them into conflict with the Romans. The Goths could not be penned north of the Balkan mountains, despite heavy fighting, so in 378 the western emperor Gratian left the Rhine frontier for the Danube, while the eastern emperor Valens brought up his own field army from the Euphrates.

The Battle of Adrianople (378)

That summer, advanced elements of both armies were in action, but Valens fatally decided to risk a decisive battle before Gratian could arrive, perhaps because faulty reconnaissance persuaded him that only half the Goths were actually present. Thirteen kilometres (8 miles) north of Adrianople (modern Edirne, near the conjunction of the borders of Greece, Bulgaria, and Turkey, west of Istanbul) he advanced in column of march against the Gothic encampment, a wagon circle, which hindered the deployment of infantry in line of battle with cavalry on both wings. The Roman army was suffering from heat, thirst, and hunger, and in the absence of the Gothic cavalry a truce was being negotiated, when a disorderly assault by Roman cavalry units provoked a general engagement. This assault failed, and suddenly the Gothic cavalry returned and charged the exposed left flank of the Roman infantry, whose ranks were crushed together by attacks from both flanks until they broke entirely. Two-thirds of the Roman army died in the rout, including Valens, whose body was never found.

In 441, the Huns broke into the western Balkan provinces and took Sirmium in 442, but it was only when Attila, the Scourge of God, appeared on the scene in 433 that the Huns became a serious threat. In 447, they devastated Thrace and threatened Constantinople. In 451, the Huns crossed into Italy, but were forced north of the Alps into Gaul by a combination of plague and Roman resistance led by the *magister militum* Aetius.

The Battle of Châlons (451)

The battle of Châlons is also known as the battle of the Catalaunian Plains. In Gaul in 451 the Huns sacked and burned more than a dozen cities before halting to besiege Orléans.

Aetius convinced the Visigoth King Theodoric of their common danger and their combined army advanced on Orléans. Attila was forced to raise the siege and retreated towards the Seine, looking for a suitable place to give battle, which he believed he had found near Châlons, where the open grasslands of the Champagne plains were suitable for his Hun cavalry. Nonetheless Attila, although allied with a force of Ostrogoths, was considerably outnumbered and a small Visigoth force under Theodoric's son Thorismond occupied the tactically important single piece of high ground overlooking the Hun left flank. Aetius and Theodoric had placed their most suspect force, a contingent of Alans, in the centre, where they were promptly broken by a Hun cavalry charge. The Huns then wheeled left and fell on Theodoric's Visigoths. Theodoric was killed in the mêlée, but a ferocious counter-attack by Thorismond drove Attila's Ostrogoth allies from the field. Meanwhile Aetius' Romans held off fierce Hunnish attacks on their own positions. Staring defeat in the face, Attila fell back into his camp, and allegedly prepared to die on a pyre of saddles. However, his archers managed to keep the Romans at bay and the Huns were able to retreat.

Although the battle of Châlons was not a catastrophe, it was of considerable significance as the first time that Attila had been defeated and suffered serious casualties. Châlons dispelled the myth of invincibility that had worked so potently on both his enemies and allies. Attila died in 435 and his successors were unable to recreate the formidable force he had commanded.

THE CAROLINGIAN EMPIRE

Charles Martel (Hammer) was a uniquely successful general who laid the foundations for the Carolingian empire built by his son Pippin III and grandson Charlemagne. Charles faced his greatest threat in 733 or 734 when the ruler of Arab Spain, Abd ar-Rahman, crossed the Pyrenees and defeated Duke Eudo. Responding to his plea for help, Charles defeated the Arab army at or near Tours.

The Battle of Tours (733 or 734)

The traditional location and date of the battle of Tours—at Poitiers in 732—are due to misinterpretations of the near-contemporary Frankish continuation of the Chronicle of Fredegar. That source states that, having burnt Poitiers, the Arab army was advancing towards Tours when it was met by Martel's force. It also implies that the battle took place in the year before the death of Eudo, duke of Aquitaine, commonly accepted as 735. On both points this account is supported by the Mozarabic Chronicle of 754, which, however, disagrees with the continuator of Fredegar in its account of the aftermath: far from 'scattering them like stubble before the fury of his onslaught', it alleges that Martel allowed the Arabs to slip away by night.

This victory allowed Charles to intervene south of the Loire, establishing his supporters in Burgundy and Provence.

The scope of Charlemagne's activity reflected the size of his empire: he campaigned from the Ebro to the Danube, the Elbe to the Po, against Byzantines and Muslims, Avars and Danes, Saxons and Slavs. These military successes owed much to Charlemagne's ability as a strategist and a diplomat. The cream of the Frankish army was the heavy cavalry, but it made up perhaps a tenth of Frankish armies, which were probably numbered in tens of thousands. The complex organization which equipped and supplied the army, and maintained lines of communication, was the real basis of Carolingian success.

Ronceval (778)

Roncesvalles is a high Pyrenees pass and the site of a defeat suffered by Charlemagne on 15 August 778. Among the Franks who died was Roland, a high-ranking aristocrat, who was later immortalized as the subject of a superb Old French poem, *The Song of Roland*, the surviving manuscript of which dates from *c*.1100. The *Song* tells an epic tale of honour, loyalty, and betrayal against the backdrop of Christian–Muslim conflict. Its value lies in the vivid insights it allows into the aristocratic mentality of the age in which it was composed; it can add nothing to our knowledge of the historical Roland.

The campaign of 778 was a response to an embassy received by Charlemagne from the Muslim ruler of Barcelona in 777. A large army which was assembled from across Charlemagne's empire at Easter 778 crossed the Pyrenees by two separate routes, before reassembling outside Saragossa, where there were protracted negotiations with the Muslims. In early August Charlemagne suddenly decided to withdraw. The problems of conducting a campaign in a hostile and strange countryside distant from the Frankish heartland are well illustrated by the disaster of 15 August. As the Frankish army reached the heights of the Pyrenees, it was ambushed by Basque forces seeking plunder (all contemporary accounts agree that the Franks' opponents were the Basques, not the Muslims of *The Song of Roland*). With the Frankish formation drawn out by the pass, the Basques cut off and then butchered the Frankish rearguard and baggage train, before melting into the hills. These tactics put the Franks, heavily armed and used to pitched battle rather than skirmishing, at a disadvantage.

After the final defeat of the Saxons in the first years of the ninth century, the constant campaigning ended. The years from 800 until Charlemagne's death in 814 were devoted to the consolidation of his frontiers.

ANGLO-SAXON WARS

In 793, a group of Scandinavian warriors, Vikings, sacked the monastery at Lindisfarne, off the north-east coast of England, unleashing two and a half centuries of turmoil on Western Europe. The technological breakthrough which made Viking raids possible was in shipbuilding; the typical Viking craft was a low, sleek, clinker-built vessel, designed with a prow at either end for rapid relaunching and fitted with a sail, but capable of being rowed. Viking techniques of warfare were, like those of the Anglo-Saxons, in the mainstream Germanic tradition of mobile infantry engagements. Generally, Viking armies, whose main advantages were speed and surprise, avoided open battle, preferring the swift raid against a wealthy, unsuspecting target followed by orderly withdrawal.

In 911 Norsemen were granted territory on the coast of northern France where they set up a state; this province was the source of the last successful invasion of England 155 years later. From the late 980s a fresh wave of raiding from Scandinavia hit western Europe.

The Battle of Maldon (991)

One of the most serious encounters between Vikings and Englishmen during these attacks took place on the banks of the Blackwater river near Maldon, Essex. A Viking force had first sacked Ipswich before being confronted on 10 or 11 August 991 by the levies of Essex under their ealdorman Byrhtnoth. Details of the ensuing battle are provided by the Old English poem generally entitled *The Battle of Maldon*, which survives substantially only in an eighteenth-century transcript. There is no agreement as to the historicity of its account, which suggests that the English chivalrously allowed the Vikings to cross onto the mainland before attacking them, but it is clear that the English were defeated and Byrhtnoth slain.

The English King Æðelred II Unræd (*c*.966–1016) (Ethelred the Unready) decided to buy the Vikings off. Taxes were raised to pay this 'Danegeld'. From 1003, the Danish king Sweyn Forkbeard began a conquest of England at the expense of Æðelred. Sweyn's son Knut (or Canute) continued his father's conquest, while Æðelred's son Edmund Ironside took over the English army on the death of his father in 1014 and drove him from a siege of London in 1016, forcing the Danes into Essex.

The Battle of Assandune (1016)
The location of the battle of Assandune (Ashdon, Ashingdon) is controversial: it may have been near Southend-on-Sea between the Crouch and Roach rivers, or further north, in the Stour valley inland from Harwich: in either case Knut had moved his forces there by sea. On 18 October 1016 Knut and Edmund met in battle, and although its events cannot be described with any confidence, it was probably treachery that led to Edmund's defeat. Many Saxon nobles were killed, and Edmund died the following month, whereupon Knut was proclaimed king.

The last great Viking leader must be Haraldr Harðráða (1016–66), whose invasion of the north of England was crushed by Harold Godwinson's Saxons at Stamford Bridge, near York, a battle that may have weakened them sufficiently to make the difference at Hastings 21 days later against the Normans.

The Battle of Hastings (1066)
Fought on 14 October 1066, between the forces of William the Conqueror, duke of Normandy and King Harold (Godwinson) II of England, Hastings was one of the most decisive battles in the history of Western Europe. William had a claim to the English throne and Harold expected him to invade, but William fortuitously landed on the Sussex coast when Harold was preoccupied with the Viking invasion in the north. On hearing of William's arrival, Harold immediately began a forced march south from York, refusing to wait in London for reinforcements, and arriving in the vicinity of Hastings on the night of 13 October. He had defeated Haraldr Harðráða when he had caught him completely by surprise. Now he hoped to repeat this successful strategy against William, but the latter was forewarned by his scouts and attacked Harold's force in a strong but confined defensive position on Senlac ridge. Harold, moreover, had lost some of his best men in the earlier battles of Fulford Gate and Stamford Bridge on 20 and 25 September: not all had kept pace with his swift march southwards, and much of the fyrd (militia with various degrees of weapons and equipment) had yet to come in. He probably had about 1,000 housecarls, professional

warriors, perhaps as many thegns, and perhaps 6,000 or 7,000 fyrdmen to his opponent's 2,000 cavalry, 4,000 heavy infantry, and 1,500 archers.

The Norman archers, supported by heavy infantry, began the battle, but made little headway against the close infantry formations of the Anglo-Saxons, so densely arrayed, noted Duke William's biographer William of Poitiers, that the dead could not even fall. Assaults by the Norman cavalry initially fared little better, and the well-equipped house-carls did terrible execution with their great two-handed axes. William's left, comprised of Bretons, broke in panic amidst rumours that the duke was slain, and William narrowly avoided catastrophe by rallying his fleeing men and raising his helmet to show he was still alive. Launching a counter-attack, the Normans cut down those Saxons who had broken ranks in pursuit, and, exploiting the efficacy of this manoeuvre, they probably executed several 'feigned flights' with considerable success, although we cannot be sure of the details. Renewed assaults by Norman archers and knights gradually thinned the remaining English formation, which lacked sufficient archers to neutralize the Norman missilemen. Harold's death effectively ended the battle; wounded first in the eye by an arrow, he was then cut down by Norman knights.

Hastings was by no means the inevitable triumph of feudal heavy cavalry over 'out-moded' Germanic infantry; the battle raged from dawn to dusk, the Normans came close to complete disaster, and it was little more than chance alone that Harold, not William, was slain. Contemporaries regarded the battle as so closely fought that only divine inter-vention could explain William's eventual victory.

THE CRUSADES

The era of what are generally regarded as *the* Crusades began in November 1095 when Pope Urban II (1088–99) proposed a military expedition to seize Jerusalem. It was ideological warfare in the purest sense, Holy War, and the crusade was preached to them in terms comprehensible to a landowning aristocracy, of recovery of wrongly taken land. Religious enthusiasm was undoubtedly the driving force of the crusade, but it was spiced by the hope of gain. In the end about 100,000 joined the crusade and about 60,000 entered Asia Minor in 1097.

The Battle of Antioch (1098)

On 3 June 1098, an alliance of Frankish leaders seized the originally Byzantine city of Antioch, strategically situated within massive walls on the Orontes river (also used as a name for this battle) in north-west Syria, from its Turcoman occupiers. Almost imme-diately, a large force under Kerbogha, the Turcoman ruler of Mosul in what is now Iraq, appeared and took up position on the Orontes in order to invest the city. Preoccupied with a military threat in Anatolia, the Byzantine emperor Alexius was unable to assist his Frankish allies in protecting his possession, and their situation became desperate. But the

---

Duke William raises his helmet, showing his face to dispel rumours of his death, during the battle of Hastings. The horsemen use stirrups and are supported by archers.

discovery of a supposed holy relic raised the crusaders' morale, and a perilous sortie from the city turned into a decisive victory over the besiegers on 28 June. With Antioch relatively secure, the main body of crusaders was able to proceed to their principal goal of recovering the Holy Land. Using the Byzantine emperor's absence from the battle as a pretext, one of the Frankish leaders, Bohemond de Hautville, claimed Antioch for himself, and established an independent principality that was to play an important part in the subsequent history of the Crusades.

The First Crusade entered the Middle East at a moment of acute political fragmentation. This in part explains its success, but even so its achievement in liberating Jerusalem in July 1099 was remarkable, because it defeated powerful enemies—the Seljuks of Rhum, the successor states of the Seljuks in Syria, and the Fatimid caliphate of Cairo—all of which were capable of fielding great armies and outnumbering the crusaders, who had lost many men crossing Asia Minor. Moreover many of the crusaders' horses had perished on the march, so that their vital cavalry force was quite small. Able leadership—especially in the person of Bohemond (c.1050–1111), who was a fine soldier—effective unity, and an unquenchable spirit of righteousness explain their success. They also enjoyed the support of allies. Sea power was essential, especially to the sieges of Antioch and Jerusalem. The seizure of these cities laid the basis for Latin rule in the Holy Land. The establishment of Latin bridgeheads in the Middle East at Edessa, Antioch, Jerusalem, and later Tripoli was a remarkable achievement; however a quarrel with Byzantium meant that there was no land bridge to Jerusalem and so the flow of pilgrims and settlers from the west was limited to those coming by sea. As a result the Latin colonies needed support in the form of further crusades—crusading became an established part of medieval life.

The First Crusade received considerable help from the Byzantine empire, but when Bohemond decided to keep Antioch he opened a breach with the Byzantines, who were cool towards the crusades of 1101 and 1147 and downright hostile by the time of the Third Crusade, when the Germans who started out under Frederick Barbarossa had to fight their way through the empire. The Third Crusade had a great fleet, and all subsequent crusades relied totally on sea power to reach the Middle East: the Fourth Crusade failed largely because its leaders lacked ships of their own. The maritime superiority of the Italian city states was the basic condition which made crusades possible: after the First Crusade the Latin footholds in the Middle East desperately needed to control the Levantine ports and by 1124 all except Ascalon had fallen with the aid of Italian fleets. But the most significant change affecting the Crusades was the revival of the Islamic spirit which awoke as it became apparent that Islam faced a long-term threat. This was fostered by important leaders like Zengi (d. 1146) who recaptured Edessa in 1144, Nur ad-Din (1146–74) who united Syria and Egypt, and Saladin (1174–93).

The Battle of Hattin (1187)

On 2 July 1187 Saladin attacked Tiberias with an army 30,000 strong including 12,000 cavalry. King Guy of Jerusalem gathered the entire army of the kingdom, 15,000–18,000 including 1,200 knights and many other cavalry, at Saffuriya. On 2 July the leaders, bitterly

The siege of Antioch.

divided by personal and political feuds, debated whether to attack Saladin or to suffer the loss of Tiberias and wait for Saladin's army to fall apart. Guy decided to challenge Saladin, although his precise intentions are not known.

On 3 July the army marched east in three great divisions with the infantry protecting the cavalry for a fighting march. It was essential to reach water. All through 3 July Saladin harassed the crusaders, especially the rearguard under Balian of Ibelin. This forced the crusaders to camp with little water at Maskana. On 4 July the army deployed for battle close to the Horns of Hattin. Our sources are confused so it is impossible to reconstruct events but ultimately the demoralized infantry fled to the Horns of Hattin and the cavalry, despite valiant charges, simply could not break out of the trap in which they were held. The army of the kingdom of Jersusalem was killed or captured in its entirety and King Guy was taken, enabling Saladin to conquer the kingdom.

The reconquest almost extinguished the Latin kingdom of Jerusalem and was the stimulus for the Third Crusade.

The Battle of Arsuf (1191)

After the capture of Acre in July 1191 the Third Crusade needed a base at Jaffa for its attack on Jerusalem. Richard the Lionheart of England had never commanded a great army in battle, but his military reputation ensured that he was the commander when the army left Acre on 22 August. He faced a march down the coast road in the face of a powerful army under Saladin. This necessitated a fighting march, familiar to the Latins in the Middle East but novel for a western commander. Richard revealed his military skill by marshalling his heterogeneous army very skilfully. The cavalry were in three great squadrons, the Templars at the front and the Hospitallers at the rear. Foot and archers on their left kept the Turkish mounted bowmen out of range of the cavalry and guarded the baggage on the seaward right. The army thus resembled a mobile fortress. Saladin's attacks reached a crescendo on 7 September but Richard kept tight order, hoping to lure the enemy into a position where they could be destroyed by a single cavalry charge. In the end the pressure on his rearguard led to a premature charge which defeated but did not destroy Saladin's army. The victory had inconclusive results: Christian prestige was restored and Jaffa seized but Saladin's army remained in being.

Under the Ayyubids, Saladin's descendants, the divisions of Islam reappeared, particularly between Syria/Palestine on the one hand and Egypt on the other, and the crusades of the thirteenth century tried to profit from this. Frederick II in 1229 exploited the divisions between Damascus and Egypt to negotiate the restoration of Jerusalem and much of the kingdom, and Theobald of Champagne did the same in 1240. However after the failure of St Louis's crusade in 1249, the rise of the Mamelukes in Egypt and their ambitions in Syria made such exploitation impossible. The Mongol irruption into Syria in the 1250s offered the crusader kingdom the opportunity to play them off against the Mamelukes, but the Franks hesitated to ally with such terrible people and in 1260 the Mamelukes defeated the Mongols at Ain Jalut. Ultimately the Mameluke creation of a regular army and their defeat of further Mongol attacks doomed the crusader states, whose last bastion of Acre fell to the Mameluke sultan Khalil in 1291.

The fall of Acre in 1291 was not the end of crusading and the recovery of Jerusalem continued to be a preoccupation within Christendom, but it became less and less of a force in the politics of the Christian west. Crusading was never confined to the Holy Land: as early as 1114 a crusade was proclaimed to Spain and Innocent III launched one against the heretics of southern France. The conquest of Constantinople by the Fourth Crusade was welcomed in the west as the restoration of orthodoxy and sustaining the Latin states of Greece which enjoyed the rewards of crusading. The conquest of the pagans of the Baltic and eastern Europe was one of the great triumphs of crusading. The Church recruited vigorously to support the tiny Christian settlements of the area. A number of military monastic orders were founded to carry the brunt of the fighting, notably the Sword-Brothers in Livonia. By the end of the thirteenth century the Teutonic order moved the focus of its activities from the Holy Land to become a great political force leading the crusade and establishing a principality out of which grew Prussia. The papal right to launch a crusade was undoubted, but failure in the Holy Land, manipulation of crusading for papal interests in Italy, and the problems of the papacy in the fourteenth century undermined the whole movement. The Crusades ultimately failed in their primary theatre, the Middle East, but their history illustrates the remarkable durability and adaptability of European military methods.

The Battle of Bouvines (1214)

On 27 July the French king Philip Augustus secured Capetian mastery in northern France by decisively defeating a coalition led by Otto IV of Germany at Bouvines, 14.5 km (9 miles) west of Tournai. Philip himself narrowly escaped death when Otto's infantry broke through the French centre. The battle was won by the superior discipline and close combat skill of the more numerous French knights who routed the cavalry of the allied right, drove Otto from the field, then annihilated the now isolated infantry on the allied left. With the capture of the counts of Boulogne and Flanders, the alliance collapsed, embroiling King John of England, who had organized and funded the coalition, in political repercussions that led directly to Magna Carta.

SCOTS WARS OF INDEPENDENCE

In 1295, the Scots negotiated a mutually defensive treaty with Edward's enemy King Philip of France, as a prelude to regaining independence by force. The first engagements were profoundly traditional, resulting in a Scots capitulation following their defeat at Dunbar in April 1296. Spontaneous revolts throughout Scotland were subsequently coordinated by Andrew Murray and William Wallace, who led a Scots infantry army to victory against an overconfident English force at Stirling Bridge in September 1297.

The Battle of Falkirk (1298)

After Stirling Bridge Edward I, determined on revenge, led an army of over 28,000 northwards. On 22 July the English engaged the Scots under Wallace at Falkirk. The Scots formed up their army in four defensive schiltroms. The schiltrom was a group of some

1,000 spearmen, in semicircular formation, hemmed in with ropes, each man holding his iron-tipped spear outwards across his chest. These succeeded in repelling the initial English cavalry charge, but were finally broken by archers, at a cost of perhaps 2,000 English casualties. Edward's discontented Welsh infantry, numbering almost 11,000, took little part in the battle, joining in only when it became clear that the English had gained the upper hand. Wallace's defensive tactics had failed.

The war became one of attrition. The Scots wearied first, submitting in 1304, although England was also exhausted. However, two years later Robert Bruce, earl of Carrick, seized the throne and reopened hostilities. Initially, the Bruce failed against the combined might of England and Scots outrage at his violent usurpation of kingship, but he kept his cause alive until the death of Edward I provided political relief. English political divisions in the early years of Edward II's reign allowed the Bruce to deal with his enemies in Scotland.

The Battle of Bannockburn (1314)

An agreement had been reached in 1313 that Stirling castle would capitulate at midsummer the following year if the English failed to relieve it. The Scots prepared a strong position near the castle to meet Edward II's relieving force. The fighting took place over two days on 23 and 24 June. On the first day the Bruce killed the English champion Bohun in single combat, after which a mounted force under Robert Clifford failed to outflank the Scots, and could not break through their schiltroms. On the second day a dispute between the earls of Gloucester and Hereford over who should lead the van underlined the weakness of the English command structure. Gloucester died in a futile charge into the Scots schiltroms. The Scots had the upper hand in the fighting that followed; the boggy ground was unsuitable for the English cavalry, and when Edward II himself fled, the English forces disintegrated. The battle demonstrated, as in other fourteenth-century examples, the deficiencies of cavalry when faced with well-organized infantry in a strong defensive position.

Bannockburn crowned the Bruce's success but did not win the war. Attempts to force Edward II to accept Scots sovereignty subsequently centred on the systematic raiding of the north of England and the opening of a second front in Ireland. A few years after the Bruce's death in 1329 the claims of those who had lost out relaunched the war, ostensibly under the leadership of Edward Balliol, son of the King John ousted by the Bruce.

THE HUNDRED YEARS WAR

Hundred Years War is the term coined in France in the early 1860s to describe the wars between England and France from 1337 to 1453. In reality, there was not a constant state of warfare; conflict was punctuated by several truces and by full peace between 1360 and 1369.

The first major English victory on land in the Hundred Years War was achieved by dismounted men at arms and archers, using tactics which became classic. Edward III had landed at La Hogue in Normandy on 12 July 1346 with some 15,000 men, of whom less than 3,000 were men at arms, about 4,000 mounted archers, and perhaps 8,000 foot soldiers. The expedition developed as a ferocious *chevauchée*, a massive, plundering, and destructive raid by mounted troops. His shipping kept abreast to carry home the

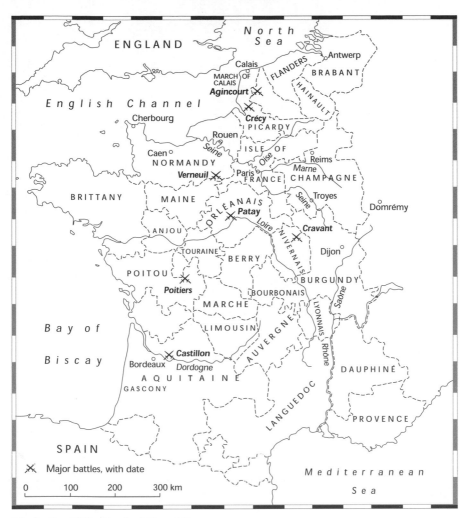

The battles of the Hundred Years War

enormous booty. After Caen fell (26 July), Edward announced he would seek out Philip VI of France and his army, then gathered around Paris. He then marched up the Seine, reaching Poissy (13 August), whence he attacked Paris, before turning north, pursued by the enraged French.

The Battle of Crécy (1346)

Edward was at first unable to cross the Somme, but a ford at Blanchetacque, below Abbeville, was traversed on 24 August despite opposition. A few miles to the north-east, on a gentle slope between Crécy and Wadicourt, with a wood behind them, the English took up a position probably reconnoitred in advance. With about 25,000 men, Philip VI left Abbeville early on 26 August, catching the English around midday. By late afternoon

his troops had formed three main divisions (battles), one behind the other, with 6,000 Genoese crossbowmen in the first rank, the main cavalry force in the second, and the king in the third. The English also formed three battles. Whether these were disposed in line abreast, with archers thrown forward on the two outer flanks; or whether the longbowmen were placed to either side of each battle (the tactics of Dupplin Moor (1332) and Halidon Hill (1333)); and whether the two battles were in the front line, with the third, commanded by Edward, in the centre but to the rear as a reserve, are matters still hotly disputed: contemporary sources are ambiguous.

When the Genoese began the attack at 17.00, they were quickly repulsed, whereupon the count of Alençon, commanding the main cavalry, rode through the retreating archers only to meet the English archers' same devastating fire, while primitive cannon (this may have been their first use in the field) caused further panic. The English right wing briefly wavered, and in the centre the Black Prince, who was 'winning his spurs' as his father wished, was hard pressed. But the French were broken, Philip VI fleeing the field. English casualties were light but there were thousands of French dead, among them the counts of Flanders, Alençon, and Blois, the duke of Lorraine, and blind King John of Bohemia, whose retinue, in a supremely quixotic gesture, had, at his own request, led him into battle with their bridles tied together. If the strategic gains for Edward III were slight (it needed the capture of Calais in 1347 to consolidate Crécy), for Philip VI the battle was not only a military disaster but also a political catastrophe.

Edward's victory dealt a major blow to French morale, as did the English victory over the Scots at Neville's Cross (17 October 1346), and the surrender of Calais in the following year. Calais was subsequently developed as an English military and trading base, and was not retaken by the French until 1558. Papally sponsored negotiations at Guines in 1354 failed and the war began again in 1355. Edward, prince of Wales (the Black Prince) carried out a raid across southern France from Bordeaux almost to the Mediterranean coast. In 1356 the duke of Lancaster was active in Normandy and the Black Prince raided northwards. Forced to give battle at Poitiers, he won an emphatic victory, capturing John II. Edward launched what turned out to be his last major attack in 1359, probably hoping to take Rheims and to be crowned French king. But his plan failed and he agreed instead to a settlement, the Treaty of Brétigny, 8 May 1360.

The Battle of Nájera (1367)

When the Treaty of Brétigny halted fighting, England and France continued their rivalry in other theatres. Both sides intervened in the war between King Peter the Cruel of Castile and his illegitimate brother Henry of Trastamara, who in 1365 gained the support of mercenaries led by Bertrand Du Guesclin. Peter riposted by allying with Edward the Black Prince, who in early 1367 led a battle-hardened force from Guyenne to Peter's aid and defeated Henry and his allies at Nájera, between Burgos and Pamplona, on 3 April. Using the classic English tactic of dismounted men at arms and archers, they won the day but their bloody success was reversed two years later when Henry murdered Peter and seized the Castilian crown.

The battle of Crécy.

In the next period of conflict (1369–89) the English did badly, losing almost all of their recent gains. In 1396 a long truce (due to last to 1426) was agreed, as was the marriage of Richard II to Charles VI's daughter Isabella. This situation was thrown into disarray by Charles's insanity, which led to civil war in France which, by 1410, had reached such a height that the two parties sought English assistance. This convinced the English that time was ripe for a new initiative in France. Thus in 1415 Henry V launched his first invasion.

The Battle of Agincourt (1415)

The battle fought near Agincourt (Azincourt) in northern France on 25 October 1415 (the feast of Sts Crispin and Crispinian) ranks high on any list of English victories. Having invaded France in August and captured Harfleur by the end of September, and now intent upon returning to England, Henry V was marching to Calais when his force was challenged by a French army blocking his advance. The king had little choice but to fight. Under his command he had some 6,000 fighting men; the enemy army may have been three times the size, although good recent research tends to downplay its superiority. Following a night of rain, the English drew up their battle line, with several large groups of archers, to await the French attack.

Some French knights charged on horseback, but the majority advanced on foot over land rendered soft by the recent rain. As they approached, probably in close formation, they were met by a hail of arrows which killed or wounded large numbers of mounts and horsemen, as well as heavily armoured knights trudging forward on foot, so lessening the force of the attack, impeding those wishing to retire, and obstructing those advancing from the rear. Having thus sown confusion in the French ranks, the English, mostly fighting on foot, moved in to the kill. While the English dead may have numbered some 300–400, the French lost several thousand men, including many nobles, either killed or taken captive. Fearing a French counter-attack Henry ordered his men to kill their prisoners, although his order was not universally obeyed. The battle is an excellent example of a small, well-disciplined, well-led, and highly motivated force with little to lose overcoming a larger one lacking discipline and proper leadership, and overconfident of victory.

Successes followed apace over the next few years, not only due to the military genius of Henry V and his commanders but also because of divisions within France. By the Treaty of Troyes (21 May 1420) Henry became heir to Charles VI (the dauphin, later Charles VII, 1422–61, was disinherited) and regent of France. Those acting on behalf of his son Henry VI, who was only 9 months old at his father's death in 1422, had the difficult task of attempting to extend the area under their control. Victories in battle at Cravant (31 July 1423) and Verneuil (16 August 1424—a battle where the dauphin's armies were boosted by Scots allies) assisted, and by 1428 the frontier had been pushed to the Loire. But the dauphin's forces managed to raise the siege laid to Orléans, partly through the boost to morale given by Joan of Arc. Charles's army went on to defeat the English at Patay (18 June 1429) and to recapture much of the land to the east of Paris, enabling the dauphin to be crowned at Rheims a month later.

From then onwards the English were forced onto the defensive. What was left of English Normandy fell in 1450, Gascony following suit in 1451. A rebellion against the French in Bordeaux in 1453 encouraged the English to send an army under the veteran John Talbot, earl of Shrewsbury.

The Battle of Castillon (1453)

On the field of Castillon on 17 July the English lost Gascony. An Anglo-Gascon attack on a French fortified artillery park on the Dordogne, upstream from Castillon la Bataille, was probably launched without knowledge of the strength of its defences. For a short while, despite the hail of shot and ball, the rampart was gained. But the assault was repulsed and the attackers overrun, their legendary John Talbot being killed in the rout. Thus, in an action not unlike the Charge of the Light Brigade, the Hundred Years War came to an end.

The Battle of Kosovo (1389)

The most important battle in Serbian history took place at Kosovo Polje (Kosovo field) on St Vitus' Day, 28 June 1389 (or 15 June according to the old Orthodox calendar) between armies led by the Serbian prince Lazar and the Ottoman sultan Murad. The result, though inconclusive, has been celebrated since in Serbian epic poetry as a defeat of great mystical significance, ushering in four centuries of Ottoman domination. No accounts by participants in the battle survive, though it is accepted that both Murad and Lazar were killed. Recent historians put the strength of the armies at about 30,000 on the Ottoman side and 15,000–20,000 on the Serb side. Serb oral legend has it that Lazar chose defeat, after being offered a choice between a heavenly and an earthly kingdom on the eve of the battle.

The Battle of Tannenberg (1410)

Also known as the battle of Grünwald, the battle of Tannenberg, fought in what is now northern Poland, was the decisive engagement of the Great War of 1409–11, in which Polish–Lithuanian–Russian forces defeated the military monastic order of the Teutonic Knights, who ruled the region from their vast, forbidding castle-monastery at Marienburg (Malbork). The Polish King Władisław II Jagiełło led a multinational force of about 30,000 Poles, Lithuanians, Russians, Czechs, and even Mongols towards Marienburg. On 14 July 1410, moving north-west, they encountered the grand master of the Teutonic order, Ulrich von Jungingen, commanding a slightly smaller force between Grünwald and Tannenberg (Stembark). His knights, with some Swiss and English mercenaries, took up position on a crest.

The battle began with a salvo from the Teutonic order's bombards but, like most artillery of the time, they had little effect in the open field. The Tartar cavalry then attacked the order's right flank, but was driven off. The Lithuanian prince Vitovt also attacked but was driven off, and the knights began to pursue. The Russians held the centre, however, and the Poles then attacked, again from the right, this time breaking the knights' formation. All the order's senior officers, including the grand master, were killed in a crushing defeat that halted its eastward advance permanently. This decisive defeat of the Teutonic Knights also gave encouragement to the Hussites in their struggle against the Holy Roman Empire.

Hussite Wars (1419–34)

There were three elements in the fourteenth and early fifteenth centuries that signalled the decline of the armoured knight: archers using the longbow, the Swiss pikemen, and the Hussite wagenburg. While the first two are well known, at least in the west, the third remains somewhat obscure.

By means of truly revolutionary tactics the vastly superior forces of the Holy Roman Empire were beaten by a gang of peasants and freemen fighting for a cause they believed to be just. These victories can be ascribed to the one-eyed visionary Jan Zizka. In an age not known for military innovation, he introduced armoured warfare and massive fire-power onto the battlefield by combining cavalry and infantry into a flexible forma-tion impervious to the charge of armoured knights. With a force of around 25,000 he was able to defeat forces two or even three times his own strength. He trained a third of his men with handguns that could penetrate steel plate armour. The Hussite strain of militant Christian fundamentalism, derived from the teachings of Jan Hus who had been executed as a heretic in 1415, gave them a firm conviction in the next life and an insouciance about leaving this one.

Although the idea of a defensive wagon laager was not new, its use as a mobile offensive weapon was. Furthermore these were no civilian ox-carts but stoutly built and fireproofed wheeled constructions, designed solely for war. They were iron reinforced, and liberally provided with loopholes from which the twenty or so crew could keep up a devastating handgun fire, with the added luxury of having all their ammunition carried for them. In defence they could be chained one to another for added solidity. Other wheeled devices transported larger artillery pieces of varying calibres, two of which were Hussite inven-tions: the *tarasnice* and *houfnice*, translated into German as *Haufnitze* or *Haubitze*, from where we get the English howitzer.

The whole body, wagons, guns, men, and horses, was trained to operate as a unit and could rapidly adopt any desired formation to meet an attack, or act as a piledriver forward into the enemy's ranks. There was also a mounted element of crossbowmen equally adept at reconnaissance and pursuit. The only method to defeat the Hussites was to induce them to leave the safety of their vehicles.

The Hussites were successful at Prague in 1419, where they repelled a frontal assault on a hill outside the city. The cleverly sited Hussite artillery caught their assailants in a withering crossfire. At Kuttenburg in 1422 the German knights were baulked by the wagon forts, and a wild countercharge supported by artillery utterly destroyed them. After the death of Zizka, the Hussites were again victorious at Aussig in 1426 under Procop the Bald, attacking with a combination of wagons and cavalry.

When Zdnek of Sternberg led an anti-Hussite crusade from 1464 to 1471, many dis-reputable Bohemian mercenaries were brought in to make up for a lack of numbers, and the true Hussite army was nothing but a glorious memory.

THE WARS OF THE ROSES

The name 'Wars of the Roses' is given to the sequence of plots, rebellions, and battles that took place between 1455 and 1487. They are so called because of the notion that, being fought between the dynasties of Lancaster and York, Lancaster was represented by a red rose, York by a white.

There were three distinct phases: between 1455 and 1464, between 1469 and 1471, and between 1483 and 1487. The first began as a conflict between rival factions for control of the kingdom under the weak and vacillating Lancastrian King Henry VI, but became a war for possession of the crown in 1460, settled for a brief period in favour of Edward IV of the house of York. The second was similar in pattern to the first, in which factional conflict led eventually to renewed dynastic war between Edward IV and supporters of Henry VI (briefly restored). The third was entirely dynastic and led to the accession of Henry VII.

When Richard, duke of York, supported by the Neville earls of Salisbury and Warwick, defeated the duke of Somerset at the first battle of St Albans on 22 May 1455, he secured control of the king and the government for a short while. He rose once more in rebellion in 1459. Athough he was outmanoeuvred at the rout of Ludlow in September 1459, his son Edward and Warwick the Kingmaker recovered power at the battle of Northampton on 10 July 1460. Thereafter York was declared heir to the throne by the victorious faction.

The Battle of Wakefield (1460)

In October York declared that his son Edward was his heir, and in December he gathered a small army at Sandal castle, outside Wakefield. The Lancastrians, under the formidable Queen Margaret, moved up to Pontefract. On 30 or 31 December 1460, after a Christmas truce, a Lancastrian force under Lord Clifford, with detachments under the duke of Somerset and the earl of Northumberland close behind, approached Sandal castle. For reasons which remain unclear, York emerged from the castle. Perhaps he was taken by surprise, or was running short of supplies and some of his men were out foraging. Out in the open, York's outnumbered men had no chance. They were cut to pieces: York, his son Edmund, and allegedly 2,800 Yorkists were killed.

Warwick was then beaten at the second battle of St Albans on 17 February. The Yorkist cause was saved by Edward of York, who, although only 18, having first defeated a Lancastrian army at Mortimer's Cross in the Welsh Marches, seized London and made himself king.

The Battle of Towton (1461)

The battle of Towton was fought over two days, 28–29 March 1461: it involved the largest numbers and was not only the bloodiest engagement of the Wars of the Roses, but almost certainly the most costly on British soil. But as if to compensate for its scale, it is also appallingly documented. Fighting began when Lord Fauconberg, a veteran of the wars in France, forced the passage of the Aire at Ferrybridge on the 28th. Edward IV followed up the next day, his initial attack possibly assisted by flurries of snow driving into the enemy and giving his archers extra range. The battle, whose details are obscure, was long and exceptionally hard fought, and was decided late in the day when the duke of Norfolk threw 'a fresh band of good men' against the Lancastrian left flank. Many Lancastrians died in flight trying to cross the Cock Beck behind their lines. There were many notable casualties, both killed on the field and massacred afterwards, but contemporary estimates of 28,000 killed are probably too high, and it may be that the battle was about as bloody as Marston Moor, the largest battle of the Civil War, fought only a short distance away in 1644.

Sporadic war continued in the far north until 1464 and Harlech castle remained in Lancastrian hands until 1468. By then Edward IV had fallen out with Warwick, his principal supporter. The following year Warwick took to arms and destroyed his enemies at the battle of Edgcote on 26 July. But in the spring of 1470 he fled to France. There he made his peace with the remaining Lancastrians led by Henry VI's queen, Margaret of Anjou. With French support Warwick landed in the name of Henry VI that autumn. Deserted by his troops, Edward IV fled to the shelter of his brother-in-law the duke of Burgundy. Henry VI, who had been a prisoner in the Tower, was restored to the throne. But Edward IV returned in the spring of 1471 and, in a brilliant campaign, defeated his divided enemies, first Warwick at Barnet on 14 April and then Margaret of Anjou at Tewkesbury on 4 May. At Tewkesbury the heir to Lancaster was killed, and his death sealed the fate of Henry VI, who was murdered by his captors.

The wars would have come to an end in 1471 had not Edward IV's youngest brother Richard, duke of Gloucester, assumed the throne on his brother's death in June 1483 arguing that Edward IV's sons were the product of a bigamous marriage and were thus illegitimate.

The Battle of Bosworth (1485)

A three-week campaign by Henry Tudor, earl of Richmond, in his bid for the throne of England culminated near the small Leicestershire town of Market Bosworth. The armies met on the plain called Redemore on the morning of 22 August 1485. The sparse sources make it difficult to reconstruct the action's course or even to be sure of its precise location, but it is likely that Richard drew up his much larger army in the customary three 'battles' (large divisions of troops) across Henry's line of advance, protected by a marsh. Probably attempting to turn his enemy's flank, Tudor's vanguard under the earl of Oxford was attacked by the duke of Norfolk commanding Richard's right. At first Oxford's mainly French contingent gave way, but then reforming they counter-attacked and drove Norfolk back. At this moment, seeing Tudor standing a little way off with only a small guard, Richard charged. The velocity of his attack carried him close to his enemy, but Sir William Stanley, who had held his contingent back and was in collusion with Tudor, chose this moment to show his hand. Richard was cut down and killed, having thrown away a battle he should have won. Although its traditional location is very well commemorated, in 1990 Peter J. Foss argued convincingly in *The Field of Redemore* that the battle's actual site was further to the south, and there are other, scarcely less persuasive, suggestions. Henry survived a challenge from the earl of Lincoln, assisted by a force of German mercenaries, at Stoke Field, near Newark, in 1487.

The Battle of Cerignola (1503)

The battle of Cerignola took place during the early French–Italian wars when Louis XII of France invaded Naples. It was the first to be won by infantry firepower. Gonzalo de Córdoba, commanding the battle-hardened Spanish army, engaged a Franco-Swiss army

Armoured knights with couched lances attack cross-bowmen, supported by archers armed with the longbow; a scene depicting the Earl of Warwick in battle.

some 32 km (20 miles) from Barletta on the southern Adriatic. An assault led by Swiss pikemen and French *gens d'armes* was shattered by the Spanish arquebusiers firing from the protection of pikemen behind a ditch and palisade. A deft counter-attack completed the victory and the French were forced to abandon the kingdom of Naples.

3 The Renaissance to the French Revolution

Although the Renaissance, 'the revival of art and letters under the influence of classical models', spanned the fourteenth, fifteenth, and sixteenth centuries, medieval warfare ended more swiftly. Historians often date its demise to 1494, when the French king Charles VIII invaded Italy, taking with him a train of bronze guns which were light enough to trundle along primitive roads but strong enough to sustain powerful charges and so to rip away the stonework of castles, sliding wall into ditch and leaving the place 'storm-ripe'. Charles thundered through Italy in the blitzkrieg of his age, levelling the symbols of Spanish and Habsburg power as he went.

The key to his success was mobile artillery, and gunners were to struggle for the next three centuries to achieve a workable balance between the effect they craved and the weight of the weapon required to deliver it. The mighty cast-iron bombard Mons Meg, made for the duke of Burgundy in 1449 and subsequently taken to Scotland, fired a 45-cm (18-inch) stone ball. But when she took the field in 1497, despite scores of oxen and a large team of workmen, Meg broke down just outside Edinburgh and it took three days to get her on the road again. The barrel of a modest field-piece, throwing a ball weighing 1.5 kg (3 lb), required two men to lift it, and bigger guns were correspondingly cumbersome. It was not simply the availability of fodder for animals that tended to restrict campaigning to the summer season (not for nothing is March named for the Roman god of war): moving heavy guns along winter roads was all but impossible. Water transport helped enormously, and a single line-of-battle ship, the decisive instrument in naval warfare by the eighteenth century, could carry more heavy guns than the whole of a field army.

Monarchs paid increasing attention to the construction and maintenance of roads, not simply because they facilitated commerce, but because they enabled gunners to move more easily. Part of the significance of fortresses, so characteristic of the age, was their ability to house battering trains of heavy guns within striking distance of a hostile frontier. They were not simply defensive, but pivots for offensive manoeuvre too, storing artillery and rations as part of the 'magazine system' that could enable an army to move between friendly fortresses as a parrot uses claws and beak to swing between the bars of its cage.

Just as modern artillery enabled an attacker to make short work of obsolete fortresses, so too it allowed monarchs to deal swiftly with contumacious subjects. In 1523 the Rhineland knight Franz von Sickengen was in dispute with his master, the Holy Roman Emperor, and retired disdainfully to his castle of Landstuhl. Once he might have expected to stand siege until the emperor lost interest. But now the emperor's gunners brought his walls down about his ears in a single day, and killed him.

Gunpowder was slower to make its presence felt on the battlefield. But just as the fall of Constantinople and the 1494 Italian campaign were to change the face of fortress warfare, so battles like Ravenna (1512), Marignano (1515), and Pavia (1525) showed the way that things were moving in the field. In the first two battles, field artillery helped convert camps into fortifications which could not be taken by assault, and in the latter Spanish infantry with hackbuts (forerunners of the musket) blew away the flower of French

March with your rest in your hand.

March, and with your Musket carry your rest.

Unshoulder your Musk

Poize your Musket

Join your rest to your Musket.

Take forth your Match

Blow off your Coal.

Cock your Match.

Try your Match

chivalry. Yet transition was gradual, and the period was an uneasy blend of old and new. Men plying pikes needed deep formations to administer shock and maintain momentum: soldiers of the British Civil Wars of the 1640s and 1650s were to speak of 'push of pike', and the phrase emphasizes the scrum-like characteristic infantry battle. However, soldiers using hackbut or musket were best deployed in line to maximize their firepower. From the early sixteenth to the early seventeenth century most infantry fought in phalanxes which would not have astonished Alexander the Great, with lines of musketeers (the expression 'sleeves of shot' has it perfectly) on their flanks.

The Spanish tercio (so called because it was nominally one-third of an army) was developed by Gonzalo de Córdoba, who beat the Swiss at Cerignola in 1503, arguably the first battle to be won by musketry. The tercio contained both pikemen and arquebusiers, and was divided into twelve companies. It did not simply hark back to classical military patterns (it might well have been called a legion had François I of France not chosen that name for his own very similar bodies of foot), but pointed the way ahead to subsequent organizations. Indeed, the terminology of rank was emerging. A column was commanded by a *colonello*, hence colonel, whose deputy, or lieutenant, gives us lieutenant colonel. Captains commanded companies, with lieutenants as their deputies. The most junior officers (ensigns in the infantry, and cornets or guidons in the cavalry) were so called because they carried their company's identifying flag or colour.

Cavalry had always found it difficult to break determined infantry, and the development of infantry firepower complicated their task. By about 1540 German heavy cavalry, known as reiters, were abandoning the lance for a pair of wheel-lock pistols. These were used in a manoeuvre called the caracole, in which a column of horsemen rode up to within range of their opponents and opened fire, usually with successive ranks firing both pistols and then trotting to the rear of the formation to reload. Although this might succeed against infantry who were poorly provided with firearms, it would fare badly against a tercio or similar body of foot. Against other caracoling cavalry the result was too often wholly inconclusive, with trampling horses and squibbing pistols—but no decision.

If artillery revolutionized the attack of fortresses, the development of engineering was no less significant in their defence. Interestingly, the antidote to the new artillery was being developed shortly before the disease was fully apparent. The defining characteristic of what has come to be called 'artillery fortification' was the bastion, an arrowhead-shaped work stepping out from the main curtain wall of the fortress. One of the first examples of this is at Poggio Imperiale in Tuscany, and dates from 1487. It already shows what we might term the DNA of a breed that was to be genetically engineered over the next two centuries.

The bastion's walls presented flat surfaces with sharp angles to help deflect shot. They were thick, with deep earth confined by the stone face of the scarp, protected by a ditch, which might be wet or dry. Across the ditch rose the counterscarp, topped by a covered way deep and broad enough for men to walk along it without being seen. From the timber palisade topping the covered way (robust enough to deflect storming infantry, but offering no cover from the defenders' fire) the ground sloped gently away in the glacis,

The military manual became commonplace in the early 17th century. Jacob de Geyn published his instruction book in 1607 and the illustrations were copied once again to show the exercises of a musketeer in Grose's *Military Antiquities* in the early 19th century.

sculpted so that artillery fire from the ramparts would sweep it like some deadly besom. Conversely, the glacis, counterscarp, and ramparts between them were so carefully engineered that an attacker looking up from the foot of the glacis would see only the top of the parapet, perhaps pierced by splayed embrasures for the defender's guns. Bastions were mutually supporting, with the guns on the flank of each bastion covering the curtain wall between them, and the cannon on their angled faces snarling out across ditch and glacis.

The basic design of the bastioned trace was subject to almost infinite elaboration, and some of the most significant features are associated with the careers of those two masters of the game, the Frenchman Sebastien le Prestre de Vauban and his Dutch opponent Menno van Coehoorn. Detached bastion-like works called ravelins or (from their shape) *demi-lunes* were thrown out in front of the trace to defend the gaps between the bastions. Elaborate outworks might strengthen gateways or natural approaches; extra gun batteries called cavaliers could be built up within the bastions to multiply firepower; and earth banks known as *tenailles* lurked in the ditch to hinder an attacker's artillery, even if it had been brought very close, in its assault on the base of the scarp. A dry ditch might be defended by a squat little fortification called a caponier (from the Spanish for chicken-house), and the attacker's attempts to undermine the covered way might be thwarted by pre-dug countermine galleries.

None of this made fortresses impregnable, for attackers developed techniques of their own. First they would try to cut off the fortress from outside help and establish their own park for guns and the other impedimenta of siege warfare. Then they would open a first line of entrenchment, the first parallel, out of effective range of the defender's artillery, and then sap forward, trenches zigzagging so as not to present an end-on shoot to hostile artillery, to reach a second parallel. More sapping took them to a third parallel, whence they might be able to undermine the work facing them, or erect batteries to dismount the guns in the chosen sector, prior to assaulting the covered way. Once that was carried, breaching batteries would be established to hammer away at the base of the scarp, cutting a long groove called a cannelure. Eventually gravity would bring scarp and rampart into the ditch, creating not simply a gap in the defences but also a rough slope that the attackers could use to scale it. A wise governor, axiomatically offered the opportunity to capitulate, would seek what terms he could get, because if the defender was put to the trouble of mounting a storm his furious soldiers could not be expected to respect the property of the citizens or the bodies of their womenfolk.

Much could go wrong for either side before this moment came. A relieving force might compel the attacker to raise the siege; a sortie might do serious damage, perhaps by wrecking irreplaceable siege guns; or one of the mortar bombs lobbed high-angle by both sides might set off a powder magazine. In 1687 the Venetians took the acropolis at Athens from the Turks after two magazines were blown up, though not before a good deal of 'collateral damage' had been incurred by the Parthenon. Nevertheless, in general a fortress would be able to impose perhaps a month's delay on an attacker, no mean feat given the shortness of the campaigning season. In 1708 the energetic Marshal Boufflers defended Lille against the duke of Marlborough and Prince Eugène of Savoy, and it took the allies 120 days to take it, soaking up the entire season which followed their victory at Oudenarde.

The importance of artillery fortification reached its peak by the early eighteenth century when, as Christopher Duffy observes, 'the business of sieges had been the central, formative experience of warfare—the school of soldiers and captains—and when the military art had been understood to consist largely of operations relating directly or indirectly to the attack or defence of strongholds'. The proliferation of fortresses acted as a brake on war. A Spanish general, writing from the Low Countries in 1574, told his royal master: 'There would not be time or money enough in the world to reduce the twenty-four towns which have rebelled so far in Holland if we are to spend as long in reducing each one of them as we have over similar ones so far.'

But although fortresses remained important even beyond the French Revolution, their overall significance declined. Armies grew increasingly adept at cross-country movement, bypassing choke-points, and grew in size so that they were often able to 'mask' irritating fortresses and get on with other tasks at the same time. As early as 1552 Henri II of France was able to use one army to watch Metz, under siege by the Emperor Charles V, and to use another one to snap up the emperor's fortress at Hesdin in northern France. This compelled Charles to relinquish his grip on Metz, generously quipping as he did so that fortune far preferred young heroes (a reference to the duke of Guise, the city's governor) to old emperors.

This growth in armies and their increasing professionalism was one of the features of the age. It is notoriously hard to be sure of the size of medieval armies but the English had perhaps 6,000 men at Agincourt in 1415 and the French possibly 12,000. In 1567 the duke of Alva set off to coerce the Netherlands with 10,600 men, and just over 50 years later both Gustavus Adolphus and Albrecht von Wallenstein each commanded 100,000. The French army had 30,000 men in 1672, when it expanded to 120,000 to fight the Dutch War, and at the start of the War of Spanish Succession it maintained some 360,000. Frederick the Great had more than 160,000 troops under his hand in the spring of 1757, and during the whole of the Seven Years War he lost some 180,000 men killed. All this was made possible by a dramatic and sustained increase in economic activity and by a sharp growth in both population sizes and surplus resources which could be devoted to war.

As armies grew, so they changed in character. At the beginning of the period mercenaries were widely used. They could be hired when needed and (at least in theory) laid off when they were not, and so constituted no lasting charge upon the state. They could be chosen as masters of a particular technology, like the Viking axemen in the Varangian guard of Byzantine emperors, German *Landsknechte*, or Genoese crossbowmen. And the losses they incurred did not damage the native population. But as the Florentine statesman Niccolò Machiavelli, writing in an age when *condottieri* had a disproportionate impact on politics, complained: 'The present ruin of Italy is the result of nothing else than reliance upon mercenaries.' Widespread use of mercenaries by all sides during the Thirty Years War sharpened the edge of that conflict, and afterwards states relied increasingly on native-born soldiers, with the burgeoning power of their bureaucracy now able not only to conscript men but even, through institutions like Louis XIV's Invalides and Charles II's Royal Hospitals at Chelsea and Kilmainham, to give a measure of care to some veterans. Although mercenaries did not disappear during the period, they became increasingly anomalous in the age of mass national armies.

The final key characteristic of the age remains a matter of dispute. Between 1600, when infantry still fought in dense hedgehogs and cavalry caracoled about the battlefield, and 1700, when musket-armed infantry fought in line and cavalry charged home with the sword, there were changes so marked that Michael Roberts, writing in 1956, identified what he called a 'military revolution'. Armies were no longer 'a brute mass in the Swiss style nor a collection of bellicose individuals in the feudal style'. An army was now an 'articulated organism'. Tactical changes, inspired by Maurice of Nassau and Gustavus Adolphus, had altered the way they fought. Their growing size and evolving composition had transformed their relationship with a state which was in itself changing, and 'the conjoint ascendancy of financial power and applied science was already opened in all its malignancy'.

The 'military revolution' thesis did not long stand unchallenged. Geoffrey Parker argued that it had been much wider, and was in fact the key to understanding the establishment of European overseas empires. Jeremy Black later maintained that while there were indeed revolutionary periods in 1470–1530, with the advent of gunpowder, and again between about 1660 and 1720, with the arrival of the flintlock musket and the socket bayonet, the overall process was evolutionary, and so 'Roberts' emphasis on 1560–1660 is incorrect'. Moreover, he suggested that many tactical developments were hardly original: what happened was 'the clever adaptation of existing ideas to suit local circumstances'.

Some commentators, writing in the 1980s or 1990s, saw the period as a metaphor for their times, when, or so it seemed to many, another military revolution was taking place. Indeed, there are now several separate definitions, like 'Revolution in Military Affairs' and 'Military-Technical Revolution'. The wise military historian Cyril Falls had already warned that observers tended to see the warfare of their own age as marking a break with the past, and suggested that instead military affairs evolved more or less continuously, albeit with occasional jerks as social attitudes and organization moved to catch up, or a particular technology caused a change.

In one sense the debate is fruitless. Military affairs did not change so quickly and comprehensively that the process constituted, in terms of speed and totality, a genuine revolution. Yet there can be no doubt that on the eve of the French Revolution the armies of monarchical Europe looked wholly dissimilar to those of the Thirty Years War or the British Civil Wars, and the centralized nation-states that raised, paid, and equipped them looked very unlike what it is now fashionable to call the 'pre-Westphalia' states that existed before the 1648 treaty that ended the Thirty Years War. Michael Roberts may have exaggerated when he wrote that: 'The road lay open, broad and straight, to the abyss of the twentieth century.' But the ingredients were in place for an explosion of military activity whose dust has still not wholly settled.

The Battle of Flodden (1513)

In 1513 James IV of Scotland invaded England with some 40,000 men, including 5,000 Frenchmen, and five great cannon while Henry VIII was away in France. Thomas Howard, earl of Surrey, responsible for the north of England, gathered 20,000 men to oppose him. In medieval style, he challenged James to battle at Milfield, south of Flodden. However, the battle owed more to the fact that the English had cut off the Scots' line of retreat northwards, ignoring the south-facing prepared positions the Scots occupied on Flodden Edge and making a forced march to the east before turning south to Branxton. Witnesses recalled seeing cartloads of arrows being ferried north for the English army. James had to abandon his fortified line and turn about to Branxton Hill. Late in the afternoon of 9 September 1513, the Scots attacked. The 2.5-m (8-foot) English bill proved handier than the 4.5-m (15-foot) Scots pike but the victory was won by the English archers. King James and 10,000 of his soldiers and officers, including the flower of the Scots aristocracy, were killed. The lament 'Flowers of the Forest' recalls the tragedy which befell the Scots nation.

OTTOMAN WARS

The Ottomans or Osmanlis established themselves in north-western Anatolia, expanding at the expense of Byzantium and the Italian trading colonies of the Aegean shores. They then overran much of the Balkans, extinguishing ancient monarchies there, and forming these lands into the province of Rumelia, European Turkey. Their advance was delayed for a generation by an incursion by Timur, but in 1453 Mehmet II the Conqueror captured Constantinople. The extinction of the Byzantine empire alarmed Christian Europe, but disunity prevented any concerted effort to stem the momentum of Ottoman conquest. The sultans of the sixteenth century went on to conquer further territory.

The Battle of Mohacs (1526)
The battle of Mohacs was a decisive defeat of Hungarian forces by the Ottoman Turks, effectively destroying the Hungarian monarchy. Suleiman the Magnificent demanded tribute from a failing Hungarian state. When it refused to pay, he advanced, capturing Sabac and Belgrade (then lying within the Hungarian dominions). The Hungarian King Louis II assembled a puny army of 20,000 and advanced from Buda (one of the twin cities which became Budapest). On 29 August 1526 he ill-advisedly attacked 100,000 well-armed, -trained, -paid, and -motivated Ottoman Turks. Unsurprisingly, he was killed and his army annihilated. Suleiman took Buda but then withdrew, taking with him 100,000 prisoners as slaves.

The Siege of Vienna (1529)
Suleiman again invaded Hungary in 1528–9, adding the greater part of that realm to the Ottoman empire. He then went on to besiege the Habsburg capital Vienna and ravaged its suburbs (27 September–15 October 1529), but the early onset of winter plus lack of supplies and armaments compelled him to lift the siege and return to Istanbul.

The Battle of Lepanto (1571)
Lepanto was the largest ever sea battle in the Mediterranean, fought between the Ottoman Turks with about 275 ships and the Holy League of Venice, the Habsburg dominions, Malta, Genoa, and other Italian states led by the papacy, with about 210. Sultan Selim the Sot had a passion for Cyprus wine, and in 1570 the Turks captured the island. The west's reaction was unprecedented. A massive and well-appointed fleet was formed under the command of Don Juan of Austria, a bastard son of Charles V. He sighted the Ottoman fleet off Lepanto (Navpaktos) on the Gulf of Patras, in western Greece. Almost all the ships were galleys but the league also had six galleasses, big hybrid ships between a galley and a galleon, with oars and guns along the broadside. The Turkish galleys were

rowed by slaves: some of the Christian ships were rowed by volunteers. Whereas the Turks still favoured ramming, the Christian galleys had large guns pointing forward above the ram, and were well protected against the Turkish arrows. In the ensuing carnage, up to 200 of the Turkish ships were sunk or captured, as against just fifteen of the league's galleys, the Turks' first major defeat in two centuries and the largest number of sinkings in any sea battle. The near-complete destruction of the Ottoman fleet resounded round Europe. But the western states reckoned without the efficiency of Ottoman administration. The Turks cut down a forest and rebuilt their fleet within a year, and held on to Cyprus when the war ended in 1573.

FRENCH WARS OF RELIGION

The Wars of Religion were much more than a confessional dispute. They embodied dynastic, factional, social, and personal frictions, set against a European financial, political, and religious crisis. The Peace of Cateau-Cambrésis (1559) ended a long period of Habsburg–Valois rivalry and France already displayed a certain homogeneity, summed up as 'une foi, une loi, un roi' (one faith, one law, one king). However, the monarchy was not absolute, but relied on the support of a powerful and divided nobility, which, though exempt from taxation, had been beggared by the wars. Some capitalized on patronage exercised by the crown and high nobility to enter the Church: others joined those already demanding church reform. Calvinism was also attractive to lesser men who saw it as an attack on the old order. The royal commander in Guyenne, Blaise de Monluc, wrote that a local Huguenot (French Protestant) leader had claimed: 'We are the kings, and he that you speak of is a little turdy roylet; we'll whip his breech and set him to a trade, to teach him to get his living as others do.' Huguenot communities placed themselves under the protection of sympathetic noblemen, and by 1560 were organized on quasi-military lines, each church with its captain and each synod with its colonel.

The first war (1562–3) and the second (1567–8) were inconclusive. The third war (1568–70) involved more serious fighting. The Catholics beat the Huguenots at Jarnac and Montcontour (1569) but the new Huguenot commander, Admiral Gaspard de Coligny, prolonged the war by skilful manoeuvre which stretched the crown's finances beyond sustainable limits. After peace was negotiated, the queen mother, Catherine de' Medici, attempted to achieve unity by marrying her daughter Margaret to Henri of Navarre, the future Henri IV. She also tried to create good relations with England's Elizabeth I. This failed and the success of the Spanish in the Netherlands restored their influence. The brief peace collapsed entirely when Coligny was murdered and a massacre of Huguenots began on the feast of St Bartholomew, 24 August 1572. The fourth war followed.

The longest of the wars—sometimes called the War of the Three Henries, from Henri III, Henri of Navarre, and Henri, duc de Guise—raged from 1584 to 1589. The last of the wars, the War of the League (1589–98), began with the league consolidating its grip on many cities. In September 1589 Henri IV met the duc de Mayenne near Arques, south of Dieppe.

The battle of Lepanto.

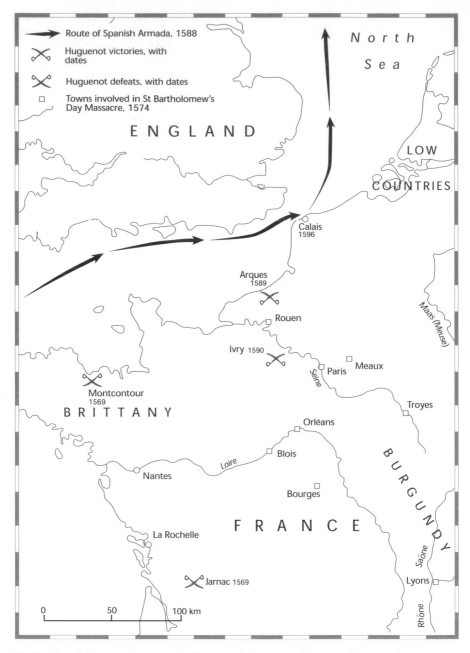

The battles of the French Wars of Religion and the route of the Spanish Armada

The Battle of Arques (1589)

Mayenne's vast army was encamped around the village of Martin-Église, east of the river Béthune and north of a lesser stream that flowed into it. It is reported he had, in this impregnable position, possibly as many as 30,000 men. Henri's force was very much smaller, perhaps 8,000. From the village a road ran east of the Béthune's marshy course southwards before turning to Arques and to the east was the Forest of Arques. Henri had two trenches dug astride the road across the narrow fields and placed his infantry, including 1,200 Swiss, in the trenches and in a chapel between the trenches. The 600 cavalry were divided into two, one detachment under Henri himself between the road and the wood, the other under the duc de Sully in the space between road and marsh. The next day, in fog, Mayenne attacked, although the narrow front meant that he could never deploy more than a small proportion of his army. His vanguard gained control of the front-line trench, possibly by similating surrender, while Sully's horse fought a series of attacks on the left, being eventually forced to shelter around the chapel. Mayenne's foot then forced Henri's troops out of that position and things looked distinctly perilous. The Swiss, however, held firm. An attempt by Mayenne's cavalry to outflank the position to the west led to their floundering in the marsh, but the huge numbers at his disposal still threatened to swamp Henri's men. Then the fog thinned, the sun broke through, and the gunners in Arques had a clear view of the attackers. Although Henri had only four cannon, five close-range salvos threw Mayenne's men into disorder and retreat, leaving the field to Henri.

The respite allowed Henri's reinforcements to arrive, not only French, but some 4,000 English and Scots provided by Elizabeth I. In the following year, having taken Honfleur, March found Henri besieging Dreux and planning the relief of Meulan on the Seine, where he expected to encounter Mayenne once more. Then the news came that his enemy had crossed the Seine and was only a few miles away.

The Battle of Ivry (1590)

On Monday 12 March Henri left Dreux and withdrew westwards to Nonancourt. The next day he occupied the billets his opponents had marked down for themselves and, that morning, arrayed his troops in a fine, open plain, but found himself too far away from Mayenne's force. That night he moved again and the next morning, the 13th, it turned out Mayenne had pulled back even more towards Ivry on the river Eure. Between ten and eleven that morning Henri, leading 2,000 cavalry and 8,000 foot, closed with them and Mayenne threw his men into battle. In less than an hour the league's cavalry had charged two, perhaps three, times and then broke, abandoning their infantry. Mayenne's Swiss mercenaries took the prudent course of throwing themselves on Henri's mercy while the rest of the infantry were shattered by attacks Henri led in person and either surrendered or fled into the woods. Four or five hundred horsemen were made prisoner and almost a thousand slain. Men attempted to flee by swimming the Eure and were pursued to the gates of Mantes.

Unable to seize Paris, Henri IV declared that he was prepared to return to the Catholic Church. Allegedly quipping that 'Paris is well worth a Mass', he was received into the Church at Saint-Denis in July 1593 and crowned at Chartres—for Rheims, where French kings were traditionally crowned, was in league hands. His conversion removed a major obstacle to peace, and Henri exploited his position with skill. He entered Paris in March 1594. He declared war on Spain in 1595, but the Spaniards had the better of it. The war ended with the Treaty of Vervins in 1598, the year the last of the league's leaders made peace with Henri. The Edict of Nantes, granted that year, gave the Huguenots freedom of conscience and wide rights of worship, and the right to garrison some hundred places of security at royal expense. It was a compromise which permitted the existence of two sects in one body politic, and was to last for the best part of a century.

Atrocities had been frequent, sometimes reflecting deliberate policy inflamed by religious passions, and sometimes demonstrating the casual brutality of a society at war for too long. Civilians had died in large numbers. Perhaps 12,000 of the inhabitants of Paris starved to death during the siege of 1590, and another 30,000 died of disease subsequently. In all, some two to four million perished.

The Spanish Armada (1588)

The voyage of the *Gran Armada* in the summer of 1588 is the subject of controversy on both the strategic and tactical levels. The Spanish plan, devised largely by Philip II himself between 1586 and 1588, involved an amphibious operation in which a fleet from Spain commanded by the duke of Medina Sidonia would occupy the anchorage in the Downs off the Kentish coast and protect a landing by an expeditionary force from the army of Flanders under the duke of Parma. The English, faced with a number of potential invasion sites, adopted a counter-strategy of intercepting the Armada in Iberian waters, but several attempts to do so between May and July 1588 were driven back by storms. Later in July the Armada (122 ships) sailed past the English fleet (66 ships) while it was replenishing in Plymouth harbour. The running battle up the Channel was inconclusive (two Spanish ships lost through accident) and only the English fireship attack on the Armada's anchorage off Calais broke the stalemate. The Armada lost four important warships at this point, but the rest had to cut their cables and the prevailing wind drove them into the North Sea. They were then obliged to sail around the British Isles to return home, at the cost of 35 of the weaker ships.

The 1588 campaign was a major English propaganda victory, but in strategic terms it was essentially indecisive.

THE THIRTY YEARS WAR

The Thirty Years War (1618–48) had its roots in the dynastic and imperial ambitions of the house of Habsburg and its leadership in the Counter-Reformation. In 1619 Ferdinand succeeded to the imperial throne on the Emperor Mathias's death, and Frederick, elector palatine, rashly agreed to stand as rival king of Bohemia. The Palatinate bordered on the Spanish Netherlands and Catholic Bavaria, providing two further flashpoints in addition to Bohemia itself, and Spanish troops soon occupied the Lower Palatinate while the Bavarians occupied the north. The Dutch and English, both supposed champions of the Protestant cause, were reluctant to become involved.

The Battle of White Mountain (1620)

The battle of White Mountain was fought at Bila Hora, west of Prague. On 8 November a 48,000-strong Bavarian-imperial army of the Catholic League defeated Frederick's 33,000-strong Protestant force. The latter mostly comprised foreigners who had no particular interest in defending the Czech people. As a result of the defeat what is now the Czech Republic came under the rule of the Habsburg empire for 300 years. Rebellious Bohemia was thoroughly ravaged by the imperial mercenary army, and forcibly restored to the Catholic faith.

A grand Protestant league was formed consisting of some German states, England, and Holland, secretly supported by France, and led by the imprudent Christian IV of Denmark, who began the attack in 1626. The Danes were sorely tried for three years by the more numerous imperial and Bavarian armies, led by the Bohemian mercenary Albrecht von Wallenstein, and by 1629 they had had enough of fighting without effective support from their allies, and sued for peace. The alliance collapsed, and it seemed that the Protestant cause was lost.

But by seeking to exploit their victory over the Danes to obtain an outlet to the Baltic, from which to strike at Dutch maritime commerce, the Habsburgs provoked their nemesis. Gustavus Adolphus, king of Sweden, offended by Habsburg behaviour and rescued from an inconclusive war against the Poles by French mediation, declared war in 1630.

The First Battle of Breitenfeld (1631)

At the first battle of Breitenfeld on 17 September 1631 Gustavus Adolphus with 30,000 Swedes and John George of Saxony with 10,000 electoral troops faced 32,000 imperialists under Graf Johan Tserclaes von Tilly. Gustavus intended to capture Leipzig, but found Tilly's troops drawn up in the rolling country 8 km (5 miles) to the north. After some desultory artillery fire from both sides, the imperialists mounted a cavalry attack on both flanks. The Saxons standing on Gustavus' left were soon put to flight, but on the opposite flank Graf Gottfried Heinrich von Pappenheim and his much-vaunted black cuirassiers could make little progress against the disciplined Swedish horse. The Swedes were able to extend their line, protecting their exposed left flank, and smash their way through Pappenheim's cavalry into the imperialist infantry. The Swedish centre under General Gustav Horn ground forward to meet Tilly's sixteen large infantry formations or tercios, denying them the space to manoeuvre, and eventually gaining the upper hand by dint of much hard fighting.

The imperialists lost over 7,000 killed or wounded, and a similar number of prisoners, against Swedish losses of 1,500 and Saxon casualties of 3,000. Tilly pulled back westward across the Weser, leaving Gustavus a free hand in Bohemia and the valley of the Main. Military pundits often cite first Breitenfeld as demonstrating the superiority of the smaller and handier Swedish battalion system over the imperial tercio, but in truth this was a victory for combined arms: infantry, cavalry, and guns (in this case captured and turned on their former owners) working together.

The Battle of Lützen (1632)

Gustavus Adolphus caught up with the imperial army under Albrecht von Wallenstein entrenched at Lützen, south-west of Leipzig, on 16 November 1632. The latter had split his force, sending the best of his cavalry under Graf von Pappenheim to Halle, and Gustavus seized the opportunity. The ground around Lützen was flat on either side of a road running east to west, with a ditch on the northern side, and further north there were three large windmills. Wallenstein had drawn up his forces, some 12,000–15,000 strong, between the road and the windmills, with a large body of camp followers in the rear to give the impression of greater numbers. Gustavus, with some 20,000 men, came up to the south of the road. Both armies faced each other from 08.00 until about 10.00, while the artillery kept up a harassing fire. Gustavus opened the proceedings by leading an attack with his right-wing cavalry, breaking the imperial horse, driving them through their own guns, and panicking the camp followers in the rear. On the opposite flank the imperial Croatian cavalry, covered by smoke from the burning village of Lützen, conducted a spirited attack against Bernhard of Saxe-Weimar's men.

Sometime after midday, and accounts disagree as to the exact time, Pappenheim rejoined the army, summoned by an urgent dispatch from the beleaguered Wallenstein. His cuirassiers plunged into the thick of the fray at once, driving the Swedes pell-mell back across the ditch and road. Pappenheim was shot and killed and Gustavus' horse was seen careering about the field riderless. When the Swedes learned that their king was down, they boiled forward in an unstoppable attack. After dark, Gustavus was found dead from a number of wounds, which made it an excessively expensive victory.

Constant campaigning and attrition had deprived the Swedes of their best native troops, who had been replaced by inferior local freebooters, and this contributed to their defeat at Nördlingen in August 1634, where the Swedish General Horn and the new champion of Protestantism, Bernhard of Saxe-Weimar, were roundly defeated by the veteran Spanish-imperial army with the loss of 14,000 men, and all their artillery. The last hope for the Protestant German princes was that Catholic France, fearing Habsburg hegemony, would come to the rescue, and thus render the ascendancy gained by the Habsburgs after Nördlingen short-lived.

The Battle of Wittstock (1636)

The battle of Wittstock was fought around a little village on the Dosse river some 93 km (58 miles) north-west of Berlin on 4 October 1636 by the Swedish army under Johan Baner to keep open its communications with the Baltic. Baner enticed an imperial, Saxon, and Bavarian army of 20,000 under John George of Saxony out of its entrenchments, while Scots mercenaries in Swedish service conducted a wide encircling movement, hitting the imperialists in the flank and rear and routing them, inflicting 5,000 casualties and capturing all their artillery. The Swedes lost about 3,000 of 15,000 engaged.

Meanwhile, the Dutch were able to roll back the Spanish, who were crippled by an economic collapse and revolt at home. The Spanish Atlantic fleet was destroyed by the Dutch Admiral Tromp at the battle of the Downs in 1639, and Portugal declared herself independent in 1640.

The Second Battle of Breitenfeld (1642)

In the spring of 1642 the ruthless Swedish commander Lennart Tortensson was ravaging the imperial lands, coming to within 40 km (25 miles) of Vienna. Archduke Leopold and Prince Ottavio Piccolomini forced him back through Silesia into Saxony, where Tortensson attempted to capture Leipzig, and the imperialists caught up with him nearby. The second battle near Breitenfeld on 2 November was preceded by a roaring imperial cannonade as the horse moved into position on Leopold's wings. Beset by whirring chain shot, the Swedes did not wait for the imperial army to complete its deployment, but mounted a hasty attack on the enemy's left, catching it in disarray and putting it to flight almost at once.

Meanwhile on the other flank the imperialist cavalry had repulsed the Swedish horse, and the imperial infantry was moving up in support. Tortensson was obliged to bring his victorious right-wing squadrons to the aid of the hard-pressed Swedish foot, stemming the tide of the imperial advance, and pushing the infantry back, which left their mounted colleagues surrounded. Seeing that they were alone and unsupported some fled, while others threw down their arms and surrendered. More than 5,000 imperial troops were captured, and as many again were killed. This defeat marked the nadir of imperial fortunes in the later stages of the war. The Spanish then tried to renew the offensive.

The Battle of Rocroi (1643)

Francisco de Melo advanced from the Spanish Netherlands to besiege Rocroi with a Spanish army of 25,000 men. The 22-year-old duc d'Enghien with 23,000 French troops decided to attack the Spanish before they could receive reinforcements. Enghien took considerable risk in approaching through narrow forest defiles, but was in position in the open country before Rocroi by the evening of 18 May 1643. Enghien initiated the battle the next morning by personally leading the cavalry of his right wing against the squadrons of the enemy's left. There Enghien's troopers succeeded, but on the other flank, French cavalry attacked in contravention of orders and was repulsed. Learning that a crisis loomed on his left, Enghien marshalled his victorious horsemen and rode round the rear of the Spanish army to collide with the enemy right-wing cavalry and drive it from the field. This success isolated the infantry of Melo's centre. At first, the Spanish infantry, which enjoyed a reputation as invincible, defied the French. However, facing the full fury of French artillery, the Spanish foot finally called for quarter late in the day, but when someone mistakenly fired on Enghien, his infuriated troops attacked the Spanish, charged into their midst, and cut down most of them before taking the rest prisoner. More than any other single battle, Rocroi stripped the Spanish tercio of its aura of invincibility and presaged the military pre-eminence of France. The young Enghien would soon succeed his father as the prince of Condé, and be known as 'the Great Condé' because of his victories.

War exhaustion now led to a desire for peace, but there was no consensus on how this was to be achieved, and the fighting dragged on. The breakthrough came in 1648, when Spain and the Netherlands concluded their 80-year war, which had become enmeshed in the wider conflict of the Thirty Years War, and the other combatants followed suit and settled their differences one after another.

The Thirty Years War had a lasting impact. One of its most obvious effects was the loss of life. Perhaps 8,000 of the imperialist troops at Breitenfeld were killed, while almost half the Swedish force of 25,000 was killed at Nördlingen. Civilians also suffered appallingly: some parts of Germany were laid waste, and the population may have fallen from around 20 million to around 16–17 million.

Armies grew bigger and were often better organized, with a premium attached to the marshalling of infantry firepower and the improvement of artillery. They also became notably more costly.

BRITISH CIVIL WARS

In financial expense, physical devastation, and loss of life, the Civil Wars (1638–52) were the costliest conflict ever waged on British soil. Deaths amounted to 11.5 per cent of the population; the figure for World War I was 3 per cent. Charles I had an exalted conception of his role as monarch, and denied that he was accountable to the people or their elected representatives. His pretensions to absolutism were challenged by a rebellion in Scotland against his attempt to impose an Anglican brand of worship on that nation. The two 'Bishops' wars' which resulted depleted Charles's treasury and exposed the unpopularity of his regime in both kingdoms. The first conflict, in the late spring of 1639, ended in a bloodless stand-off between the Scots and English armies. A year later the Covenanting army, 14,000 strong, under Alexander Leslie routed a demoralized English army of only 4,500 at Newburn and seized the nearby city of Newcastle-upon-Tyne. Forced to summon parliament, the king found it unsupportive of his war against the Scots and determined to reform the abuses of prerogative government.

In January 1642, having failed to arrest the ringleaders of the parliamentary opposition, Charles fled London leaving it in the hands of his enemies. With the more prosperous and populous part of the kingdom under its control, parliament was from the beginning in a better position to conscript men and pay them. For his part the king drew strength from Wales, the west Midlands, Lancashire, Yorkshire, and Cornwall. Royalist finances were always more fragile than those of parliament, with the consequence that royalist armies resorted more frequently to free quarter and straightforward plunder in order to keep themselves alive.

By October 1642, when the first Civil War effectively began, the king had mustered about 12,500 men, whereas the main parliamentary army under the Earl of Essex had reached nearly 14,000.

The Battle of Edgehill (1642)

Edgehill was the first major battle of the wars. The main royalist army, under Charles I, left Shrewsbury on 12 October to march on London. Parliament's main army, commanded by the earl of Essex, left Worcester on 19 October and attempted to get between the king and the capital. On the morning of 23 October it became clear that the royalists had won the race, and were at the foot of Edgehill, north-west of Radway in south Warwickshire. The parliamentarians formed up south-east of Kineton. Both armies were drawn up in two main lines, with infantry in the centre and cavalry on the flanks.

After an ineffective artillery duel the royalists advanced. On the flanks their cavalry drove their opponents from the field but disappeared in pursuit. The infantry battle was finely balanced, both sides fighting bravely hand to hand. Sir Edmund Verney, who bore the Royal Standard, was cut down: the standard was taken, and then recovered by Captain John Smith. Both sides lost perhaps 1,500 men apiece.

The battles of the British Civil Wars and Monmouth's rising

At the end of the day Essex remained in possession of the battlefield, but strategically the victory was the king's, since the road to London was now clear. Charles's slowness in approaching the capital gave parliament the time to mobilize an army of some 24,000 men to bar his way at Turnham Green. The king wisely pulled his men back and returned to Oxford for the winter.

In 1643 Charles consolidated his position around Oxford, while his general Sir Ralph Hopton recruited a formidable little army in Cornwall. At Roundway Down, near Devizes (13 July), he and Lord Wilmot routed Sir William Waller, leader of the parliamentary forces in the west. This was the low point of the war for parliament. With its grip on the Severn valley broken, Bristol and Gloucester were imperilled. In the south Essex's army had wasted away to 5,500, while the earl of Newcastle dominated the north with his royalist army of 8,000, many of them crack infantry. His cavalry were an elite force, led by Sir Marmaduke Langdale and George Goring. The northern parliamentary army, never more than 6,000 strong under Ferdinando Lord Fairfax and his son Sir Thomas Fairfax, was always dangerous, but after a number of lesser engagements, Newcastle beat it at Adwalton Moor near Bradford (30 June), and drove the Fairfaxes back to Hull.

The arrival of the queen in Oxford with 3,000 troops and supplies at last gave Charles numerical superiority over Essex. This infusion of strength enabled Prince Rupert of the Rhine with 12,000 men to overrun Bristol, the second port of the kingdom. Instead of pressing home his advantage with an immediate attack on London the king chose to protect his rear by turning and besieging Gloucester. When Essex came to the relief of the city Charles abandoned the siege, and tried to block Essex's way back to London. The two armies, about equal at 14,000 men each, fought a pitched battle at Newbury, where many royalist cavalry were lost, and Essex's reputation was temporarily restored. Meanwhile, parliament recovered more ground in the north and south. But by the end of 1643 the armies of both sides were nearly at the end of their tether. The following year would see the arrival of outside help.

In the autumn of 1643 the parliamentary leader John Pym managed to persuade his reluctant colleagues to forge an alliance with Scotland, and in January 1644 the earl of Leven crossed the Tweed with 21,500 troops. Meanwhile in Ireland the marquess of Ormonde had concluded a truce or 'Cessation' with the Roman Catholic Confederates. This enabled Charles to bring in several thousand troops, mainly infantry, from that kingdom. Whatever military advantage he gained by this access of strength was offset by the propaganda defeat he suffered for his apparent appeasement of Roman Catholicism and Irish nationalism.

The Battle of Marston Moor (1644)

Marston Moor was the largest and most important battle of these civil wars, although its results were not immediately decisive. The earl of Leven's army had advanced southwards, first meeting parliamentarian forces under Lord Fairfax and his son Sir Thomas Fairfax, and then being joined by the earl of Manchester's forces from East Anglia. The marquess of Newcastle, royalist commander in the north, fell back into York. Charles I regarded the city as crucial to his cause, and told his nephew Prince Rupert to relieve it at all costs. In a finely executed manoeuvre, 'Yorke march', Rupert duly crossed the Pennines and outmanoeuvred the allies to join Newcastle.

The allies decided to block Rupert's route south, and on 2 July their rearguard was on Marston Moor, south-west of York, when it became clear that the royalists had marched out of the city to offer battle. Not all royalist commanders shared Rupert's wish to fight. Newcastle's fine infantry was slow in arriving, and this prevented Rupert from attacking the allies while they were strung out on the line of march. Both armies were drawn up by late afternoon, their foot in the centre and their cavalry on the flanks, with the Long Marston–Tockwith road between them and a ditch and some cultivated ground just in front of the royalists. The allies, with around 27,000 men, outnumbered the royalists, with perhaps 17,000.

A desultory cannonade began at about 14.00, and as it seemed likely that there would be no battle that day Newcastle retired to his coach. But at about 19.00 the allies advanced, their attack providentially screened by a shower which impeded the royalist musketeers in the ditch. On the allied left Oliver Cromwell's cavalry beat their opponents after 'a hard pull of it'. On the allied right, however, most of Fairfax's horse were beaten by George Goring, and their defeat dragged some of the infantry back too. The royalist infantry had rather the better of the fighting in the centre (and but for the dogged action of two Scots regiments might have won altogether), persuading several allied generals, and not a few of their men, to leave the field hurriedly.

Cromwell still had his victorious cavalry in hand. Fairfax, already wounded, had made his way behind the royalists to join him, and they now came in against the royalists from the rear. One of Newcastle's regiments fought to the end in the Hatterwith enclosures, on the north-east edge of the battlefield. A parliamentarian captain admitted that 'he never in all the fights he was in, met with such resolute brave fellows'. Some isolated parties of royalist horse stayed in the field until midnight, but the battle was clearly lost. Rupert had allegedly been forced to take refuge in a bean field as Cromwell's men swept past, and his dog Boy was among the killed. The royalists lost at least 4,000 killed and 1,500 captured, the allies perhaps 2,000 killed. Newcastle 'would not endure the laughter of the court' and went into exile. Rupert got away with perhaps 6,000 men, and York surrendered on terms on 16 July.

The result was the shattering of the royalist infantry, and the end of the war in the north. On the other hand parliament was in danger of losing the south. Despite beating the royalists at Cheriton (29 March 1644), Sir William Waller failed to come to the help of Essex who was recklessly plunging deep into royalist territory in Cornwall in the hope of finishing off the royalist forces under Prince Maurice and Sir Ralph Hopton. Charles had decided to pursue him with his main Oxford army, which at 10,000 was now equal to Essex's. The forces in the west brought the king's strength up to 16,000. All through August the royalists skilfully closed the net around the dispirited parliamentarians. At Lostwithiel Essex reached the end of the road. As defeat stared him in the face he ordered his cavalry to cut their way through the enemy lines and escape to Plymouth. The earl slipped away by boat, leaving Major General Philip Skippon to surrender the 6,000 infantry. It was the most resounding royalist victory of the war.

Discontent with the lacklustre performance now boiled over in London. The war party in the Commons amalgamated the three southern armies into a new force, the New Model Army, under the command of Sir Thomas Fairfax.

The Battle of Naseby (1645)

This was the occasion when the New Model Army was blooded, when Oliver Cromwell's Ironsides confirmed that parliamentarian cavalry could now meet and defeat royalist horse, and when the weaknesses and rivalries that had bedevilled Charles I's cause finally doomed him. The royalists, under the command of Prince Rupert, were outnumbered (approximately 10,000 to about 13,500) although enjoying near-parity in cavalry. Not waiting for a detached force under George Goring, they drew up south of Market Harborough to await attack. Thomas Fairfax and Cromwell, their forces making rendezvous at the Naseby windmill, saw them but decided to move west, for they also wished to invite attack. Observing this, Rupert moved as well to face his adversaries across Broadmoor, the bulk of his artillery left behind. The galling fire of dragoons Cromwell had posted behind the thick hedge on the west precipitated a premature charge by the royalist cavalry, Rupert with them, while Sir Marmaduke Langdale's horse covered the left on terrain that restricted the enemy advance.

Rupert's troopers broke through and he returned to the king's side. Had his brother Prince Maurice been able to rally the horse, he might have decided the battle by falling on the rear of the parliamentarian foot, hard pressed by the determined attack of the out-numbered royalist infantry. He could not, however, and the impetus of the charge led his main body instead to the enemy baggage train and a fatally wasted two hours.

Meanwhile in the centre the royalist infantry almost broke Colonel Pickering's and Sir Hardress Waller's regiments. The situation was saved by the intervention of the parliamentarian reserves and by, on the right, Cromwell's keeping his men well in hand, overthrowing Langdale, and turning to take the royalist infantry in the flank and rear. The king, in Rupert's view, had committed his cavalry reserve too early and although his Bluecoats 'stood like a wall of brasse' the parliamentarians' greater numbers and steadi-ness remorselessly prevailed. Recent research, based on the discovery of musket balls on the battlefield, proves that the infantry battle developed into a fighting retreat which continued as far as the Welland river valley. The wonder is not that the royalists were defeated, but that they came so near to snatching victory from a situation they should have avoided.

The price of victory was relatively cheap: only perhaps 150 parliamentarian soldiers were lost, against nearly 1,000 for the king, in addition to 4,500 prisoners, mainly infantry, and the capture of the king's file of secret letters. The publication of these letters, with their evidence of his dealings with the Irish rebels, would do irreparable damage to Charles's reputation in England. After Naseby, the king's cause was doomed.

The events of the next year were essentially a mopping-up operation for the New Model Army. Royalist strongholds tumbled like ripe fruit into its lap: Bristol, Plymouth, Exeter, and many others. By June 1646 the west was sewn up, and Oxford had surrendered. Before this last humiliation was played out, Charles had slipped away and delivered him-self into the hands of the Scots army at Newark. He would spend the next year and a half negotiating and plotting.

Thanks to the king's stubbornness the second Civil War erupted in the spring of 1648. The New Model had little trouble annihilating the ill-coordinated series of uprisings in Kent, south Wales, Yorkshire, and East Anglia. A more serious threat was posed by a sec-tion of the Scots nobility, who signed an Engagement with the king, and led an invasion of England in July. In August Cromwell brilliantly outmanoeuvred and demolished their forces at Preston. When parliament persisted in negotiating, the army occupied London, purged parliament of moderates, and oversaw the trial and execution of the king.

Once the republic had been proclaimed the grandees of the army turned to deal with the long-festering rebellion in Ireland. Cromwell was dispatched with an invading force of 12,000, but before his arrival the parliamentarian Colonel Michael Jones had crushed the royalist army under the marquess of Ormonde at Rathmines, just outside Dublin. This 'astonishing mercy', as Cromwell dubbed it, meant that he did not have to fight a single field battle while he was in that country. When Drogheda refused the summons to capitulate he stormed it, and allegedly put the entire garrison of 3,500 to the sword though both numbers and circumstances were the subject of propaganda. Similar punish-ment was meted out to Wexford in October, when civilians and clergy were also caught up in the mayhem. Royalist resistance collapsed by the end of 1650, but the Catholic

Confederates continued to wage a bitter guerrilla war. By 1651 it required 33,000 English troops to occupy Ireland and cope with the continuing resistance. However, divisions within Confederate ranks brought them formally to capitulate in the autumn of 1652.

Meanwhile in the spring of 1650 Cromwell had returned to England to prepare for an apprehended invasion from Scotland, where the Kirk had recently proclaimed Charles II monarch of both kingdoms, setting the scene for the third Civil War. Rather than wait for the Scots, Cromwell decided on a pre-emptive strike. Taking an army of 16,000 across the Tweed in July, he found the Scots general David Leslie (son of Alexander) maddeningly elusive. Having stripped the counties south of Edinburgh of food and fodder, Leslie retreated behind fortified redoubts and declined Cromwell's invitation to a pitched battle. His numbers worn down to barely 10,000 by desertion and disease, Cromwell decided to return to England, but at Dunbar he found Leslie blocking his way. Thanks to excellent reconnoitring he perceived that the infantry on Leslie's left wing were wedged against a steep ravine and unable to manoeuvre quickly. Under cover of rain and darkness he therefore brought his army across the front of Leslie's regiments and launched a surprise attack on his right wing before dawn on 3 September. The reward for this masterstroke was a devastating English victory against an army twice their size. Charles II, considering it hopeless to continue the war in an impoverished and exhausted land, led a Scots royalist army into England. The royalists knew they were marching to their doom, but, as the duke of Hamilton put it, 'we have one stout argument, despair'. Cromwell allowed them to hole up in the stronghold of Worcester, and then unleashed his overwhelming might against them on 3 September 1651. Charles fled the country and remained in exile until, in 1660, the collapse of the Commonwealth led to the restoration of the monarchy.

The Battle of Sedgemoor (1685)

When the Catholic James II succeeded to the throne in February 1685, his half-brother the duke of Monmouth was pressed to lead a rising which would be synchronized with a rebellion by the earl of Argyll in Scotland. Monmouth landed at Lyme Regis on 11 June and was proclaimed king in Taunton. Local men—but few notables—flocked to join him, and he had the best of a clash with the earl of Feversham's royal army on the 27th. He then heard that Argyll had been executed, and fell back to Bridgwater. Feversham followed, establishing himself at Westonzoyland. He had about 2,700 regulars (including John Churchill, the future duke of Marlborough, who was in effective command of the royal army during the battle) to Monmouth's 3,500 largely untrained men.

Monmouth decided on a night attack, but his men were detected by a cavalry vedette and discovered that a wide drainage ditch, the Bussex Rhine, lay between them and Feversham. Although they fought with courage they were no match for the firepower of the royal infantry, and as they broke Feversham's horse cut many of them down. The rebellion was suppressed with a savagery still remembered in the West Country. Monmouth himself was captured, and executed by a headsman who botched his job.

The Battle of Killiecrankie (1689)

While James II was fleeing Ireland after the defeat of his forces at the battle of the Boyne, a Jacobite victory was gained in Scotland on 27 July over a government army of about 4,000 men under General Hugh Mackay. This was marching from Perth to occupy Blair castle when it was ambushed by a smaller force of Highlanders led by John Graham of Claverhouse, Viscount Dundee. Six and a half kilometres (4 miles) south of Blair, by the deep gorge of Killiecrankie, they charged downhill at the English, whose plug bayonets, stuffed into the muzzles of their muskets, prevented them from firing effective volleys. The Highlanders pushed the English back into the gorge, killing half their number. Mackay retreated to Stirling to regroup, but the irreplaceable Bonnie Dundee had been killed.

THE LEAGUE OF AUGSBURG WAR

The war of 1688–97 is also known as the Nine Years War or the War of the Grand Alliance. Spurred on by fear of the expansionism of Louis XIV of France, the Holy Roman Emperor, the electors of Bavaria, Palatinate, and Saxony, and the kings of Sweden and Spain created the League of Augsburg in 1686. Louis took on this coalition, soon reinforced by the Netherlands and England united under William of Orange, when he invaded Germany in September 1688. Given this Grand Alliance arrayed against it Louis's France was surrounded by enemies and was forced to fight on several fronts, including the European colonies in the New World.

The Battle of the Boyne (1690)

Louis XIV determined to support an Irish rebellion seeking to reinstall the deposed James II on the English throne. James landed in Ireland in March 1689 to find most of the country held by his supporters. William of Orange disembarked a large army of seasoned Dutch, Danish, French Huguenot, and English troops at Carrickfergus in June 1690. They joined William's existing troops in Ireland under the duke of Schomberg, bringing their total strength to some 40,000 men.

When they met on the river Boyne, west of Drogheda, William had 36,000 men to James's 26,000. On 1 July William attacked across the river at Oldbridge while an outflanking force marched upstream to Rossnaree. James sent too many troops—including all his French infantry under the duc de Lauzun—to meet the flank attack. His centre was broken after hard fighting in which James's cavalry earned widespread admiration. William's commander-in-chief, the veteran duke of Schomberg, was among the killed. James lost about 1,000 men, William perhaps 500. James was hustled away, and left Ireland shortly afterwards. His supporters fought on with a courage worthy of a better cause.

By 1692, the Anglo-Dutch had regained control of the seas and the French were limited to privateering. The land war in Europe was marked by indecisiveness. Only a few major battles took place, with the French more often than not emerging victorious, but without achieving a crushing enough victory to be able to dictate peace terms. In many ways, it was a war of logistics, resulting in a characteristic manoeuvring of armies for position, forcing an enemy to withdraw rather than seek a decision on the battlefield. Another result was the large number of siege operations because fortresses were often vital to the smooth supply of an army.

Nonetheless, battles were fought. The land war opened with a minor alliance victory at Walcourt (25 August 1689) in Flanders. An alliance army of 35,000, including 8,000 English troops under John Churchill, then earl of Marlborough, inflicted 2,000 casualties on the French army under the marquis d'Humières while only suffering 300 themselves. The defeat resulted in d'Humières being replaced by the duc de Luxembourg.

The Battle of Fleurus (1690)

The French victory at Fleurus, on 1 July 1690 north-east of Charleroi, saw Marshal Luxembourg with 35,000 troops thrash General George Frederick, prince of Waldeck and his 38,000 Dutch and German soldiers. Taking great risks, Luxembourg divided his army in two as he approached Waldeck's position and then struck both of the enemy flanks simultaneously. In the fighting that followed, the French killed, wounded, or captured half of Waldeck's army. The French force suffered 2,500 casualties to the alliance's 6,000 dead and 8,000 prisoners, but Luxembourg was unable to exploit his victory as Louis ordered him to coordinate his army with other forces. Despite Louis's constraints, Luxembourg managed to win another series of engagements in the Low Countries. On 8 April 1691, he took the fortress of Mons and followed this up by seizing Halle in June.

The Battle of Aughrim (1691)

The Jacobite forces survived in Ireland and in 1691 William appointed Godert de Ginkel as his field commander there. James II's supporters now fell to this advancing army, being driven to the west and south-west of the country. Ginkel then advanced to besiege Athlone, which fell on 10 July. The marquis de Saint-Ruth had been appointed to command the Jacobites in James's absence, and he decided to meet Ginkel at Aughrim on 12 July. In the ensuing bitterly contested battle, Saint-Ruth was killed and the French–Irish army collapsed, and along with it James's war effort in Ireland. Nevertheless, it was not until 3 October 1692 that Limerick, the final centre of resistance, fell. Subsequent negotiations resulted in the Articles of Limerick which provided for the freedom of religious belief in Ireland, the voluntary transporting of Irish troops (to become known as the 'wild geese') to France, and a general amnesty. The treaty was rejected by the mainly Protestant Irish Assembly who introduced harsher anti-Catholic penal laws.

The French had better fortunes closer to home with the routing of Waldeck's army in September. Through the use of a bold night march, Luxembourg was able to catch Waldeck's army unprepared at Leuze as it retired for winter quarters and inflict heavy casualties. At the battle of Staffarda on 18 August, a French force commanded by Nicolas Catinat defeated the army of Victor Amadeus II of Savoy, allowing the French forces to capture most of Savoy. In September, French armies under Duc Anne-Jules de Noailles seized Ripoll and Urgell on the Spanish front.

The French were again largely victorious in 1692. Luxembourg was successful against the alliance army, now commanded by William of Orange. At daybreak on 3 August,

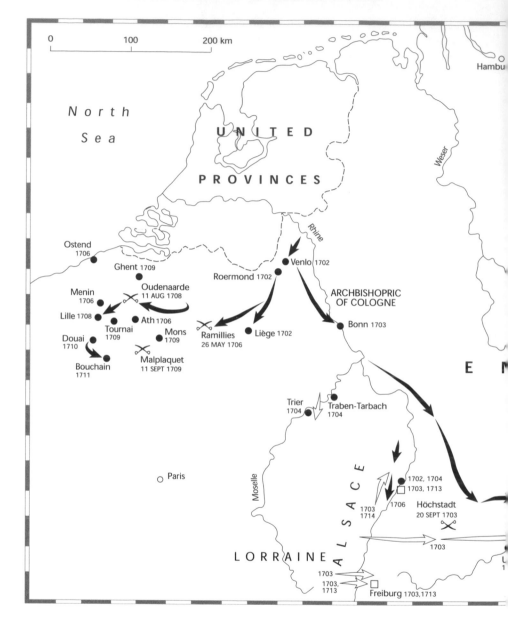

William's 63,000 men attacked Luxembourg's fortified camp at Steenkerke, between Brussels and Mons. After initial successes, the French, numbering around 57,000, were able to drive off the allies in a savage close-quarter battle. William ordered the British Guards to cover the withdrawal of his army, and in a stiff rearguard action they lost Generals Mackay and Lanier. The alliance suffered 8,000 casualties and the French 6,800.

The year 1693 saw the last large-scale battles of the war. Its biggest clash occurred on 29 July 1693 at Neerwinden, north of Namur. There, Luxembourg attacked William's

French offensives, with date

Attack by Anglo-Dutch-Austrian alliance, with date

☐ Towns captured by French and their allies, with date

● Towns captured by allies, with date

Allied victory

Allied defeat

○ Leipzig

○ Dresden

H E

P I R E

Prague ○

Donauwörth
1704

Danube

Blenheim
13 AUG 1704

> ☐ Augsburg
1/03

B A V A R I A

The War of the Spanish Succession

entrenched army of 50,000 with a force numbering 80,000. After eight hours of hard fighting and three assaults, the French were able to drive the alliance troops from the field. The French suffered 9,000 casualties, while the alliance lost 19,000 killed, wounded, and captured. Given the damage suffered by his own army, Luxembourg was unable to exploit this victory. After Neerwinden, the war became almost totally one of manoeuvre and siege, with neither side willing to risk high losses in battle. Bottled up in the Netherlands, William was joined in the summer of 1697 by the Holy Roman Emperor and between 20 September and 30 October the powers negotiated a peace settlement, the Treaty of Ryswick.

The Battle of Zenta (1687)

Eugène, prince of Savoy, was refused service in the army of Louis XIV and fled France to join the imperial army. By the age of 30 he had risen to the rank of field marshal. He fought against the French in Italy in the League of Augsburg war and was then sent to counter the increasing threat of the Turks. At Zenta on 11 September 1697, Eugène found himself facing a Turkish army marching north from Belgrade towards Hungary as it attempted to cross the river Theiss (Tisza). He allowed the Turkish cavalry to cross onto the west bank and then attacked while their infantry were marching across a temporary bridge, which was destroyed leaving the advance guard on the wrong side of the river. They were soon overcome for a loss of some 20,000 killed, wounded, and captured, many being drowned as they attempted to swim the river. The Turks also abandoned all their baggage and artillery. Eugène's reputation was assured, and the Austrians went on to raid Bosnia, sacking Sarajevo.

THE WAR OF THE SPANISH SUCCESSION

While the Treaty of Ryswick ended the League of Augsburg war in 1697, it did nothing to alter the underlying tensions within Europe. On 7 September 1701, the alliance against Louis was formally brought into being, consisting of the Habsburg empire, England, the Netherlands, Brandenburg-Prussia, and most of the other German states. Louis could count on the support of Savoy, Mantua, Cologne, and Bavaria, in addition, of course, to Spain. Upon the crowning of his grandson Philip as king of Spain, Louis marched his troops into the Spanish Netherlands and provoked the Habsburg empire to declare war.

The first moves were made in Italy, as Louis sent an army under the command of Marshal Nicolas Catinat to occupy Rivoli. The French intention was to prevent the Austrian army of Prince Eugène from entering Italy. However, Eugène was able to outmanoeuvre Catinat. Louis replaced Catinat with François Villeroi, who in turn was captured by an Austrian raid on Cremona on 1 February 1702 and replaced by the duc de Vendôme. The remainder of the campaign in Italy is an excellent example of the manoeuvring that dominated much of early eighteenth-century warfare.

The alliance became aggressive in 1702. In July, the Austrians invaded Alsace with an army under the direction of Prince Louis, margrave of Baden. While this army threatened Alsace, an Anglo-Dutch force under the command of John Churchill, earl of Marlborough, captured the French fortresses along the river Meuse between 15 September and 15 October, for which he was created a duke.

However, in September Louis concluded an alliance with Bavaria, which declared war on the Habsburg empire. In the spring of 1703, Marshal Claude Villars advanced through the Black Forest to meet Maximilian of Bavaria at Ulm with the intention of advancing on Vienna. However Maximilian engaged in an abortive invasion of the Tyrol while Villars remained in the Danube valley to hold off the alliance armies of Louis of Baden and General Herman Otto von Limburg-Styrum. Villars manoeuvred successfully to keep the two armies from joining, and defeated each in detail at the battles of Munderkingen on 31 July and Höchstädt on 20 September. Villars once again urged Maximilian to join with his army in a drive on Vienna, but Maximilian demurred and operations came to a halt for the year. The clash of opinions between the two commanders resulted in Villars being replaced by Ferdinand, comte de Marsin.

By the beginning of 1704, the Franco-Bavarian forces were well positioned to invade Austria and take Vienna. Maximilian and Marsin had collected around 55,000 men at Ulm and this force was to be reinforced by Marshal Count Camille de Tallard's army of 30,000 for the invasion. Thus, the main task of the alliance was to prevent this and to draw off French forces from the main theatre. The first of their operations resulted in the British capture of Gibraltar in August. The second step resulted in one of the largest battles of the war.

The Battle and Campaign of Blenheim (1704)

The name 'Blenheim' is the Anglicized version of Blindheim, a village in Bavaria on the left bank of the river Danube. The duke of Marlborough's route was chosen to mislead the French into pursuing him, rather than marching directly to reinforce the elector of Bavaria. It required a miracle of logistic planning. Such long marches in the eighteenth century usually resulted in mass desertion, while those who remained with the colours were soon in poor condition. Margrave Louis of Baden and Prince Eugène of Savoy met Marlborough briefly on 10 June at Mondelsheim, and it was agreed that Eugène (10,000 men) should distract the French under François Villeroi from intervening in Bavaria, while Baden (30,000 men) accompanied Marlborough (35,000 men). On 2 July, Marlborough and Baden carried Donauwörth, an important crossing point over the Danube, in the swift but costly storming of the Schellenberg. They then proceeded to devastate the vicinity in an effort to draw their opponents into battle. Eugène, on discovering that the French army under Marshal Comte Camille de Tallard had slipped away, himself marched to join Marlborough. They joined forces on 12 August at Blindheim, 16 km (10 miles) west of Donauwörth. Baden having been dispatched with 15,000 men to besiege Ingolstadt, their combined strength was about 56,000.

Their Franco-Bavarian opponents, Ferdinand, comte de Marsin, and the elector of Bavaria under the overall command of Tallard, slightly outnumbered the allies at 60,000. Advancing in nine columns, Marlborough and Eugène spent the morning of 13 August deploying, covered by artillery fire. Tallard, who was taken by surprise, deployed hastily to a poor position between Blindheim, on the Danube, to his right and Lützingen on his left. In the centre was a third fortified village, Oberglau. Eugène faced Marsin and the elector between Lützingen and Oberglau, while Marlborough stood opposite Tallard from Oberglau to Blenheim. Each Franco-Bavarian force deployed with infantry in the centre and cavalry on the wings, the two cavalry wings meeting in Oberglau. At 12.30 battle commenced when Lord John Cutts attacked Blenheim twice, which drew in French reserves, while Marlborough tried to break through at Oberglau, the hinge of Tallard's two armies. Eugène meanwhile attacked the elector and Marsin in a classic fixing operation, which prevented them from supporting Tallard elsewhere. While Eugène's attack distracted Tallard's attention, Marlborough got his infantry across the Nebel stream,

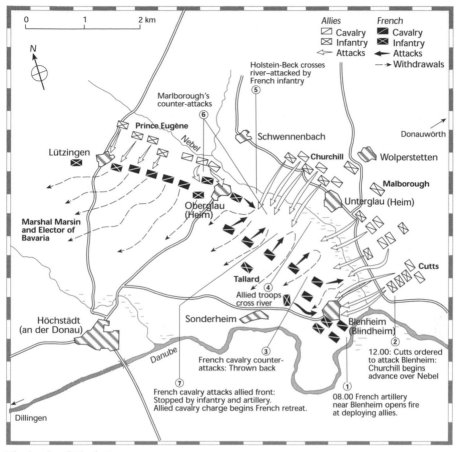

The battle of Blenheim

which ran across the battlefield between the armies. Once across, his men deployed in a unique formation—two lines of infantry sandwiched between two lines of cavalry—which was able to beat off French cavalry charges. Marlborough personally led a cavalry countercharge and by 17.30 had breached Tallard's centre, his forces pouring through the gap. Blenheim surrendered, after fierce fighting, to General Charles Churchill, the duke's brother, at 23.00.

In a model of coalition warfare, the armies of the two great allied commanders had acted in perfect harmony with one another to inflict a crushing defeat on the Franco-Bavarian force, whose losses totalled 38,000, the blow to their prestige being even more fundamental. Marlborough and Eugène suffered 12,000 casualties and the former's prestige and that of his army was without precedent. But it had been a costly affair: 43 per cent of all troops engaged had been killed, wounded, or taken prisoner. With this battle,

The battle of Blenheim.

the safety of Vienna was assured and the French armies were driven from Germany. Maximilian was forced into exile and his state was annexed by the Austrian empire.

The Battle of Ramillies (1705)

In 1705 the duke of Marlborough's allied army penetrated the Lines of Brabant, field fortifications intended by the French to defend the frontier of the Spanish Netherlands, and destroyed a section between Zoutleew and Merdorp. The following spring, anxious to bring François Villeroi to battle before he was reinforced, Marlborough advanced through the damaged section. Villeroi at once raised the siege of Zoutleew and marched to meet him. Early on Whit Sunday, 23 May 1706, Marlborough's scouts found the French in a good position on open countryside behind the marshes of the Little Geet with their right on the river Mehaigne and the village of Ramillies in their centre. Both armies were equal, at around 50,000 men apiece, and the French were unusually confident.

Marlborough's guns opened on the French centre at about 13.00 and he struck at both flanks shortly afterwards. He pushed back the French right, and though he made poorer progress against the French left, Villeroi reinforced it with troops from his centre. Nevertheless, the centre remained very strong, and Marlborough could make little impression on it. In mid-afternoon he withdrew troops from his right, using a re-entrant to enable them to move unseen, and their unexpected arrival gave him the decisive advantage. The French right was pushed back, and by 18.00, although Villeroi still had troops facing a non-existent threat to his left, he had none to spare to reinforce Ramillies, which was taken after heavy fighting. He tried to form a second line but allied cavalry swept him away: by dawn on the 24th only about half his army was intact, suffering 8,000 casualties and 7,000 prisoners. Marlborough had lost just 4,000 men, and exploited success by taking Louvain, Brussels, and Antwerp and shepherding the French field army back to the Flanders frontier.

The Battle of Almanza (1707)

The battle of Almanza (Almansa) is best remembered for the fact that the British-allied army was commanded by a Frenchman, the Huguenot Henri de Massue de Ruvigny, earl of Galway, and the Franco-Spanish army by an Englishman, James FitzJames, duke of Berwick, illegitimate son of James II and Arabella Churchill—and thus the duke of Marlborough's nephew. But it was a decisive battle in its own right. There was extensive campaigning in Spain during the war, and it proved as detrimental to the allied war effort as it was to Napoleon's a century later. In 1705 the earl of Peterborough captured Barcelona, the following year Galway took Madrid. He was outmanoeuvred by the capable Berwick, gave up Madrid, and fell back to the coast to retain the support of the fleet.

On 25 April 1707 Galway, with a British, Dutch, and Portuguese force, advanced on Berwick at Almanza, between Albacete and Alicante. Although things went well at first, the Portuguese on Galway's right broke, and Berwick seized the opportunity to outflank and encircle the survivors. Despite the valour of Galway's British contingent—the 6th and 9th Foot bore themselves especially well—almost all Galway's 15,000 men were killed or captured. The battle led to the allied claimant to Spain, the Archduke Charles, losing all except Catalonia, and left the French claimant, Philip V, secure on his throne.

French attempts to retake the Spanish Netherlands in 1708 resulted in another severe defeat for the French at the battle of Oudenarde (11 July 1708), after which Louis sued for peace. However, the negotiations broke down over Louis's refusal to join the alliance against his grandson Philip of Spain, and in 1709 he made a final effort to regain the Netherlands.

The Battle of Malplaquet (1709)

Malplaquet was the most costly and least useful of the duke of Marlborough's four great victories. In August 1709 he and Prince Eugène of Savoy took Tournai and moved on to besiege Mons. Marshal Claude Villars, ordered to raise the siege, approached from the south-west with 80,000 men. He took up a strong position north of Malplaquet, where a main road to Mons passed between thick woods, and Marlborough advanced against him with 110,000 allied troops. He hoped to repeat his favourite ploy of attacking his enemy's flanks to persuade him to weaken his centre. However, the late arrival of a force from Tournai meant that he could not make his left as strong as intended.

He attacked on 11 September and made slow progress on his right, while on his left the prince of Orange launched two costly attacks to little effect. Villars eventually thinned his centre to support his left, and was wounded shortly afterwards. The earl of Orkney's infantry then advanced through the French redoubts in the centre, and the allied horse moved up into a bitterly contested cavalry battle. The duc de Boufflers, who had succeeded to command, eventually fell back, in good order, on Le Quesnoy, having lost 17,000 men to the allies' 25,000. Mons surrendered in October, but it was a prize too dearly bought, although Louis was forced to give up his attempt to reconquer his lost territory.

After several more years of indecisive manoeuvring, the principals again entered into peace negotiations. On 11 April 1713 the Treaty of Utrecht was signed between all the participants, save the Habsburg empire which finally signed treaties in 1714.

The Battle of Poltava (1709)

The battle in which Peter the Great of Russia defeated Charles XII of Sweden during the Great Northern War established Russia as a European power. In early 1709, after an appalling Russian winter, the Swedes, whose military reputation was high and their self-esteem even more so, marched south-east into Ukraine with about 22,000 men and 32 guns and besieged Poltava, a supply depot with a 6,700-strong garrison. Peter, at the head of a relief force of 42,000 men and 72 guns, approached and built fortifications behind the besiegers. While Charles was sidelined by an infected wound received earlier while scouting, the Swedes launched a pre-dawn attack in four columns directed by General Rehnskjold, a veteran commander but one neither as inspiring nor as readily obeyed as the king would have been. The attack on the Russian fortifications succeeded after fierce fighting, but the Swedes then had to advance 600 m (660 yards) under withering artillery fire before closing with the Russian infantry, which outnumbered them two to one. Seven thousand Swedes died in the battle and 2,500 were captured, to be joined by the 10,000 who retreated in good order but were cornered a few days later against the Dniester river. Charles was carried off in a stretcher towards Turkey. By destroying the previously almost invincible Swedish army and separating Charles from his kingdom, Peter won the war and signalled the arrival of Russia as a military power in Europe.

The Battle and Siege of Belgrade (1717)

In August 1717 the Austrians, commanded by Prince Eugène of Savoy, were laying siege to the Turkish-held fortress of Belgrade. On the 16th a massive relieving force numbering some 150,000 attacked the imperial lines. The grand vizier, Ibrahim Pasha, opened the proceedings with a bombardment from higher ground. Eugène swiftly decided on a surprise assault with 60,000 men, covered by the early morning fog. The Turkish army was routed, losing around 15,000 men. Belgrade surrendered on 21 August, clearing the way for the Treaty of Passarowitz (21 July 1718).

The Austrian Habsburgs had secured a foothold in the Banat of Temesvar, Wallachia, and northern Serbia, and Austria had emerged from its decline of the previous century. This victory, coming hard on the heels of Eugène's equally stunning success at Peterwardein, also in the Danube valley, in the previous year, seemed to offer to the Austrians the prospect of replacing the Turkish administration in Moldavia and Wallachia, and simultaneously blocked Russian access to this strategic area.

THE WAR OF THE AUSTRIAN SUCCESSION

The loosely related and indecisive series of struggles involving the leading European states called the War of the Austrian Succession lasted eight years from 1740. Though extending overseas, to the West Indies, North America, and the Indian subcontinent, it was fought mainly in central Europe, the Italian peninsula and, latterly, the southern Netherlands. Fought between two frequently changing alliances, it was as much a series of manoeuvres by the diplomats as operations by armies, and was remarkable principally for Prussia's emergence as a leading military power. It resolved little, and the peace settlement in 1748 was rightly seen as merely a truce.

The struggle took its name from the failure of Charles VI, ruler of the Habsburg monarchy and Holy Roman Emperor (1711–40), to father a male heir, and when he died suddenly in October 1740 the military challenge to his daughter Maria Theresa came from the unexpected quarter of Prussia, now ruled by the young and ambitious Frederick the Great. Within a fortnight of Maria Theresa's accession, Frederick determined to invade populous and economically advanced Silesia, part of the Bohemian lands and connected by a thin strip of territory to the central Hohenzollern province of Brandenburg.

The invasion was launched on 16 December 1740, and within six weeks the Prussian army had overrun and occupied most of Silesia. In spring 1741 an attempted Austrian counter-attack was defeated at the battle of Mollwitz (10 April), a fortuitous success for Frederick but one with enormous political repercussions. The victory gained by the Prussian infantry encouraged the formation of a European alliance against Maria Theresa which was joined by France, the leading continental power. In the following year Prussia abandoned its allies. By the Treaty of Berlin (July 1742) Frederick secured Habsburg acceptance of his gain of Silesia and left the war.

The Battle of Dettingen (1743)

In the summer of 1743 the so-called 'Pragmatic Army' (Austrian troops with British and Hanoverian auxiliaries, in all about 35,000 men) moved up the Rhine valley towards Bavaria. Its advance was checked by a French force of 70,000 men under Marshal Adrien Maurice Noailles, and they were forced to push up the river Main to secure their supply line. The marshal cut that route also and the allies decided to retreat northwards to Hanau on the night of 26–7 June. At daylight they discovered that Noailles was already blocking their retreat, putting the allies in a 'mousetrap' between the river and the Spessart hills and exposed to the French guns west of the river.

At that point the French advantage was thrown away by Noailles's nephew, the comte de Gramont, who led the northern blocking force of 26,000 men from their position commanding the only route through the village of Dettingen, to attack the allies. An inferior French force was thus committed to a series of uncoordinated cavalry and infantry attacks against the allied main body. The allies' superior musketry, with artillery support, eventually broke the French infantry which retreated in considerable disorder, recrossing the Main. The allies made no attempt to pursue but continued their withdrawal northwards. French casualties, including prisoners, were about 4,000 men; the allies lost half that number. Dettingen was hardly a decisive battle, although it was a severe blow to French prestige. It is most often remembered as the last time a British king commanded his army in battle, but George II, despite demonstrating personal courage, showed no talent as a general.

In 1744 both Britain and France formally entered the conflict as principals: until then they had simply fought as auxiliaries. The war consequently became more of a purely Anglo-French struggle. Frederick re-entered the conflict in August when he invaded Bohemia. The campaign which followed was notably unsuccessful, and his winter retreat was little short of a disaster. In 1745 the king won notable victories at Hohenfriedberg (4 June) and Soor (29 September), in the process establishing his own reputation as a commander. At the end of 1745 the veteran Prussian general Prince Leopold of Anhalt-Dessau won a stunning victory over the Saxons (now the allies of Vienna) at Kesseldorf (15 December), one of the conflict's very few decisive battles, and this forced Austria to come to terms. Prussia now abandoned the war, for a second time.

In 1745–6 British attention was diverted by the final Jacobite rising, led by Charles Edward Stuart, the Young Pretender, who quickly proved to be an even less able leader than his father. Despite this his army reached Derby before turning back, and the Hanoverian government was forced to undertake large-scale military operations within the British Isles, involving the recall of regiments from the Continent.

The Battle of Culloden (1746)

Fought on 16 April 1746 on Drummossie moor near Inverness, the battle of Culloden marked the culmination of the Jacobite uprising. It was fought by armies headed by George II's son, the duke of Cumberland, on the Hanoverian side and James II's grandson Charles Stuart, Bonnie Prince Charlie, on the other. The Hanoverians numbered about

Cronbach

HANAW

Dettingen

french Battery

Gens d'Armes   B   A

9,000 and the Jacobites about 5,000. Contrary to myth the 9,000 were neither all English nor the 5,000 all Scots. There were Scots troops with Cumberland and some French soldiers as well as English volunteers in the prince's army. The rebels were not only outnumbered but outclassed in weapons, being heavily dependent upon the Highlanders' traditional broadswords and shields while their enemies had muskets and bayonets, and above all artillery. The Jacobites also made the mistake of giving battle on ground totally unsuited to their most effective tactic, the Highland charge. Cumberland's artillery soon reduced the moor to a killing field. The Jacobites stood the fire for some time before charging, and were decimated by grape and musketry as they ran forward. Although their right wing reached the front line of the Hanoverian army they were forced to retreat. Charles fled the field and eventually escaped to France. Some 2,000 Jacobites were slain compared with only about 300 casualties on the Hanoverian side. It was a conclusive battle, ending all prospects of a Stuart restoration.

Only with the final defeat of the uprising could London's attention return to the continental war, in which it now fought in partnership with the Dutch Republic. In 1746–8 fighting only took place in the Italian peninsula, where the existing stalemate lasted for the remainder of the war, and in the Low Countries. On France's northern border the French commander Maurice de Saxe won an impressive series of victories.

The Battle of Fontenoy (1745)

The French opened the 1745 campaigning season by besieging Tournai. An allied force of 50,000 men, under the duke of Cumberland, approached from the east. The French commander, Maurice de Saxe, split his 70,000 men, leaving a detachment to carry on the siege while the remainder blocked Cumberland's line of advance between Barry Wood and the river Escaut, strengthening the gently rising ground with redoubts. On 11 May, after the failure of an attack on Barry Wood, on his right, Cumberland ordered a general advance. His British infantry, advancing between Fontenoy and the wood, came close to breaking the French line—this was the occasion when the officers of the French and British Guards invited each other to fire first—but was checked by a counter-attack in which the Irish Brigade in French service played a distinguished part. Cumberland lost 7,500 men and fell back: Tournai surrendered.

Saxe's successes at Fontenoy, Roucoux (11 October 1746), and Laufeldt (2 July 1747) led to the overrunning of great tracts of Dutch territory in 1747 and contributed to the negotiation of the Peace of Aix-la-Chapelle in 1748.

THE SEVEN YEARS WAR

The Seven Years War was in reality two separate conflicts, the first fought in Germany and central Europe between Prussia and a coalition headed by Austria, France, and Russia, and the second overseas between Britain and France, latterly assisted by Spain.

The battle of Dettingen illustrated to show the Allies between the river Main and the hills.

THE BATTLE
OF CULLODEN
WAS FOUGHT ON THIS MOOR
16th APRIL 1746.

THE GRAVES OF THE
GALLANT HIGHLANDERS
WHO FOUGHT FOR
SCOTLAND & PRINCE CHARLIE
ARE MARKED BY THE NAMES
OF THEIR CLANS.

The two struggles were linked principally by France's involvement in both. The European conflict had a clear-cut beginning which the colonial war lacked. On 29 August 1756 Frederick the Great led his troops across the border into neighbouring Saxony. He was convinced that he would be attacked in the following spring by a coalition assembled by the Austrian chancellor Wenzel Anton von Kaunitz, which aimed to recover the former Habsburg province of Silesia.

Frederick's action was, at first sight, successful. The Saxon army was speedily surrounded and disarmed. The political repercussions were more serious. It ensured that France would fight actively to defeat Prussia, and enabled Kaunitz to transform his defensive alliance into an offensive coalition, which confronted Frederick in the campaign of 1757. Encouraged by his early success and anxious for a short war because of Prussia's very limited resources, Frederick went on the offensive. He invaded Bohemia, winning a hard-fought victory at Prague (6 May) but suffering a severe reverse at Kolin (18 June), in a battle which forced him to acknowledge the progress which the Austrian army had made since the defeats of the 1730s and 1740s. Simultaneously the Russians advanced upon isolated East Prussia and, two months after the reverse at Kolin, inflicted a serious defeat on the Prussians at Gross Jägersdorf (30 August).

The Battle of Rossbach (1757)

In the autumn Prussia was invaded by Austrian, French, Russian, and Swedish armies heading for Berlin. Frederick the Great decided to deal first with the Franco-imperial army, commanded by the prince de Soubise, and met them near Leipzig in Saxony. On 5 November 1757, the Franco-imperial army attempted to envelop Frederick's left flank by marching around it laboriously in five giant columns totalling 40,000 troops. Frederick observed their approach, and, concealed by the dominating position of the Janus hill, turned his entire army to face them and simultaneously launched a massive cavalry counter-thrust, led by the redoubtable Friedrich Wilhelm von Seydlitz, that brushed aside the allied horse and went on to scythe into the unprepared Franco-imperial infantry. This was followed by an echeloned attack by the Prussian foot. In one and a half hours the allies lost 8,000 to Frederick's few hundred. French military prestige was shattered. The victory enabled Frederick to turn about and deal with the fresh threat posed by the Austrians in Silesia.

The Battle of Leuthen (1757)

Frederick the Great, with a force of 36,000 marching east from Neumarkt, encountered the 80,000 strong Austrian army under the Graf von Daun at Leuthen, west of Breslau (Wrocław), in the snows of 5 December 1757. The Austrians were formed up in a strong position 6.5 km (4 miles) wide, in an area of rolling country, with the village of Leuthen at their centre, and their flanks protected by marshy ground. Frederick feinted toward the enemy right, driving in their pickets and effectively blinding them, and then marched

---

The field of the battle of Culloden has become an iconic site for visitors. Recent work is restoring the field to its 1746 condition, and new interpretation challenges some of the enduring myths.

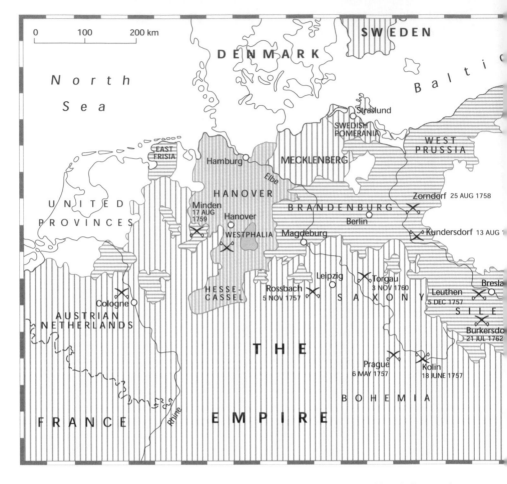

right around the enemy's left flank, protected from view by a range of low hills. He then proceeded to form his army at right angles to the Austrian line. The Austrians could only watch amazed at this rapid redeployment, and mocked it by calling it the 'Potsdamer Wachtparade'—the changing of the guard at Potsdam. They were in for a rude awakening.

Daun could not react swiftly enough and, despite a determined cavalry counter-attack, his army was torn apart by Frederick's 'walking batteries' of well-drilled infantry, losing 7,000 casualties and 20,000 prisoners. This was Frederick's finest hour. Napoleon called it a 'masterpiece of movement, manoeuvre and resolve' and said that this victory alone placed Frederick in the ranks of the greatest generals of all time.

Rossbach was the war's most decisive battle, because of its enormous repercussions within France. Louis determined to concentrate available resources on the colonial struggle with Britain. Prussia's struggle was thus reduced in scale, becoming primarily a war against Austria and, increasingly, Russia, while supported financially by Britain.

In its middle years no clear decision was evident in the war for Silesia. Despite a series of

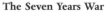

The Seven Years War

reverses, particularly at the hands of the Russians—a bloody tactical draw at Zorndorf on 25 August 1758, serious defeats at Kay (Paltzig) on 23 July 1759 and especially at Kundersdorf on 12 August of that year—Frederick retained the ability to win sufficient victories to keep the struggle going.

The Battle of Minden (1759)

The seizure of Minden, on the river Weser west of Hanover in Westphalia, by the French forced a reaction lest Hanover itself should fall to them. On 1 August a 37,000-strong Anglo-Hanoverian force under Prince Ferdinand of Brunswick met a French army of 44,000 commanded by marshal de Contades: skirmishing and artillery exchanges began at about 05.00. The French front was eventually pierced by a remarkable attack (launched as the result of a linguistic misunderstanding) by a brigade of British infantry, which shrugged off cavalry attacks and artillery fire, but suffered one-third casualties. But when the allied cavalry of five regiments was called to charge in support, Lord George Sackville thrice refused to give the order to advance, and thus lost an opportunity to influence the

battle: his conduct has never been satisfactorily explained. At a crucial moment, the Anglo-Hanoverian heavy artillery (30 guns) was moved to the left flank by a concealed route, and quickly repulsed an attack from that quarter, exploiting its mobility to the full. The same guns were then pushed forward, accompanying the final allied attack that decided the battle. The action lasted for about five hours during the early morning, and was over by about 10.00. The French suffered a resounding defeat, losing 7,000–10,000 men, while the allied casualties were fewer than 3,000.

Though Frederick had lost Hochkirch to the Austrians (14 October 1758), victories at Liegnitz (15 August 1760) and Torgau (3 November) broke Habsburg will to sustain the conflict. The continental war was effectively decided by the death of Frederick's implacable foe, the Russian empress Elizabeth, in January 1762. Her successor was the pro-Prussian Peter III, who immediately concluded first an armistice and then a peace treaty with his Prussian hero. Austria continued to fight for one further campaign, in the course of which Frederick won a final tactical victory at Burkersdorf (July 1762).

THE FRENCH REVOLUTIONARY WARS

It is the deepest irony that the French Revolution, with its ideals of liberty, equality, and fraternity, led to a quarter-century of bloody war. French royalist émigré forces began to gather at the frontiers and on 7 February 1792 Austria and Prussia signed the Treaty of Berlin against France. Exasperated, the French declared war on 20 April, initiating the War of the First Coalition. The Prussians took the powerful fortress of Longwy with ease and went on to take Verdun. The route to Paris seemed clear, and in the capital there was panic. The great revolutionary orator Danton made a stirring speech calling for 'de l'audace, et encore de l'audace, et toujours de l'audace!' (boldness, again boldness, and always boldness!), and French soldiers rose to meet the challenge.

The Battle (or, more accurately, the Cannonade) of Valmy (1792)

At Valmy, east of Rheims on the road to Verdun, on 20 September, French troops met the Prussian/Austrian invaders in a clash that established that the revolution would not be strangled at birth. The duke of Brunswick, who commanded the allied invasion, incorrectly expected his opponents to run. With elements of the Army of the North, Charles-François Dumouriez marched against Brunswick, manoeuvred skilfully, and held up the enemy advance at the Argonne forest. This bought time for François-Christophe Kellermann to bring his Army of the Centre to Valmy. Brunswick, after finally penetrating the Argonne, wheeled south with 30,000–4,000 Prussians to confront Kellermann's 36,000 republican troops.

Cannon decided the battle. The day began with an intense artillery duel, during which the French guns demonstrated their superiority. Although the Prussian infantry began to advance, it did not become seriously engaged. After seeing how steady the French

The battle of Prague, a hard-won victory for Frederick 'the Great'.

remained, Brunswick calculated that he could ill afford the casualties of a frontal assault and called off his attack. After a week-long face-off, Brunswick began a disastrous retreat to the Rhine. The day after Brunswick fell back from Valmy, the monarchy was abolished and France was proclaimed a republic.

French armies now went on the offensive in Savoy, the Rhine, and the Low Countries. Dumouriez routed the Austrians at Jemappes on 6 November, and Brussels was captured. The National Convention issued the Edict of Fraternity of 19 November 1792, calling on all oppressed peoples to rise up with the promise of French military assistance. The allied powers dug their heels in.

Recognizing that this was now a fight to the death, the French guillotined Louis XVI on 21 January 1793 and declared war on Hanoverian Britain and Bourbon Spain for good measure. Once again the borders of France were threatened. The allies swiftly took Mainz, Condé, and Valenciennes and the Revolutionary Tribunal responded with an effusion of blood known as the Terror. The British admiral Hood landed in Toulon in support of the royalists, and in the west of France the royalists of the Vendée rose in armed revolt against Paris. The combination of threats drove France to extreme measures, and a decree of *levée en masse* was issued by the Convention on 23 August 1793. All citizens were called to the defence of France. Fired with new fervour, the revolutionary armies recaptured Toulon, ejected the British from around Dunkirk, and advanced into the Alps. The organizational genius of Lazare Carnot was brought into play to help turn a revolutionary rabble into a properly equipped fighting force. The new commander in the north, a modest ex-ranker called Jean-Baptiste Jourdan, beat the Austrians in a tough contest at Wattignies on 16 October 1793, and the rebels of the Vendée and Lyons were crushed. The tough and talented Louis Lazare Hoche went on the offensive on the Rhine front, defeating the allies at Froeschwiller and Kaiserslautern in December. This success could not conceal the fact that the revolution's real military weakness was at sea. Most naval officers had either fled or been murdered by their mutinous crews. Small wonder, then, that a French fleet was mauled by the British admiral Lord Howe off Ushant on the Glorious First of June, 1794.

The Battle of Fleurus (1794)

French forces besieged Charleroi, some 10 km (6 miles) south-west of Fleurus. In an attempt to relieve the fortress, a dispirited prince of Saxe-Coburg marched with 52,000 Austrian and Dutch troops against the 73,000 republican soldiers led by Jean-Baptiste Jourdan. On 26 June Coburg split his forces into five columns to try to surround the French, but they defeated his forces in detail. After tough resistance repelled Coburg's attacks, he withdrew across the Meuse on the following day. Although suffering fewer casualties than did his French opponents, he had spent his energy. Soon the French chased the Austrians out of the southern Netherlands, which France annexed and retained for twenty years.

The French had no answer to allied sea power and Corsica was lost on 10 August. However, French armies stormed to victory in Spain and Savoy, and by the end of 1794, tired of continual war, the Austrians signed an armistice. Prussia, the Netherlands, and Spain made peace in April, May, and June 1795. The revolution had ensured its survival purely by force of arms. Further south, in Italy, the revolutionary armies under the enterprising young General Napoleon Bonaparte began to make startling progress from

March 1796. By 28 April he had conquered Nice, Savoy, and Piedmont. From there he went on the offensive into the north Italian plain, defeating the Austrians, taking Milan, and besieging the important communications nexus of Mantua in June. On the Rhine front Jourdan was making poorer progress against the redoubtable Archduke Charles and was defeated at Amberg, Würzburg, and Altenkirchen in August and September.

The Battle of Arcola (1796)

In November Austrian armies under Josef Freiherr von Alvinczy (28,000) and Paul Davidovich (18,000) advanced on Bassano del Grappa and Trento respectively to attack the French Army of Italy under Napoleon Bonaparte besieging Mantua (Mantova) with well under 40,000. A deception plan masked Davidovich's advance, and although Bonaparte saw through it, his northern wing was beaten by Davidovich, and he found himself facing two enemy armies.

Bonaparte determined to deal with the southernmost threat first, by cutting Alvinczy's communications at Villanova and forcing the Austrians to turn and fight him in difficult, marshy ground between the rivers Alpone and Adige. To reach Villanova he had to cross the Alpone at Arcola. On 15 November Pierre Augereau was checked at the bridge, and all Bonaparte's personal energy could not help him. There were no major gains the following day, but Alvinczy's nerve was shaken and his force was split to cover the river line in marshy countryside. On 17 November André Masséna outmanoeuvred the Austrians in Arcola, while Augereau crossed the Alpone further south. Alvinczy fell back with the loss of 7,000 men. Bonaparte jabbed northwards, but just missed Davidovich. Arcola is a graphic illustration of the ability of a weaker army to use interior lines to defeat stronger opponents in detail, and shows Bonaparte at the peak of his form.

Spain's entry into the war on the side of France gave planners in Paris access to a large and well-equipped navy. The British withdrew from the Mediterranean entirely. Indeed, the British Isles themselves came under threat when Louis Lazare Hoche attempted to land an army in Bantry Bay in Ireland, but was foiled by the weather: as the Irish nationalist Wolf Tone put it, England had not had such an escape since the Armada. Although Bonaparte's successes in Italy continued unabated with victory at Rivoli on 14 January 1797 and the capture of Mantua, at sea the Spanish fleet was hammered by Admiral Sir John Jervis off Cape St Vincent. However, it was not all plain sailing for the coalition: there was another French landing at Fishguard in Wales (the last invasion of British soil by foreign troops) and British sailors, supposedly infected by Jacobinism but at least as much influenced by more mundane grievances, mutinied at Spithead and the Nore.

The Austrians now began to accept the fait accompli of French presence in Lombardy, but the British continued truculent. Admiral Adam Duncan savaged the Dutch, a French ally, at Camperdown on 11 October 1797. Bonaparte was appointed to command an invasion army, but without control of the Channel his task was impossible, and so he cast his eyes toward the east. The British, in any event, had problems of their own: the United Irishmen rose in armed rebellion. Profiting from the confusion Bonaparte left Toulon for Egypt and went on to fight a glittering campaign, capturing Alexandria on 2 July 1798, routing the Mameluke army at the Pyramids on 21 July, and entering Cairo on the 25th. However, the British admiral Horatio Nelson caught up with the French fleet in Aboukir Bay and, on 1 August, utterly destroyed it in what is known as the Battle of the Nile.

Bonaparte, so successful on land, was now totally isolated from home. Furthermore, a planned invasion of Ireland had foundered: General Joseph Aimable Humbert landed in Killala Bay, but was surrounded and forced to surrender at Ballinamuck on 8 September.

Soon France's enemies were threatening its borders once more and royalist uprisings began. Such an emergency needed a desperate solution, and Bonaparte led a military coup in Paris on 9 November 1799, declaring himself first consul shortly afterwards.

Bonaparte immediately set about reversing the unpromising military situation. He descended on Italy by way of the St Gotthard pass and defeated the Austrians at Marengo on 14 June 1800, recovering northern Italy and removing the danger of an Austrian invasion of France. General Jean Moreau, meanwhile, advanced through Bavaria into Austria, and on 3 December beat the Archduke John at Hohenlinden, only 80 km (50 miles) from Vienna. The Austrians promptly made peace at Lunéville in February 1801. Bonaparte then set about isolating Britain, and a Russian-led Armed Neutrality was formed to oppose British attacks on neutral shipping.

The Battle of Copenhagen (1801)

On 2 April a British fleet under Admiral Sir Hyde Parker engaged the Danish navy under the guns of Denmark's capital city. The aim was to destroy the hostile Russian-sponsored League of Armed Neutrality that threatened to close the Baltic to British trade. The British victory knocked Denmark out of the alliance and persuaded Russia and Sweden to think again. This was the occasion when Horatio Nelson put a telescope to his missing eye when Hyde Parker's recall signal was drawn to his attention, saying that he had the right to be blind sometimes.

This, and the destruction of their French army in Egypt in August, were setbacks for the French, but in London the ministry led by William Pitt the Younger fell and its successor negotiated peace with France, signed at Amiens in March 1802. This brought the Revolutionary wars to an end, but proved to be a mere truce before the even more destructive Napoleonic wars.

4 Nineteenth-Century Europe

On 23 August 1793 the French National Convention proclaimed general mobilization for its struggle against monarchical Europe. 'Young men will go to battle,' it decreed; 'married men will forge arms and transport supplies; women will make tents, uniforms and serve in the hospitals; children will pick rags; old men will have themselves carried to public squares, to inspire the courage of the warriors, and to preach the hatred of kings and the unity of the Republic.' This *levée en masse* took the revolutionary army, already a mixture of regulars and volunteers, to over a million men, but it was not just size that distinguished it. Louis XVI had been executed that January, and it was evident that this was no mere dynastic conflict. On the French side there was a sense that war was the business of the people, not just of its leaders. Revolutionary armies were accompanied by government representatives who had unsuccessful or unlucky commanders guillotined. Captured officers were not simply hostile combatants but agents of malign regimes, and there were times when neither the French nor their opponents were inclined to take prisoners.

The scale and intensity of the war which blazed out across Europe from 1792 and lasted, with brief interludes, until 1815, were wholly new. But some of its ingredients had deep roots. Revolutionary infantry, lacking the training and discipline of the pipeclayed warriors of old Europe, often fought in column. Columns were not new, but had long been the best means of crossing ground rapidly, for the lines which produced the most effective firepower were disorganized by inconvenient terrain. Columns generated shock by their impact (real or anticipated, for foes often ran away before physical contact), and were a useful means of keeping men together.

The eighteenth century had seen increasing interest in light infantry, so useful for reconnaissance and outpost work, who could be thrown forward to screen main bodies of infantry before they began the volleying which often decided battles. Troops like this came into their own outside Europe, especially in North America, but there had long been tension (as much social and institutional as military) between light infantry, with their more relaxed notions of discipline, and their starchier colleagues in the line. Adding a foam of skirmishers to the rolling wave of columns created a formidable tactical instrument, and battles like Jemappes (1792) and Wattignies (1793) were won by it. One of the most striking contrasts came at Jena in 1806, when Prussian infantry, symbolic of the old world, were drawn up in front the village of Vierzehnheiligen. A British historian, writing a century ago, told how:

Now followed one of the most extraordinary and pitiful incidents in military history. This line of magnificent infantry, some 20,000 strong, stood out in the open for two whole hours while exposed to the merciless case [shot] and skirmishing fire of the French, who, behind the garden walls, offered no mark at all for their return fire. In places the fronts of companies were only marked by individual files still loading and firing, while all their comrades lay dead and dying around them.

As the French Revolutionary and Napoleonic wars went on, combatants recognized the merits of being able to deliver both fire and shock, and developed formations like *l'ordre mixte*, popular with French infantry, to keep part of a regiment in line with the remainder close behind in column, able to strengthen the line if required, or to push on to take advantage of the effect of fire. Armies not only employed specialist light troops, often rifle armed and green jacketed, but also turned one company of the eight or ten in each battalion into a light company, trained for skirmishing.

Cavalry retained the conventional division into heavy and light, with light cavalry often modelled on wild horsemen on the fringes of Europe. Hussars, soon the heroes of extravagant tailoring, began as light cavalry on the Great Plain of Hungary. Light cavalry tended to grow heavier, and, despite traditional preference for outpost work, to see the battlefield charge as a major reason for its existence. Dragoons, developed in the seventeenth century as little more than mounted infantry, became part of the cavalry arm in their own right, although during the Napoleonic era they might still carry a short musket and bayonet, and expect to fight dismounted.

Artillery, too, had made significant strides in the eighteenth century. Cannon had long been cast around a removable core, but in mid-century the Swiss Jean Maritz perfected the technique of boring out barrels, giving a better fit between bore and projectile, and enabling barrels to be made thinner and lighter, and so requiring fewer horses to haul cannon. Jean Baptiste de Gribeauval used this technology to standardize French artillery from the 1760s. Guns fired roundshot, whose weight (like 6-pounder, 9-pounder) defined the calibre of the piece, with various forms of multiple shot for use at short range. Both mortars and howitzers fired exploding projectiles, and in 1784 Lieutenant Henry Shrapnel of the Royal Artillery developed the missile that was to bear his name, 'spherical case' shot, a shell packed with musket balls and gunpowder exploded by a burning fuse.

French artillery had suffered far less from the emigration of its officers than had infantry or cavalry, and was initially the most proficient arm of the revolutionary armies. Napoleon Bonaparte was an artillery officer by training and inclination, and a hallmark of his tactics was the concentration of artillery against the chosen point of his enemy's array. Napoleon also profited from the work of eighteenth-century theorists like the comte de Guibert and General Pierre Joseph de Bourcet. The *corps d'armée*, a combined arms force commanded by a marshal or senior general, powerful enough to sustain battle unsupported for some time, but small enough to make the best use of road-space and not to exhaust local logistic resources, was an essential element of his method. It enabled Napoleon to make great strategic moves, like that from the Channel coast to Moravia for the Austerlitz campaign of 1805, with corps marching separately and uniting on the battlefield.

It was his successful exploitation of the ideas of others, and the addition of his own emphasis on speed, concentration, and decision, that made Napoleon a commander with few peers. He ultimately failed because the conviction that helped make him such an outstanding general induced him to go too far, and to disdain compromise which could have left him on the throne of a France shorn of its conquests. Although he demolished successive coalitions, his opponents, who raised their own game by studying his, returned to the attack time and time again. The 'Spanish ulcer' was a constant drain on French manpower, and after the Russian campaign of 1812, in which perhaps 400,000 French and allied soldiers died, the Grande Armée was never the same again. Moreover, the emotions aroused by the revolution were not confined to France: the period unleashed the twin passions of nationalism and liberalism, and in 1814–15 the French were struggling against opponents driven on by the sort of fervour which had once animated threadbare armies of the revolution.

However profound his understanding of warfare on land, Napoleon had neither interest in, nor aptitude for, maritime affairs. His descent on Egypt was doomed when Horatio Nelson destroyed his fleet in the Nile estuary (1798). His plan to invade England in 1804 depended on gaining control of the Channel, just as German hopes in 1940 hinged on mastery of the sky above it. He had begun to move eastwards even before the battle of Trafalgar ensured that, although French raiders could still harass commerce, his fleet could not break the strong arm of blockade. In 1812 the prefect of the Lower Seine reported that the seaborne trade of Rouen had collapsed: 'Commerce is almost non-existent: it cannot prosper without maritime peace.'

The climactic battle of Waterloo (1815) was followed by a long period of peace. The French soon began, almost accidentally, the conquest of Algeria, and elsewhere in Europe armies reverted to eighteenth-century type, with the nobility generally reasserting its grip on commissioned rank, and the preservation of internal order becoming a major preoccupation. The French officer-turned-author Alfred de Vigny speculated that his own dreams of military glory would end with his being brained by 'a chamber-pot thrown from a window by a toothless old crone'.

Although the victorious powers, reordering Europe at the Congress of Vienna, had tried to return to happier times, the genies of nationalism and liberalism could not be forced back into the bottle. Italy and Germany, both 'geographical expressions' rather than unified states, were gripped by growing demands for unification. France's nostalgia for past triumphs helped bring Napoleon's nephew to power, as Napoleon III, in 1851. Although he affirmed that 'the Empire is peace', Napoleon recognized that glory was an indispensable corollary to his regime. In 1854–6 he joined Britain and Piedmont in a war against Russia, which saw inconclusive naval operations in the Baltic and a major landing in the Crimea, Russian territory on the northern shores of the Black Sea. The allies won several scrambling victories and occupied the naval base of Sevastopol.

The British had begun military reform before the Crimea, but the well-publicized miseries of their army accelerated the process, with marked improvements in medical and logistic departments. Most armies moved in the same direction by militarizing their transport and supply services. Another legacy of the Crimea was the relationship between Napoleon and Count Cavour, prime minister of Piedmont. In 1859, in the first use of the railway for large-scale military transport, the French moved an army into northern Italy and beat the Austrians, occupiers of Lombardy and Venetia, at Magenta and Solferino. Although Napoleon, horrified by his first sight of a stricken field, stopped before driving the Austrians out of Italy, the war was an important step towards Italian unification. The process required further campaigns, the most important fought by nationalists led by Giuseppe Garibaldi in Sicily and Naples in 1860–1, as well as by Austrian relinquishment of Venetia after their defeat by the Prussians in 1866, and French withdrawal from the Papal States in 1870.

The weapons used in 1859 would not have surprised the men who fought at Waterloo. The flintlock was replaced by the more reliable percussion lock in the 1830s and 1840s, and shortly afterwards the rifle ceased to be the firearm for the specialist few, but was issued to infantry as a whole. In 1859 the Austrians had a slight advantage in infantry weapons, but the battles were won, not by prolonged firefights, but by French infantry pressing on with unstoppable élan. The Austrians, anxious to take the 'lessons' of the war to heart, resolved to get to close quarters themselves, and developed shock tactics (*Stosstaktik*) in order to do so.

The north German state of Prussia had played a prominent part in the Napoleonic wars, and the arrival of the Prussians on the field of Waterloo towards the end of that long day decided the battle. However, in 1860 there seemed little reason for the French to give Prussia a second thought. Its army was small, and served largely to support the *Landwehr*, a citizen militia displaying the hallmarks of liberalism. King Wilhelm's determination to recast his army on the basis of universal conscription, with trained conscripts passing into a reformed *Landwehr*, provoked a constitutional crisis. Wilhelm was supported by war minister Albrecht von Roon and by the tough minister-president Otto von Bismarck, appointed in 1862. Bismarck proposed to unify north Germany on the basis of 'blood and iron', and Roon furnished him both those essential commodities.

As a curtain-raiser the Prussians led a force which beat the Danes in 1864, and annexed the duchies of Schleswig and Holstein. Helmuth von Moltke, a graduate of the Berlin Kriegsakademie, appointed to what was then the uninfluential post of chief of the great general staff in 1857, served as chief of staff of the allied army, and his dour efficiency was one of the campaign's notable features. Two years later Bismarck seized the chance to establish Prussian leadership of Germany by excluding Austria from the arrangement. Moltke's specialist general staff did not simply plan mobilization and deployment with meticulous care, using railways to whisk armies to the frontier, but implemented a classic plan for concentration on the field of battle. The schemes were imperilled by senior commanders who disliked seeing inky nonentities dictate their operations, and a less robust personality might have been broken by the bickering, but the pay-off came when the Austrians were roundly defeated at Königgrätz, losing 44,000 men to the Prussians' 9,000. This disparity was partly caused by the Prussian needle gun, a breech-loading rifle which had already carpeted the war's early battlefields with dead and wounded. The victory ensured Prussian hegemony in north Germany, but the south German states still stood aloof, and Bismarck realized that he needed to bring them together in a war against a common enemy.

There was little doubt who that enemy might be. The news of Königgrätz produced such a shock in Paris that one commentator noted that it might have been a French army that had been defeated. An expeditionary force was hauled back from Mexico, and the government set about recasting its army. This was no easy task, for it had beaten the Russians and the Austrians, completed the conquest of Algeria and overrun Mexico. Its fashions were widely imitated: British rifle volunteers dressed like the French chasseurs they spent their weekends training to fight, and the armies of the American Civil War wore jaunty *képis* and included *zouaves*, modelled on North African light infantry. Selective conscription gave France an army ideal for colonial campaigns and small wars, but it would not do for a major war against an opponent able to implement universal conscription backed by growing public resolve.

The debates on the new French military service law featured familiar disputes between the left, with its affection for old-style *levée en masse*, and the right, which preferred smaller, more politically reliable, armies. The law of 1868 was a compromise. It increased the annual contingent of conscripts but enabled many men to avoid the regular army and to serve with the barely organized Garde Mobile. Other reforms were more effective.

In 1866 the French introduced the handy breech-loading *chassepot* rifle, which outranged the needle gun. Thanks to Napoleon's support the *mitrailleuse* machine gun was brought into service. It was too heavy to be really successful, and matters were not helped by shrouding the weapon in a cloak of secrecy which even its owners found hard to lift. The French considered replacing their muzzle-loading artillery with breech-loaders like those obtained by the Prussians: Herr Krupp kindly drew their attention to his new steel weapons. But there was an animus amongst French gunners against steel, and the government of the new 'Liberal Empire' dared not demand too much money from its electorate.

When the French blundered into the conflict in the summer of 1870 Bismarck brought the whole of Germany into the war. Within the first six weeks it was evident that the French had failed at each of war's three levels. Strategically, they had no allies and no proper general staff: a war plan was modified at the last moment to allow Napoleon to take personal command. Combining general mobilization and concentration on the frontier produced chaos. Operationally, Moltke's small but expert general staff, working down to carefully trained chiefs of staff at formation level, and communicating by telegraph, ensured that Germans could march divided but fight united, with a logistic network that could support either dispersion or concentration. The French began the war strewn along the frontier: when they drew together to fight, the sheer weight of numbers broke their fragile commissariat.

Tactically, the *chassepot* justified its early promise, with the repulse of the Prussian Guard at Saint-Privat on 18 August as the most striking example. But French infantry firepower induced the Germans to use their artillery to reduce the defence before their infantry came into action, and the development of what we would now term 'fire and manoeuvre' went far towards enabling them to cope with a *chassepot*-based defence. Shock action by cavalry rarely achieved what its instigators sought, and the best example of its success, 'von Bredow's death-ride' at Rezonville on 16 August, was the exception, rather than the rule. Nor did cavalry redeem itself by reconnaissance: if the Germans did better than the French, they still lost contact with the Army of Châlons on its way to destruction at Sedan. Overall, German performance was by no means perfect. General Karl von Steinmetz of the First Army came close to wrecking Moltke's plan at the start of the campaign, and a competent French commander might have won the double battle of Rezonville/Vionville and Gravelotte/Saint-Privat on 16–18 August.

German victory at Sedan on 1 September removed the last field army from the French order of battle, leaving the Army of the Rhine shut up in Metz, where it surrendered the following month. Once that would have ended matters, but the world had changed. The new Government of National Defence raised forces in the provinces, bought arms and equipment abroad, and fought on with armies which were now an amalgam of regulars, *mobiles*, French and foreign volunteers, the over-age and the youthful, the quietly competent and the flamboyantly hopeless. The Germans responded with growing severity, shooting *francs-tireurs*, enforcing collective punishments, and meting out the casual destruction that reflected bitterness at the changed nature of the war. Paris was besieged and bombarded, and no sooner had an armistice been ratified in March 1871 than there was a rising in the city, whose suppression by French troops became scarcely less significant than the war itself. Most commentators were to focus on the destruction of the imperial armies: but it was the Armies of National Defence that pointed the way ahead to the wars of the twentieth century.

THE NAPOLEONIC WARS

It is possible that the treaties bringing the French Revolutionary wars to a close might have formed the basis of a more durable peace, had the powers been willing to honour them in both spirit and letter. But France and Britain were sonn at loggerheads, culminating in war in May 1803.

As France's first consul, Napoleon had made the most of the respite granted by the short-lived Peace of Amiens. Military strength called for efficacious conscription and taxation systems, administered by a suitably competent bureaucracy. Napoleon's meritocracy channelled the gifted and diligent into an educational system which was geared to serving the needs of the regime. His adversaries found themselves forced to adopt Napoleon's methods.

Some of the most striking changes occurred in the size and organization of armies. As early as 1800 Napoleon had devised a permanent structure for the French army consisting of *corps d'armée*, subdivided into divisions and brigades. Each of his corps formed a small army in its own right. Capable of independent manoeuvre, and expected to live off the land, they moved rapidly over vast tracts of Europe, cornering their opponents and compelling them to fight or surrender. For Napoleon the goal of strategy was to destroy the enemy's means to resist through battle, not attrition.

Although the Royal Navy quickly bottled the French fleet up in its ports and harried enemy merchantmen, there was a persistent fear that a hostile armada might jeopardize the British Isles or key trade outlets. The blockade stretched naval resources to the limit. Moreover, in order to move troops overseas, Britain needed ships. Entrusted with the defence of the home waters and with foreign trade, the Royal Navy already faced too many demands on its resources and tonnage was in short supply.

The Battle of Trafalgar (1805)

By the end of 1804 Russia and Austria had been sufficiently alienated by French actions in Germany and Italy to enter into a coalition with Britain. Napoleon, who had been proclaimed emperor in December 1804, assembled an army along the Channel coast in preparation for an invasion of England. He ordered Admiral Pierre Charles de Villeneuve to lure the British fleet to the West Indies and then head straight back across the Atlantic to combine with the Brest fleet and escort his invasion barges across the Channel. Villeneuve completed the first part, pursued by the British under Vice Admiral Horatio Nelson, but on his return the French admiral was unnerved by a skirmish with Admiral Calder off Cape Finisterre in July and he sailed not east to Brest but south to Vigo, and thence to join the Spanish fleet in Cadiz.

The combined Franco-Spanish fleet included several of the most powerful warships afloat, but enforced inactivity under British blockade had eroded skills and morale of officers and sailors alike. After 1700 blockade became the critical offensive instrument of British sea power, keeping inferior fleets in harbour.

The basic unit of sea power was the ship of the line or battleship, mounting as many as 100 or more guns. Because warships mounted almost all their guns on the broadside, and were vulnerable to fire from ahead or astern, actions were usually fought in line ahead. This was a strong defensive formation, especially as ships' means of propulsion (masts

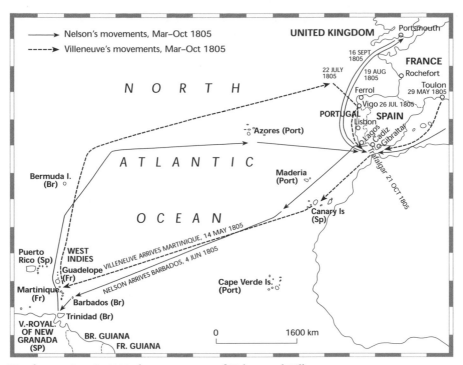

Naval operations in 1805; the manoeuvres of Nelson and Villeneuve

and sails) were much more exposed than their hulls, and they were often stopped or disabled before they could come to close quarters. The meeting of two competent fleets in roughly equal numbers usually resulted in an inconclusive action. Only during the Napoleonic wars did new tactical methods allow equal or even inferior fleets to win overwhelming victories, and these were developed by the Royal Navy, drawing on a strength of seamanship and morale conferred by overall strategic naval dominance.

The news of Villeneuve's presence in Cadiz reached London in September and on the 15th of that month Nelson rejoined *Victory* and sailed south. On 21 October he finally caught the Franco-Spanish fleet off Cape Trafalgar. Petulantly, Napoleon had ordered Villeneuve to put to sea even though the strategic justification was gone, for he had already left Boulogne, and Villeneuve duly sailed on 20 October with 33 ships of the line. He anticipated Nelson's tactics and had made provision by putting his faster ships under Vice-Admiral Count Dumanoir in the rear, to sail up and close the gaps when the British ships broke his line. But when he reversed direction the next day before the engagement, he threw his line into confusion and put Dumanoir in the van, whence he played a culpably limited role in the battle. It is doubtful whether it would have made any difference in the face of greatly superior British ship handling and gunnery. The British caught sight of Villeneuve's Franco-Spanish fleet at six o'clock in the morning of the 21st and Nelson attacked with his 29 ships of the line in two columns, breaking his enemies' line. The last of the fighting died away at half past four that afternoon. The British lost 449 killed and 1,214 wounded out of 18,000 engaged, but the price in officers was high: Nelson was killed and 22 per cent of the captains and 19 per cent of the lieutenants fell.

The carnage on the other side was indescribable: Villeneuve's flagship alone suffered 546 casualties and 18 ships surrendered, many to sink in the storm that followed, while one blew up.

Nelson's inspiration and tactical boldness may be said to have been the crowning touch in gaining the victory, but it was the long years of blockade that built the edifice, with a little assistance from an exasperated Napoleon, who threw away an arm whose value he never fully appreciated.

Even the triumph of Trafalgar in 1805 was to fail to dispel Britain's basic strategic problems; its naval supremacy was a necessary condition for France's defeat, but it was not a sufficient one. Aware of the preparations that Austria and Russia were making for war, as he prepared to invade England, Napoleon resolved to strike at them and, thus, indirectly at Britain; he too realized that, without continental allies, 'Perfidious Albion' would be almost impotent. Accordingly, amidst conditions of great secrecy, he wheeled his forces from the Channel towards the Danube. Advancing at tremendous speed, they pounced before the Russians could reach the theatre.

The Battle of Austerlitz (1805)

Fought on 2 December, Austerlitz is known as the battle of the three emperors. Napoleon faced the combined armies of Emperor Francis II of Austria and Tsar Alexander of Russia, under the nominal command of the veteran Field Marshal Mikhail Illarionovich Kutuzov. Napoleon had captured an entire Austrian army of 27,000 men under General Karl Mack at Ulm on 20 October. Hearing of this disaster, Kutuzov began to retire, leaving the French to occupy Vienna. Napoleon resolved to march north to seek out and engage the coalition forces, and allow his scattered detachments to join him on the way. He desperately needed a swift outcome to the campaign before the Austrians could reorganize, and to forestall the threatened entry of Prussia into the war. Supplies were running out, and the weather, predictably for the month of December in Moravia, was bitterly cold, adding to the discomfort of tired and hungry French soldiers.

The Grande Armée consisted of around 73,000, not all of whom were immediately available, facing nearly 86,000 Austrians and Russians. Napoleon carefully scouted the ground in person, noting salient features. He gave orders to improve defensive positions, such as the natural bastion of Santon Hill on his left. The vital ground, though, was the Pratzen Heights, a large area of high ground dominating the centre of his chosen battlefield. It was here that the violent drama of the battle would reach its climax.

Wrong footed by Napoleon's carefully laid deception, the Russian and Austrian plan called for five large columns, totalling some 59,000 men, to overwhelm Napoleon's right before he could react, thereby cutting the French off from Vienna. A secondary assault led by General Prince Piotr Ivanovich Bagration would strike on the opposite flank, held by Marshal Jean Lannes and the dashing Marshal Joachim Murat, assaulting from east to west along the Olmütz to Brünn road. A final crushing blow would be delivered to the centre, when the French were driven back on themselves into a crocheted line, by the combined force of the allied assault. It was a complex plan which would require excellent timing and perfect coordination to succeed. It was to founder in its execution.

The dawn attack on the French right was soon foiled by the timely arrival by forced march of Louis Friant's division of III Corps, whereupon the Russians and Austrians redoubled their efforts on this sector, pushing more troops through the central position of the Pratzen Heights, and across the French front. The disparate allied columns became stalled and confused as they lumbered into each other in the gloom. Seeing that the allies had, as he had hoped, exposed their flank to his attack, Napoleon ordered Marshal Nicholas Soult to lead his corps up onto the Pratzen just before 09.00, as 'the sun of Austerlitz' broke through the clouds and mist. Soult's men were still partially hidden by the fog lying in the low valley and the smoke of the breakfast fires, and achieved perfect surprise as the two divisions burst on to the plateau. By 11.00, and after a stiff fight, the French had a secure hold on this key central high ground.

Kutuzov now realized that his plan was in danger of turning to ruin, and towards 13.00 he threw in the crack Russian Imperial Guard under the Grand Duke Constantine, the tsar's brother. This attack threw the French on the Pratzen into some disarray and Napoleon's reserves were hurried forward into the fray. After a titanic clash, the allies were pushed back off the Pratzen feature. This withdrawal soon turned to rout as Soult's troops wheeled onto the flank and rear of the enemy assaulting the right of the French position. Seeing themselves surrounded, these too fled, some across the frozen Satschan lakes behind them, where it is said that guns and teams fell through the ice into the freezing water. The French *Bulletin de La Grande Armée* claimed that some 20,000 allied soldiers were killed. However, the veracity of these claims is open to question. The true figures were probably nearer 16,000 allied troops dead and wounded and 11,000 taken prisoner, still a handsome victory.

This was Napoleon's finest hour. He had effectively smashed the Third Coalition: Austria made peace at once, and the Russians retreated to the East Prussian and Polish marches to fight again the next year. Napoleon proceeded to redraw the map of Germany. Substituting around 30 sizeable states for the hundreds of entities which had constituted the Reich, he transformed the geopolitics of the region, laying the foundations of modern Germany.

This alarmed and offended Prussia. After a bout of dubious diplomacy, which was largely an attempt to buy time in which to mobilize their forces, the Prussians issued Napoleon with an ultimatum in October 1806. Provoked by Berlin's demands he again unleashed the Grande Armée.

The Battles of Jena and Auerstadt (1806)

The French army had at least 160,000 men quartered in southern Germany, and although the Prussians and their Saxon allies could produce rather more, the Prussian army was 'a walking museum piece' which had changed little since the days of Frederick the Great. In September the Prussians began a hesitant advance, initially confident that Napoleon would stand on the defensive. They were beset by divided counsels, with Prince Hohenlohe and the duke of Brunswick favouring different plans which an irresolute King Frederick William III did his best to balance.

Napoleon decided to concentrate on his extreme right and push swiftly through the difficult Thuringerwald into the area between Dresden and Leipzig. If the Prussians advanced he would outflank them, and if they fell back he hoped to catch them at a disadvantage on one of a number of river lines. He crossed the Saxon frontier on 8 October behind a cavalry screen with the Guard and six corps, a *bataillon carré* (literally 'square battalion') of 180,000 men moving in lateral columns close enough to offer mutual support. Prince Louis of Prussia, commanding a division watching the south-west

approaches to the Prussian concentration area, was caught and killed at Saalfeld. On the 13th Napoleon reached Jena, where reports from Marshal Jean Lannes, commanding his leading corps, suggested that the whole Prussian army lay on the lofty Landgrafenberg feature in front of him, though thick fog prevented accurate reconnaissance. He was confident that he would be able to move his corps up to concentrate in overwhelming strength over the next 24 hours, and decided to attack. That night he set about securing the Windknollen feature, highest point of the Landgrafenberg.

On the morning of the 14th Napoleon duly attacked, and a combination of French élan and Prussian command errors soon gave him enough room to deploy his troops as they came up. By late morning Hohenlohe realized that he was dealing with the main French army and did his best to concentrate to meet it. The turning point of the battle came when 20,000 Prussian infantry drew up outside the village of Vierzehnheiligen, under merciless fire from French in the village. A general advance, begun at about midday, pushed the Prussians from the field.

Unbeknown to Napoleon, he was in fact only facing part of the Prussian army: Brunswick's 60,000 men were at Auerstadt, 19 km (12 miles) to the north. Two French corps under Marshal Louis Davout and Marshal Jean-Baptiste Bernadotte had hooked to the east of Jena, making for Hohenlohe's rear, and collided with Brunswick early on the 14th. Davout fought a masterly battle against the odds, unsupported by Bernadotte, who turned a deaf ear to his appeals for help and was lucky to escape court martial for it. The Prussians were routed and Brunswick himself was killed. Auerstadt was a prodigious achievement, a tribute to the Iron Marshal and his troops.

The double battle of Jena/Auerstadt cost the Prussians 25,000 prisoners and 200 guns. Although Napoleon's advance had been skilful, he had made a significant error of judgement on the night of the 13th and was saved from its consequences by Prussian hesitation, by Davout's talent, and by the superb fighting qualities of the French army.

The Battle of Eylau (1807)

Napoleon advanced into Poland to meet Marshal Kamenskoi's armies, but failed to catch them in 'the manoeuvre of the Narew' in December 1806. The following month he was again unsuccessful in trapping them, now under Leonty Leontyvich, Count von Benningsen, on the river Alle, and followed them north to Preussische-Eylau. Each army eventually totalled some 75,000 men, but was smaller for the opening moves. Napoleon awaited the corps of Marshal Louis Davout from his right and Marshal Michel Ney from his left, while Benningsen would be reinforced by General Lestocq's Prussian corps.

On 8 February a bombardment began in snow which fell intermittently all day. Napoleon hoped to turn Benningsen's left flank when Davout arrived, but attempts to pin Benningsen by attacking his centre misfired: the corps under Marshal Pierre Augereau was appallingly mauled by Russian cannon and forced back by infantry. Only a desperate massed cavalry charge by Marshal Joachim Murat checked the Russians. Davout came up on the Russian left and pushed it steadily backwards: it was close to breaking when Lestocq appeared and checked the attack. Ney now arrived, but night had fallen.

Horace Vernet's romantic vision of Napoleon at Jena.

Benningsen's generals urged him to hold his ground. But he had spent the day in the saddle, and Ney's arrival depressed him. He ordered a retreat, and Napoleon was in no condition to pursue. The French may have lost 25,000 men, the Russians and Prussians perhaps 15,000; many wounded froze to death. Ney, crossing the field on the 9th, said: 'What a massacre! And without a result!'

Licking his wounds, Napoleon reduced Danzig while awaiting the enemy's next move. In early June, the allies again took the offensive, only to be repulsed by Napoleon's counterstroke which culminated in the battle of Friedland.

The Battle of Friedland (1807)

The Russian army under General Bennigsen with 61,000 men significantly outnumbered the 26,000 with whom Marshal Jean Lannes was advancing on Königsberg (modern Kaliningrad) on the Gulf of Gdansk. The Russians were crossing the river Alle at Friendland when contact was made on 14 June 1807 and they attacked at once. The stubborn resistance of Lannes's men allowed Marshal Ney to bring up 80,000 reinforcements and the arrival of 30 cannon with General Claude Victor's corps exposed the Russians in Friedland to a withering fire. In addition to the numbers drowned in the Alle, the Russians lost 11,000 killed and 7,000 wounded. The French occupied Königsberg on 16 June.

This catastrophe prompted Tsar Alexander I to make peace, regardless of the consequences for his Prussian ally. The Treaty of Tilsit was drawn up on a barge moored in the centre of the river Niemen on 25 June. The demise of the Fourth Coalition climaxed with Russia becoming France's ally, joining both Napoleon's anti-British maritime league and his Continental System.

The Peninsular War (1808–1814)

By late 1806, Napoleon's defeat of Prussia had opened up new possibilities in his continuing struggle with Britain. Unable to overcome the Royal Navy's domination of the Channel and thus bring his military strength to bear directly against England, he was obliged to resort to other instruments of policy. Britain's war effort was ultimately founded on its prosperity. By endeavouring not so much to end as to control Britain's trade with the European continent, Napoleon hoped to induce its capitulation: the entire coastline of Europe would have to be sealed off.

The Berlin Decrees of 1806 were the first in a series of sanctions against Britain's trade, known collectively as the Continental System. The French then turned their attention to Portugal, and Spain joined with France in occupying the almost defenceless kingdom. Napoleon was now able to incorporate the entire Iberian peninsula into the Continental System. The Spanish were soon to find themselves his next victims. In February 1808, French soldiers, with a mixture of trickery and force, wrested several key fortresses and towns from their astonished Spanish 'allies'. Thousands more French troops then swept

A French view of the battle of Salamanca, showing the village of Los Arapiles and, beyond it, the town of Salamanca.

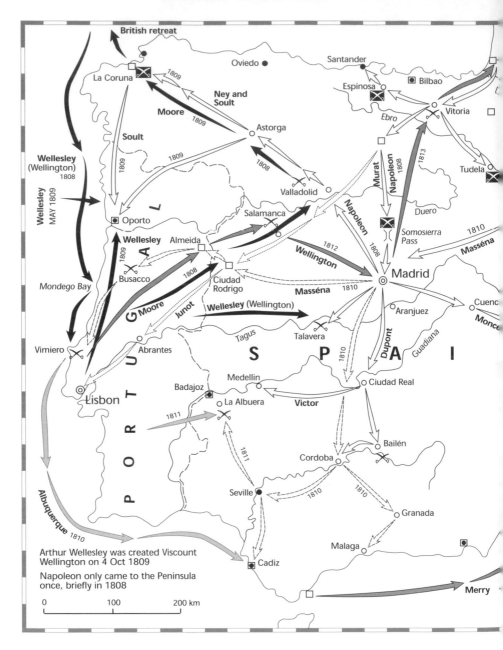

over the Pyrenees with impunity. Napoleon then contrived the replacement of the house of Bourbon by putting his brother Joseph on the throne. On 2 May, the population of Madrid turned on the French garrison. Though suppressed, this rising sparked off a general insurrection which quickly engulfed the entire country.

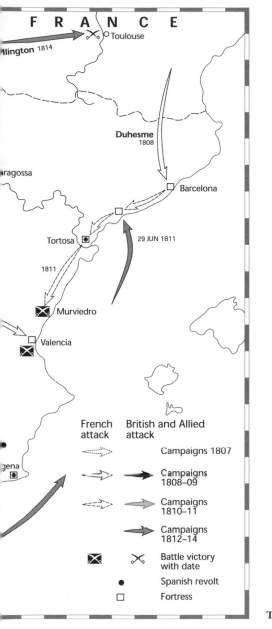

The Peninsular War

The Battle of Bailén (1808)

After the coup in May, Napoleon had ordered the forces that he had over the preceding months sent into Spain to occupy various strategic points. Among these was the port of Cadiz, the troops detailed for this purpose consisting of the first division of the army corps commanded by General Pierre Dupont de l'Étang. Led by Dupont himself, this division advanced as far as Córdoba which it sacked on 7 June 1808. However, alarmed at his growing isolation, Dupont fell back on Andujar. A further two divisions were sent to assist him and by early July over 20,000 French troops were concentrated around Andujar and Bailén (Baylen). By this time some 30,000 Spanish regulars under General Francisco Javier Castaños were attempting to envelop him from the west and south, but, though his men were poor-quality second-line troops, Dupont should still have been able to escape. However, when he finally resolved on retreat a bizarre series of accidents enabled the Spaniards to occupy Bailén and cut off Dupont and a large portion of his army. On 19 July the French general tried to fight his way out of the trap, but he completely mishandled the situation and, with overwhelming numbers of enemy troops closing on all sides, was compelled to order a ceasefire. After much argument, it was eventually agreed that Dupont's entire army—not just that part of it caught in the trap—should be repatriated by sea. This agreement was never honoured: though Dupont was sent home, his troops were eventually left to die of starvation on the barren island of Cabrera.

As the uprising spilled into Portugal, the British glimpsed an opportunity to establish a toehold on the European continent. An expedition was duly dispatched to Portugal and, on 21 August, it inflicted a sharp defeat on the occupying French forces at Vimiero. Judging the situation to be hopeless, the French commander General Andoche Junot concluded the Cintra Convention with his British counterparts. In accordance with this, and the sensitivities of the Portuguese and Spaniards notwithstanding, Junot, his troops, and all their equipment (and booty) were repatriated, leaving the British in undisputed control of Portugal.

Infuriated, Napoleon hurried across the Pyrenees to redeem the situation. Arriving in early November, he unleashed a devastating counterstroke against the astonished Spanish armies. Madrid fell and, by mid-December, the French had reoccupied the heart of the peninsula and were preparing to march on Lisbon.

The reconquest of Portugal was prevented essentially by a timely foray mounted by a British column under Sir John Moore. Their forces' earlier successes had aroused great hopes within the British cabinet; Spain, it was believed, might follow Portugal in being completely cleared of the enemy. However, like their Spanish allies, they had not reckoned with Napoleon's reaction to developments. Moore, unaware of the strength of the hostile forces confronting him, was preparing to fall on a seemingly isolated corps around Burgos when he was alerted to the approach of Napoleon himself. Diverting his army from its march on Portugal, the emperor was seeking to get behind the redcoats, sever them from the coast, and annihilate them. He all but succeeded. Slipping away, Moore went into precipitate retreat for La Coruña. Napoleon, alarmed by Austria's preparations for a renewal of the war, turned the pursuit over to Marshal Soult and hurried back to Germany. Repulsed at La Coruña on 16 January 1809, Soult failed to prevent the British evacuation, but Moore was killed and his force, which comprised much of Britain's available army, had been badly mauled.

Nevertheless, Portugal had been saved from immediate reoccupation, giving the British and the Portuguese, who completely subordinated themselves to their powerful allies throughout the war, time to prepare their defences. Soult slowly moved south, taking Oporto, while his colleague Marshal Victor, having destroyed a Spanish army at Medellin on 28 March 1809, ventured down the Guadiana. The new British commander,

Arthur Wellesley (later the duke of Wellington), had some 23,000 redcoats at his disposal and was having some 70,000 Portuguese regulars and militia trained by British officers under General William Beresford. Despite Moore's predictions, he was confident that he could cling to Portugal.

Having attacked Soult at Oporto and driven him northwards, Wellesley was free to join with the Spanish in a concentric advance on Madrid. After holding off a counterstroke by Victor at Talavera in July 1809, the British were compelled to retreat into Portugal once Soult threatened their rear, while the Spanish armies, their efforts poorly coordinated, were subsequently defeated. Moreover, the Talavera campaign highlighted the importance of adequate logistical support in the barren peninsula; living off the land in such an inhospitable environment was rarely feasible.

By the time that Napoleon had defeated Austria and another French invasion of Portugal seemed practicable, Wellesley, now elevated to the peerage as Wellington, had prepared a series of concentric defences, the Lines of Torres Vedras, to protect Lisbon. In autumn 1809 he reconnoitred the area between Lisbon, Torres Vedras, the Atlantic coast, and the river Tagus accompanied by Colonel Richard Fletcher, his chief engineer. The positions were constructed over the next year. Forts and batteries on hills commanded all likely approaches, with lengths of rampart between them to impede enemy advance. Semaphore signal towers enabled the defenders to communicate. There were three lines: the first, running for 47 km (29 miles) through Torres Vedras itself, between the Tagus at Alhandra and the coast south of the Ziandre estuary; the second, rather stronger line some 10 km (6 miles) to the south; the third, centred on Fort St Julian on the Tagus estuary, secured an embarkation beach in case all else failed.

The first line proved to be sufficient. Wellington withdrew into the Lines in October 1810. The French commander Marshal André Masséna had no knowledge of them, and could neither attack them nor supply his army if it remained before them. He soon fell back about 48 km (30 miles), but his men grew increasingly hungry, and terrorized the inhabitants in their quest for food. In March 1811 Masséna retreated at last, and Wellington pursued. The character of the war had changed.

A series of clashes along the Portuguese–Spanish frontier ensued as Masséna, and his successor Soult, together with Marshal Auguste Marmont, sought to prevent the allies seizing the fortresses commanding Spain's northern and southern gateways, Ciudad Rodrigo and Badajoz respectively. Wellington's subordinate William Beresford won a narrow and bloody victory over Soult at Albuera in May 1811 and was forced to raise the siege of Badajoz. However, early in 1812, Wellington succeeded in storming both Badajoz and Ciudad Rodruigo before French field armies could concentrate and come to their relief.

Just as Napoleon's attention and resources were turning to the invasion of Russia, the French position in Spain was becoming dire. After destroying the Tagus bridge at Almaraz so as to cut the communications between Soult's army in Andalusia and Marmont's in Leon, Wellington fell on the latter, scattering it at Salamanca.

The Battle of Salamanca (1812)

The encounter battle of Salamanca has been hailed as 'Wellington's Masterpiece' and ended a brief period of shadow-boxing between the duke of Wellington and Marshal Auguste Marmont, each with about 50,000 men. On 22 July 1812 the rival armies were marching westwards, parallel with one another south of Salamanca, across flat ground dominated by two hills, the Greater and Lesser Arapile. Marmont occupied the Greater, hoping to pin Wellington's army to its position while he hooked around its western flank, cutting Wellington's communications with Portugal. In the process his divisions, marching across Wellington's front, became too extended to provide mutual support.

Wellington, watching from the Lesser Arapile, seized his opportunity, and ordered his leading division, under his brother-in-law Edward Pakenham, to attack the French advance guard. He then fell on Marmont's divisions in succession, and a cavalry charge by Major General John Le Marchant, who was killed in the moment of victory, helped clinch the French defeat. Marmont was wounded by a shell, and although General Maximillian-Sebastien Foy's division preserved his army from rout it was very roughly handled, losing about 14,000 men to Wellington's 5,000. The battle led King Joseph to abandon Madrid, but Wellington, besieging Burgos, was threatened by superior forces under Marshal Soult and compelled to make a difficult retreat towards Portugal.

The siege of Burgos went badly. The city was relieved by the French, and by mid-November Wellington had retreated beyond the Huebra. However, the following year the balance of power in the peninsula had changed, for the strategic pendulum had swung against France, opponents seriously weakened by the disaster suffered by the Grande Armée in Russia the previous year.

The Battle of Vitoria (1813)

Wellington had moved out of winter quarters in May with an Anglo-Portuguese force of 81,000 men, crossed the Duero, and pursued King Joseph and Marshal Jourdan, who had relinquished Madrid and were falling back northwards. This time they did not try to hold Burgos, and on 21 June Wellington brought them to battle at Vitoria in the valley of the Zadorra. He combined Lieutenant General Sir Rowland Hill's frontal attack, parallel with the river, with a short left hook by the earl of Dalhousie and Sir Thomas Picton and a longer one, towards the French rear, by Lieutenant General Sir Thomas Graham. Although the French, numbering 66,000, fought well to start with, they could not cope with Wellington's veteran infantry and his wide-ranging attacks.

When the French began to fall back Graham, hooking down from the north, did his best to cut off the French retreat; his task was impossible. This was partly because some brave Frenchmen retained their cohesion to the last, but, more seriously, because the road leading eastwards out of Vitoria was packed with the thousands of carriages and wagons that constituted the baggage train of the defeated army. The pursuit melted away in the face of unrivalled opportunities for looting. Wellington thundered: 'We may gain the greatest victories, but we shall do no good until we shall so far alter our system, as to force all ranks to perform their duty.' Although he was right to lament a missed opportunity, the battle was a major victory. Wellington lost 5,000 men to the French more than 8,000. He also captured all but two of Joseph's cannon and most of his transport, doing lasting damage to French cohesion.

Their forces in northern Spain having been pushed back to the Bidassoa, the French were also obliged to evacuate Valencia and Aragon. With Wellington investing San Sebastian and Pamplona, Marshal Soult led an ultimately futile counter-offensive to try to save the fortresses. Subsequently levered out of defensive positions on the Bidassoa, Nivelle, and Nive, his battered army was worsted again at Orthez in February 1814, and driven from Toulouse on 11 April.

In 1809, believing Napoleon to be preoccupied by events in the peninsula, Austria had joined a new coalition, the fifth, and suddenly launched an offensive into southern Germany in April. Having learnt from its earlier defeats and having reformed its armed forces accordingly, it proved a more formidable opponent than in past conflicts.

The Battle of Aspern-Essling (1809)

At Aspern-Essling, 8 km (5 miles) east of Vienna, Austrian forces under the command of Archduke Charles inflicted the first major defeat suffered by Napoleon. The latter was unaware the Austrians were so close, on the north side of the Danube, and began pushing his forces across the river. The Austrians had an observation post on the Bisamberg Heights, which gave them a rare advantage: perfect intelligence of the location, movements, and even intentions of the enemy. They therefore caught Napoleon at his most vulnerable, with a third of his force across the river. Between 1300 and 1800 on 21 May 1809 five Austrian corps attacked the French bridgehead on the north side of the Danube. The villages of Aspern and Essling on the left and right of the bridgehead received the brunt of the attack. As the Austrians attacked with 95,800 men and 264 guns, the French tried to pour forces into the bridgehead. They increased their strength from 23,000 and 50 guns at the start to 31,400 and 90 guns at the end of the day, but a combination of the river's current and Austrian attacks destroyed the bridge. Overnight the French repaired it and managed to build their force up to 70,000 and 144 guns on the second day, 22 May.

At the end of the first day both villages were still in French hands. With the bridge repaired, fighting resumed at 05.00, by which time the French had about 50,000 troops across. At 07.00 the French, enjoying the advantage of interior lines, attacked the middle of the Austrian forces. But then the bridge was damaged again and Marshal Louis Davout's III Corps was stuck on the south side of the Danube. Realizing that his situation was untenable, Napoleon withdrew across the bridge under cover of darkness. Although the French withdrew successfully—remarkable, under the circumstances—they lost up to 30,000 (some sources say as many as 37,000) men to the Austrians' 20,000 out of a smaller total force.

The Battle of Wagram (1809)

Napoleon was badly shaken by Aspern-Essling, but two months later renewed his attack, this time crossing the Danube from the eastern edge of Lobau island. Early on 5 July the French crossed and secured a bridgehead, and on the 6th fought the campaign's deciding battle around the village of Deutsch-Wagram. Napoleon rose brilliantly to the numerous crises of the day. Marshal Davout took the village of Markgrafneusiedl, key to the Austrian left, but when Marshal Alexandre Macdonald attempted to roll up the Austrian right with a huge column his men were slaughtered. The French were too exhausted to pursue Archduke Charles when he fell back. The French lost at least 30,000 men and the Austrians rather more. An armistice was agreed on the 12th, and the peace treaty, signed on 14 October, was much to Austria's disadvantage.

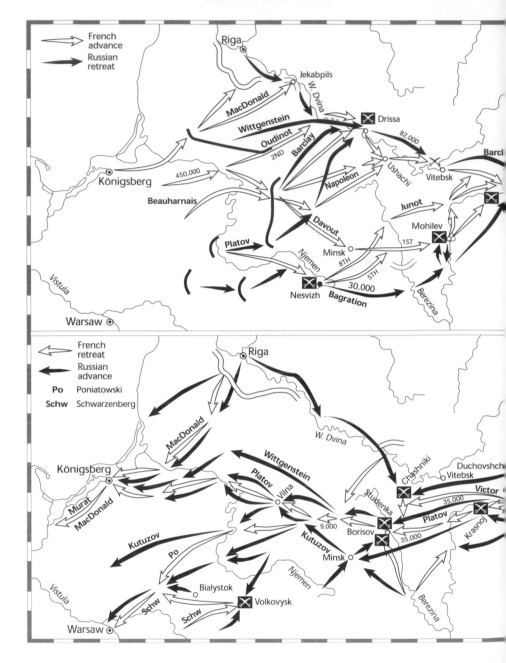

In the interim, an abortive British landing at Walcheren, an island on the northern side of the Scheldt estuary, although costing more than 23,000 lives lost to disease as against 200 from combat, highlighted both the vulnerability of the French empire's littoral to amphibious attack and the limitations of Britain's military capabilities.

Napoleon's 1812 campaign

By 1812, British endeavours to control neutral trade between the USA and France had come close to success before American fears of invasion by their former colonial masters led them to make a pre-emptive declaration of war. However, Russia and France also found themselves on a collision course over the Continental System and other divisive issues.

Invading Russia at the head of a colossal army, Napoleon sought to encircle and annihilate the Russian forces within three weeks. Obliged to venture ever further east over scorched earth, he met his enemies as he approached Moscow.

The Battle of Borodino (1812)

At the village of Borodino, on the main road 124 km (77 miles) west of Moscow, Marshal Kutuzov, commanding 120,000 Russian troops with 640 guns, gave battle to Napoleon's multinational Grande Armée with 130,000–150,000 men and 587 guns.

On 3 September, after a long retreat from the frontier which included giving up the city of Smolensk, Kutuzov dug in across a front of 8 km (5 miles) spanning the only two approaches to Moscow, the main (new) Smolensk road and the old Smolensk road to the south, with his right flank protected by the Moskva river, the left by the thick Utitsa forest, with the Kolocha stream to the front and with woods behind to conceal his reserves. In the centre was the Kurgan hill, where the Great (Raevsky) redoubt was constructed. General Mikhail Andreivitch Miloradovich commanded the right near the villages of Maslovo and Gorki, strengthened with several redoubts, and General Bagration commanded the left, near the village of Semyonov where he constructed three lunettes. The strength of the wings was designed to direct any attack into the centre, commanded by General Barclay de Tolly with the bulk of the artillery. Outflanking movement to the immediate north or south was impossible because of the forest and river.

There was nothing subtle about the Russian position: it was immensely strong and any sane general would have refused to assault it under normal circumstances. But Kutuzov calculated that after a long advance over scorched earth, Napoleon would be desperate for a decisive battle, and so it proved. The French army comprised the corps of Marshals Murat, Davout, Ney, and General Andoche Junot, plus the Old and Young Guard in reserve under Napoleon's own command. The first contact was at the Russian redoubt at Shevardino, to the west of the main position, where 40,000 French stumbled on 12,000 Russians on 5 September and were repulsed, giving Kutuzov confirmation of the main line of French advance and buying time to strengthen his position yet further. This included reinforcing Bagration, upon whom Napoleon's first hammer blow was to fall.

The French attacked at 05.00 on 7 September; seven separate assaults were beaten back at enormous cost but the eighth, at about noon, succeeded. His planned turning manoeuvre already seriously dislocated, Napoleon then attacked the Great Redoubt in the centre. As he had already discovered at Eylau, Russian infantry on the defensive fought to the death, and the battle lost any semblance of tactical refinement in an orgy of slaughter. Shaken by the carnage and perhaps suddenly aware of how far he was from home, Napoleon decided not to commit the Guard, whose bitterly ironic nickname of 'the immortals' may have been coined by the battered line infantry after Borodino. At about 18.00, as darkness approached, the fighting petered out through exhaustion. Not only the French were stunned. More than one-third of those on each side were killed or wounded. The battle itself was indecisive, and the Russians withdrew, having lost about 44,000 killed and wounded. Six days later Kutuzov informed his subordinates of his decision to give up Moscow in order to maintain the army in being. But they had inflicted a mortal wound on Napoleon's overextended army, which lost about 50,000. Napoleon proceeded to capture Moscow, but his opponents had it burned around his ears. The retreat that followed was a holocaust that, combined with the slaughter at Borodino, may have cost Napoleon as many as 400,000 men killed, and did lasting damage to French ability to sustain the war. Adam Zamoyski's recent study suggests that Russian losses were roughly similar, and in consequence 'about a million people died, fairly equally divided between the two sides'.

With the Grande Armée all but obliterated in Russia, first Prussia and then Austria turned on Napoleon, who, drawing on France's last reserves of manpower and other resources, clung to Germany throughout 1813, securing major if indecisive victories in May at Lützen and Bautzen at the head of his improvised and outnumbered army.

The Battle of Dresden (1813)

Napoleon's last great victory in the German campaign of 1813, Dresden showed how near, and yet how far, he was from beating the alliance of Prussia, Russia, and Austria. The French, initially under Marshal Gouvion Saint-Cyr, contained the allied attack on 26 August and on 27 August mounted a massive counter-attack, with three reinforcing army corps, led by Napoleon himself. The attack was spearheaded by the Imperial Guard, which stormed through the Grosse Garten, sweeping the Prussians before them. Frederick William of Prussia had insisted that the allies stand their ground, but the disparate allied armies found it hard to coordinate their defence, and their left flank was split in two by vigorous French assaults. By 16.00 it was obvious that a withdrawal to the safety of Bohemia was the only option. The pursuit was badly handled, the French lacking cavalry to harry Count Schwarzenberg's defeated army, which had lost 38,000 of its 158,000 men. General Dominique Vandamme rushed 30,000 men behind the retreating allies in Bohemia, but outpaced the main army and was himself surrounded and captured at Kulm on 30 August.

The Battle of Leipzig (1813)

Although Napoleon had won the battles of Lützen, Bautzen, and Dresden, he had been unable to take advantage of his success, and General Vandamme's defeat at Kulm raised allied spirits. Napoleon considered alternative plans—a strike against the Army of Bohemia, which had just beaten Vandamme, in the hope of driving Austria out of the war, and a drive on Berlin, which would draw the Prussians and Russians north, isolating the Austrians. No sooner had he ordered Marshal Ney to march on Berlin in early September than it became clear that Marshal Macdonald, who had been roughly handled in his pursuit of Marshal Gerbhard von Blücher's Prussians, could not could check their renewed advance, and Dresden itself could not be held in adequate strength.

Napoleon took substantial reinforcements to Macdonald, but the Prussians, discerning the reason for the latter's sudden confidence, declined to be drawn into battle. Napoleon then heard that the Austrians and Russians were threatening Dresden, and darted off to Kulm to fall on the Russians, but, seeing them in a strong position and mindful of the fragile morale of some of his conscripts, decided against an attack and retired on Dresden. There was more bad news: Ney, a brave leader whose grasp of grand tactics had never been firm, had been sharply rebuffed by Marshal Bernadotte at Dennewitz on 6 September. As the month wore on there was yet more shadow-boxing as Napoleon moved against his opponents in turn, exhausting his badly supplied troops in filthy weather and unable to strike a really telling blow. The news of Dennewitz had persuaded the Bavarians to defect, and there were ominous creakings amongst Napoleon's German allies.

Eventually Napoleon decided to leave Dresden well garrisoned and to move north with the intention of beating both Blücher and Bernadotte, still marching separately, before jinking back to deal with Count Schwarzenberg's Austrians. He narrowly failed to catch Blücher, and it was soon all too evident that his opponents were likely to meet up near Leipzig. Both Bernadotte and Schwarzenberg were decidedly cautious, but Blücher was eager to fight, and pressed the tsar of Russia, present with his armies, for decisive action.

When Napoleon entered Leipzig on 14 October he was unaware that the allies had succeeded in bringing such a substantial force into the area. He held Leipzig and its suburbs, with the rivers Elster, Pleisse, Luppe, and Parthe, most of whose bridges had been blown by his engineers, making it hard for his opponents to mount a coordinated attack, and hoped to capitalize on this central position to beat each of his opponents in turn. On the 16th there was heavy fighting in each of the four sectors created by the river system, and Napoleon's hope of smashing Schwarzenberg in the southern sector was dashed by sporadic and ill-coordinated allied attacks across the whole front which made it impossible for Napoleon to achieve the concentration he required to defeat Schwarzenberg. By the end of a day of bitter fighting the balance of casualties (some 25,000 to 30,000) narrowly favoured the French, but neither side had gained key terrain. On the 17th the allies were content to a wait the arrival of further reinforcements, and when Bernadotte's Swedes and Count von Benningsen's Russians joined the allies Napoleon recognized that he was now so badly outnumbered—over 300,000 to perhaps 175,000—that he had no option but to retreat.

On the 18th Napoleon's army began that most difficult of manoeuvres, a withdrawal in contact with the enemy. By the day's end his line was intact, but now ran through the suburbs of Leipzig, and that evening he determined to give up the city altogether. Early on the 19th it took the Allies some time to realize what was afoot, and the retirement might have gone without a hitch had the Lindenau bridge over the Elster not been blown in error by its French engineer demolition party while it was still crowded with retreating soldiers, and with the rearguard on the wrong side. Marshal Oudinot swam to safety, but Marshal Poniatowski, who had held his rank for just twelve hours, was drowned. Overall the allies had lost more than 50,000 battle casualties to the French 40,000. But another 30,000 of Napoleon's men were captured, mainly on the 19th, and perhaps 5,000 of his German troops changed sides. Scarcely less significant was the loss of 325 French guns and huge quantities of stores.

In the short term the battle ended Napoleon's hopes of fighting beyond the borders of a France bled white by repeated calls for conscripts. It struck a serious blow at his own prestige, and disintegrated the system of alliances upon which he had depended to sustain his massive armies. Even the hitherto-loyal Saxons, whose capital Dresden fell on 11 November, were compelled to make peace with the allies. It was the biggest battle of the horse and musket era, with perhaps half a million men engaged, and stretched the extant techniques of command and control to their breaking point. The 'Battle of the Nations' was the largest European clash to date, and in some of the national passions it inspired, most notably amongst the Prussians, we can see the beginnings of the process that was to spin Europe into an even deeper conflict just over a century later.

The Hundred Days (1815)

Declared an outlaw by the allies on his escape from Elba in March 1815 Napoleon decided to take the offensive against the forces massing against him. The two nearest enemy forces were the Anglo-Dutch-German army under the duke of Wellington and the Prussians under Marshal von Blücher, and he aimed to destroy them in detail before they could unite.

Napoleon crossed the frontier into Belgium in the early hours of 15 June, surprising the Prussians and British, whose forces were still dispersed; an alarming gap threatened to open up between Wellington and Blücher. Napoleon divided his Army of the North in a left and a right wing under Marshal Ney and Marshal Emmanuel Grouchy, maintaining the reserve under his own command. After taking Charleroi, he sent Grouchy towards the Prussians at Fleurus, while Ney headed up the Brussels road.

On 16 June Napoleon joined Grouchy and attacked Blücher at Ligny. The Prussians fought stubbornly, but were defeated. But the battle was not a knockout blow and the pursuit, under the command of Grouchy, was dilatory. Blücher, praiseworthily honouring his agreement to join Wellington south of Brussels, retreated to Wavre, whence on 18 June he was able to link up with Wellington at Waterloo, despite Grouchy's futile efforts to interfere.

Ney's advance on 15 June was halted by a small force under the prince of Orange just south of the key crossroads of Quatre Bras. Wellington rushed forces to the battlefield, and Ney's decision to delay attacking until the afternoon of 16 June bought the Iron Duke more time. Although there were moments when Wellington was hall pressed, by the early evening Wellington had sufficient forces to drive back the French. Thanks to confused command, Count d'Erlon's corps, which might have proved decisive at either Quatre Bras or Ligny, spent the day marching back and forth between the two battles without intervening in either. Wellington fell back on Waterloo, where on 18 June he met Napoleon in the climactic battle of the campaign.

The Battle of Waterloo (1815)

In the last battle of these wars Napoleon fielded 72,000 men and 346 guns to attack an Anglo-Dutch-Belgian army of 68,000 men and 156 guns under the duke of Wellington, drawn up along the Mont Saint-Jean ridge and blocking the road to Brussels. The numbers are deceptive: although smaller than many armies he had commanded in the recent past, Napoleon's force included a high proportion of veterans and morale was generally high. However, Marshal L. A. Berthier, his trusty chief of staff, had died under mysterious circumstances, and Napoleon was unwise to entrust the brave but headstrong Marshal Ney with command of the left wing in the campaign's opening moves and then with overall conduct of the main battle. By contrast the allied force was more heterogeneous, with a mixture of British, German, and Dutch–Belgian units. The crucial difference was certainly that Napoleon's generalship had been declining for years and on this day he was probably suffering from cystitis and prolapsed haemorrhoids, whereas Wellington— caught flat footed at the campaign's opening—was now at the peak of his form and spent fourteen hours in the saddle, riding to every crucial point to direct the battle personally.

Drenching overnight rain dictated a delay for the ground to dry out for his cavalry and in particular his artillery to be able to manoeuvre, so Napoleon spent the time deploying

his army for maximum visual effect, which did indeed dishearten some of the troops facing him across a long shallow valley. It was late morning before his younger brother Jérôme advanced to attack the fortified farmhouse complex of Hougoumont anchoring Wellington's right. Napoleon's purpose was to draw in allied reserves from the centre, where the main assault was to go in, but he failed to achieve this, and by attacking unsuccessfully seven times between 11.30 and 19.30 he reversed the equation and drew in French troops needed elsewhere.

At 13.00 Napoleon's grand battery of 84 guns opened fire on the allied centre, but as usual Wellington had deployed most of his men on the reverse slope and it had limited effect. Count d'Erlon's Corps then attacked to the east of the Brussels–Charleroi road, with his centre divisions in two giant columns 150 men wide and 25 deep. As they passed La Haie Sainte farm, standing just in front of Wellington's centre, their left came under fire from the 95th Rifles and the King's German Legion (KGL), but their right managed to take Papelotte at the left end of the allied position.

The attack in the centre came close to succeeding because of its sheer weight, but was eventually halted by concentrated point-blank volleys. Lieutenant General Sir Thomas Picton was killed at the head of his division and then, at the crucial moment, British cavalry brigades under Major General Sir Frederick Ponsonby and Lord Edward Somerset drove the French back, breaking both of d'Erlon's centre divisions.

But the horsemen got carried away and charged across the valley to attack the grand battery unsupported. After French cuirassiers and lancers had counter-attacked, Ponsonby was dead and a sad remnant on blown horses limped back to be of no further use to an exasperated Wellington. Meanwhile La Haie Sainte was besieged and the defenders were running out of ammunition when the prince of Orange unwisely sent part of the KGL forward in line, to be ridden down by French cavalry. The farm complex eventually fell and Wellington's centre was now desperately vulnerable, but Napoleon let the opportunity slip away.

This was because, from mid-afternoon, Ney was deceived, when he saw stragglers and ammunition wagons moving back, into believing that Wellington was close to breaking. He led massed cavalry charges, thinking to precipitate a rout. Disabused by steady fire from unbroken British squares, he nonetheless persisted in cavalry-only attacks. Had he brought up horse artillery or even ordered his troopers to spike the touch-holes or to break the wheels of the British guns, which the gunners had to abandon to shelter in the squares every time the cavalry rode up, it might have made sense. But he did not, and appears to have succumbed to something close to the berserk rage that his nickname 'le rougeaud' (Ginger) suggested. When La Haye Sainte fell and he asked for infantry to advance and attack the weakened centre, an understandably sceptical Napoleon refused.

By that late stage, however, Napoleon had other worries than the successive failures of his brother, d'Erlon, and Ney. On his right, Marshal Grouchy had not appeared but the Prussians had. Napoleon dispatched General Georges Lobau and the Young Guard to clear them out of the village of Plancenoit, which they did with commendable efficiency, preventing the union of the allied armies until the end. This came at 19.30, when Napoleon himself led out the Old and Middle Guard to attack up the slope now littered

French cuirassiers attack infantry squares at the battle of Waterloo.

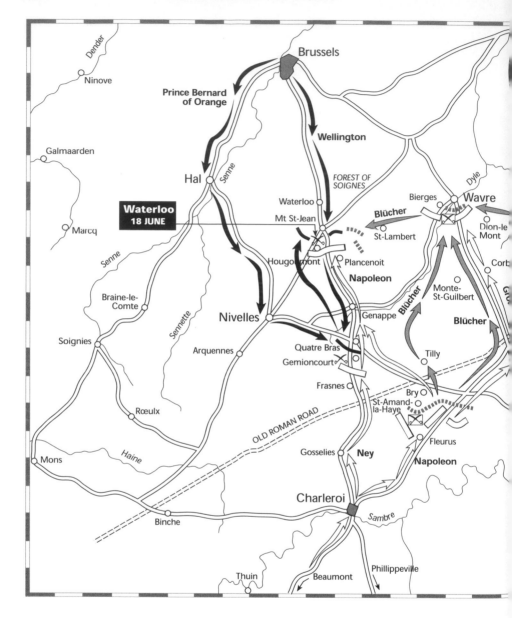

with the bodies of Ney's troopers. The attack evolved into an assault by several distinct columns, one of which collided with Sir Peregrine Maitland's Guard Brigade, with Wellington himself to hand. He ordered 'Up Guards! Make ready! Fire!' directing what were perhaps the day's decisive volleys. Recent research, however, suggests that even more serious damage was done by Colonel Sir John Colborne of the 52nd Light Infantry, who threw his fine battalion out at right angles to the main line, mercilessly raking the French column as it advanced.

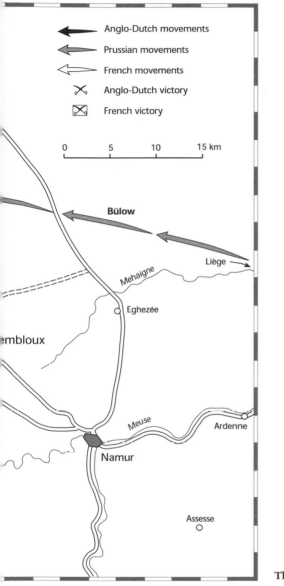

Anglo-Dutch movements

Prussian movements

French movements

✗ Anglo-Dutch victory

☒ French victory

0 5 10 15 km

Bülow

Mehaigne

Liège

Eghezée

embloux

Meuse

Ardenne

Namur

Assesse

The Waterloo campaign

The sight of the Guard falling back stunned the French, and Wellington waved his hat to gesture what was left of his army forward. The mainspring of Napoleon's army snapped at last, and for most it was *sauve qui peut*. Wellington's army was exhausted, but Marshal von Blücher's cavalry had scores to settle and its pursuit prevented all hope of an organized fighting retreat. Protected by the remnants of his Guard, Napoleon left the battlefield and at 21.30 Wellington and Blücher were embracing in the courtyard of the farmhouse aptly called La Belle Alliance.

ITALIAN INDEPENDENCE WARS

taly's struggle for independence (1821–70) is known as 'il Risorgimento' (resurgence). In 1815 the Italian peninsula reverted to its pre-war tripartite division with the newly revitalized Austrian empire holding Venetia and Lombardy in the north, the Papal States in the middle, and the retrograde kingdom of the Two Sicilies in the south. Additionally there was the north-western kingdom of Sardinia, Savoy, or Piedmont (we will use the last designation), which was possessed of the sense of nationalism that was the great legacy of the French Revolutionary wars. Among the riots and revolutions that convulsed the continent in 1848 were two popular uprisings in Lombardy and Venetia. King Carlo Alberto of Piedmont believed that Austria would be too distracted to oppose him, and invaded in support of those he declared to be fellow Italians. The war began badly for the Piedmontese when the Austrian commander, Field Marshal Count Josef Radetzky von Radetz, jabbed forward to take the fortress of Mortara. A Piedmontese army under General Chrzanowksi offered battle and was roundly defeated at Novara on 23 March.

The First Battle of Custoza (1848)

Custoza, a hill town in Venetia, close to the river Mincio, south of Lake Garda, was the site of two important battles in the struggle for Italian independence. The first, in July 1848, was a display of brilliant generalship by Radetzky, 82 years old but still a formidable opponent. Carlo Alberto pushed him across the Mincio river into the powerful Quadrilateral forts of Mantua, Peschiera, Legnago, and Verona, in Venetia. There he waited until, on 24 July, Carlo Alberto attempted to cross the Mincio and take Custoza and its surrounding heights with 22,000 men. In a two-day battle, Radetzky concentrated 33,000 troops, took Custoza with the bayonet, and crushed the Piedmontese army. The battle forced Piedmont out of the war and effectively ended the national revolution of 1848 in Italy.

Carlo Alberto was forced to abdicate in favour of his son, who became Vittorio Emanuele II. The noisy patriot Giuseppe Mazzini and the less noisy but equally patriotic soldier of fortune Giuseppe Garibaldi seized Rome in February 1849 and announced the formation of the Roman republic, which was promptly suppressed by troops from France, Austria, and Naples.

The battles of Magenta and Solferino (1859)

In 1858, Count Camillo Cavour, the Piedmontese foreign minister, negotiated a treaty with Napoleon III which promised French assistance in freeing northern Italy from Austrian rule, and the following year he encouraged revolts in Venetia and Lombardy to precipitate a war with Austria. On 4 June the French won an encounter battle at Magenta, clearing the town house by house with that 'furia francese' which was a characteristic of their infantry during this war. At the pitched battle of Solferino (24 June 1859), a combined Franco-Piedmontese force defeated the Austrians in a series of assaults on bravely defended positions. The suffering of the wounded at Solferino shocked Jean-Henri Dunant, a Swiss merchant. The bitter fighting had resulted in almost 40,000 casualties, many of whom were left to die in agony. In 1862 he published *Un souvenir de Solferino* and set about devising formal procedures for the care of wounded and prisoners.

In the peace that followed, Austria was forced to cede most of Lombardy (except for the important fortresses of Peschiera and Mantua) to Piedmont. In addition the duchies of Parma, Tuscany, Modena, and Romagna agreed to union with Piedmont. As agreed France annexed Nice and Savoy.

In April 1860, King Francis II of the Two Sicilies bloodily suppressed revolts in Naples and Sicily and in response Garibaldi led his Thousand Redshirts (with the covert support of Piedmont) in an invasion of Sicily and crossed the Straits of Messina on 22 August with the help of the Royal Navy. Naples fell on 7 September and Garibaldi marched north, defeating the last Neapolitan army at the battle of Volturno (26 October). It was perfectly clear that he intended to march on Rome, and it was equally clear that if he did Napoleon III, self-appointed guardian of the papacy, would intervene. So the Piedmontese army marched south, defeating a papal army at Castelfidardo on 18 September but carefully skirting Rome, and interposed itself between Garibaldi and his objective. On 17 March 1861 a united kingdom of Italy was proclaimed, its capital in Florence and Vittorio Emanuele its first constitutional monarch.

Garibaldi was unreconcilable and in August 1862 gathered another army of patriots and marched on Rome. The same reasons that led him to the Volturno in 1860 caused Vittorio Emanuele to block him, and this time there was a battle at Aspromonte where the great patriot was wounded, and after which he had to flee the country. He tried again in 1867 and was again defeated, this time by the French.

In April 1866, Italy signed a treaty with Count Otto von Bismarck's Prussia against Austria and attacked across Lombardy towards Venetia at the outbreak of the Austro-Prussian war. However, things did not go well.

The Second Battle of Custoza (1866)

On 24 June, King Vittorio Emanuele tried to force his way across the Mincio with 127,000 men, but was roundly beaten at Custoza by 75,000 Austrians under Field Marshal Archduke Albrecht. Then the technically superior Italian navy was trounced at Lissa by an Austrian commander who scorned technology and pressed home to ram his opponent. This made no difference to the outcome, decided at the battle of Königgrätz in Bohemia, and in the post-war settlement Austria was obliged to relinquish its Italian provinces to the new kingdom of Italy.

THE CRIMEAN WAR

In March 1853 the Turkish government declined an ultimatum demanding that the Orthodox Church in Turkey should be placed under Russian protection. The Russians occupied the Danubian principalities, and when they refused to withdraw Turkey declared war. On 30 November a Turkish squadron was destroyed off Sinope in the Black Sea, and this helped push Britain and France towards war, declared in March 1854.

Britain and France both sent expeditionary forces to the east, the former under Field Marshal Lord Raglan and the latter under Marshal Saint-Arnaud. The British army was

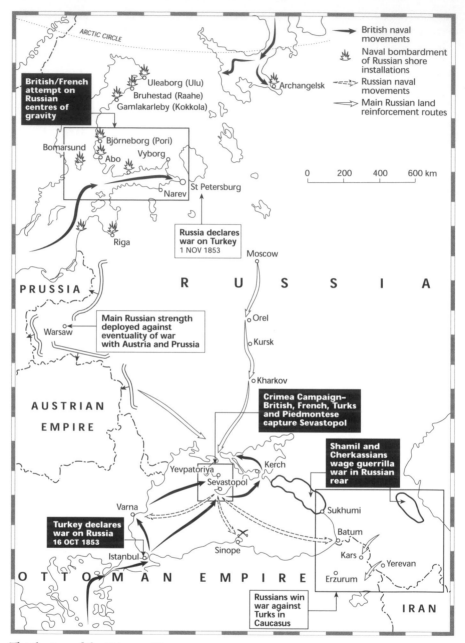

The theatres of the Crimean War

either being reformed or, more pertinently, reforming itself, in the period 1830 to 1854, but there remained areas of weakness. Raglan had some 26,000 men, many of them raw recruits, and no reserves. Transport and supply were ill suited to a distant campaign in bleak and unproductive terrain, and army administration was chaotically decentralized.

Raglan's force comprised five infantry divisions (four commanded by Peninsular War veterans aged between 60 and 70) and Lord Lucan's cavalry division, its light brigade under Lord Cardigan and its heavy brigade under Sir James Scarlett. The French had gained experience during their conquest of Algeria, and their first contingent of four infantry divisions and two cavalry brigades (about 40,000 men) included many units from North Africa. The French contingent was larger, and in many respects more efficient, than the British. The Russian army loomed large in the mind of Tsar Nicholas I (in the 1820s he was spending about three-quarters of his day on military matters) but it was unimaginatively trained and lacked an experienced general staff. Although it had a total regular and reserve strength of perhaps 1,400,000 men, it was wholly unprepared for modern war.

The Russians withdrew from the Danubian principalities, depriving the allies of a target. The British government believed that the Russian naval base of Sevastopol should now be attacked, and ordered Raglan to take it unless he felt the task to be impossible. Accordingly the allies sailed for the Crimea, and landed at Calamita Bay, north of Sevastopol, on 14 September. The Russian commander, Prince Menshikov, had not believed that the allies would invade, and when they did so he prepared to receive them inland, with more than 35,000 men in a strong position on the river Alma. The British spent two nights without tents, and when they were eventually ready to advance too few wagons had been commandeered for their baggage and the men, many of them sick, were heavily laden.

The allies set off on 19 September, about 60,000 strong, with the British on the left and the French on the right. Some men dropped with cholera on the march, and even the fit found the advance exhausting. There was a cavalry skirmish on the little river Bulganak, and the allies spent the night in the field, aware that Menshikov was in position on the river Alma. Raglan and Saint-Arnaud agreed that night that the French would attack the high ground on the Russian left, which Saint-Arnaud believed to be strongly held, while the British swept round the Russian right.

The Battle of the Alma (1854)

The battle began at about 13.30, and it became clear that the British were facing the main Russian positions, where two redoubts—the Great and the Lesser—covered the slopes leading down to the river. Obedient to the allied plan the French attacked first, enabling the Russians to shift some of their guns to rake them, provoking demands that the British should attack. The Russians fired the village of Bourliouk as the British advanced, causing some confusion, but the attackers were soon across the Alma and on their way up the slopes behind it. Cannon fire from the Great Redoubt caused casualties, but the guns were withdrawn prematurely, and the Light and 2nd Divisions, drawn up in line, then became involved in a firefight against Russian columns. Some British regiments gave ground against counter-attacks, but the 1st Division came up, and its Guards and Highlanders pushed back the Russians, who withdrew in good order; Lord Raglan declined to unleash his cavalry against them. Some Russian combatants blamed their defeat on lack of orders. One wrote that 'During the five hours of fighting we neither saw nor heard from our divisional general, our brigade or regimental commanders, nor did we receive any orders to advance or retire.' Another shrewdly observed that the rifles carried by most allied infantry were far more effective than the muskets carried by the majority of Russians. The allies had lost over 3,000 casualties and the Russians more than 5,000. The

allies might have mounted an immediate attack on Sevastopol, whose defences were incomplete, but Saint-Arnaud, who was mortally ill, was not enthusiastic. Instead they marched around the city, establishing themselves on the uplands to its south, supplied through the little ports of Kamiech and Balaclava.

Raglan and General François Canrobert, the new French commander, agreed to bombard Sevastopol before mounting an attack. Heavy guns were landed and batteries prepared, and on 17 October the bombardment began. British and French warships, standing inshore to take on the forts, were badly knocked about, and although the land bombardment seemed more promising, it too was strenuously opposed. The defenders, many of them sailors, were inspired by Admiral Kornilov, who was mortally wounded on 17 October, and Colonel Eduard Todleben, an engineer officer sent down to assist Prince Menshikov, played a leading part in repairing damaged defences and building new ones. The allied rear, where the Woronzoff road ran eastwards, was secured by a number of Turkish-manned redoubts. Suspicions that Menshikov's field army, which had slipped away from Sevastopol and been reinforced by fresh troops marching down from Bessarabia, might approach from this quarter led to frequent alarms.

The Battle of Balaclava (1854)

On 25 October about 25,000 Russians advanced from the east, taking the redoubts on the Woronzoff road and sending a force towards Balaclava, whose capture was probably Prince Menshikov's objective. It was checked by the 'thin red line' of the 93rd Highlanders, and Sir James Scarlett's Heavy Brigade successfully charged Russian cavalry north of Balaclava. Lord Raglan, on the edge of the escarpment between Sevastopol and Balaclava, could see that the Russians had brought up horses to take the cannon from the captured redoubts, and decided to use Lord Cardigan's brigade of light cavalry to prevent them.

But his order to the Light Brigade was misunderstood. Raglan and his quartermaster general, General Sir James Airey, who drew up the loosely worded order, had a good view of the field, but failed to appreciate that commanders in the valleys below would see less. Captain Lewis Nolan, an impetuous aide-de-camp, delivered the order to Lucan, commanding the cavalry division, and the latter sent him on to Cardigan. The personal feud between their lordships, and Nolan's provocative insolence, did the rest. Cardigan was presented with a formal order to attack the only guns visible to him, a battery at the end of a shallow valley with riflemen around it and cavalry in support. In the ensuing charge the Light Brigade took the battery but could not hold it, and had 247 of its 670 officers and men killed or wounded. French Chasseurs d'Afrique carried out a well-executed charge to help the survivors withdraw. Overall, though, the day was a disappointing one for the Russians: they had failed to disrupt the progress of the siege.

The Battle of Inkerman (1854)

The day after Balaclava the Russians mounted a sortie from Sevastopol against British lines on the complex series of ridges where the river Chernaia entered Sevastopol harbour. 'Little Inkerman' failed, but it provided the Russians with useful information,

---

The Scots Fusilier Guards (later the Scots Guards) at the battle of the Alma.

and 5 November they launched a much bigger attack, with 20,000 men advancing from Sevastopol while 16,000 from the field army crossed the Chernaia to attack the British from the east and another 22,000 men swung south to threaten the French. The battle of Inkerman was fought on difficult ground in thick fog. It was decided by the dogged determination of the British defenders, supported, as the day went on, by the French. 'The French are saving the English at Inkerman,' commented a bitter Russian officer, 'as the Prussians did at Waterloo.' Its results were terrible: the hardened General Pierre Bosquet described the much fought-over Sand Bag Battery as an abattoir. The British lost 2,500 men, the French 1,700, and the Russians perhaps 12,000. After Inkerman, Prince Menshikov, deeply unpopular with his subordinates, was replaced by Prince Gorchakov, who struck many of them as scarcely an improvement. Admiral Nakhimov was the soul of Sevastopol's defence: morose and fatalistic, alone among the garrison's officers he still wore his gold epaulettes.

The allies spent an uncomfortable winter before Sevastopol, and growing concerns about the British army's inadequate administration provoked attacks on Lord Raglan in both press and parliament, although opinion in the army was more evenly divided. Keenly sensitive to these insults, Raglan had to grapple with a French command whose sense of purpose seemed infirm. On 16 May General Canrobert, exasperated by order and counter-order over the telegraph from Paris, resigned command and was replaced by the hard-driving General Aimable Pélissier. Things improved at once. Kerch, at the eastern end of the Crimea, was taken by an allied force which did much damage and opened the way into the Sea of Azov, destroying the Russian naval squadron there.

On land, Raglan and Pélissier agreed to attack two of Sevastopol's outworks, the Quarries, in the British sector, and the Mamelon, in the French, as a prelude to the assault on the Great Redan and the Malakoff. The Quarries and the Mamelon were duly taken on 7 June. However, ten days later the British were repulsed from the Redan with the loss of 1,500 men. The repulse greatly cheered the Russian defenders, but the gallant Nakhimov was mortally wounded. Raglan died on 28 June: a recent biographer blames a broken heart. The Russian field army made a last attack at the Chernaia on 16 August. On 8 September Raglan's successor, General Sir James Simpson, attacked the Redan again, sustaining almost 2,500 casualties. But the French stormed the Malakoff that morning, and Sevastopol was untenable: the Russians withdrew on the night of 8–9 September.

Although the Crimea was the war's main theatre, the allies also sent support to Shamil, whose Muslim zealots were fighting the Russians in the Caucasus, and embarked upon a more ambitious strategy in the Baltic in March 1854. The allies attacked the fortress of Bomarsund, on the land Islands, quickly knocking it into submission. Plans for an attack on Sveaborg, on the Finnish coast, were aborted in a flurry of mutual recrimination, and the main allied squadrons withdrew. Peace was concluded in Paris in 1856.

THE AUSTRO-PRUSSIAN WAR

This conflict was a violent solution to the nineteenth-century German and Italian independence questions. Emperor Franz Josef I of Austria declared war in June 1866 and fought on two fronts: in Bohemia against the Prussians, in Venetia against the Italians. Although the Austrian army (400,000 men) was outnumbered by the combined armies of Prussia (300,000 men) and Italy (200,000 men), it was highly rated, and Franz Josef entertained ambitious war aims.

The Austrians failed to reckon with military reforms enacted by Prussia's chief of general staff Field Marshal Graf Helmuth von Moltke. The most portentous reform was adoption of the breech-loading needle gun and small unit fire tactics in the early 1860s. This was revolutionary; the Austrian, French, and Russian armies were still using muzzle-loading rifles (to conserve ammunition) and battalion-sized columns (to deliver 'shock') in 1866.

Austria's North Army of 240,000 men was commanded by Field Marshal Ludwig von Benedek, who chose General Alfred Henikstein, a jovial but inept boon companion, to be his chief of staff. When both Benedek and Henikstein failed to produce plans for a war with Prussia, Emperor Franz Josef added a second chief of staff: General Gideon von Krismanic. This bureaucracy stifled all initiative, and as Moltke's mobilization roared ahead, deploying 260,000 men by road and rail to the frontier of Bohemia in six weeks, Benedek's limped along so slowly that Krismanic decided to deploy the bulk of the North Army at Olmütz in Moravia. This was a fateful decision. Krismanic left a single corps (and two allied Saxon divisions) in Bohemia; this 60,000-man detachment (the Iser Army) was supposed to hold the Prussians long enough for Benedek to complete his mobilization in Olmütz and march westward to their rescue. It was a bad plan whose defects Moltke fully exploited.

The Prussians invaded Saxony and Bohemia on 16 June on a broad front in three armies: the Elbe Army at Halle (46,000 men), First Army at Görlitz (93,000 men), and Second Army at Breslau (115,000 men). Four hundred and eighty kilometres (300 miles) separated the Elbe and Second armies, which many considered reckless, but Moltke planned either to smash Benedek's widely separated armies in detail, or sweep them into a great, crushing 'pocket battle' (*Kesselschlacht*) in the vicinity of Königgrätz on the Elbe.

In the last days of June, the Prussian armies passed through Saxony (obligingly vacated by the Saxon army, which was on the Iser) and into Bohemia. Once the Prussians were through the Bohemian mountains, the North Army exhausted itself marching westward to engage them. The first battles of the war demonstrated the awesome effectiveness of the needle gun, and the obsolescence of Austrian shock tactics. At Trautenau and Vysokov on 27 June, whole Austrian corps launched repeated bayonet attacks on isolated Prussian advance guards, with catastrophic results. At Trautenau, the Austrians lost 5,000 men, the Prussians just 1,300. The death toll among professional officers was as alarming; the Austrians lost 191, the Prussians 56. At Vysokov, a plateau that commanded a principal highway from Prussia to Austria, the Austrians spent 5,720 men in futile charges against a well-concealed Prussian division, which lost only 1,122 men. On 28 June, the Austrians attempted to hold the village of Skalice at the foot of the Vysokov plateau, but were routed again, losing 6,000 men to Prussia's 1,300. Austrian casualties at Skalice were so dreadful that Benedek resolved never again to employ shock tactics, which partly explained his later paralysis.

On the line of the river Iser, where 60,000 Austro-Saxon troops awaited the approach of the 140,000 men of the Elbe and First armies, the Prussians hardly needed the advantage conferred on them by the needle gun. They routed the Iser Army in three successive battles: at Podol on 27 June, at Münchengrätz on the 28th, and at Jicin on the 29th. In these battles, the Prussians benefited from mass desertion among Austria's Italian regiments, which had been shifted from Venetia to Bohemia to no good effect. On 3 July, Benedek united the remains of the Iser and North armies on the hills between the fortress of Königgrätz and the village of Sadowa.

The Battle of Königgrätz (1866)

Austria's army of 240,000 men awaited the approach of 245,000 Prussian troops grouped in three armies under the nominal orders of Prussia's King Wilhelm I and the operational command of Field Marshal Helmuth von Moltke. Moltke intended Königgrätz (Sadowa) to be a classic 'pocket battle'. Heavy rain on 3 July nearly ruined his plans. His First and Elbe armies arrived before Sadowa wet and exhausted. The Second Army did not reach the field until late afternoon. Field Marshal von Benedek therefore enjoyed a considerable advantage for most of the battle; his men faced just 135,000 Prussians. Yet he did nothing with this advantage, and stopped an attempt by a subordinate (General Anton von Mollinary) to swing the North Army's right wing forward to encircle the two Prussian armies at Sadowa before the arrival of the third. This Austrian flanking attack, pushed forward by Mollinary and pulled back by Benedek, foundered in Swib Forest, where small parties of Prussian riflemen lacerated the confused columns of Austrian infantry moving in and out of the wood.

Saved by Benedek's inaction, Moltke had time to await the arrival of the Prussian Second Army, which struck Benedek's weakly guarded right flank at dusk. Hit from all sides, the North Army dissolved in a defeat which the gallantry of its cavalry and artillery rearguards mitigated but could not avert. Königgrätz ought indeed to have been the classic pocket battle, a 'second Cannae'. With the Elbe at his back, Benedek had no line of retreat. Yet Moltke's pursuit was too slow. Prussian reserves of infantry and cavalry were stuck in a muddy knot of wagons behind the lines, and did not come up in time to seal shut the pocket at Königgrätz. Most of Benedek's army escaped across the Elbe in the night. However, the Austrians lost 44,000 men in the course of the day, compared with Prussian losses of just 9,000. The North Army retreated to Vienna in such a weakened, demoralized state that the Austrian emperor had no option but to agree to an armistice on 22 July 1866.

THE FRANCO-PRUSSIAN WAR

C ount Otto von Bismarck, chancellor of Prussia, did his best to goad France into declaring war, and it did so on 15 July 1870, without allies. Over the next two weeks the armies mobilized and moved to concentration areas. In Germany reservists reported for duty and rattled off to the frontier by rail. Field Marshal von Moltke deployed three armies between Luxembourg and Switzerland: the First, under General Karl von Steinmetz, on the lower Moselle; the stronger Second, under Prince Frederick Charles, on the Saar, and the Third, which included south German contingents, under the crown prince of Prussia, in the Bavarian Palatinate. The French attempted to save time by

Prussian batteries prepare to bombard Paris.

combining mobilization and concentration. Confusion followed, but such was the resilience of the French army that by late July it had six corps on the frontier. VII Corps was at Belfort near the Swiss border, I to the north at Strasbourg, and V north-west of I between Sarreguemines and Bitche, south-east of Saarbrucken. In or around Metz were II, III, and IV. The Guard soon joined them, while Marshal François Canrobert prepared to move VI Corps forward from Châlons. Plans for concentrations at Strasbourg, Metz, and Châlons had been changed to enable Napoleon, who reached Metz on 28 July, to assume personal command of a quarter of a million men with a view to launching an offensive when concentration was complete. The Germans already had more than 300,000, and the balance tilted remorselessly against France in the weeks that followed.

Operations began with two minor actions. On 2 August the French took the heights above Saarbrucken. There were two far more significant engagements on 6 August. Moltke hoped to use the Second Army to meet the expected French attack while the First and Third swung in from the flanks. However, he found it hard to keep the headstrong Steinmetz under control, and in the north the First Army blundered into General C. A. Frossard's II Corps at Spicheren. Uncertain command left II Corps unsupported, while German units marched to the sound of the guns to outflank it.

The Battle of Spicheren (1870)

Like the battle of Wörth, also fought on 6 August, the action at Spicheren (Forbach) set the tone for what was to come. General Frossard's three divisions held a strong natural position dominating the slopes leading down to the Saar valley, and the four divisions of Marshal François Achille Bazaine's III Corps were close enough to support him. The first ill-considered Prussian attacks were beaten off with ease, in a clear justification of French faith in the *chassepot* breech-loading rifle. But while all German formations within earshot marched to the sound of the guns, and their artillery drenched French positions with a fire to which French gunners could make no effective response, a dreary series of order and counter-order left Frossard unsupported. Although his men held their ground, the threat to his flanks forced him to pull back at nightfall. He had inflicted 4,500 casualties on the Germans and lost only 2,000 during the battle, but had another 2,000 missing, most of them captured, in a dispiriting retreat.

The Battle of Wörth/Froeschwiller (1870)

On 4 August the Germans had beaten an outlying French division, at heavy cost, at Wissembourg, to the north-east of Wörth. Marshal Marie Edmé Patrice de MacMahon, with his own I Corps—good troops from North Africa—and a division of VII Corps took position on high ground north of Strasbourg and west of the Sauerbach, around the villages of Froeschwiller and Wörth, expecting that V Corps would march to his support. He was attacked by the German Third Army, and though his infantry fought very well his artillery was pounded into silence and the Germans, comfortably superior in manpower, lapped round his flanks. MacMahon committed a cuirassier division to help his infantry break clear, but the charge—much featured in post-war paintings—bought little except honour. Both sides lost about 11,000 killed and wounded, but the French lost almost as many prisoners as their position collapsed. Much of the beaten army reached Châlons by train, to form part of the Army of Châlons.

On 12 August Marshal Bazaine was given command of the force around Metz, the Army of the Rhine, though while Napoleon remained there was doubt as to how far his authority went. The next day his old corps held the First Army at Borny, east of Metz, but Bazaine, intent on crossing the swollen Moselle to march west for Châlons via Verdun, would not permit a counter-attack. Bazaine's army moved slower than he or his opponents expected.

The Battles of Rezonville/Vionville and Gravelotte/Saint-Privat (1870)

The battles of Rezonville/Vionville and Gravelotte/Saint-Privat were the decisive engagements of the war. The Army of the Rhine, over 160,000 strong, retreated through Metz and across the Moselle towards Châlons, where the defeated French right wing was being reconstituted. Two German armies were involved, General von Steinmetz's First, advancing on Metz, and Prince Frederick Charles's Second, moving to its south.

On 16 August most of Marshal Bazaine's force was ready to move off for Verdun. A cavalry division was at Mars la Tour and Vionville, 8 to 10 km (13–16 miles) west of Metz, with II and VI Corps around Rezonville, 6 km (10 miles) west of Metz. III Corps was at Verneville and the Guard at Gravelotte, just behind it, while IV Corps marched up from Metz. Bazaine's sloth confused Field Marshal von Moltke. Lieutenant General von Rheinbaben's cavalry division, leading the right wing of Second Army, had no idea that it faced the main French force. It shelled French cavalry out of Mars la Tour at about 09.00, but when the German III Corps arrived its capable commander, Constantin von Alvensleben, soon grasped what had to be dealt with. He engaged II Corps, taking Flavigny and Vionville, but was soon fought to a standstill.

Early in the afternoon Alvensleben ordered Major General von Bredow's cavalry brigade to charge north of the Verdun road to buy him much-needed time while other German corps came into action. It overran VI Corps's gun-line, and helped assert moral superiority over Bazaine. Yet French infantry made good progress towards Verdun, and it was more Bazaine's failure to inspire his corps commanders than German resistance that stopped them. A cavalry mêlée north of Mars la Tour ended the day. The Germans lost almost 16,000 men to almost 14,000 French, but had cut the Verdun road. Bazaine, worried about ammunition shortages, ordered his exasperated men to fall back to restock.

The French took up a strong position running north from the high ground just east of Gravelotte, with II and III Corps to the south, both well dug in on open slopes, IV in the centre, VI (short of both digging tools and artillery) in the north at Saint-Privat, and the Guard in reserve. On the 18th Moltke, imagining that he was facing only part of the French army and that the bulk of it had slipped away northwards, sent the Second Army curling up to the north while the First Army pushed in from Gravelotte. Steinmetz's assault, delivered head on into unshaken defenders, was a bloody failure, and further north the Prussian Guard, attacking VI Corps, lost over 8,000 men in another cruel demonstration of the effectiveness of the breech-loading rifle in defence. But Bazaine neither counter-attacked the shaken First Army, nor committed the Guard in time to reinforce VI Corps, eventually outflanked by the Saxon Corps. When VI Corps at last broke it took the Guard with it, and Bazaine had to retire on Metz. The Germans lost over 20,000 and the French at least 12,000 men, but the battle sealed Bazaine's fate: he capitulated in October.

Moltke left Frederick Charles with the First Army and four corps of the Second Army to blockade Metz. The crown prince of Saxony was given the new Meuse Army, comprising three of the First Army's corps and two cavalry divisions. On 23 August the Germans set off, looking for Marshal MacMahon's Army of Châlons, comprising the battered I, V, and VII Corps from Alsace, as well as the fresh XII Corps, a total of over 100,000 men. MacMahon was beset by contradictory instructions from Paris, encumbered by the emperor, who had left Metz just before the Germans cut the Verdun road, and was logistically dependent on the railway. Eventually ordered to relieve Bazaine, he stumbled north-eastwards and on 1 September was crushed between the Third Army and the Meuse Army at Sedan.

The Battle of Sedan (1870)

The Germans, with 250,000 men and 500 guns, attacked Sedan at first light on 1 September. Under accurate fire from artillery on the surrounding heights which outranged their own, the French, many of them drawn up in the open, were soon in difficulties, though the gallant defence of the outlying village of Bazeilles, just west of Sedan, by their fine Infanterie de Marine showed that this was still a force to be reckoned with.

Marshal MacMahon was wounded by shellfire early on and named General Auguste Ducrot, the senior corps commander, as his successor. Ducrot ordered a withdrawal westwards, but General Félix de Wimpffen, who had been privately appointed to take MacMahon's place by the war minister, arrived and countermanded this. The Germans, meanwhile, completed the encirclement of Sedan by midday. After final, desperate cavalry charges seeking to break out to the west in which the Chasseurs d'Afrique distinguished themselves, by early evening with 20,000 French already captured, a truce was arranged to negotiate surrender terms.

King Wilhelm I, Marshal von Moltke, Otto von Bismarck, their staff, and foreign observers, including William Howard Russell of *The Times*, had watched the battle from a clearing above Frenois. When the king watched the Chasseurs d'Afrique charge to immortality he exclaimed (and somehow only French would do) 'Ah! Les braves gens!' Wimpffen formally surrendered at the Château de Bellevue the following morning, and the remaining 83,000 French, including Napoleon III, became prisoners: the Prussians lost just 9,000.

After just two months of campaigning, the victory at Sedan and Napoleon's capture precipitated the fall of the Second Empire and the proclamation of the Third Republic. Jules Favre, foreign minister, met Bismarck at Ferrières on 18 September, but found armistice terms impossibly harsh. The new government had already set about calling the nation to arms.

As the Germans closed in on Paris a delegation was established at Tours to carry on the government's business. On 7 October Léon Gambetta left in a balloon to take charge of the delegation. He hurled himself into creating the Armies of National Defence. Civilian specialists were swept into service, arms contracts were placed abroad and domestic production was stepped up, and restrictions on promotion and appointment were swept away. It was a towering achievement, but for every Frenchman who fought there were more who stayed at home.

For the remainder of the war operations focused on the siege of Paris and attempts by French provincial armies to bring succour to the capital or limit penetration. Proximity to

Paris made the activities of the Army of the Loire the most important. It was reconstituted, after the fall of Orléans in October, by the veteran General Louis d'Aurelle des Paladines. By December the Germans had broken his army and taken Orléans. The two divided portions of the army were reorganized but were defeated in January. The Army of the North, under General Louis Faidherbe, fought well at Bapaume that month, but could not prevent the fall of Péronne. Finally, attempting a limited offensive to distract German attention from Paris, it was beaten at Saint-Quentin.

The Germans had encircled Paris on 20 September. They did not assault, which forced the French to attempt, unsuccessfully, a number of breakouts, most notably in a brave but mishandled attempt around Champigny on 29 November. It was not until 5 January that German siege guns opened fire, and although the bombardment devastated outlying forts, its effect on morale was perverse: not for the last time, citizens became bitter rather than cowed. In response to popular demands for a *sortie torrentielle*, on 19 January the French launched 90,000 men against Buzenval, on the western edge of Paris. The venture was hopeless from the start, and its collapse was the last straw: after a flurry of civil unrest, Favre asked Bismarck for terms.

Negotiations began on 23 January, an armistice was signed five days later, and preliminaries of peace were agreed on 26 February. France lost Alsace and Lorraine, and Europe entered a dangerous era when military power rested upon universal conscription, relentless technological improvement, and general staff honing plans for a war whose likelihood entered deep into the spirit of the age.

5 World War I

Between 1914 and 1918 what Barbara Tuchman called 'the Proud Tower' was demolished in the most destructive conflict the world had so far seen. Chief amongst its causes were tension between the great powers, the curdling of Franco-German relations after France lost Alsace and Lorraine in 1871, Anglo-German naval rivalry, and squabbling over colonies as Germany sought its place in the sun. A precarious alliance system, linking France and Russia on the one hand and Germany and Austria on the other, left Germany sensitive to the risk of attack from two sides, and linked it, through its relationship with Austria, to the instabilities of the Balkans. Britain was not formally entangled in the web, but had an unofficial understanding with France, and guarantee of the treaty establishing Belgium seventy years before left it obliged to defend Belgian neutrality, compromised by the wheeling march of German armies.

The wars of 1866 and 1870–1 had emphasized prompt mobilization, and concentration by railway. The creation of huge armies, sustained by conscription, nerved by national enthusiasm, directed by powerful general staffs, and armed by burgeoning economies, all contributed to the tension. Generals feared that an opponent might steal a march, and warned that when the crisis came there could be no hesitation. In Germany, they argued that comparative strength would decline as the Russian army completed reforms begun after the Russo-Japanese War of 1904–5. The Austrian high command itched to take on Serbia, which had made the most significant gains, largely at Turkish expense, in the Balkan wars of 1912–13. Fear that windows of opportunity were closing and the balance of power was shifting was as important as bellicosity, and few men making key decisions in the summer of 1914 matched the dimension of the challenge they faced.

Most observers believed that the war would be short: after a decisive clash, soldiers would be 'home before the leaves fall'. There was no doubt that modern weapons make this clash a costly one. In 1912 General Friedrich von Bernhardi warned: 'Anyone who thinks that great tactical successes can be achieved in modern war without staking a great deal of human life is, I believe, mistaken,' and his was not an isolated view. Yet there was widespread conviction, even amongst those who had studied the second Boer War and the Russo-Japanese War, that the side with highest morale would be best placed to sustain the shock, and to win the war by offensive action. The French, with their belief in 'a conquering state of mind' were more extreme than their allies or opponents, but their views found abundant answering echoes.

Rapid victory was important because the alternative was too terrible to contemplate. In 1898 the Polish banker Jan Bloch had predicted that in future war the weight of firepower would paralyse movement. He was a civilian, so professional soldiers gave him short shrift, but their own analysis was often similar: it was their deductions that were different. Since war could not be avoided, they argued, the only escape from paralysis would be offensive action. If this failed, then armies would, just as Bloch had suggested, entrench themselves, and the result would be national collapse. Economies and financial structures were intimately linked, and the home front might not bear the strain. When we look at the armies that fought the war and the communities that supported them, we can only admire their durability. On the eve of 1914, however, this could not be taken for granted. There was fear that the growing strength of socialism would influence both military morale and political support, and it would be impossible to sustain a long war: so better a short one, bloody though it must be.

In the quarter-century before 1914 weapons had changed beyond measure. The development of smokeless powder in the 1880s gave rifles extra range with smaller calibre rounds, now contained in a magazine, enabling the user to fire as many as fifteen a minute. The same technology underpinned the development of the machine gun, and by 1914 the belt-fed machine gun, its barrel housed inside a water-filled jacket, was universal. Smokeless powder provided the propellant which sped shells on their way, and instead of bursting charges of black powder they now contained the more efficient high explosive. In 1897 the French 75 mm gun embodied a buffer, which absorbed most of the recoil, and a re-cuperator, which pushed the barrel back to its original position: it no longer bounded backwards when fired. Although in 1914 gunners still thought mainly in terms of 'direct fire', hitting targets they could see, the ingredients of 'indirect fire', engaging targets invisible to the gun-line, were already there, and had been used in the Russo-Japanese War. Field telephones now permitted displaced observers to correct fire. Although the military aircraft was still in its infancy, an Italian pilot had dropped bombs from the air in Libya. It was a short step from using aircraft for reconnaissance to getting them to spot for artillery, although it was not until well on in the war that radios, large, unreliable, and relatively uncommon, could be used to facilitate the process.

The steam-powered armoured warship, its heavier guns mounted in turrets, had become the main currency of naval power in the last quarter of the nineteenth century. British development of the turbine-engined, big-gunned *Dreadnought*, built in just one year, rendered all other battleships obsolescent, and accelerated the Anglo-German naval race. Germany's desire to build a High Seas Fleet said more about its quest for super-power status than about strategic logic. When war came the High Seas Fleet was unlikely to mount a successful challenge to the command of the sea exercised by Britain and its allies, while concentration on the development of submarines might well have enabled Germany to inflict intolerable damage on the maritime lines of communication upon which British power depended.

Part of the problem confronting commanders, at sea or on the land, was that before 1914 all these developments had not yet been brought together in a conflict which could not be made to seem a special case. For instance, cavalry armed with sword or lance had distinguished themselves in neither Manchuria nor South Africa: but might things not be different in a European campaign against a first-rate opponent? It was to take the war itself to show the real significance of these changes, and throughout it one simple truth emerged. Improvements in communications lagged behind weapon technology. Unless the attacker could administer a blow that decided the struggle at a stroke (like Erich von Falkenhayn's campaign against Romania in 1916) it was usually easier for the defender, pushed back on his own communications, to cauterize his failure than it was for the attacker, his advance stretched across a blighted battlefield, to reinforce his success.

Seldom had battle been less decisive. Even impressive German victories over Russia at Tannenberg and the Masurian Lakes in 1914 were not conclusive. The remarkable thing about the Russian army is not that it was eventually defeated, but that it plodded on, repeatedly mauled, for so long. As late as the Brusilov offensive of 1916 it could still inflict serious damage on the Austrians, compelling the Germans to reinforce them and so helping to change the balance of forces on the western front while the battle for Verdun raged on. Armies were able to absorb dreadful punishment. On 1 July 1916, the first day of the battle of the Somme, British casualties amounted to almost 60,000, more than half the total strength of the British army at the time of writing. Even in the Russian case, eventual military collapse was a consequence of revolution at home rather than the other way about.

Battle at sea was also indecisive in the short term. There was only one major engagement between the Grand Fleet and the High Seas Fleet, off Jutland in 1916. Its outcome was both a disappointment for the British public, which hoped for a new Trafalgar, and a condemnation of British tactics and training methods. Yet it neither altered the balance of sea power, nor loosened Britain's grip on the world's shipping lanes, and against the eventual defeat of Germany on land must be set its slow throttling by blockade. In contrast, German submarines played havoc with British trade, leading the first sea lord to announce in June 1917 that 'There is no good discussing plans for next spring: we cannot go on.' The prospect of starving Britain to death encouraged the Germans to adopt unrestricted submarine warfare on 1 February 1916. It was a calculated risk, and had the German submarine arm been more powerful it might have succeeded. However, it brought America into the war, tilting the manpower balance so firmly against Germany that even by making peace with Russia and concentrating in the west, the Germans faced an uphill struggle against American demographic and economic strength.

We cannot be sure whether Field Marshal Sir Douglas Haig, the British commander-in-chief in France and Belgium in 1916–18, was being wise after the event when he affirmed in his final dispatch that the battles on the western front were 'one great continuous engagement', but he was stating an incontrovertible truth. The German army in the west had been ground down by a long series of allied offensives, and finally spent its own strength, from March to June 1918, in a desperate effort to win the war before the Americans arrived in Europe in large numbers. But even when it was being elbowed back across France in the last hundred days of the war, it remained a formidable adversary, its rearguards snarling out to the last.

Even though the war's early battles had shown the futility of massed attacks in the face of unshaken defence (the French lost almost half their officers and a quarter of their mobilized strength in the first month) they did not annul the strategic requirement to attack. The German advance left most of Belgium and wide tracts of France, including the mines of the Lens–Douai plain and the city of Lille, in German hands. The front line ran southwards, bulging out to Noyon, as close to Paris as Canterbury is to London, before snaking off to the east. Both ends were firmly anchored, one on the North Sea coast and the other on the border of neutral Switzerland, prohibiting large-scale turning movements, and the abundant quantities of young men ensured that both sides could hold the front so densely that a decisive breakthrough was unlikely.

For Britain and France, any strategy which did not envisage the expulsion of the Germans from captured territory was fundamentally suspect. There were some, known as 'Easterners', who argued, as did Lord Kitchener, British secretary of state for war, that the German lines had become 'a fortress which could not be carried by assault' and that the Allies should seek a decision elsewhere: this logic encouraged the opening of fronts in Gallipoli and Salonika. It remains a matter of dispute as to whether inflicting a severe defeat on an ally would have compelled Germany to relinquish its hold on France and

Belgium, but the question remained academic, for in Gallipoli, Salonika, and northern Italy alike the conditions of the western front, characterized by trenches, barbed wire, machine guns, and massed artillery, asserted themselves. In Palestine too, where the British and Turks faced one another in a narrow coastal strip, there was a locked front, levered open only when the British manoeuvred around the desert flank.

For the 'Westerners' the essence of the problem was the development of offensive tactics to meet the strategic requirement of recovering lost territory. Given that most developments in the pre-war period had favoured the defender rather than the attacker, the process was never going to be simple. It was complicated by the difficulty of identifying key changes and accommodating them within existing structures or devising new frameworks, and of overcoming the experiential and institutional constraints. Although the debate over generalship continues to rage, these factors were more significant than stupidity or callousness amongst commanders, however unattractive they may seem across the pockmarked glacis of history. In part it became attractive to blame the generals because such a catastrophe needed scapegoats, and in the post-war period political leaders were successful in shifting the blame. In part, too, dislike of generals has been fuelled by so much of the war's poetry and literature, and by the anti-authoritarian sentiments of the 1960s when the 'Lions led by Donkeys' historiography was at its most compelling.

The British and, though they entered the war only in 1917, the Americans too faced particular difficulties. While conscript armies had a broad base of trained manpower, the British and Americans expanded a small professional force into a mass national army, a gigantic challenge in itself, and also identified and embodied tactical and technological change. The complexities of this dual task go far towards explaining British conduct of battles like the Somme in 1916 and third Ypres a year later, and although American battles like Saint-Mihiel and Meuse-Argonne were not on the same scale, they were marked by similar factors.

The Germans attacked less often than the Allies, for their initial gains gave them bargaining counters should there be a negotiated peace. Their defences tended to be more robust, for they usually thought of staying put while the Allies hoped to move on, and they were able to give terrain relative importance rather than absolute value, for it was not their own territory. However, their own experience in launching attacks on both eastern and western fronts, together with the lessons they learnt in facing Allied offensives, enabled them to develop tactics based on a short but overwhelming bombardment, a 'creeping barrage' (first used on a significant scale by the British on the Somme), and specialist assault infantry, well supplied with mortars and machine guns, seeking gaps in the defence and pressing on into the depth of the enemy's position. These tactics came very close to inflicting irreparable damage on the British in March 1918, and had the Germans reached the rail junction of Amiens it is hard to see how the British could have continued to sustain their forces. However, the Germans did not focus tactical excellence into a campaign plan at what we would now call the operational level of war. The casualties of their spring offensives fell most heavily on their specialist storm troops, and the salients they had punched into Allied lines were themselves vulnerable.

Although Allied development of the art of the attack did not look as dramatic, it followed similar lines, with growing recognition of the importance of physically and psychologically dislocating the defence with artillery fire, and using infantry in 'worms' better suited for penetrating gaps rather than lines which could be held up by isolated strongpoints. The learning process was painful, and for the British it was inextricably linked with raising the biggest army in their history. The tank, first employed on a small scale on the Somme in September 1916 and then used en masse at Cambrai in November 1917, was as much a weapon of future promise as of immediate practicality, for early tanks were unreliable and slow. However, by the summer of 1918 they were used not simply to crush barbed wire and cross trenches, but, as 'whippet' tanks, to begin to take on roles of pursuit and exploitation once entrusted to cavalry. By this stage, too, aircraft had been fully integrated into the battle, some spotting for artillery, others keeping the skies swept of hostile machines, and still others strafing front-line defenders or reaching deeper to attack road and rail junctions. Indeed, although soldiers had little idea of the fact, heavier aircraft (and, in the German case, airships too) were attacking strategic targets in the enemy's homeland.

There was not one war but many. On the western front troop density was at its highest: in mid-1917 the British had 1.7 million men holding about 160 km (100 miles) of the line (less than a third of the front's whole length), although the changing ratio of the administrative 'tail' as opposed to the combat 'teeth' meant that perhaps one-third of these soldiers were rarely within field artillery range of the enemy. Density on the eastern front was lower, defences were rarely as comprehensive, and there was, to put it simply, more 'room for manoeuvre'. Yet while there were important objectives (notably railheads) immediately behind the front in the west, it was harder to discern objectives of similar status in the east, and although manoeuvre there removed huge slices of enemy man-power, it struck no vital nerve.

The campaign in north Italy came to resemble the fighting on the western front with the satanic addition of appalling terrain. The Italian army bled itself white in successive battles on the Isonzo, and although the Austrians and Germans beat it at Caporetto in 1917, decisive exploitation eluded them. The fighting on the Gallipoli peninsula in 1915 was characterized by missed opportunities, and there is room to doubt whether, even had the Allies got through the Dardanelles and reached Constantinople, they would have driven Turkey from the war or delivered aid to a munition-hungry Russia. This was precisely the moment when the Allies were labouring painfully to match industrial supply to their own military demand. For the Turks, Gallipoli was one front of a wider war. They fought the British in Palestine and Mesopotamia and the Russians in the Caucasus, where their defeat at Sarikamish in the winter of 1914–15 did not simply secure the Russian frontier, but did fatal damage to attempts to inspire a holy war that might have flared out across British India. British and German soldiers and locally recruited forces contended for German colonies in Africa. The honours of the war in German East Africa went to Paul von Lettow-Vorbeck, who surrendered only after the news of the armistice in Europe reached him.

THE EASTERN FRONT

The German strategy in 1914 was to defeat France quickly and only then turn to the east. The calculation was disrupted when, at the urging of the hard-pressed French, the Russians advanced into East Prussia earlier than they had planned or the Germans had anticipated. While this succeeded in distracting the Germans, the price was appalling.

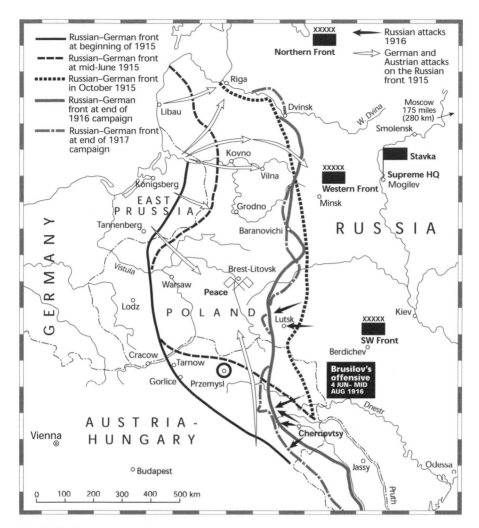

World War I: the eastern front

The Battle of Tannenberg (1914)

On the outbreak of war the Russian First Army advanced west from the Nieman river; the Second moved north-west from the Narew. Coordination between them was poor, due to inadequate communications, bad staff work, and the geographic barrier of the Masurian Lakes. Nevertheless the Russian plan of using their significantly superior numbers to encircle the German Eighth Army had good prospects of success, especially when German commanders panicked after being defeated by the First Army at Gumbinnen on 20 August. The First Army, however, failed to follow up its victory while poor logistics and worse intelligence handicapped the Second's advance. As a result the Eighth Army's new command team of General Paul von Hindenburg and Major General Erich

Ludendorff was able to implement plans, already outlined by the Eighth Army's staff officers, to concentrate their entire force against the Russians coming from the south.

The German railway network achieved rapid movement of men and supplies between the theatre's two sectors. Further, the commander of the German I Corps refused to attack until his artillery arrived, a delay that gave the Russians two more days to push forward into a tightening German noose. On 27 August I Corps crushed the Second Army's left wing. Two more corps, who had reached their position by hard marches in the August heat, drove in the Russian right. The Second Army's commander saw neither of these local defeats as decisive and sought to master the situation by driving forward with the five divisions of his centre. The Russians came closer to success than is generally realized, but proved unable to break through their opponents. By the evening of 28 August, German forces advancing on the flanks had closed a circle around the Second Army. The final balance sheet showed 50,000 Russians dead or wounded and another 90,000 prisoners of war. While Russian losses were severe, for the Germans it established a model of decisive victory that discouraged realistic assessment of what could be achieved by military means under the conditions of 1914–18.

The Battle of the Masurian Lakes (1914)

The destruction of the Russian Second Army at Tannenberg left another Russian army deep in East Prussia, with the Germans badly out of position to deal with it. Erich Ludendorff, Paul von Hindenburg, and their brilliant operations officer Max Hoffmann immediately began coordinating redeployment. The Eighth Army now consisted of thirteen divisions, two cavalry divisions, and about five more divisions' worth of fortress and garrison troops. The Russian First Army, under General Pavel Rennenkampf, had fourteen divisions, a rifle brigade, and five cavalry divisions. Supporting it on the left, moving into the hole created by the Second Army's defeat, was a new Tenth Army with the equivalent of a half-dozen first-line divisions—and more en route.

The Eighth Army's command team saw their best chance as concentrating against the First Army's left wing, in the air since Tannenberg. The German operational concept was based on a right hook through the Masurian Lakes, driving north-east against the Russian lines of communication while the rest of the army fixed the Russians in place by a frontal attack. Rennenkampf had held his ground partly because he did not believe the Germans could redeploy as quickly as they did. Instead, replicating their earlier performances, the Eighth Army staff and the railways within a week mustered eight divisions on the First Army's front and five more, with two cavalry divisions, for the flank attack.

This relatively even division of forces suggests willingness to accept Russian retreat, as opposed to thinking in terms of double envelopment. On 7 September, three divisions drove in the Russian left against scattered opposition, but the cavalry, blocked by the leading units' supply trains, could not get forward. The XVII Corps, expected to support the initial advance, was stopped by determined Russian resistance, as were the four corps that went against the First Army's front. The flank attack's commander responded on his own initiative by swinging two of his divisions hard left, routing the Russians in front of XVII Corps.

The Eastern Front. Railways played a crucial part in the mobilization of Russian forces, as they also did for the German army.

The way to the First Army's rear seemed open, but Rennenkampf reacted with an energy and decision in sharp contrast to his earlier lethargic behaviour. On 10 September he committed two divisions to a counter-attack that bought the rest of his army time to disengage.

Marching over 30 km (20 miles) a day in brutally hot weather on roads blocked by their own transport, the Russians managed to run faster than the Germans could chase them. Ludendorff, expecting a general battle, kept his flanking force close to the main army on the 10th. Given more latitude on the 11th, they were too tired and too disorganized to do more than push the Russians across the frontier in the face of determined rearguards. The Russian Tenth Army made no significant effort to intervene. By 14 September, the battle of the Masurian Lakes was over. The Russians had lost over 125,000 men and around 200 guns. They had not lost the war.

The Battles of Galacia (1914–1915)

Simultaneously, Russian arms were far more successful against the Austro-Hungarians, who were distracted by the failure of their initial offensive into Serbia and badly directed by General Conrad von Hötzendorf. The Russians were almost, but not quite, equal in the ineptitude of their leadership. Their Fourth Army crossed the Austrian border to attack Kraśnik on 23 August and was held, then forced to withdraw by the Austrian First. The pursuit ran into trouble and both sides summoned reinforcements. A series of clashes led to a battle at Komarów on 28 August from which the Russian Fifth Army was rescued by the quick thinking of General Wenzel von Plehve who pulled it out northwards with the loss of 20,000 prisoners and 100 guns. General Nikolai Ivanov attempted to hurry his Third and Eighth armies from the east to help but they made poor progress, which was perhaps why the Austrian General Brudermann underestimated their strength and attacked with his Third Army. The Russian Third Army, under General Nikolai Ruzski, was too slow to prevent Austrian withdrawal to the river Gnila Lipa where it was joined by the Second. The two attacked on 30 August, confident the reported superiority of the Russians of three to two was mistaken. It was not. With the loss of 20,000 men and 70 guns, the Austrians retreated once more. Conrad's errors increased his armies' sufferings, culminating in defeat at Rawa Ruska on 8 September, and another defeat was suffered by his Fourth Army the next day. Retreat became general, and only the sluggishness of the Russians prevented the casualties rising further from the 300,000 killed and wounded the Austrians had had in the five weeks' campaign. Russian losses amounted to two-thirds of that figure, but they had gained Galacia. On 22 March the Austrian fortress of Przemyśl fell and 120,000 men were made prisoner.

The western front settled down by November 1914 into trench warfare. By contrast a war of movement continued in the east for another year, partly because of the expanse of the theatre of operations: the western front was only about 720 km (450 miles) in length, whereas the front line in the east was over twice as long. Despite the ambivalence of the new chief of staff Erich von Falkenhayn, Berlin temporarily reversed its grand strategy and tried to win victory in the east. After inconclusive or unsuccessful offensives elsewhere on the front General August von Mackensen won a critical victory in May 1915 in the area of the Galician towns of Gorlice and Tarnow. The local breakthrough, achieved with the aid of operational surprise, a concentration of fresh German troops, and a heavy artillery bombardment masterminded by Colonel Alfred Ziethen, shattered the whole Russian line. By the end of September the Russians had abandoned most of Galicia and all of Russian Poland, retreating up to 400 km (250 miles). The defeat, did not, as Falkenhayn had hoped, force St Petersburg to the peace table, but these battles, on top of those of 1914, saw the destruction of the Russian pre-war regular army. Another fateful result of these reverses was that Tsar Nicholas II replaced Grand Duke Nikolai Nikolaevich as supreme commander of Russian forces.

A second, more static period began in 1916, with a situation superficially similar to that on the western front. Without the Polish salient the eastern front was now only 1,130 km (700 miles) long, running roughly north–south from Riga on the Baltic to the foothills of the Carpathians at the eastern tip of Galicia, along the western edge of today's Belarus and Ukraine; with Moscow over 700 km (450 miles) in the rear. The Russians achieved one successful offensive in June 1916, through a combination of surprise, innovative tactics, and Austro-Hungarian demoralization.

The Brusilov Offensive (1916)

General Aleksei Brusilov's meticulously planned offensive in summer 1916 was one of the most successful breakthrough operations of World War I. He first commanded the Eighth Army, and in 1916 the South-West Front (army group), where he organized his offensive to coincide with the British offensive on the Somme. The offensive, also called the battle of Lutsk, lasted from 4 June to 13 August. The front, with 573,000 men and 1,770 guns, broke through Austro-Hungarian forces with 448,000 men and 1,300 guns along a 550-km (342-mile) front and penetrated between 60 and 150 km (37–93 miles). The artillery preparation, planned by Lieutenant Colonel V. F. Kirey who had studied Colonel Alfred Ziethen's bombardment of 1915, was meticulously organized. Although the Russians were short of guns and ammunition by western front standards, they were concentrated on very narrow breakthrough sectors and targets were carefully picked and accurately surveyed. The infantry were assembled in underground bunkers very close to the enemy trenches, to maximize surprise. Although the Austrians eventually stopped the offensive, they lost 1.5 million killed and wounded to 0.5 million Russians and they and their allies had to pull 30 infantry and three cavalry divisions from the western and Italian fronts.

The Russian success encouraged Romania to enter the war, but a combination of delay and the low quality of the Romanian army meant this turned out to be of little value. Romania was overrun that autumn, and in effect the eastern front was lengthened 480 km (300 miles) from the Carpathians to the mouth of the Danube.

The onset of the March 1917 revolution in Russia was influenced by the war, but the provisional government, far from being defeatist, was committed to prosecuting the fighting more effectively than the tsar had. The revolution started among civilians and rear garrisons, and the front-line Russian army was disrupted but not disbanded. The Central Powers, for their part, adopted a passive strategy. The Russian attempt under the socialist war minister Aleksander Feodovorich Kerensky to regenerate fighting spirit took the form of another offensive in Galicia in July 1917, but this made little progress before a German-led counter-attack pushed the Russians back beyond their starting point. It only ceased because the Germans lacked the logistical means to sustain it.

The Battle of Riga (1917)

The port of Riga, on the Baltic Sea, remained in Russian hands, held by General Vladislav

Klembovski's Twelfth Army. On 20 August, as the German Eighth Army under General Oskar von Hutier prepared to attack, the Russians sent away the sick and shortened their line by evacuating some positions south-west of the city, but morale was low.

The Germans used new infantry tactics and new artillery fire control systems. The infantry employed numerous small groups instead of long lines of men in the attack and they were precisely coordinated with the artillery fire plan. The artillery used the initial bombardment phase to register on selected points before switching their attention to the actual targets. An orchestrated selection of gas and high explosive was used, the former to immobilize manpower and the latter to destroy fortifications and enemy gun positions. The architect of this bombardment was Lieutenant-Colonel Georg Bruchmüller.

At 04.00 on 1 September the German barrage on Russian batteries began and after two hours the infantry became the target. At 09.10 German forces crossed the river Duna and advanced behind a creeping barrage controlled so the troops were able to keep contact. Again protected by covering fire, pontoon bridges were constructed so the German artillery could cross the river and the final advance could take place. By noon the Russians were at the end of their strength and by 3 September the city had fallen. The Russians lost 25,000 killed, wounded, and captured while German casualties came to 4,200 men.

A strange third period of the eastern front began with the November 1917 Bolshevik revolution. A December armistice was followed by peace negotiations, and when these failed the Central Powers attacked against Russian trenches emptied by self-demobilization. The Bolsheviks capitulated in March 1918 at the Peace of Brest-Litovsk.

THE WESTERN FRONT

Field Marshal Graf Alfred von Schlieffen (1833–1913) spent much of his time concocting a solution for the strategic problem facing Germany: a war on two fronts against France and Russia. He decided to leave a holding force in the east and to throw most of his army against France. The French had fortified their border, and a frontal attack was not to Schlieffen's taste. He decided instead to send the right wing through Belgium, violating Belgian neutrality, to swing behind the French armies and fight a decisive battle in Champagne.

'The Schlieffen plan' was a series of yearly memoranda, whose changes reflected staff rides and war games as well as recent military events. With retirement looming, he drafted 'War against France', a detailed guide for his successor, which dwelt on the need for the left wing to fall back before the French, drawing them deeper into the trap. Having won in the west, Germany could then use interior lines to shift armies to the east to beat the Russians, who would then sue for peace. Recent research, however, suggests that the term 'Schlieffen Plan' is altogether too mechanistic, although there was indeed a strategic logic to German actions in August 1914.

The French also had a project, Plan XVII for an all-out assault on Germany through Alsace-Lorraine, and it was with this that they began the war. The French First Army (256,000 men) faced the Vosges mountains, with the Second Army (200,000 men), based on Nancy, to its left: the front to the north-east of Verdun was that of the Third Army (168,000 men). To the west the Fourth Army (193,000 men) and Fifth Army (254,000 men) stood on the border up to Charleroi. Their opening offensive, called the battle of the Frontier, was a shocking defeat for the French. On 17 August, two weeks after the Germans made their first move, the French First and Second armies attacked, advanced and retreated to find themselves where they had started six days before. The Third and Fourth armies moved into the Ardennes on 22 August and two days later had been thrown back across the Meuse.

The Battle of Mons (1914)

The battle of Mons was infinitely smaller by comparison, but was the first time British soldiers had fought a battle in Western Europe since Waterloo. In late August 1914 Field Marshal Sir John French's force of a cavalry division and two corps of the British Expeditionary Force (BEF) advanced into Belgium on the left of the French Fifth Army. Sir John was unaware that the French offensive was in difficulties, and that German armies were moving through Belgium in strength. On the evening of 22 August his westernmost II Corps, under General Sir Horace Smith-Dorrien, arrived on the Mons–Condé canal east and north of Mons, with Lieutenant General Sir Douglas Haig's I Corps echeloned back on its right. General Alexander von Kluck's First Army, in superior strength, was approaching the canal from the north, but neither side had much knowledge of the other's dispositions.

Early on 23 August the Germans mounted courageous but disconnected attacks: most foundered in the face of fierce rifle fire. Smith-Dorrien recognized that the troops on his right, where the line bulged out north of Mons, risked being cut off, and in the afternoon pulled back south of Mons. On the following day the BEF began its long retreat to the Marne. The battle cost the BEF 1,642 casualties, and the Germans up to 10,000. It gave early proof both of the quality of the BEF's soldiers and of the shaky state of its staff work.

The Battle of Le Cateau (1914)

On 25 August the British Expeditionary Force was divided by the Forest of Mormal, with General Smith-Dorrien's II Corps passing to its west and Lieutenant General Haig's I Corps to its east. Smith-Dorrien had been told that the retreat was to continue, and at 22.15 he issued orders for a retirement the following morning. At about midnight he heard that the Cavalry Division had pulled back off the long ridge to his north: unless he was away by first light the Germans would be upon him. Smith-Dorrien concluded that if he tried to withdraw as planned he would be caught in the open by superior forces. He decided to stand and administer 'a stopping blow' and then to continue the retreat.

This was a courageous decision, for Smith-Dorrien got on badly with the commander-in-chief. Sir John French's chief of staff had collapsed from overwork that night, and French himself was preoccupied with the threat to I Corps at Landrecies rather than II Corps at Le Cateau. Smith-Dorrien spoke to headquarters on the phone and was given grudging permission to stand. Major General Edmund Allenby of the Cavalry Division, not formally under Smith-Dorrien's command, agreed to fight under his orders, as did Major General Sir Thomas Snow, whose newly arrived 4th Division had come up on his left. The British were fortunate in that a French cavalry corps appeared on the left flank, where its 75 mm field guns made a useful contribution to the battle.

There was no time to lay out a defensive position. Most of Smith-Dorrien's men fought close to where they had spent the night, and were in action soon after dawn. The

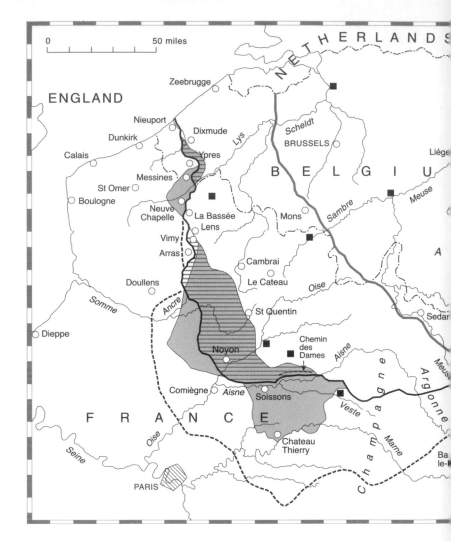

Germans, with no clear idea of British positions, launched repeated assaults. For many of the British the battle resembled Mons: determined infantry assaults prepared by heavy shellfire, met with accurate rifle fire. Smith-Dorrien's artillery commanders had decided that the infantry might not stand without intimate gunner support, and many batteries fought close to the front line.

The most vulnerable point in Smith-Dorrien's position was the knoll on his right above Le Cateau, and in the early afternoon he ordered a withdrawal, beginning with the hard-pressed right. It was difficult to get the guns out: three VCs were won in the process. The battle cost the British 7,812 men killed, wounded, and captured, as well as 38 guns, most of them from the 5th Division, on the right. German losses were around 5,000. Smith-Dorrien's decision to stand and fight had paid off: the German pursuit was not quite so pressing again.

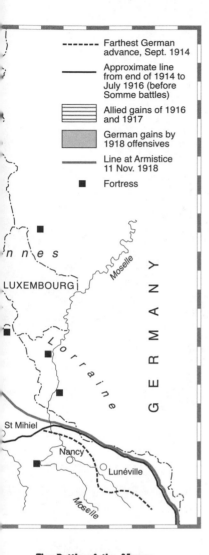

Legend:

- - - - - - Farthest German advance, Sept. 1914

———— Approximate line from end of 1914 to July 1916 (before Somme battles)

Allied gains of 1916 and 1917

German gains by 1918 offensives

———— Line at Armistice 11 Nov. 1918

■ Fortress

World War I: the western front

The Battle of the Marne (1914)

The stately Marne, which joins the Seine on the edge of Paris, offers a barrier to invaders entering France from the north. By September the German invasion plan, which had initially gone well, was in difficulties, partly because of the weakness of General Helmuth von Moltke the Younger, the German commander, and partly because of the effects of a long advance upon his troops. The Germans had planned to send their westernmost army (Kluck's First) west of Paris, but a counter-attack by the French Fifth Army at Guise on 29 August persuaded Moltke to edge it eastwards to support General Karl von Bülow's Second Army, and subsequently to order it to follow in echelon behind the Second Army—east of Paris.

General Joseph Joffre, the French commander-in-chief, realized that the main threat was to his left, around the Marne, and drew troops from his right to form two new armies,

General Michel Manoury's Sixth and General Ferdinand Foch's Ninth. An aviator from the Paris garrison brought news of Kluck's wheel in front of Paris, and Joffre planned a counterstroke, with the Sixth Army attacking the German flank north-east of Paris, the armies in the curve of the salient standing firm, and in the east the Third Army jabbing in across Champagne.

The battle did not go as planned. General Joseph Galliéni, governor of Paris, sent troops to join the Sixth Army in taxicabs, but Kluck, fighting with remarkable skill, swung round to check the attack. In the east the attack failed to materialize, and in the centre, in the stifling valley of the Marne, the fighting was fierce but inconclusive. Joffre was not helped by the fact that the British Expeditionary Force, sandwiched between the Fifth and Sixth Armies, was not under his command, and Sir John French, bruised by previous French failures, required a direct order from his government to remain in the line.

The battle hung in the balance when Moltke sent a trusted staff officer, Lieutenant Colonel Richard Hentsch, to the front with 'full powers to act on my own initiative'. Persuaded, by pessimism at the Second Army and the chaotic state of the rear areas, that a retreat was essential, Hentsch ordered the First Army to fall back to conform with the Second. Most historians agree that the battle could have gone either way, and that it was a failure of nerve in the German high command that lost it. The Germans withdrew from the Marne and made a stand on the Aisne.

The Battle of the Aisne (1914)

The British Expeditionary Force, placed between the French Fifth and Sixth armies on the Allied left, endeavoured to force its way across the Aisne, from south to north, on 13 September. That day set the pattern for what was to follow. The Germans, dug in on spurs overlooking the river, enjoyed artillery superiority, and the British infantry, attacking repeatedly with a bravery worthy of more realistic plans, made little headway. The seizure of crossings was in itself a remarkable feat, but it soon became evident that both terrain and balance of forces made it impossible to dislodge the Germans. On 15 September Sir John French recognized that 'it is no longer a question of pursuit, but of a methodical attack, using every means at our disposal and consolidating each position in turn as it is gained'.

Although French hoped to continue the advance when circumstances permitted, it was clear that the BEF lacked the strength to break the German position. The fighting settled down into trench warfare, with the Germans now on the attack, but unable to dislodge the BEF. The weather was appalling, and German artillery made life unpleasant for the British. Meanwhile, both belligerents began to shift troops to the north-west (the Race to the Sea) in the hope of turning the enemy flank. French informed General Joseph Joffre that a move to the north-west flank would shorten the BEF's line of communications and in early October the BEF left the Aisne for Flanders.

The First Battle of Ypres (1914)

Ypres lies in the centre of a shallow saucer, with higher ground to the north (a complex of

---

A German Maxim machine-gun firing from a trench on the western front.

ridges including Passchendaele ridge), east (Menin road ridge), and south (Messines ridge), although the sensation of height is rarely marked.

Ypres was entered by a German cavalry patrol on 13 October 1914, but the British Expeditionary Force arrived the next day. The area became important during the Race to the Sea as both Germans and Allies extended to the north in the hope of finding an open flank. The first battle of Ypres took place as British and Germans, both attacking, clashed on the axis of the Menin road. It soon became evident that the Germans were in over-whelming strength, and the battle embodied moments when the British and French held on by the narrowest of margins. On 31 October the Germans took Gheluvelt and were checked only by an improvised counter-attack, and much the same happened on 11 November at Nonne Bosschen. The Cavalry Corps defended (though it ultimately lost) Messines ridge with a skill which bore tribute to the British army's pre-war emphasis on dismounted training. The Germans committed newly raised divisions of reserves, includ-ing some student volunteers, whose losses were severe. The legend that they went forward into the teeth of the BEF's scorching musketry bravely singing patriotic songs—in fact those songs that were sung were to recognize friendly units in the dark—caused the Germans to call the battle the 'Kindermord zu Ypern' (the massacre of the innocents at Ypres). Fighting died away at the end of November, with losses equal at more than 50,000 each, leaving a substantial Allied salient bulging out into German lines.

The Battle of Neuve Chapelle (1915)

In order to disrupt German railway communications running through Lille and Cambrai, General Joffre asked Sir John French to attack the Aubers Ridge at Neuve Chapelle. The British First Army, commanded by Sir Douglas Haig, undertook the assault with General Sir Henry Rawlinson's IV Corps and Sir James Willcocks's Indian Corps. Aerial photog-raphy helped the artillery lay down accurate and swift fire to assist the attack at 08.05 on 10 March 1915. It was at first generally successful, taking the village and pushing on to the line of the Layes brook beyond it, though a single stretch of unshelled trench in front of Neuve Chapelle resulted in the virtial destruction of two attacking battalions. But the British were not well placed to follow up their initial success—an observer saw follow-up troops 'packed like salmon in the bridge-pool at Galway'. By the time Rawlinson could issue new orders German reinforcements were in place and, and over the next two days, the fighting achieved little apart from equal loss. Some 13,000 casualties were sustained by each side. The battle helped the Germans recognize that a defence based on 'one line, and that a strong one' would not survive a determined attack, well supported by artillery, and began to think in terms of holding in depth. The British, whose artillery had succeeded in part because of the sheer weight of its fire, had unwittingly stumbled on the 'lightning bombardment', but were unable to identify and institutionalize this lesson.

The Second Battle of Ypres (1915)

On 22 April 1915 the Germans began the second battle of Ypres, attacking the northern flank of the salient between Poelcappelle and Bixschoote, using chlorine gas for the first time on the western front. They achieved a breakthrough by mauling two French divisions, but were unprepared to exploit it, and were then checked by desperate resist-ance in which Canadians played a distinguished part. The fighting then became an expensive see-saw of attack and counter-attack, which ended with British with-drawal to a line closer to Ypres and was followed by the loss of Hill 60, south-east of Ypres. In all the Allies lost over 60,000 men to 35,000 Germans. For the next two years the Ypres salient remained one of the most active parts of the western front. In July 1915 the Germans used flame-throwers to gain the crest-line at Hooge on the Menin road, and in the spring of 1916 there was heavy fighting around Mount Sorrel, at the southern end of Sanctuary Wood.

The Battle of Loos (1915)

In the summer of 1915 General Joffre planned a repetition of the strategy used that spring, an assault on each flank of the great German salient bulging out in the centre of the western front. His Tenth Army was to attack in the Vimy sector, and he pressed Sir John French to support this by attacking around Loos, to the immediate north. French looked at the ground in July and was not impressed by the numerous mines and miners' cottages, which he believed to be well suited to defence. However, Lord Kitchener, sec-retary of state for war, made it clear that the French were to be supported even if the British suffered 'very heavy casualties' by doing so.

French then seemed to warm to the scheme, in part because he hoped that the use of chlorine gas on a large scale would paralyse the German defence. The attack was en-trusted to the First Army under Sir Douglas Haig, which was to attack with two corps, each of three divisions, side by side on a front running from Loos to La Bassée. French de-cided to keep the general reserve, two of whose divisions were inexperienced 'New Army' formations, at his own disposal rather than to entrust it to Haig, possibly because he feared that it might be committed prematurely.

The battle began early on 25 September, and although the gas was not as successful as had been hoped the attack went well in the south and Loos was taken. However, the reserves were too far back to reinforce success, and the German second position—constructed following the experience of receiving British offensives at Neuve Chapelle and Aubers Ridge that spring—remained untouched. When the reserves appeared on the 26th, after a difficult approach march, they could make no impression on it and lost heavily. Although the battle did not end until 4 November, there was no real prospect of success after its first day. The British lost over 60,000 casualties to about 20,000 German. Three British major generals were among the killed, as was the only son of the poet Rudyard Kipling. The failure inspired serious disappointment in Britain, and the issue of the reserves became a cause célèbre. Haig used official papers, some of them shown to the king, to demonstrate French's unfitness for high command, and succeeded as commander-in-chief in December.

The Battle of Verdun (1916)

In terms of casualties and the sheer suffering of combatants, Verdun has good claim to being one of the most terrible battles of history. The little town of Verdun lies in a circle of hills where the main road to Paris crosses the river Meuse. The destruction of the Liège forts in the German invasion of Belgium encouraged the French to remove most of the guns from the forts. By 1915 Verdun formed a quiet salient jutting into Ger-man lines.

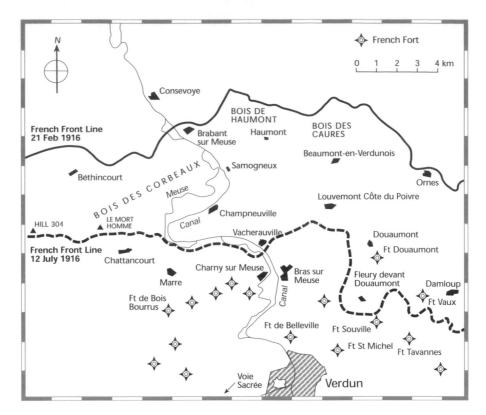

Verdun

Late in 1915 the German chief of general staff Erich von Falkenhayn decided to attack Verdun. He later claimed that he selected a spot of such importance that the French would have to 'throw in every man they have. If they do so the forces of France will bleed to death'. However, no original copy of this memorandum survives. It is possible that he sought to justify a lost battle.

The state of Verdun's defences alarmed not only General F. G. Herr, its governor, but also Lieutenant Colonel Émile Driant, a former regular officer turned parliamentarian, recalled to service and now commanding two chasseur battalions in the Bois des Caures on the right bank of the Meuse. A commission was sent to Verdun as a result of Driant's protests, but General Joffre angrily dismissed its findings.

Bad weather forced the German Fifth Army under Crown Prince Wilhelm of Prussia to delay its attack until 21 February 1916. It began with a carefully orchestrated bombardment in which some guns reached out to destroy distant targets while others knocked out batteries and smashed infantry positions. When the infantry went forward of the right bank that afternoon they made good progress everywhere save in the Bois des Caures. Driant was killed when it fell the next day, and soon the German tide was lapping against the ridge crowned by Douaumont, strongest of Verdun's forts. It fell to a small detachment of Brandenburg grenadiers on the 25th, its caretaker garrison unreinforced after a crucial order went astray.

Joffre decided that Second Army would be sent to hold Verdun, and his deputy, General Noël Castelnau, went to see things for himself. General Philippe Pétain, a big, wintry infantryman, close to retirement when the war broke out, was given command. Castelnau suggested that he should be ordered to hold both banks of the Meuse—a withdrawal from the right had been considered—and Pétain set up his headquarters at Souilly on the Bar-le-Duc road late on the 25th. Next morning he awoke with pneumonia, but had put in train the techniques which saved Verdun: no more costly counter-attacks, and the use of artillery to take the strain. The Bar-le-Duc road became an artery pumping lifeblood into Verdun. In the week beginning 28 February 190,000 men and 25,000 tons of supplies passed along it, and troops worked almost shoulder to shoulder to keep it open. It richly deserved its title 'la Voie Sacrée' (the Sacred Way).

Checked on the right bank, in March the Germans attacked on the left. In April they assaulted both banks at the same time, and though they took the heights of the Mort Homme and Hill 304 on the left, there was no breakthrough. The importance of artillery observation gave new emphasis to the war in the air, and above the battlefield fighters struggled for a superiority eventually won by the French.

Losses were now so serious that the crown prince would have discontinued the attack had he not been pressed to continue. There were also divisions in the French leadership, and in April Pétain was promoted away and replaced by General Robert Nivelle. The Germans launched more attacks. On 7 June they took little Fort Vaux after a heroic defence, and in July a final burst took them momentarily to the top of Fort Souville, within sight of Verdun. But they could not continue: on 1 July the Allies attacked on the Somme, and on 23 August Falkenhayn was dismissed. That autumn the French retook the lost ground, and Nivelle's recapture of Douaumont on 24 October marked him as the army's rising star.

We cannot be sure of casualties, but each side lost more than 300,000 men, the French rather more than the Germans. Verdun epitomized the dogged defence of French soil against the invader and was etched deep on the French psyche.

The Battle of the Somme (1916)

The Somme has a unique place in British social and military history. Battalions from every infantry regiment in the British army fought there at some time during the battle, and the losses, the more than 70,000 missing commemorated on the soaring arch at Thiepval, lacerated the whole of British society, from Raymond Asquith, the prime minister's son, through George Butterworth the composer and H. H. Monro (Saki), to the miners, shopkeepers, and sportsmen of the 'Pals' battalions' that bled there.

Although Sir Douglas Haig would have preferred to attack in the north, where he thought operational results were more likely, he was persuaded to mount a major attack with the French astride the Somme, where the Allied armies joined. However, the Germans attacked Verdun in February and the Somme battle was therefore launched early, to draw off German pressure, and never involved as many French troops as had been intended. Bisected by the Albert–Bapaume road, the battleground was a series of gentle chalk ridges, into which the Germans had dug extensive fortifications. Haig's plan was for Sir Henry Rawlinson's Fourth Army to break through in the centre, capturing the Pozières ridgeline, while General Sir Hubert Gough's Reserve Army (later renamed the Fifth Army), including cavalry, exploited this gap, took Bapaume, and then rolled up

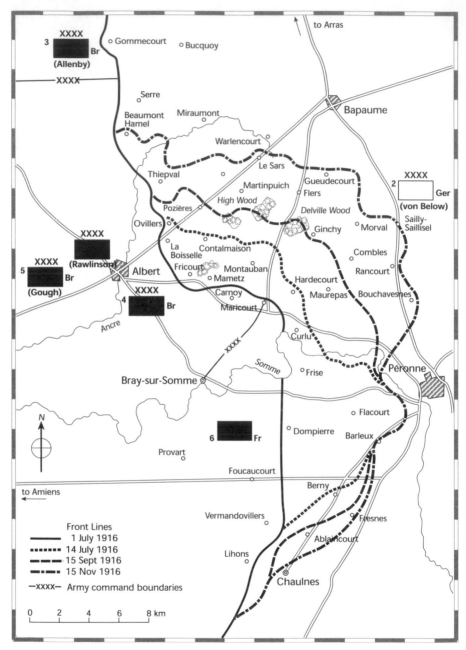

The battle of the Somme, 1916

German defences to the north. General Sir Edmund Allenby's Third Army was to mount a diversionary attack on Gommecourt, to the north.

Preparatory bombardment to destroy the German wire, trenches, and dugouts started at 06.00 on 24 June: 1.7 million shells were fired, while tunnelling companies hollowed out chambers under the key German strong points and filled them with explosives. Perhaps 30 per cent of the shells did not explode, while others failed to destroy the barbed wire or dugouts as planned. The shelling started on U-Day, continued throughout the subsequent days, and the assault should have gone in on Z-Day, 29 June. However, heavy rainstorms, which obscured artillery observation and made the approach roads muddy, meant that Z-Day was postponed until 1 July.

As the attack went in, seventeen large mines were exploded under German strong points, and the barrage lifted and began to 'creep' ahead of the intended infantry advance. However, in most cases the British were unable to get across a fire-swept no man's land and the barrage roared its way ahead to no purpose. Although there were local gains—36th Ulster Division was briefly successful near Thiepval, and on the southern end of the line Montauban was taken—the picture was bleak by the day's end. The British had lost 57,470 officers and men—19,240 of them killed, 2,152 missing, the rest wounded. This casualty rate was an unprecedented experience for the British army. Martin Middlebrook has identified 32 battalions that lost over 500 men on 1 July. Twenty of these were New Army battalions of 'Pals' or 'Chums' units—groups of friends who enlisted together. The French attack on the British right, although smaller in scale than initially planned, went far better, and the preponderance of heavy guns in the French sector proved a real help to adjacent British formations.

The shocking images of 1 July tend to cloud the overall Somme campaign. The British army's casualties of that day need to be seen against its overall losses for the 142 days—some 415,000 men. The perception is of disproportionate British casualties; in fact, the Germans are calculated to have suffered much more—possibly 650,000, although the methods used to arrive at this total are themselves controversial. Spread over the 142 days, therefore, the average British casualty rate was under 3,000 per day. The historian John Terraine argues persuasively that 1 July should be seen as a freak day of battle, an unrepresentative snapshot of 1916, and certainly not a typical day of war.

There were twelve separate battles that together constitute the 1916 Somme campaign, which ended on 18 November 1916, when the 51st Highland Division took Beaumont Hamel (which had been a Day One objective). After the initial setback, Gough's Fifth Army took over attacking Pozières in the north, while Rawlinson's Fourth concentrated on securing a series of ridgelines in the Mametz–Montauban area, to the south. The 38th (Welsh) Division suffered particularly taking Mametz Wood, and fighting up to 13 July cost the Fourth Army 25,000 more men. Longueval and Bazentin fell to a well-conducted night attack on the 14th, opening a hole in the German second line, but Delville Wood took longer to subdue, the South African Brigade suffering heavily. However, German reserves arrived in time to hold a line between High Wood and Delville Wood, on the crest of Longueval Ridge, and remained there for the rest of the summer. On 15 September, tanks made their first ever appearance in war, supporting the attack on Flers-Courcelette. This led to the capture of High Wood, and the break-in to the German third line, though it was too late in the year to exploit this effectively.

While 1 July did not bring the breakthrough hoped for by Haig, by November he could claim a victory, though only in attritional terms. Territory had been taken, and his enemy pushed back and badly mauled: one German officer called the Somme 'the muddy grave of the German field army'. That eleven French divisions also fought on the Somme between July and November is often overlooked, along with the 200,000 casualties they sustained.

The battle remains deeply controversial. Paddy Griffith emphasizes that the British army that emerged from it was a better-trained instrument of war than that which entered it, and John Terraine points out that the 'true texture of the Somme' included failed German counter-attacks as much as failed British attacks. However, it is impossible to exonerate Haig and Rawlinson from having fundamentally different conceptions of the battle: the latter had initially advocated modest 'bite and hold' tactics, and had little real confidence in the breakthrough he was bidden to achieve. There was also a distressing lack of grip by the Fourth Army for much of the battle, when the same objectives were repeatedly attacked, with too little originality, behind too light a barrage. In principle Haig had no alternative but to fight on the Somme; but in practice it was not a well-handled battle. And its human cost, even in this terrible war, still has the power to shock.

The Battles of Arras and Vimy Ridge (1917)

The result of Allied discussions in early 1917 placed the British army, controversially, under French command for the spring offensive. Robert Nivelle, the French commander-in-chief, championed what he saw as a war-winning offensive on the Aisne and in the Soissonais, and Sir Douglas Haig, who had been placed unhappily under French command for the operation, was directed to attack at Arras on 9 April to draw in German reserves before the main French attack began.

The battle, launched at 05.30 on a sleety morning, began very well. In the north Lieutenant General Sir Julian Byng's Canadian Corps, attacking with its four divisions side by side, took Vimy Ridge in a well-prepared operation which left it dominating the Douai plain. This success had wide implications; it was a proud demonstration of Canada's nationhood. When Byng was promoted shortly afterwards, Major General Sir Arthur Currie of 1st Canadian Division took over, becoming the first Canadian lieutenant general.

To the south, the Third Army under General Allenby attacked from the suburbs of Arras towards Monchy-le-Preux and Fampoux. German defences, laid out in three main lines, were strong, but a well-orchestrated counter-battery programme crippled artillery support. Heavy and accurate bombardment smashed defences, but tanks were a disappointment on the churned-up ground. North of the Scarpe, XVII Corps took Fampoux and the Point du Jour Ridge. The day ended with some attackers up on the German third line, leading Ludendorff to write: 'The battle of Arras . . . was a bad beginning for the decisive struggle of this year.'

Allenby was in a position to do even more serious damage to the Germans, possibly compelling them to withdraw to the Drocourt–Quéant switch-line behind their front position. But he misread the battle, sending cavalry forward into the snow flurries around Monchy on the 10th, and it proved difficult to coordinate fire support for fresh attacks with guns stalled behind captured trenches and communications cut. At Bullecourt, south of the main attack sector, a promising Australian attack broke down when its tank support failed, leading to long-lasting recriminations between Australians and the Tank Corps.

By this stage some of Allenby's commanders were horrified by the losses suffered in what had become a grim attritional battle in filthy weather, and three divisional commanders took the unusual step of protesting directly to Haig. The operation was called off on 15 April having cost the Allies 150,000 men—a heavier daily loss rate than the Somme or Passchendaele—and the Germans some 20,000 fewer. While it succeeded in drawing in their reserves as intended, the losses incurred in the later stages were unconscionable.

The Nivelle Offensive (1917)

General Robert Nivelle had succeeded General Joseph Joffre as commander-in-chief of the French army in December 1916. Nivelle's plan was based on tactics he had used on a much smaller scale at Verdun. It involved mass infantry attacks on a broad front, supported for the first time by tanks, and preceded by a swift, rolling artillery barrage, unlike previous assaults which had been heralded by long bombardments. His plan might have had some chance of success had not the Germans withdrawn suddenly in the spring of 1917 to the Hindenburg Line, taking up a much shorter and cunningly sited defensive line. This left Nivelle's plans dangerously up in the air, but he did not change them. News of the threat reached the Germans, who fortuitously captured a copy of the plan. They widened their trenches in the crucial Aisne sector to confound the tanks, built extra concealed machine-gun bunkers, posted additional artillery nearby, and circulated information which would enable them to shell French trenches at their most crowded.

The 'lightning' bombardment fell on a 40-km (25-mile) stretch of front between Rheims and Soissons on 5 April 1917, but the infantry attack was postponed several times due to the weather. French troops eventually slithered out of their trenches in appalling conditions on 16 April, by which time the Germans were fully alerted. The French tanks were halted and destroyed by artillery fire and the 'creeping' barrage moved forwards too fast for the accompanying infantry. German machine guns and artillery exploited the window of opportunity after the hurricane of shells had passed, and caused 134,000 French casualties between 16 and 29 April, 80 per cent during the first day's fighting. Penetrations were made in some places and 11,000 prisoners taken, but the 48-hour victory was undeliverable.

Nivelle's failure caused troops in 68 of France's 112 infantry divisions to mutiny. The government, alarmed by the scale and consistency of the mutineers' grievances, summoned General Philippe Pétain to take command of the army. Nivelle was sacked on 15 May. The French breakdown reaffirmed the need for the British to take the initiative, and this played a part in persuading Haig to fight the third battle of Ypres three months later.

The Battle of Messines Ridge (1917)

The preliminary battle of the third Ypres campaign was meticulously planned by General Sir Herbert Plumer, whose Second Army had held this sector for two years. Its aim was the removal of the Germans from the Wytschaete–Messines ridge, which ran due south from Ypres for 8 km (5 miles) and overlooked Ypres sector. From early 1916, 22 tunnels were dug under German positions on the ridge by British and Dominion tunnelling companies and 470 tonnes of explosives laid in them. One mine was discovered by the Germans and blocked, but at 03.10 on 7 June 1917, the rest were fired. Nineteen actually exploded on time, causing a shock wave felt in London. The twentieth was accidentally triggered by a bolt of lightning 38 years later in 1955, while the twenty-first remains unaccounted for. The mines had been preceded by a seventeen-day bombardment of unprecedented ferocity, and as the earth of the mines was still falling, the IX, X, and II Anzac (Australian and New Zealand Army Corps) Corps attacked, supported by gas and tanks.

The ridge itself was seized straight away: the town of Wytschaete fell to the combined efforts of 16th (Irish) and 36th (Ulster) Divisions, and in 1998 a memorial commemorating this symbolic joint effort was unveiled. The New Zealand Division took Messines, and by mid-afternoon, the reserve divisions and tanks had leapfrogged through to ward off counter-attacks. This was Plumer's finest hour.

The Third Battle of Ypres (1917)

The Ypres salient was chosen as the scene of the principal British offensive of 1917. Sir Douglas Haig had always believed that Flanders, where there were important objectives like the German railhead of Roulers within striking distance, offered better prospects for an attack than the Somme, and was under pressure from the Admiralty to get German submarines off the Flanders coast. It was launched—rather too late, for the momentum had been lost—by the attack of Sir Hubert Gough's Fifth Army north of Ypres, which began on 31 July. It formed three phases, more distinct to historians than they were to participants. First, in the battles of Pilckem Ridge, Gheluvelt Plateau, and Langemarck, the Fifth Army pushed its way into a salient made more than usually boggy by unseasonable weather and shelling which had destroyed the land drainage system. Next, the Second Army took over for the battles of Menin Road Ridge, Polygon Wood, and Broodseinde, and made good progress in the crucial central sector. Finally, in the battles of Poelcappelle and Passchendaele the exhausted attackers—British, Australian, and Canadian—fought their way up onto Passchendaele ridge in appalling conditions: the Canadians took the village on 6 November. In all the British and Germans lost about 260,000 men each. The battle did very serious damage to the morale of combatants on both sides, although on balance it probably hit the Germans hardest, and the conditions in which it was fought make it a byword for suffering.

The Battle of Cambrai (1917)

The British tank attack, by the Third Army under General Sir Julian Byng against the Hindenburg Line west of Cambrai, had mixed parentage. The Tank Corps, under Brigadier General Hugh Elles and his chief of staff Lieutenant Colonel J. F. C. Fuller, saw the rolling downland as offering excellent opportunities for the use of tanks, and Fuller proposed a large-scale raid with the aim of getting tanks onto the German gun-line. Brigadier General H. H. Tudor, commanding the artillery of the 9th Division, had developed a system for marking targets by survey rather than adjusting them by fire, so that an attack would not be heralded by artillery preparation. Surprise would be lost, however, if guns cut the belts of barbed wire in front of German trenches, and Tudor proposed that these should be crushed by tanks. These ideas were synthesized, and the Third Army, recently eclipsed by operations around Ypres, supported the project. In September Sir Douglas Haig gave Byng outline permission to proceed with planning, but it was not until the third battle of Ypres had ended that the plan was approved. Even then it was one of limited liability: the Third Army was to break the German line with tanks, push cavalry across the Saint-Quentin canal, and seize Bourlon Wood, Cambrai, and other objectives. If early results were not encouraging, the operation would be called off after 48 hours.

Four hundred and seventy-six tanks were assembled in the strictest security, and their crews practised battle drills with the infantry which would accompany them. There were two main types of tank, 'males', armed with a pair of 6-pounders, and 'females' with machine guns. They were to carry fascines (bundles of sticks or pipes) to drop into trenches too broad for tanks to span. Thus equipped, they would gap the wire for the infantry following close behind, cross trenches, and then, while some tanks drove parallel with them to kill or neutralize their defenders, others were to push on to the next trench while the infantry mopped up in their wake. Over 1,000 guns supported the attack from positions which had been meticulously surveyed, opening fire at 06.10 when it was barely light enough for the horrified defenders to see the tanks and infantry bearing down upon them.

Many of the defenders were shocked into surrender by the dual impact of the stunning bombardment and the unexpected arrival of the tanks. However, at Flesquières in the centre of the attack sector, there were at least two German batteries that had recently been trained in the anti-armour role and were not destroyed in the short but very intense bombardment that preceded the attack. While elsewhere the tanks rolled over trenches and achieved their first-day objectives by noon, at Flesquières they were checked, suffering heavy loss as they crested the ridge; in this sector well-handled guns, unfavourable ground, and a difference of tactical opinion between the tanks and the local infantry commander all contributed to the disappointing result. In all, 179 of 378 fighting tanks were lost, 65 destroyed by direct hits. Nevertheless, the day had seen the German defences penetrated at their strongest point to a depth of some 8 km (5 miles), and church bells were rung in England for the first time in the war.

For the next week there was a bitter struggle for Bourlon Wood, whose whaleback mass still dominates the battlefield. The British were tired and off-balance, with most unit commanders ordered out of the line for a well-earned rest, when the Germans counter-attacked on 30 November, and though they were eventually checked, they recovered about as much ground as they had lost. Both sides lost about 45,000 men.

The Ludendorff Offensive (1918)

The first phase of Germany's final bid for victory on the western front between 21 March and 15 July was divided into a series of operations: Army Group Crown Prince Rupprecht opened the campaign with an advance on both sides of the Scarpe river (code-named MARS); General Otto von Below's Seventeenth Army pushed toward Bapaume (MICHAEL I); General Georg von der Marwitz's Second Army advanced south-west from Cambrai (MICHAEL II); and General Oskar von Hutier's Eighteenth Army drove forward on both sides of Saint-Quentin (MICHAEL III). General Hans von Boehn's Seventh Army was held in reserve south of the Oise river. It was primarily an infantry operation as the Germans were outnumbered in aircraft (4,500 to 3,670), guns (18,500 to 14,000), trucks (100,000 to 23,000), and especially tanks (800 to 10).

Major General Erich Ludendorff, effectively in charge of the whole German war effort, was convinced that unrestricted submarine warfare had failed to defeat Great Britain and that Germany had used up its last manpower reserves. On 11 November 1917 he decided to play his 'last card', that is, 'to deliver an annihilating blow to the British before American aid can become effective'. He selected 44 full-strength 'mobile' divisions for MICHAEL, and equipped them with the best available machine guns, trench mortars, and flame-throwers; he also shifted more than 40 largely reserve divisions from Russia to France. The assault forces were trained in infiltration tactics according to Captain Hermann Geyer's manual, *The Attack in Position Warfare*, and patterned on Captain Willy Rohr's storm troops. No

deep strategic/operational design lay behind MICHAEL. Instead, Ludendorff opted simply to 'punch a hole' into the Allied line. 'For the rest,' he declared, 'we shall see.'

Bruchmüller's plan for the artillery involved seven major and four minor phases of high explosive, gas and registration fire; a level of sophistication previously unparalleled in warfare. The western front erupted in a hurricane of fire at 04.00 on 21 March as 6,608 guns and 3,534 trench mortars announced the opening of MICHAEL. Five hours later, 76 German divisions assaulted the Allied lines between Arras and La Fère. By the third day, they had opened an 80-km (50-miles) gap in the Allied lines and were heading into open fields. In the process they sent General Gough's Fifth Army reeling and drove the British 64 km (40 miles) behind the Somme. During the next three days, the Germans advanced another 32 km (20 miles). Sir Douglas Haig's armies were pushed back to the outskirts of Amiens and special 'Paris guns' with a range of 120 km (75 miles) shelled the French capital. A further attack was aimed against Arras (29 March). But Ludendorff failed to sever the British from the French and on 28 March the American commander General John J. Pershing reluctantly agreed to release formations to plug the holes in the Allied lines.

Ludendorff had asked too much of his troops and MICHAEL degenerated into position warfare north of the Somme. Starving German troops all too often had stopped the advance to raid rich Allied supply depots. They became demoralized as victory receded from view. Nonetheless, Ludendorff mounted more assaults. Operation GEORGETTE was directed against the British on the Lys river (9 April). Operation BLÜCHER was launched on the Chemin des Dames (27 May).

The Battles of Château-Thierry and Belleau Wood (1918)

The Germans successfully crossed the river Aisne and reached the Marne. At Château-Thierry on 30 May machine-gunners of the US 3rd Division helped French troops check the German advance. Belleau Wood, taken in the offensive, was recaptured by the US 2nd Division, its attack led by the 4th Marine Brigade. It cost the USA over 9,000 casualties, in part because of tactical inexperience. However, both victories, together with a third, won by the US 1st Division at Cantigny, south of the Somme, on 28–9 May, were of enormous psychological importance. The Germans revised their hitherto low opinion of the American Expeditionary Force, and Allied morale received a much-needed boost.

The final assaults on the Oise river (9 June), and Rheims (15 July) were more easily rebuffed. In the meantime, the Allies had appointed General Ferdinand Foch commander-in-chief of the Allied armies in France. On 18 July Foch launched a counter-attack near Villers-Cotterêts that caught the Germans unprepared. Allied forces quickly ruptured the German front and penetrated deep behind the lines, while Allied aircraft mercilessly strafed the retreating Germans. This second battle of the Marne formally ended the German advance in France. Step by step, they fell back upon the Hindenburg Line. Cases of desertion skyrocketed. Some soldiers openly refused to obey orders; entire units lost any sense of discipline; others wildly fired their weapons out of moving trains; thousands simply surrendered to the Allies. The last of the well-equipped, fit units had been squandered and skeletal divisions manned by badly clothed and undernourished soldiers

---

Men of A Company, 7th Machine-Gun Battalion, 3rd Division, American Expeditionary Force, in action with a Hotchkiss gun at Château-Thierry, 1 June 1918.

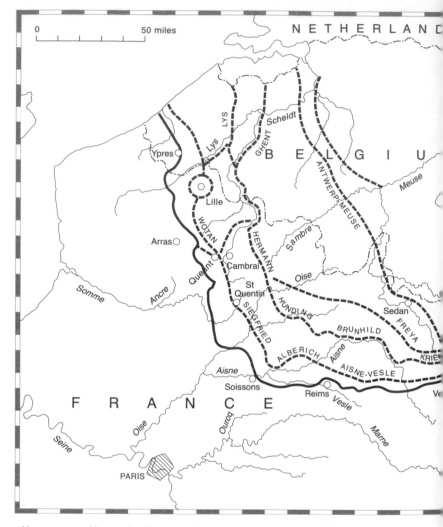

and powered by emaciated horses had been unable to complete the task of driving the best-equipped and best-fed armies of Britain and the empire, France, and the USA back beyond the gates of Paris. All they had achieved, in the words of the German official history of the war, were 'ordinary victories'. Nowhere had they possessed sufficient manpower or logistical support to turn it into the extraordinary breakthrough that Germany required.

The Battle of Amiens/Montdidier (1918)

One of the most significant battles of World War I, the first day was what Erich Ludendorff called 'the black day of the German army in the history of the war'. For the British army, having shouldered the main burden of combat after the French mutinies and the Russian Revolution of November 1917, and before American strength could make itself felt on the battlefield at Saint-Mihiel the following month, Amiens is a distinguished, if poorly

The successive defences of the Hindenburg Line

remembered, battle honour. And for the Australian and Canadian troops who played a leading part in the battle, Amiens was yet more proof of New World valour on the battlefields of the old.

By August 1918 the Allied artillery had established dominance over the German but the Germans still held the salient bulging out towards the main railway from Paris to Amiens. The Allied command planned to clear the salient of Germans along a 32-km (20-mile) front. The British Fourth Army, under General Sir Henry Rawlinson, comprising the British III Corps, the Australian Corps, and the Canadian Corps, plus XXXI Corps of the French First Army, concentrated for the attack: a total force of 18 infantry and 3 cavalry divisions, with 3,532 guns (2,070 of them British), 534 tanks—the largest number in any battle of the war—and about 1,000 aircraft of which 800 were British, from the newly formed Royal Air Force. The opposition in this area was the German Second Army with 7 weak infantry divisions, 840 guns, and 106 aircraft. On 8 August the British and French attacked without

the customary long preliminary bombardment, achieving surprise. For some days the sound-ranging sections and flash-spotting observation posts and the RAF had been engaged in plotting the positions of the German artillery. Using tanks in coordination with the well-adjusted artillery fire and aircraft, the British penetrated 11 km (7 miles) on the first day, killing or capturing 28,000 Germans and taking 400 guns. On the second day the full strength of the French First Army was brought in to the south, and on 10 August part of the French Third Army was engaged even further to the south. However, heavy losses of Allied tanks slowed the advance, and the Germans fought well in the air. By the end of 13 August the British and French had penetrated up to 18 km (11 miles) on a 75-km (47-mile) front, killed or wounded 18,000 Germans, and captured 30,000.

The Battle of Saint-Mihiel (1918)

General Pershing, in accordance with instructions given by the US secretary of war Newton B. Baker, had consistently resisted Allied attempts to feed his divisions into the front piecemeal, under foreign command, although he was prepared to commit them to meet genuine emergencies, like that on the Marne. The US First Army, with five French and fifteen US divisions, was activated on 10 August 1918. South of Verdun the German-held Saint-Mihiel salient followed the eastern bank of the Meuse, and in their four years of occupation the Germans had tunnelled extensively into the hilly and wooded terrain, creating a defensive system which remains one of the best preserved on the western front. In the first major offensive by the US army, Pershing hoped to pinch out the salient and then, if German resistance faltered, to push on against the defences around Metz. Foch persuaded him to adjust his aim, mounting the Saint-Mihiel offensive as a discrete operation before moving north to attack into the Argonne.

Pershing planned to use the US I and IV Corps to drive northwards from the southern flank of the salient while V Corps attacked its western flank. Two divisions of the French II Colonial Corps would advance across the nose of the salient to take Saint-Mihiel itself. The Americans were inexperienced and required considerable French tank and air support, but the determination of their assault would not be denied, and they secured all their objectives, taking 16,000 prisoners and 443 guns for the loss of 7,500 men. Pershing thought they could have gone on, though his staff doubted it.

In September 1918 attacks were launched in the Argonne by the Americans and on the Hindenburg Line between Cambrai and Saint-Quentin by the British and Australians, with two American divisions added to their strength. The Saint-Quentin canal, a significant part of the German defensive system, was crossed on 29 September. In the Argonne the American attack stalled within three weeks, having made an advance of 16 km (10 miles). Pershing promoted Hunter Liggett to lieutenant general and relinquished command of the US First Army to him. The attack resumed on 1 November and made better progress, while in the west Sir Douglas Haig's armies also forged ahead. For some weeks it had been clear to the German commanders that the war was lost, and an armistice was negotiated which came into force at 11.00 hours on 11 November.

The Saint-Quentin canal, incorporated in the German Hindenburg Line, was broken when the Riqueval Bridge was taken on 29 September 1918. 137 (Staffordshire) Brigade reassembled there to be congratulated on 2 October.

THE ITALIAN FRONT

The Treaty of London, signed on 26 April 1915, brought Italy into the war with promises of territorial gains at the expense of the Austro-Hungarian empire. The conflict began in two distinct theatres, the Trentino and the Izonzo. The former was in the incredibly hostile terrain of the Alps and the Dolomites, the latter ranged from the Julian Alps in the north through the plateaux of the Bainsizza to the stark land of the Carso. These were fields of battle daunting in the extreme.

The Battles of the Isonzo (1915–1917)

Of these areas the north-east was the least unattractive for conquest, although the river Isonzo, rising in the Julian Alps and making its way down a steep-sided valley before emerging onto Friulian Plain, and to the east of it two so-called plateaux, the Bainsizza and the Carso, tortured landscapes of ridge and stone, are challenging terrain for military operations. The whole of this area was, at the time, well within the Austrian border.

The first five battles undertaken in the area gained virtually nothing and cost Italy more than 175,000 casualties against the Austro-Hungarian army's 130,000. What did become clear was that the positions of Monte Nero in the north and the Carso in the south were crucial, for without possessing them an attacker would be exposed to enfilading fire. In June 1916, while the Austrian offensive in the Trentino was still in progress, the Italian commander-in-chief, General Luigi Cadorna, told the duke of Aosta, heading the Third Army, that a fresh assault was to be made on the Isonzo with Gorizia as its objective. By the end of July twelve divisions, a cavalry division, 32 heavy artillery batteries, and 37 mortar batteries had been relocated to the Isonzo undetected by the Austrians. This gave Italy 22 divisions against Austria's nine.

The Sixth Battle of the Isonzo (1916)

In the sixth battle the advance began on 6 August at 16.00 hours after a nine-hour bombardment. The Italians crossed the Isonzo and were faced with the trenches and barbed wire entanglements of the Austrians. On 8 August Gorizia fell to the Second Army. On 10 August the Third Army assaulted the Carso and by 18.00 hours on 17 August they had reached a line between Monfalcone and Vipacco, but there they halted. In the opinion of General Cadorna they were by then too exhausted to sustain the advance. Austrian commentators were of the opinion that the Italians were on the verge of a breakthrough, had they but known it.

The Seventh, Eighth, and Ninth Battles of the Isonzo (1917)

On 4 September the seventh battle began with diversionary attacks by the Second and Fourth Armies followed by an assault in the Carso by the Third Army supported by 432 heavy guns and 558 mortars on a 10-km (6-mile) front. The weather closed in and the

Arming a German aircraft before the battle of Amiens, 1918.

fighting stuttered to a halt with little gained. On 10 October the next effort was made and was abandoned after three days. On 30 October the ninth battle opened with offensives east of Gorizia by the Second Army and on the Carso by the Third Army. Heavy losses and foul weather halted that on 4 November. The Italian casualties in these three battles totalled about 75,500 while Austrian losses were some 63,000 men.

The Tenth Battle of the Isonzo (1917)

During the winter plans were made by General Robert Nivelle for a massive attack on the western front in spring 1917 and Cadorna was pressed to mount a fresh campaign at the same time. He created a special force by taking the left corps of the Third Army and the three right corps of the Second to make the Gorizia Zone Command led by the energetic General Luigi Capello. In all 28 divisions were to attack with a further ten in reserve. In the event the tenth battle of the Isonzo fell into two battles, north and south, as no progress at all was made in the centre around Gorizia. Two days' bombardment preceded Capello's attack on 14 May and he took the Monte Kuk-Vodice Ridge, held it and drew off two Austrian reserve divisions in time to assist the Third Army's attack on the Carso on 23 May. Their advance was halted and pushed back by an Austrian counter-attack on 28 May and another, supplemented by three more Austrian divisions sent from the Russian front, secured the line about 15 km (9 miles) from Trieste. The three weeks' fighting had inflicted heavy casualties. The Italians lost 26,000 killed, 96,000 wounded, and in the counter-attacks had 27,000 men taken prisoner. The Austrians had been weakened to the extent of 7,300 dead, 35,000 wounded, and 23,000 made prisoner.

The Eleventh Battle of the Isonzo (1917)

The last Italian attack took place in late August. Six new divisions had been squeezed from the Italian people and more artillery obtained. General Capello became the commander of the Second Army and took over the front from the Vipacco river to Plezzo, north of Tolimino; a distance of 56 km (35 miles). Capello had seventeen divisions, 850 heavy guns, and 960 mortars, and a significant number of storm troops, *arditi*, for special operations. The preliminary bombardment lasted a full day and in the night of 18-19 August five divisions poured over the Isonzo on a 13-km (8-mile) front near Auzza. The Austrians reeled under the shock and on 20 August renewed Italian attacks broke their line. By contrast the Third Army's efforts in the Carso were repulsed and Cadorna called a halt there, moving as many troops as possible to reinforce the success at Auzza. On the advice of the new Austrian chief of staff, General Arz von Straussenberg, General Boroevich withdrew across the Bainsizzia Plateau. The broken country hampered the Italian pursuit and the Austrians were able to establish a new defence line. His heavy artillery still far to the rear, Cadorna was obliged to suspend the action.

Italian casualties had once again been numerous; 40,000 killed, 108,000 wounded, and 18,000 taken prisoner. The Austrians had lost 10,000 killed, 45,000 wounded, and 30,000

Mark V tanks carrying cribs to cross trenches as they move up to support the attack on the Hindenburg Line at Bellicourt, 29 September 1918.

3026 F.

prisoners. Both sides were near exhaustion and it was the Austrians who were to benefit from being reinforced from elsewhere.

The Battle of Caporetto (1917)

Erich Ludendorff sent six German divisions to reverse the situation. On 24 October two Austrian armies attacked the Italian salient from the south-east while the Germans and nine Austrian divisions struck from the north-east. Italian resistance promptly collapsed amid scenes immortalized in Hemingway's *A Farewell to Arms*. There were about 700,000 casualties, many of them caused by surrender and desertion.

Unprepared for the magnitude of their success, the Austro-Germans gave General Luigí Cadorna just enough time to reform his remaining 300,000 along the Piave river north of Venice, where they held until reinforcements were rushed to their support, including British and French units from the western front. The defeat prompted a conference of Allied political and military leaders at Rapallo in November, from which unified military command emerged. Under their new commander General Alberto Díaz, the Italians beat back a further Austrian attack in June 1918.

The Battle of Vittorio Veneto (1917)

The last offensive on the Italian front was mounted to assault the Austrian forces sitting astride the Piave river in north-east Italy. During the night of 26/7 October 1918 the Twelfth (Franco-Italian), Tenth (Anglo-Italian), and Eighth (Italian) armies, totalling 41 divisions (22 forward, 19 in reserve), began to throw bridges across the Piave at eleven places. Engineers had earlier occupied a midstream island, but a heavy rise in the river had delayed the assault by 24 hours. The 33 Austrian divisions (23 in line with another 10 in reserve) formed into two armies and fought well in some places, though the Tenth Army (two British and two Italian divisions) under the earl of Cavan had advanced 3 km (2 miles) on 6-km (4-mile) front by the 28th. This was the greatest success, as floodwater destroyed the bridges of the Eighth and Twelfth armies. Eventually the Eighth Army commander detached a corps to cross by the British bridges in the early hours of the 28th and manoeuvred around to clear the Eighth Army's front. By the close of 29 October the bridgehead for the three Allied armies measured 16 km (10 miles) wide and 6 km (4 miles) deep, a wedge had been driven between the Fifth and Sixth Austrian armies, and 33,000 prisoners were taken. Now the attack began to yield results, as an Italian column took the town of Vittorio Veneto that evening. The Austrian withdrawal became a rout on 30 October, and senior Austrian commanders began requesting an armistice, which was eventually signed on 3 November, coming into force at 15.00 on the following day. Allied casualties amounted to over 35,000, but the final Austrian prisoner count alone was over half a million, full revenge for Caporetto.

The terrain in which the Italians and Austrians fought was amongst the most extreme of any encountered in the World War I.

THE MIDDLE EAST AND BALKAN FRONTS

The Gallipoli Campaign (1915–1916)

The attempts first by British and French warships and then troops to force the Dardanelles in 1915 constitute one of the most fascinating and controversial campaigns of World War I. The Allies hoped to pass through the Dardanelles, drive Turkey out of the war, and deliver assistance, through the warm water ports of the Black Sea, to a hard-pressed Russia. It was the first major amphibious operation in modern warfare, using aircraft (and an aircraft carrier), aerial reconnaissance and photography, steel landing craft, radio communications, artificial harbours, and submarines. Its lessons, positive as well as negative, were studied by the British planners for Normandy and were even remembered in the Falklands conflict of 1982.

The naval assault was the inspiration of the young first lord of the Admiralty, Winston Churchill. It foundered on 18 March, when three battleships—two British, one French—were sunk and three others badly damaged when they ran into an undetected minefield. Churchill wanted to persevere, but his senior naval colleagues refused.

The British admiral at the Straits, Vice Admiral John de Robeck, shaken by the events of 18 March, agreed with them. So did General Sir Ian Hamilton, the newly appointed commander of the Mediterranean Expeditionary Force. Thus, the two senior commanders on the spot decided on a land campaign to capture the Gallipoli peninsula, which kicks out like a dog's leg between the Aegean and the Sea of Marmora, opening the straits by controlling the littoral.

Given the troops at his disposal, which included only one regular division, the 29th, the shortage of time, the nature of the rugged peninsula with its central spine, the Sari Bair ridge, its few accessible beaches, and severe logistical difficulties, Hamilton's plan for the Gallipoli landings was imaginative. The Turkish commander, the German Field Marshal Liman von Sanders, was totally deceived by the feint landing by the Royal Naval Division at Bulair and confused by the French one at Besika Bay and a real French landing at Kum Kale. Out of the six divisions at his disposal on 25 April, only two were on the peninsula itself.

But they turned out to be enough. Only two of the landings by the 29th Division were opposed, but that at Sedd-el-Bahr—V Beach—was definitely, and bloodily, repulsed, and there were failures of nerve and initiative elsewhere. The commander of the 29th, Major General Aylmer Hunter-Weston, should have used those of his forces safely ashore to take Sedd-el-Bahr from the rear, but did not. It fell on the 26th, but by the time the advance began the momentum had been irretrievably lost.

The Australian and New Zealand Army Corps (Anzac) had been given what had seemed to be the easier task of landing further north on the western coast between the promontories of Gaba Tepe and Ari Burnu. The Anzac commander, Lieutenant General Sir William Birdwood wanted a surprise dawn landing with no preliminary naval bombardment, which required the warships carrying the troops to anchor in pitch darkness. They did so 1.6 km (1 mile) to the north of the intended landing area, and so the troops were landed from boats on the wrong beach. The Australians, with the New Zealanders rapidly behind them, moved inland, meeting little resistance.

But von Sanders's 2nd Division, commanded by the then unknown Colonel Mustapha Kemal (later known as Atatürk), was based only a few kilometres away. Realizing that this

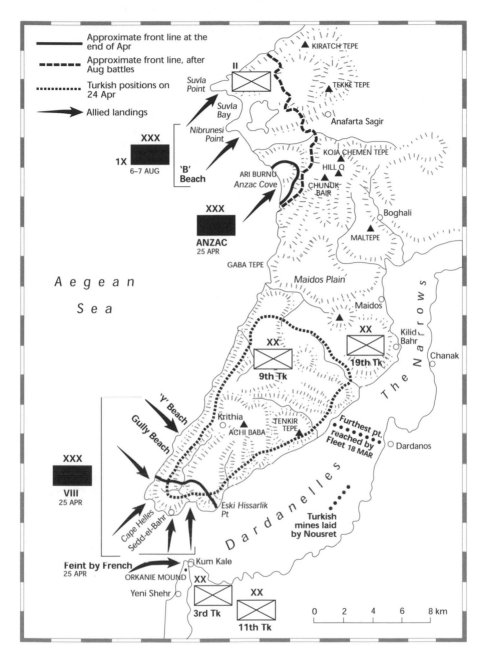

The Gallipoli landings

was a serious invasion, Kemal, without higher authority, committed his entire division to driving the attackers into the sea, and very nearly succeeded. After a day of ferocious fighting, much confusion, and varying fortunes, the Anzacs were left clinging to a fragment of land, and Birdwood was urging evacuation. Hamilton refused, and the epic of Anzac had begun.

Between the beginning of May and end of July, in torrid heat and plagued by dysentery and then typhoid, while the Anzacs clung on grimly to their tiny perimeter and inflicted brutal losses upon the Turks' daylight attacks, the British and French advanced with agonizing slowness and heavy losses. But a change of heart in London, despite the downfall of Churchill (removed from the Admiralty in May), now brought Hamilton almost excessive reinforcements.

The August plan stemmed from the night reconnaissance of the New Zealander Major P. J. Overton which proved that there was a feasible route from the north of the Anzac position to the key peak, Chunuk Bair, and that it was undefended. The Anzac garrison was reinforced by 20,000 men, primarily British and Gurkhas, secretly over three nights.

The assault on the Sari Bair mountains on the night of 6/7 August was preceded by the attack of the 1st Australian Division under the command of its British commander, Major General Harold Walker on the supposedly impregnable Lone Pine position towards the south of the Anzac sector. As a result of meticulous and imaginative planning and the barely credible ardour of the Australians, Lone Pine was taken, albeit at a heavy cost.

For the main battle, the Right Assaulting Column got to Chunuk Bair, but was ordered to pause, and this delay was to prove fatal. The Left Column got hopelessly lost, but some units of British and Gurkhas got close to their objective of Hill Q and captured it on the 8th, only to be driven off it by 'friendly' artillery fire. At first light on the 10th, in a near-suicidal charge led by Kemal, the British reinforcements were hurled off Chunuk Bair. The great gamble, which had so nearly succeeded, had definitely failed.

The landings at Suvla, north of Anzac and on ground dominated by Chunuk Bair, on the night of 6/7 August were an addition to the main August Plan, and were to be made of the three extra divisions now at Hamilton's disposal. Their commanders were old and cautious, but to be fair to them their orders emphasized landing successfully, which indeed they did. When it was at last realized that they had not advanced much further Hamilton furiously demanded an advance, but it was too late, for the Turks were ready and the battlefield was overlooked. The greatest battle of the campaign was fought on the Suvla plain on 21 August, but, despite grievous losses, the Turks held their ground.

Hamilton was recalled, and his replacement, Lieutenant General Sir Charles Monro, advised evacuation. After much anguish in London this was agreed. It was left to the men on the spot to organize the evacuations, first of Anzac-Suvla, and then of Helles. This they did with real brilliance in December 1915 and January 1916, not a man being lost, to the stupefaction of the unsuspecting Turks.

The campaign had cost the Allies 46,000 dead, of whom 26,000 were British. The Turkish dead are unquantifiable, but an estimate of 200,000 is considered to be conservative. The campaign casts a long shadow even by the standards of World War I. Just as the April 1917 capture of Vimy Ridge was to define Canadian nationalism, so Anzac did the same for Australia. This is not a wholly accurate reflection of history: the French, for instance, had more men at Gallipoli and sustained more casualties. But nations are not created by bald facts alone: on Anzac Day, 25 April, each year there are so many young antipodeans at the Lone Pine memorial that it is impossible not to share their fierce pride and deep grief.

The Salonika Campaign

When a campaign based on the Greek port of Salonika finally got under way in October 1915, it did so ostensibly to bring aid to the hard-pressed Serbian army, but in large part as the result of the determination of the French to find gainful employment for the politically influential 'republican general' Maurice Sarrail, who had recently been relieved of his command on the western front, not without cause. The Anglo-French army arrived too late to assist the Serbs, whose survivors were ferried to safety in Corfu, and throughout its duration the campaign was opposed by the British military hierarchy, who believed that it was doing nothing to win the war against Germany.

As the months passed the Allied commitment to the Salonika campaign steadily increased with the addition of the reconstituted Serbian army as well as Italian and Romanian forces. Further reinforcements in the shape of Greek forces were added after the Allies had deposed King Constantine in June 1917.

At its peak the Allied army numbered some 600,000 men. By contrast, the Germans progressively withdrew from the campaign. In March 1916 Erich von Falkenhayn abandoned plans for a large-scale offensive in the Balkans leaving a largely Bulgarian force of about 450,000 men to make use of the difficult terrain to hold down the numerically stronger Allies. The grateful Germans thus came to look upon Salonika as 'the largest internment camp of the war'. The campaign was largely irrelevant to the war's outcome, at least until the last few weeks of fighting. Then, in mid-September 1918, an advance under the new Allied commander, General Louis Franchet d'Espérey, produced a rapid disintegration in the Bulgarian forces, which the German commander Erich Ludendorff later alleged to have been a significant factor in his country's defeat.

The Caucasus Campaigns

The region south of the Caucasus Mountains, between the Black Sea and the Caspian Sea, had been disputed between Turkey and Russia since the nineteenth century. Enver Pasha, the Turkish minister of war and effective ruler of the country, initiated hostilities with the attacks by the former German light cruisers *Goeben* and *Breslau* on 29 October 1914 in the Black Sea. Enver also sent the Turkish Third Army under Hasan Izzet Pasha to the border north of Erzurum with 189,562 men, 60,877 horses, and 160 guns. The Russians were also prepared for war. Their Caucasus Army had its headquarters at Tbilisi and had bases at Kars and Ardahan. Under General Mishlaevski there were some 100,000 men of whom 15,000 were cavalry, and 256 guns. The terrain in the region is daunting, consisting of substantial mountains cut with steep-sided valleys, snow covered in winter and at all times a nightmare for logistics officers.

The Turkish decision to commence hostilities in October led, inevitably, to a winter campaign. The Russians moved forward as soon as they declared war on 2 November and advanced until they were blocked east of Erzerum. The Turks, however, were losing men to the cold rather than to enemy action, and the advance of their Second Army on Ardahan was ponderous. On 14 December Enver himself arrived in front of Köprüköy to take command of the Third Army offensive he demanded. In spite of heavy snowfalls on

19 December, 95,000 Turks attacked the Russians two days later, recovering Köprüköy and pushing the Russians back. To the north-west at Oltu the Turkish X Corps ejected a Russian brigade from the salient on the frontier on 23 December.

The Battle of Sarikamish (1914–1915)

On 26 December the battle began with General Mishlaevski, recently arrived from Tbilisi, in command of the Russian forces. Enver's 29th Division was repulsed and in the attempt to come to his support with a nineteen-hour forced march his X Corps lost more than 7,000 men. The Bardiz Pass was hotly contested and Russian reinforcements struggled from Kars to lend their strength to their comrades. By 31 December the Turkish IX Corps was reduced to a mere 2,500 men still able to bear arms. To the north the Siberian Cossack Brigade regained Ardahan on 3 January and at Sarikamish the battle ended the next day. The Turks had lost over 38,000 men against the Russians' 15,000. The terrible weather saved the Turks from further damage. The battle of Sarikamish can rightly be considered decisive. It turned the tide of war in the Caucasus, and effectively ended German and Turkish plans to unleash a pan-Islamic movement which might have weakened Britain's hold on India.

This fighting in the border mountains loosened the Turkish grip to their rear, encouraging Armenian rebels to organize. Their raids cost some 120,000 Turkish lives that winter. In February 1915 a force of some 30,000 Armenians, eager for independence, formed up at Sivas and part of it took Van on 20 April, proclaiming themselves a government. The consequent Turkish action against the Armenians amounted to genocide and, before the end of the war, between 700,000 and 1,000,000 men, women, and children were to die at the hands of their own government.

General Nikolai Yudenich, who had distinguished himself at Sarikamish, was promoted to the command of the army in January. He dealt with the Turkish offensive of July 1915 at Malazgirt and mounted an offensive in 1916, taking Erzurum in February, Trabzon in April, and Erzincan in July. The 1917 February revolution in Russia stalled operations and, for the Russians, it was fortunate that thereafter the campaign in Palestine preoccupied the Turks.

The Mesopotamian Campaign

On 6 November 1914, a force of Indian and British infantry landed at the head of the Persian Gulf, in modern Iraq, ostensibly to protect imperial oil interests, now threatened by Turkey, who had joined the Central Powers on 28 October. Oil had been discovered in the area just prior to 1914. Moreover, Britain was anxious to preserve its established position in the Gulf, to prevent Turkish agents from stirring up trouble amongst India's Muslims, and to encourage Arab resistance to Turkish rule.

Until early 1916 the campaign was directed by the government of India, which left much of the decision-making to its own military authorities and to the commander-in-chief, General Sir John Nixon, who took over in March 1915. Both recognized that as long as they retained only a toehold in Mesopotamia the Turks were at liberty to move down the Tigris and Euphrates against them, and early successes encouraged them to believe that an advance inland would be easy.

Despite the campaign's lack of clear strategic focus, its early signs were promising.

Basra (which the Turks had already evacuated) was taken on 22 November, and El Qurnah, at the junction of the Tigris and Euphrates, fell on 9 December. In May 1915 two British columns moved off, one following each river upstream. The 6th Indian Division under Major General Charles Townshend moved up the Tigris towards Baghdad, while Major General G. F. Gorringe took his 12th Indian Division to An Nasiriyah on the Euphrates, which fell on 25 July.

These easy successes encouraged Nixon to aim for Baghdad, convinced that he could take it, though Townshend disagreed. The latter's men were unused to the local climate and had begun to tire after the long advance while lines of supply came under increasing strain. Despite pleas for reinforcement, the 6th Division was ordered to continue its progress along the Tigris. The Turks evacuated their 10,000-strong garrison, and Townshend occupied Kut Al Amara, just 190 km (120 miles) from Baghdad, on 28 September 1915. Although Nixon knew that the Turks had been reinforced, he told Townshend to press on.

The Battle of Ctesiphon (1915)

Major General Townshend resumed his advance, and though he had to wait six weeks to resupply, by 22 November he was 39 km (24 miles) from Baghdad, where he attacked a strong Turkish defensive line at Ctesiphon. He was supported by four Royal Navy gunboats, but Turkish artillery prevented them getting close enough to give adequate covering fire for his attack. The British succeeded in breaking through the Turkish line in spite of being outnumbered by four to three but they lost over 4,000 men, one-third of their force. Townshend had pushed his luck too far. He was without reserves, and, faced with the arrival of fresh Turkish troops, was obliged to fall back on Kut Al Amara. At Umm-at-Tubul on 1 December his rearguard fought off 12,000 Turkish troops, twice their number, but the gunboats *Comet* and *Firefly* were lost.

The Siege of Kut Al Amara (1915–1916)

Major General Townshend was encircled by Colonel Nur-Ud-Din's forces on 7 December. He had ordered the cavalry back to Basra and, calculating he had supplies for two months, determined to hold out. He had 10,000 men but was encumbered with 2,000 sick and wounded, 3,500 non-combatants, and 6,000 local people. The relief attempt by Lieutenant General Sir Fenton Aylmer's Tigris Corps failed on 21 January in the battle of Hanna and Townshend put his garrison on half-rations. In March 1916 Aylmer failed again, and, his supplies exhausted, Townshend surrendered with 10,000 men in late April. Many of Townshend's soldiers perished in their harsh captivity.

In August 1916 General Sir Stanley Maude took over as commander-in-chief and resumed the offensive up the Tigris in December with two corps, an impressive force of 166,000. By 25 February, he had retaken Kut, and pressed on to the prize, Baghdad, which his main force entered on 11 March 1917. To secure Baghdad, Maude formed three columns, and sent them further up the Tigris, Euphrates, and Diyala rivers, with the aim of destroying the Turkish field army. Each column won a series of engagements, but Maude died of cholera on 18 November and was succeeded by Lieutenant General Sir William Marshall. In January 1918, a small British force under Major General L. C. Dunsterville (Dunsterforce) moved north from Baghdad in a race with the Turks to seize the Russian oilfields at Baku, some 800 km (500 miles) distant. Dunsterforce arrived only in August, and had to withdraw the following month after Turkish attacks.

In Mesopotamia, the river advances continued throughout 1918. Five thousand Turkish prisoners were taken in an engagement on the Euphrates at Khan Baghdad on 26 March, and Turkish troops gradually lost their enthusiasm for fighting. In late October 1918, faced with an impending Turkish armistice, a British force under Alexander Cobbe pushed up the Tigris to seize the oilfields at Mosul, fighting their last battle with the Turks near the ruins of the ancient Assyrian city of Asshur. The armistice with Turkey of 30 October brought about the surrender of Asshur (Ash Sharqat), but Cobbe moved on to occupy Mosul in early November. In 1918 Mesopotamia assumed its modern name of Iraq, under a British mandate, and imperial forces remained garrisoned there to subdue dissident tribesmen, a task which, with a foretaste of a later conflict, proved far from easy. The campaign cost the British army 27,000 fatalities, 13,000 of whom died of disease.

The Palestine Campaign

At the beginning of World War I the Suez Canal, an essential link with India, was the chief cause of Britain's desire to hold Egypt. In February 1915 a small Turkish force crossed Sinai and attacked the canal but was easily repulsed, and in 1916 the British gradually moved into Sinai, defeating a Turkish attack at Rumani on 3 August. The well-prepared Gaza position, stretching about 50 km (30 miles) from Gaza, near the coast, to Beersheba, blocked further advance.

The Battles of Gaza and Beersheba (1917)

On 26 March 1917 General Sir Archibald Murray, commander-in-chief of the Egyptian Expeditionary Force, attacked the Gaza position frontally with little success, and a second battle on 17–18 April was no more fruitful. Murray was replaced by General Sir Edmund Allenby, who inherited a more ambitious plan prepared by Lieutenant General Sir Philip Chetwode and Brigadier General Guy Dawnay. Leaving part of his army to fix the Turks and their German allies at Gaza, Allenby hooked round the desert flank, taking Beersheba and its all-important wells on 31 October. Lieutenant General Sir Henry Chauvel's Desert Mounted Force arrived as dusk fell and the 4th Australian Light Horse Brigade, lacking swords, charged with bayonets. The Gaza position had already been penetrated by a tank attack, and the Turks had no option but to withdraw to escape encirclement.

On 16 November the New Zealanders rode into Jaffa, cutting links between Jerusalem and the coast. Allenby had not merely taken the Gaza–Beersheba position, but had defeated the Turkish Eighth Army and brought Jerusalem within his grasp as well.

The Battle of Megiddo (1918)

Following the loss of Jerusalem on 9 December 1917 the Turkish Seventh and Eighth armies had regrouped on a well-fortified line from Jaffa to the Jordan. Sir Edmund Allenby deceived Liman von Sanders into believing that the attack would fall inland, whereas he attacked on the left, on the coastal plain, on 19 September 1918. An intense artillery bombardment opened a breach for the British XXI Corps, through which Allenby then pushed his cavalry, the Desert Mounted Corps. Local Jewish settlers helped by showing them the way through the marshes, enabling them to penetrate the Turkish positions and then exploit the breakthrough using cavalry, armoured cars, and aircraft. The RAF attacked the retreating Turkish columns, and helped force the Turks back to the Jordan. In just under a month the British and Commonwealth forces destroyed three Turkish armies (Seventh, Eighth, and Fourth, to the east), advanced 550 km (350 miles), and took 36,000 prisoners at a cost of only 853 dead.

The Turkish front had collapsed and the advance to Damascus was swift. On 1 October at 06.30 the 3rd Australian Light Horse entered the city. At 07.00 Colonel T. E. Lawrence arrived. Both claimed to be first. On 4 October the Turks informed the Germans that they were going to make a separate peace and an armistice was signed on 30 October.

THE GERMAN EAST AFRICAN CAMPAIGN

In 1914 Germany possessed four colonies in sub-Saharan Africa: Togoland, the Cameroons, South-West Africa (now Namibia), and East Africa (now Tanzania). It is the fight for the fourth of these that has most captured the public imagination. The last German troops did not surrender until two weeks after the armistice in Europe, on 25 November 1918. Their commander Major General Paul von Lettow-Vorbeck, became a German hero, the symbol of an army that deemed itself undefeated in the field. By the 1960s he had acquired another reputation, that of guerrilla leader. Neither interpretation can be fully sustained.

The German colonial troops, the *Schütztruppen*, were equipped and trained only for internal policing duties, but Lettow-Vorbeck, appointed through the influence of the German general staff, aimed to contribute to the main struggle in the event of war in Europe by drawing British forces away from their principal theatres and sought battle rather than shunned it. However, his isolation from Germany meant that neither trained European soldiers nor stocks of munitions were easily replaced. After the battle of Mahiwa, which Lettow-Vorbeck began on 15 October 1917, the Germans had exhausted all their smokeless cartridges and had to abandon German territory for Portuguese in the search for ammunition.

British strategy in Africa was much more limited. On 5 August 1914 it was decided that the principal objectives were to eliminate Germany's wireless stations and to deprive its navy of bases. Heinrich Schnee, the governor of German East Africa, anxious to protect the fruits of German colonialism, effectively cooperated in the achievement of both these objectives. The principal German cruiser in the region, SMS *Königsberg*, was unable to enter Dar es Salaam, and took refuge in the delta of the Rufiji river, where she was eventually located and sunk on 11 July 1915. The British colonial office lacked the troops to do much more, and it therefore called on the Indian army. Indian Expeditionary Force B, principally made up of second-line units, landed at German East Africa's second major port, Tanga, on 2 November 1914. Lettow-Vorbeck had concentrated his forces to the north, with a view to launching an attack into British East Africa, but was still able to redeploy and inflict a humiliating defeat on the British. The latter, hamstrung by overlapping administrative authorities and now deprived of any faith in the available Indian troops, did nothing in 1915, while the Germans raided the Uganda railway.

The campaign was reactivated in March 1916 with the arrival of South African reinforcements under General Jan Smuts. Like the Indians, the South Africans were not all easily deployable to the western front (though some fought there with great distinction), and to that extent Lettow-Vorbeck's strategy was not working. However, Smuts's aims were much more extensive than those of London. He wished to conquer the entire German colony and then trade territory with Portugal, so as to extend South Africa's frontier into Mozambique at least as far as the Zambezi. He therefore invaded German East Africa from the north, cutting across the axes of the two principal railway lines and neglecting the harbours on the coast. He had earned his military reputation as the leader of a Boer commando and conducted his campaign as though his mounted rifles could move as fast through regions infested with tsetse fly as they could across the veld, and accorded little recognition to the difference between rainy and dry seasons. His advance, although rapid, failed to grip and defeat the German forces. His troops entered Dar es Salaam on 3 September 1916, and were astride the Central railway, running from there to Tabora and Lake Tanganyika. Smuts should have paused but he did not, plunging on to the Rufiji river, and claiming that the campaign was all but over when in reality it had stalled.

Worrying for Smuts were Belgian territorial ambitions in the west. Debouching from the Congo into Ruanda and Urundi, the Belgians had reached Tabora in August 1916. Smuts's sub-imperialism was challenged even more fundamentally by the contribution of blacks to the campaign. The *Schütztruppen*, although officered by Europeans, were predominantly native Africans, and yet they had proved formidable opponents for the whites. On the British side the South Africans were particularly susceptible to malaria, and by early 1917 they were being replaced in the British order of battle by the black units of the West African Frontier Force and the King's African Rifles. Moreover, the collapse of animal transport meant that supply was largely dependent on human resources; the British ended up recruiting over a million labourers for the campaign. The long-term impact for Africa—in the development of the cash economy, in the penetration of colonial rule into areas hitherto unmapped, and in the erosion of chiefly or tribal authority—was immense.

Smuts was summoned to London in January 1917 to join the War Cabinet, and handed over his command to Major General Sir Arthur Hoskins. Hoskins set about remedying the worst of the health, transport, and supply problems, but in doing so aroused impatience in the War Cabinet in London, which could not understand why a campaign which Smuts had said was over was still continuing to drain Allied shipping: this was the one area in which Lettow-Vorbeck most nearly fulfilled his overall strategy. In April Hoskins was replaced by J. L. van Deventer, another Afrikaaner, who implemented Hoskins's plan but still failed to prevent the German remnants from escaping into Portuguese East Africa in November. For the next year, Lettow-Vorbeck's columns marched through Portuguese territory, fighting largely to secure supplies and munitions. The Allies still had a ration strength of 111,371 in the theatre at the war's end, but far fewer men actually fit to fight.

The campaign for German East Africa was effectively confined to a period of eighteen months, from March 1916 to November 1917. Its commencement had been delayed by the under-appreciated efforts of Lettow-Vorbeck's colleagues in South-West Africa (who had engaged the South Africans until 1915) and in the Cameroons (who had tied down British West African forces until 1916). The inadequacies of Portuguese military administration, rather than the failings of the British, go far to explain Lettow-Vorbeck's continued survival after all political purpose in continued fighting had been removed.

THE WAR AT SEA

At the outbreak of the war the German East Asiatic Squadron was in China and more ships were at various locations in the Pacific and the South Atlantic oceans. The German commander, Admiral Maximillian Graf von Spee, sent the cruiser *Emden* on a raiding voyage into the Indian Ocean where she was eventually sunk by the Australian cruiser HMAS *Sydney* on 9 November 1914. The rest of his squadron, including the modern ships *Scharnhorst*, *Gneisenau*, and *Nürnberg*, steamed eastwards. A squadron under Rear Admiral Sir Christopher Cradock moved from the South Atlantic to oppose them while the old battleship HMS *Canopus* and the modern armoured cruiser HMS *Defence* sailed to join him. When *Canopus* met Cradock at the Falklands he was told that she needed urgent work on her engines. If he waited while this was carried out he might miss Spee altogether, but if he left without he would lack the firepower to deal with *Scharnhorst* and *Gneisenau*. In the gallant but now misguided tradition of his service, Cradock put to sea.

The Battles of Coronel and the Falklands (1914)

On 1 November 1914 Admiral Maximilian von Spee was moving southwards down the coast of South America in search of HMS *Glasgow*, which had been reported as being at Valparaiso. At 16.40 she was sighted by *Leipzig* but soon identified the larger German ships and hastened to report to Cradock. The admiral signalled *Canopus* to join him, assumed, wrongly, that *Defence* was already on her way, and moved immediately to attack, hoping to get within range while the light favoured his gunners. But his squadron was held back by the slow *Otrano*, and Spee kept out of his reach until the sunset favoured his own gunners, and opened fire at 19.00. It was a hopeless fight: the British guns were mounted low, and many could not be used in the heavy sea. Both HMS *Good Hope* and HMS *Monmouth* were sent to the bottom. Only *Glasgow* and *Otrano* survived, and 1,654 men, including Cradock, were lost.

On 11 November Vice Admiral Sir Doveton Sturdee with the battlecruisers *Invincible* and *Inflexible*, three armoured cruisers, and two light cruisers sailed for the South Atlantic. They entered Port Stanley in the Falkland Islands on 7 December to take on coal. Spee had, in part, the same aim and also intended to destroy the port. He arrived on 8 December and discounted the reports of tell-tale tripod masts which indicated the presence of the battle cruisers, which could both outfight and outrun him. At first, when the elderly *Canopus* opened fire, he was confident he could out-steam his adversaries, but when he saw the battle cruisers he knew that he was doomed, and courteously signalled to his second in command, who had warned him of their presence: 'You were perfectly right.' Sturdee allowed time for his ships to get up steam and then set off in pursuit. The battle was as hopeless as the earlier action off Coronel, although this time the roles were reversed, and of the German light cruisers only the *Dresden* escaped, and the scant 200 survivors of the German squadron were pulled from the sea by their enemies. Spee and both his sailor sons died.

In the European theatre the British aim was to keep the German High Fleet confined to the North Sea and to do what damage opportunity and cunning could make possible. Poor planning and communications hampered an attempt in August 1914 to trap capital ships in the Heligoland Bight by endangering German torpedo boats. A German assault in January 1915 on British ships guarding fishing vessels on the Dogger Bank resulted in the sinking of the *Blücher*, but allowed most of the others to get away. A lucky shot from HMS *Lion* entered the aftermost turret of *Seydlitz* and caused explosions in the ammunition supply system. The Germans modified their ships to prevent this happening again. The British desire to achieve high rates of fire led to their leaving their magazines open to the same danger.

The Battle of Jutland (1916)

Fought between the British and German fleets in the North Sea about 120 km (75 miles) from the Danish coast, Jutland (31 May–2 June 1916) was the biggest naval battle of World War I, and in terms of the forces engaged, close to being the largest naval battle ever fought. Vice Admiral Reinhard Scheer, the German High Seas Fleet commander, aimed to reduce the overall quantitative superiority of the Royal Navy by ambushing part of the Grand Fleet, perhaps Vice Admiral Sir David Beatty's battlecruiser force. For his part, Admiral Sir John Jellicoe hoped to bring the whole of his Grand Fleet to bear and to destroy the German fleet, once and for all. Jellicoe needed to be cautious, however, for, as Churchill aptly said, only he 'could lose the war in an afternoon'.

Scheer undertook a number of operations to draw the British out. In April 1916 an assault on Lowestoft was intercepted by Commodore Reginald Tyrwhitt's Harwich Force and the planned shelling of Yarmouth was abandoned. An attack on Sunderland scheduled for 17 May was imperilled by German delay, and Scheer decided instead to attack Scandinavian shipping of the Danish coast. The fleet sailed on 31 May.

British Naval Intelligence (Room 40) reported the imminent German sailing to Jellicoe and the British Grand Fleet put to sea some four and a half hours before the Germans, but without knowing where Scheer's ships were going. Beatty's battlecruiser force was screening the approach of the Grand Fleet just as Rear Admiral Franz Hipper's Scouting Groups were running ahead of the High Seas Fleet.

The German battlecruiser force under Hipper engaged Beatty at 15.48. *Lion* was hit and only saved by the swift closing of the magazine doors to Q turret. *Indefatigable* was not so lucky and blew up with the loss of all but two of her complement. Beatty turned to increase the range as well as to draw his adversaries into the grasp of the Grand Fleet and was joined by Rear Admiral H. Evan-Thomas's 5th Battle Squadron of four fast battleships. Next the battlecruiser *Queen Mary* exploded, but the newly joined British battleships were by this time hitting Hipper hard.

At 16.40 the rest of Scheer's fleet joined. Beatty's losses were unsurprisingly heavy but he drew the whole German fleet behind him as he fought his way towards the British Grand Fleet speeding south towards the battle.

Jellicoe had received signals too sparse to convey the course of the action and it was the chance encounter of *Iron Duke* with the embattled *Lion* that revealed Scheer's presence to him. He turned south-east by east to cross the German line in an enveloping curve and to get between them and their base, silhouetting them against the setting sun. Scheer, realizing he had now encountered the whole of the British fleet, sought to extricate himself from this perilous situation by ordering, at 18.33, a 'battle turn'. The rearmost ship immediate turned, followed by the next nearest the end of the line, and so on; within ten minutes they were heading west. It was half an hour before Jellicoe had understood what was happening and altered course. At 18.55 Scheer turned again, inadvertently heading for the centre of Jellicoe's line. When he realized his peril he ordered 'Battlecruisers at the enemy! Give it everything!' and then ordered another sharp turn, covering his retreat with a destroyer attack. The Grand Fleet turned away at 19.04 to minimize the danger from torpedoes. Although many of Scheer's ships had been badly damaged, the greater part of the High Seas Fleet escaped. The Germans had the better of some confused fighting at night, and reached port early on the afternoon of 1 June.

Aided by a combination of British signalling blunders, cautious tactics, and luck the Germans had managed to avoid destruction. Inadequate shells, design faults in the British battlecruisers, and their lack of effective damage control made for a disappointing result for the British, who lost 3 capital ships (all battlecruisers), 3 cruisers, and 8 destroyers, and 5,069 dead. The Germans lost 2 capital ships (1 battleship and 1 battlecruiser), 3 cruisers, 5 destroyers, and 2,115 dead. But the losses were proportionate to those engaged, and the force ratio for the Germans the day after the battle was worse than it had been before, and the High Fleet did not sail thereafter. The strategic situation in the North Sea, which made a German defeat eventually inevitable, was confirmed. Nonetheless the British, expecting another Trafalgar, were grievously disappointed at the battle's outcome.

The German submarines, U-boats, were the most effective arm of the service and the conduct of submarine warfare became an issue that eventually brought the USA into the war. They had ten modern boats in 1914 and a slightly greater number of superannuated submarines for training and coastal work; 134 new U-boats were built during the war as well as 132 UB-boats, which were smaller and with a short range, and 79 mine-laying UC-boats.

The Germans used their boats against merchant shipping. In the early days the U-boat surfaced and allowed the victim's crew to take to their lifeboats before torpedoing their prey, but such courtesies were soon forgotten and the attack came as a complete surprise. The U-boat campaign slackened after the sinking of the *Lusitania*, a passenger liner correctly believed to be carrying munitions of war, on 7 May 1915. America perceived it to be a murderous attack on innocent civilians and, lest the USA declare war, the Germans reined in their campaign. In the hope of bringing Britain to its knees before American intervention could tip the balance of the war against her, Germany resumed unrestricted submarine warfare in February 1917. The Royal Navy finally agreed to what proved to be the effective counter-strategy, the convoy system, on 10 May and shipping losses declined dramatically. German U-boat losses, sunk and captured, had risen to 192 by the end of the war. The Royal Navy had seventeen modern, and 40 older, submarines in service in 1914 and by November 1918 there were 137 boats in operation. Wartime losses amounted to 54.

6 World War II

World War II flared up from the embers of World War I. Indeed, there is a case not simply for connecting the two world wars by what was in effect the long truce of the 1920s and 1930s, but for marking their real end, not with the defeat of Germany and Japan in 1945, but with the end of the Cold War and the reunification of Germany a generation later. However, while World War I had certainly deserved the global implication of its title, its origin lay in Europe, and what happened in the rest of the world reflected this. World War II, in contrast, had two separate sources, one in Europe and the other in the Far East. Although these conflicts were linked because they shared some common combatants, and presented Britain and America with conflicts of strategic priorities, they were the result of distinct processes of development, and resulted in two different sorts of war.

Both can be traced back to World War I. The Treaty of Versailles, which ended it, embodied the passions of US president Woodrow Wilson, creating new states like Czechoslovakia and Yugoslavia and reviving Poland. Wilson hoped that international order would be preserved by the League of Nations, which would apply sanctions to rogue states, but America declined to accede to the League, and it never grew the teeth it needed. Moreover, the USA was a net creditor on a grand scale, and demanded payment in full: 'They hired the money, didn't they?' observed President Calvin Coolidge.

Versailles was a calamity for Germany. It acknowledged 'war guilt', was ordered to pay reparations to reflect the damage its armies had caused, and had sharp limits imposed upon its military strength. These factors might not in themselves have caused a crisis had it not been for the repercussions of the Wall Street crash of 1929, and in particular the hyperinflation which undermined the political centre and contributed to support for the Nazi party, whose leader, Adolf Hitler, became chancellor in 1933. He swiftly repudiated Versailles, declared his intention of rearming, and looked towards ethnic German populations now within post-Versailles states.

Italy, which had eventually entered the war on a refined calculation of self-interest and made territorial gains at its end, had already turned its back on democratic institutions, with the Fascist leader Benito Mussolini attaining dictatorial power, achieving material progress at the price of stifling dissent and debate. He leant hard on both Greece and Yugoslavia, and invaded Ethiopia in 1935: when the League fumbled with ineffectual sanctions he resigned from it. There was mutual sympathy between Hitler and Mussolini, and both sent troops and aircraft to support the Nationalists in the Spanish Civil War of 1936-9. By this time Hitler had taken the first aggressive step of his own, sending troops into the Rhineland, demilitarized by Versailles. We know now, as contemporaries did not, that he had ordered his generals not to persist if they were opposed by the French. However, the alliance which had won the war had not survived its conclusion. France was racked by

Sherman tanks of the 40th Tank Battalion near St Vith in the battle of the Bulge, December 1944.

economic depression and political extremism, and the last decade of the Third Republic, the Republic of Pals, saw a succession of weak coalition governments unwilling to take firm action. Britain had been wrestling with a depression of its own and, haunted by the bloodletting of 1914–18, had many politicians, like Neville Chamberlain, who was to become prime minister in 1937, anxious to maintain peace almost at any price.

Japan had supported the Allies during World War I, but had gained less than it thought it deserved by doing so, and it too had suffered from the effects of the great depression. At the Washington Conference of 1922 and the London naval treaty of 1930 the Japanese accepted limitations on the size of their fleet, but proceeded to produce warships of the utmost technical sophistication. The Tokyo government found it hard to control factionalized and nationalistic armed forces. In 1931 officers of the Kwantung Army, the Japanese force which had remained in Manchuria since the war, manufactured an 'incident' which led to the invasion of the whole of Manchuria. International condemnation followed, and increasing American pressure, which included an embargo on the supply of fuel and scrap metal, actually strengthened the hand of the war party. After the outbreak of war in Europe and initial German victories, Japan concluded a Tripartite Pact, recognizing 'the leadership of Germany and Italy in the establishment of a new order in Europe', while German and Italy supported Japanese aims in 'Greater East Asia'.

War came to Europe after a series of crises: the remilitarization of the Rhineland, the *anschluss*, the union of Germany and Austria, seizure of the German-speaking parts of Czechoslovakia after the Munich agreement of 1938, and eventually the invasion of Poland in September 1939. Hitler had prepared the way for the latter by concluding a non-aggression pact with the Soviet Union, whose troops also entered Poland to partition the country. The first phase of the war ended with the German invasion of France and the Low Countries in the spring of 1940. Winston Churchill, who had taken over from Chamberlain while fighting was in progress, rallied Britain and rejected any suggestion of making peace, and the RAF's victory in the battle of Britain made it impossible for the Germans to invade.

And then, like Napoleon in 1805, Hitler turned east, launching an attack on Russia in June 1941. He was encouraged to do so by the remarkable success achieved by the combination of tanks and air power in 1939 and 1940. In fact blitzkrieg, as these tactics became known, was never a deeply considered doctrine, but relied as much on enemy flaws as on German skills, and in mechanizing only the smaller part of their army the Germans left the rest of it with horse-drawn transport. The Germans came close to beating Russia in 1941, but the very philosophies which helped endue Hitler's armed forces with such powerful resolve also made them unable to take advantage of the fragility of the Soviet Union. They made no attempt to exploit national and ethic tensions until it was too late, and Stalin, cruel and ruthless though he was, was able to convert this epic struggle into 'The Great Patriotic War', restoring officers' titles and badges of rank, abolished after the revolution, and, on a wider scale, summoning up old Russia to reinforce communism.

World War I was ultimately decided by a long attritional contest on the western front, which left its enduring mark upon the British, French, and German armies. Although the dual character of World War II meant that its events were never absolutely analogous with those of the First, it was the eastern front in 1941–5 that eventually ripped the guts out of the German army in a long and bitter struggle which, for scale, duration, bitterness, and intensity, has no equal in history. German defeat at Stalingrad in the winter of 1942–3 marked the turning of the tide, and with the failure of their attack at Kursk in the summer of 1943 the Germans squandered their last major armoured reserve. However, even when it was straining every nerve to hold the creaking front together the German army never ceased to be a dangerous opponent, and after the western Allies had landed in Normandy and southern France in mid-1944 it fought resolutely on two fronts, though there was little doubt the eastern front enjoyed primacy, swallowing up the most front-line divisions and war production. Berlin was finally taken by the Russians in early May 1945: Hitler committed suicide amongst its ruins.

Important though it was, the eastern front might not have led to the defeat of Germany in and of itself. First, other theatres of war helped syphon off German strength. Expulsion from France in 1940 had left the British fighting against German and Italian forces in North Africa, where victory at El Alamein in 1942 was speedily followed by the Anglo-American landings, code-named operation TORCH, in French North Africa. The Germans and Italians, caught between the British and Americans advancing from the west and the British from the east, eventually surrendered in May 1943. The Allies moved on to invade Sicily, clearing it after a lacklustre campaign which did, however, drive Italy out of the war. In September the Allies invaded the Italian mainland, and spent the next twenty-one months fighting their way up it against stiff German resistance across a landscape of ridges and river lines that might have been made for defence. Rome fell on 4 June 1944, just before D-Day banished news of Italy to the inside pages, but it was not until 2 May the following year that German commanders in Italy surrendered. The campaign remains controversial. Major General J. F. C. Fuller maintained that 'for lack of strategic sense and tactical imagination' it was 'unique in military history'. The Germans suffered more casualties than the Allies, and the troops they deployed in Italy might have made a substantial difference had they fought elsewhere. But so too could the Allied soldiers who fought in Italy, and it is far from easy to decide who was fixing whom and to what overall effect.

Neither the Mediterranean campaign nor Allied invasion of Europe (nor, indeed, Britain's very survival) would have been possible without victory in the battle of the Atlantic. This, at its height between 1940 and 1943, ebbed and flowed as the Allies brought in fresh countermeasures to deal with improving German submarines and tactics. It cost the lives of more than 80,000 Allied sailors and saw the German submarine service become the most dangerous major branch of any armed service. But as long as the Atlantic lifeline was held open, then America's burgeoning might could be shipped to Europe, confronting the Germans with a war on two fronts.

The strategic bombing offensive against German also played its controversial part. It grew from modest beginnings, through the first thousand-bomber raid in May 1942, to the full-fledged Combined Bomber Offensive, whose policy of 'progressive destruction and dislocation of the German military, industrial and economic system, and the under-mining of the morale of the German people' was enshrined in a directive of the January 1943 Casablanca conference. The RAF's Bomber Command attacked by night and the American Eighth Air Force by day, reducing Germany's cities to rubble. The campaign did not, as some of its authors had hoped, bring about the complete collapse of either civilian morale or industrial production, though it did terrible damage to both. It was also costly for the attackers (Bomber Command lost over 55,000 aircrew killed), and, especially at the end of the war, when the details of destruction became clear, there was growing unease at the morality of the campaign. Nations make war as they must, not as they might wish to. Bombing was the only way in which Britain could contribute meaningfully to the war in its first years, and the campaign not only reduced German production but forced the diversion of vital aircraft and anti-aircraft guns to the defence of the Reich. The destruction of Dresden in February 1945 was perhaps the most shocking example of this cruel necessity, and the rebuilding of the city's Frauenkirche, completed in 2005, helped citizens of Dresden, as well as bomber crews and their relatives, continue the process of understanding and forgiveness.

Even the struggle against Germany presented Allied leaders with conflicting priorities. Winston Churchill was by instinct and experience inclined to seek an indirect approach, and preferred to postpone the cross-Channel invasion until he was absolutely sure that it would succeed. The Americans, in contrast, favoured a direct approach, and although Churchill succeeded in punching above his weight in the early Anglo-American conferences he had lost the ability to do so by the time he met President Roosevelt at Casablanca in early 1943. Here he did not simply agree to a target date for D-Day, in the summer of 1944, but found himself upstaged by Roosevelt's declaration that the only terms the Allies would accept would be unconditional surrender.

The United States had begun to supply Britain with military equipment, albeit on a commercial basis, before it entered the war itself. However, Roosevelt's countrymen fought shy of entangling relationships, and he succeeded in getting conscription through Congress by a single vote. The Japanese attack on the naval base of Pearl Harbor changed all that. Although some historians suggest that Roosevelt had foreknowledge of the attack and took no action so as to guarantee American entry into the war, it was probably error, not conspiracy, that prevented the Americans from parrying the stroke. Germany adhered to the terms of the Tripartite Pact and declared war on the USA, greatly simplifying Roosevelt's task, and the Americans agreed to put 'Germany First' in their strategic priorities. Such was America's military and economic strength that it was in fact able to wage war on two fronts, one in the Pacific and the other in Europe and the Mediterranean, and eventually to prevail in each.

However, the war in the Pacific began with a series of reverses for the USA, Australia, Britain, and the Netherlands, with the loss of Hong Kong, Malaya, Singapore (the scene of the greatest surrender in British military history), the Dutch East Indies, and the Philippines. In the summer of 1942 the battles of the Coral Sea and Midway, in which carrier-borne aircraft played the leading role, underlining a fundamental change in the character of war at sea, showed that the tide had begun to turn, although it was not until the Japanese decided to evacuate Guadalcanal in January 1943 that the current was really running against them. The Americans and their allies attacked along two distinct axes, with General Douglas MacArthur thrusting from New Guinea (the scene of some dogged fighting by the Australians) through the Dutch East Indies and on to the Philippines and thence to Okinawa. Admiral Chester Nimitz, meanwhile, proceeded by way of 'island-hopping', taking first the Marshalls and then the Marianas before securing the tiny island of Iwo Jima, whose defence typified the routinely suicidal courage of the Japanese: of the garrison of more than 20,000 men, only 216 were captured.

While the Americans were pushing inexorably across the Pacific to Japan, the British, bundled unceremoniously out of Burma by the first surge of Japanese conquest, stemmed the wave on its northern borders. In early 1943 the first Chindit expedition showed that British soldiers could face the Japanese on equal terms in the jungle, but it was not until June 1944 that the Japanese began to fall back from Imphal and Kohima. In the meantime, Allied pilots had flown supplies to embattled China (whose part in the ultimate defeat of

Japan deserves more recognition than it generally receives) 'over the hump', across some of the worst flying country in the world.

Although the war's theatres were not directly linked, June 1944 was hugely significant in four of them, and does enable us to discern a broad pattern of rise and fall. It marked the last of the Japanese offensive in Burma; saw the Western Allies land in Normandy, and witnessed both the fall of Rome and the beginning of operation BAGRATION, in which the Russians destroyed the German Army Group Centre and liberated Belarus.

Like Germany, Japan too was bombed, first by Colonel James Doolittle's carrier-launched bombers in April 1942, then by aircraft based on Chinese airfields, and lastly, as the American advance brought Japan within range, by bombers flying from Pacific islands. Japanese cities, where factories were often surrounded by crowded wooden houses, were particularly susceptible to incendiary bombs, and an attack on Tokyo on March 1945 killed at least 83,000 people. Shattering conventional attacks on Japanese cities helped set the context of what was to come. The resolute Japanese defence of Okinawa and Iwo Jima showed just how costly the invasion of the home islands was likely to be. There was a feeling, especially marked in America, that the Japanese were worthy of harsher treatment than the Germans because of their 'sneak attack' on Pearl Harbor and their treatment of Allied prisoners. In September 1944 Roosevelt and Churchill had agreed that when an atomic bomb was finally developed, 'it might perhaps . . . be used against the Japanese'. President Truman, who succeeded Roosevelt in April 1944, admitted in his diary that 'even if the Japs are savages, ruthless, merciless and fanatic, we as the leader of the world for common welfare cannot drop this terrible bomb on the old capital [Kyoto] or the new [Tokyo]'.

The first atomic bomb was dropped on Hiroshima on 6 August, killing perhaps 100,000 people instantly, and a second bomb was dropped on Nagasaki three days later. Russia declared war on Japan shortly before the second bomb fell, and its troops jabbed down into Manchuria in a bravura display of operational art honed on the eastern front. The Japanese government surrendered unconditionally on 14 August. One young officer, destined for the invasion of Japan, reflected that: 'We were going to live. We were going to grow up to adulthood after all.'

THE EUROPEAN THEATRE

The Polish Campaign (1939)

The invasion of Poland in 1939 may have been very likely, sandwiched as it was between Germany and Russia when both were under the absolute dominion of the most ruthless rulers in their histories; but it was not inevitable. The rulers of the USSR (Josef Stalin) and of Germany (Adolf Hitler) concluded the Molotov–Ribbentrop Pact, a non-aggression pact whose secret clauses dealt with the dismemberment of Poland, and a week later, on 1 September, after a fabricated border clash involving concentration-camp inmates dressed in Polish uniforms, the Germans introduced Poland and the world to blitzkrieg—lightning war. Operation WEISS involved Army Group North, with fifteen divisions in East Prussia and Pomerania under General Fedor von Bock, and the main Army Group South with 26 divisions in Silesia under General Gerd von Rundstedt. Between 1 and 6 September the Luftwaffe destroyed the Polish air force (a remnant fled to Romania) and thereafter Stuka dive-bombers flew freely over Polish territory, hammering communications neural points and any sign of organized resistance ahead of the two panzer-led pincers that encircled and destroyed the Polish army.

Correctly calculating that the Maginot Line and the passive mentality that produced it precluded a direct advance by France into Germany, and that Belgian neutrality would inhibit any other incursion, Hitler denuded his western frontiers and committed his military forces to a campaign designed to achieve swift results. Britain's ultimatum and declaration of war on 3 September was discounted in advance and on 17 September another reason for swiftness was revealed when the Soviets attacked Poland on the Belorussian and Ukrainian fronts.

Things did not all go the Germans' way. The fast-moving mechanized columns proved vulnerable to flank attacks, and the Poles managed one such on 9–12 September at Kutno, mauling a division from General Johannes Blaskowitz's Eighth Army before themselves being defeated. By contrast, the Red Army encountered little opposition, having waited until the Poles were defeated before rolling in to pick up the spoils. Warsaw held out until 27 September and technically the campaign continued until 5 October, but it was really all over by mid-September. There are no accurate estimates of Polish losses, but the Germans had only 8,000 dead among their 50,000 casualties.

The Norwegian Campaign (1940)

Britain and France resolved in early 1940 to mine Norwegian inshore waters and land troops at Narvik and other ports to strangle the flow of iron ore and minerals to Germany. Suspicions were afoot that Germany was in any case planning to occupy Norway, to protect its economic interests. The mining went ahead directly, but before Allied troops could be landed, the Germans invaded Denmark on 8 April and Norway on the 9th, but were surprised to encounter opposition since the collaborator Vidkun Quisling had suggested that Norway might fall without a fight. The cruiser *Blücher* covering an amphibious landing force was sunk off Oslo, but Norway's capital fell to the first ever combat use of airborne forces, which captured the airport and then the city. Other airborne troops seized Stavanger, while Bergen (though with the loss of the cruiser *Königsberg*), Kristiansand (with the loss of the *Karlsrühe*), and Trondheim were also captured. Narvik, where ten German destroyers quickly landed 2,000 mountain troops under Lieutenant General Eduard Dietl, fell almost without a struggle.

Before the German warships could leave, a Royal Naval destroyer force attacked them, sinking two and damaging five. Three days later another flotilla, led by the battleship *Warspite*, sank the remaining vessels, crippling the tiny Kriegsmarine (which had possessed only 22 destroyers) and stranding Dietl. Although the powerful Royal Navy deployed several vessels off the Norwegian coast to support the mining, German air power proved decisive: the first occasion in which air power cancelled out naval power. In mid-April, in poorly planned operations, Anglo-French forces landed 12,000 men at Namos and Andalsnes, north and south of Trondheim respectively, but were unable to be resupplied due to the attentions of the Luftwaffe, and were driven back by German ground troops. Both were evacuated by 2 May. Another overwhelming Allied force landed to retake Narvik on 13 May but was more frustrated by disagreements between army and navy commanders than by any opposition from Dietl's mountain troops. Although the port was captured a fortnight later, Dietl had been supplied by air, in the first campaign where aerial supply was an influential factor, and managed to tie down a large Allied-Norwegian force. Under constant Luftwaffe bombardment and unable to sustain the Narvik force due to the German invasion of France, all Allied troops were evacuated from Narvik on 8 June, but much valuable equipment and stores had to be left behind.

The Fall of France (1940)

In the history of warfare few campaigns between great and approximately equal powers have been decided so swiftly and conclusively as the German conquest of western Europe in May and June 1940. Within five days of the opening of the campaign on 10 May, the Netherlands had surrendered, the French defences on and behind the Meuse had disintegrated, and the French prime minister was already talking of defeat.

The original plan, for a hook through Belgium, was very similar to that adopted in 1914, except that the objectives were the capture of the Channel ports and the subjugation of the Low Countries rather than the conquest of France. The credit for perceiving the defects of this plan and devising an alternative to secure a decisive victory belongs chiefly to Erich von Manstein, Army Group A's chief of staff. It should be added that by the early weeks of 1940 the German army high command (OKH) and some senior commanders had also become dissatisfied with the original plan. Essentially, Manstein proposed to transfer the principal role and the bulk of the armoured units (initially seven out of ten panzer divisions) to Army Group A, and to stake everything on a surprise attack through the Ardennes against what was known to be the weakest sector of the French defences (the Sedan–Dinant sector of the Meuse). Army Group B still had the important task of drawing the Allied First Army Group into Belgium and holding it there, but the role of deep penetration now fell to Army Group A.

On 10 May 1940 Germany had 136 divisions in the west of which only 10 were armoured (panzer), 7 motorized, 1 cavalry, and 1 airborne. The French and British together had 104 divisions (94 and 10 respectively) to which 22 Belgian divisions were added on 10 May. The French total included 3 armoured divisions, 3 light-mechanized divisions (as powerfully equipped as the panzer divisions), and 5 cavalry divisions. On the question of total comparative tank strengths on the western front, the French by themselves had more tanks than the Germans—3,254 against 2,574. As for quality, many French tanks proved inferior to the Germans because they were slower, had a more limited radius of action, and were poorly provided with radius.

The only respect in which the Allies were markedly inferior was in the air, but here German superiority has sometimes been exaggerated. German air strength in May 1940 was as follows: 1,016 fighters, 248 medium bombers, 1,120 bombers, 342 Stuka dive-bombers, and 500 scout planes, a total of 3,226 aircraft. The French air force then possessed only some 1,120 modern aircraft of which 700 were fighters, 140 bombers, and 380 scout planes. To these must be added the British contribution which initially consisted of the air component of the British Expeditionary Force (BEF) (4 fighter squadrons, 4 bomber squadrons, and 5 army cooperation squadrons) and the Advanced Air Striking Force (10 bomber and 2 fighter squadrons); in all 220 bombers and 130 other aircraft. Again the German air forces were better organized for their immediate purpose. The Stukas had serious defects in slow speed and vulnerability, but they played a vital part in the crucial first days.

The decisive breakthrough occurred on Army Group A's front. By the evening of 12

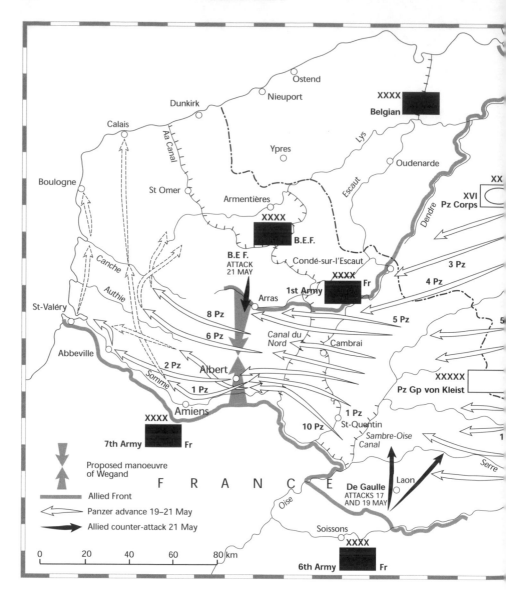

May, the leading German armoured divisions had reached the Meuse in two places, at least two days earlier than the defenders had thought possible. Sedan—on the east bank— had been captured by the 1st and 10th Panzer Divisions (General Heinz Guderian), while the 7th Panzer Division (Major General Erwin Rommel) had reached Dinant. It was typical of the Germans' offensive spirit that they pressed straight on with the crossings on 13 May, again to the bewilderment of the French. All the bridges had been blown and French opposition was stiff, yet by the end of the day four precarious bridgeheads had been established on the west bank. At Sedan, especially, the French artillery was almost paralysed by Stuka air attacks.

World War II: the fall of France, 1940

There was still an opportunity for the Allies to launch a counter-attack while the Germans were confined to congested bridgeheads and makeshift bridges, but it was not taken. The Germans had deliberately struck at the junction of the two French armies (Second and Ninth) which contained many poorly trained reserve units. On the evening of 14 May General André Corap, commanding Ninth Army, mistakenly ordered a general retreat to a new defensive position about 16 km (10 miles) to the west. Ninth Army's withdrawal turned into a rout, while to the south General Charles Huntziger's Second Army fared little better. By nightfall Guderian's bridgehead was already some 48 km (30 miles) wide and 24 km (15 miles) deep. That same day British and French bombers with

French fighter cover made heroic but vain attempts to destroy the vital bridges at Sedan. Out of 170 bombers (the majority of them Blenheims) about 85 were shot down.

Thus by the evening of 15 May the Germans had already gained a decisive advantage. All three panzer corps had broken clean through the Meuse bridgeheads and were thrusting westward virtually unopposed in the chaotic rear areas behind the French Ninth Army. Although the dynamic panzer leaders, particularly Guderian and Rommel, were full of confidence and already were thinking of driving relentlessly to the Channel coast, which the 2nd Panzer Division reached on 20 May, some of their senior commanders, and Hitler himself, were astonished by the speed of the advance and became day by day more anxious about overextension.

With every passing day the Allies' prospects of launching an effective counter-attack diminished. General Maurice Gamelin had been slow to see the need to pull back his forces from Belgium to avoid being cut off, and only on 19 May, the day of his replacement by General Maxime Weygand, did he issue a directive for a combined counter-offensive from north and south of the Somme to pinch off the German corridor and so isolate panzers from infantry. The one minor action which temporarily worried the Germans and had some long-term effect was the British counterstroke at Arras.

The Battle of Arras (1940)

On 21 May 1940, the 7th Panzer Division under Major General Rommel, leading the inner flank of the thrust from the Meuse, was temporarily checked south of Arras by an improvised British formation, 'Frankforce'. Due to hurried assembly the counter-attack was initiated by only two columns of tanks (4th and 7th Royal Tank Regiments), followed closely by two battalions of the Durham Light Infantry, but with little artillery and no air support. That morning the columns moved from Vimy to the west of Arras and then swung eastward across the Arras–Baumetz railway, striking the 6th and 7th Rifle Regiments and the SS Totenkopf regiment just as they were beginning a disorderly advance through the villages of Wailly, Ficheux, and Agny. Impervious to much German antiarmour fire the British tanks wrought havoc among the chaos of troops, guns, and transport.

Although anticipating a counter-attack, Rommel was so shaken that he thought five British divisions were attacking. To stem the retreat Rommel himself took command of the German guns at Wailly: his aide-de-camp was killed at his side. Only on the arrival of the 25th Panzer Regiment at dusk, and after twelve hours' fighting, did the few surviving British tanks and infantrymen withdraw north of Arras. The town was finally abandoned on the night of 23 May. The results of the British attack were ephemeral, but the wider significance of the Arras episode was that it reinforced the apprehension already displayed by General Gunther von Kluge, General Ewald von Kleist, and General Gerd von Rundstedt that the armoured spearhead was running too many risks.

The experience helped to influence the fateful decision to halt the panzers on 24 May until the morning of the 27th. There were both political and operational reasons for the halt order: the need to let the Luftwaffe deliver the *coup de grâce*; to rest the armoured divisions before the second phase of the offensive; and to define the roles of Army Groups A and B in destroying the Allied forces in the shrinking pocket around Dunkirk. Often neglected is the yet more important fact that the German maps and handbooks described the terrain as unsuitable for both wheeled and tracked vehicles, save on the roads. It is clear that it was not Hitler's intention that the BEF should escape: rather he shared the widespread German belief that escape by sea was impossible.

The Evacuation of Dunkirk (1940)

When the British Expeditionary Force (BEF) was cut off from the bulk of the French armies by the German panzer drive, Field Marshal Lord Gort began to consider a withdrawal to the coast. At the same time the War Office envisaged the evacuation of non-combatants and key specialists from the Channel ports. Preparations were entrusted to Vice Admiral Sir Bertram Ramsay, and the fact that a room in his headquarters below Dover castle had housed electrical generators may have persuaded his staff to christen the evacuation DYNAMO.

On 21 May preparations were increased to include large-scale evacuation, and on the 25th Gort made the courageous decision—for he was then acting without political authority and in the face of French pressure to counter-attack—to evacuate from Dunkirk. The evacuation began on 26 May, and over the days that followed vessels of all sorts—including warships, passenger ferries, and privately owned 'little ships'—took off troops from the east mole in Dunkirk itself and the open beaches to its north under fierce air attack.

In all 338,000 men, 120,000 of them French, were evacuated. Of the 693 British ships which took part, about 200 were sunk and as many again damaged, while RAF fighter Command, whose efforts were usually invisible to troops on the beaches, lost 106 aircraft. British prime minister Winston Churchill warned that 'wars are not won by evacuation', but Dunkirk was both psychologically and materially vital to the British war effort. Although the BEF had lost its equipment, it formed a nucleus of trained manpower, and its almost miraculous survival, as much a consequence of unseasonably fine weather and German errors as British gallantry, reinforced popular resolve. Many Frenchmen, however, were less enthusiastic about the operation, seeing it as evidence of British self-interest.

Although Dunkirk was treated as something of a triumph in Britain, from the continental viewpoint it marked the brilliant climax of the first phase of a whirlwind campaign. In three weeks the Germans had taken over a million prisoners at the cost to themselves of only 60,000 casualties. The Dutch and Belgian armies had been eliminated, the latter surrendering on 28 May after a far more gallant resistance than is normally ascribed to it. The French had lost 30 divisions—nearly a third of their total strength and including virtually all their armour. They had also lost the support of twelve British divisions. General Maxime Weygand was left with only 66 divisions (many of them already depleted) to defend an unprepared front, longer than that originally attacked, stretching from Abbeville to the Maginot Line.

When the second phase of the German offensive (code name FALL ROT) began on 5 June, the French military situation was already hopeless. Guderian had been promoted to the command of his own Panzergruppe as part of Army Group A operating east of Rheims while Army Group B, including Major General Rommel's 7th Panzer, attacked across the Somme in the west. The resistance offered by British and French forces south of Amiens and Abbeville in the last days of May had been fierce, and the newly promoted Brigadier General Charles de Gaulle had commanded an assault on the Mont Caubert, south of Abbeville, which came within a hand's breadth of success on 29 May. On 5 June Rommel

crossed the Somme north of Hangest and raced towards Rouen, cutting off the 51st (Highland) Division which was obliged to surrender at Saint-Valéry-en-Caux on 12 June. The reinforcements the British sent to Cherbourg, the Canadian Division, and the 52nd Division were ordered to evacuate on 13 June as Army Group B poured through the gap between the French Army of Paris and their Tenth Army to the west. The next day the Germans entered Paris, Guderian entered Langres, and Army Group A began operations against the Maginot Line.

For some time the military leaders had been talking of 'saving their honour' rather than victory, and those who felt with de Gaulle, now Under Secretary for War, that resistance must be continued even, if necessary, outside metropolitan France, found themselves in a minority. The French cabinet had discussed the possibility of seeking an armistice independently of Britain even before Dunkirk, and thereafter Prime Minister Paul Reynaud steadily lost ground to those, including Marshal Henri Pétain and Weygand, who favoured an immediate ceasefire to save France from further loss. Reynaud's resignation in favour of Pétain on 16 June had signalled the end of any surviving hopes that the struggle could be continued in Brittany or in North Africa. On 22 June the French capitulated at Compiègne.

The Battle of Britain (1940)

In the summer of 1940 the Luftwaffe attempted to win air superiority over Britain as a sine qua non for an invasion code-named SEALION. On 30 June Reichsmarschall Hermann Göring issued multiple directives to draw the RAF into combat over the Channel by attacking coastal convoys (which the Admiralty unwisely continued to run), and bombing the British aircraft industry and RAF airfields. This dispersion of effort was the first of a triad of reasons why the RAF won the battle. The second was Air Chief Marshal Sir Hugh Dowding, in charge of Fighter Command since 1937. He had been involved in the procurement of the Spitfire and the Hurricane, and in the development and deployment of radar. He resisted demands by Churchill to send his reserve of fighters to France, and refused to commit them in strength to defending the convoys, or indeed to involve them in mass battles at all. The third was that the Luftwaffe was not well equipped for a sustained air superiority campaign. Like the RAF's Hurricanes and Spitfires, the Messerschmitt Bf 109 was a short-range aircraft, but the former were fighting over their own bases. Likewise a downed pilot who survived was lost to the Luftwaffe but returned immediately to his RAF squadron. But underlying these three was the existence of radar (radio detection and ranging), without which the work of the Royal Observer Corps and the operations rooms would have been impossible. It took fifteen minutes for a German raid to reach a target just south of London, and seventeen minutes for the British Spitfire squadron to respond and gain enough height to attack; the raiders had only a slight advantage at the outset of the battle and the increasing skill of the radar operators soon overcame it.

The battle officially began on 13 August. The RAF had about 700 operational fighters and during August the Luftwaffe believed that, by 19 August when bad weather

---

The evacuation of Dunkirk. Queues of men wait to be taken off the beach by boats ferrying men to ships offshore. The majority embarked on vessels moored alongside the harbour mole.

temporarily halted the raids, they had destroyed 500 of them, whereas the number of operational aircraft was still as high as 600. Realizing that the fighters were still able to resist, Göring redirected the attacks onto RAF fighter stations, sending small groups of bombers to hit the airfields and large fighter formations to destroy the fighters that were bound to hurry to defend them. The new tactics came very close to success, but, perhaps in retaliation for an air raid by the British on Berlin late in August, the Germans switched their attention to London. On 7 September the Blitz began with a daylight raid of 300 bombers escorted by 600 fighters and took the RAF by surprise. The fires that raged in London guided 180 night bombers to increase the damage. Large formations of bombers and their attending fighter screen took time to assemble and were easily observed by radar. This gave the RAF the time to mount counter-attacks in strength. The fight reached its climax on 15 September when 60 German aircraft (not the 185 claimed) were shot down, bringing the weekly total to 175. On 17 September, Hitler postponed SEALION, the operation for the invasion of England, although air raids continued. The invasion plan was quietly forgotten.

In the period July to October the RAF suffered 1,140 aircraft totally lost and 710 severely damaged. German figures, including bombers, were 1,733 and 643 respectively.

The Battle of Crete (1941)

In 1941 the first airborne assault on a major island took place. The defenders, mainly Commonwealth forces withdrawn from the Greek mainland at the end of April, outnumbered their attackers, but of Lieutenant General Bernard Freyberg's 42,460 men, barely half were properly formed and equipped. The New Zealand Division was deployed west of Canea up to Maleme airfield, the British 14th Infantry Brigade defended Heraklion airfield, and two Australian battalions covered Rethymnon airfield. The attack was no surprise. Likely dropping zones had been identified in November 1940. ULTRA intelligence (gained from deciphering Enigma encoded messages) confirmed them as targets two weeks before the invasion. Freyberg's defence plan was distorted by his fixed idea that a seaborne invasion would follow rapidly behind the airborne assault. Operation MERCURY, planned by General Kurt Student, was spearheaded by the 7th Airborne Division on 20 May. From well-prepared positions, the British and Commonwealth forces killed or wounded nearly two-thirds of the division. A total of over 3,000 paratroopers were killed. Student's superiors believed the battle lost. In a last-ditch attempt early on 21 May, Student sent reinforcements to Maleme. The New Zealand commander, still expecting a seaborne invasion, delayed sending in a counter-attack and the battalion responsible for the airfield withdrew. Student dropped his last paratroop reserves, then started to land the 5th Mountain Division. That same day, 21 May, Freyberg misread ULTRA message OL 15/389. He took it to mean that the Germans were going to land troops by sea near Canea. In fact only a small convoy of caiques, bearing a single battalion of mountain troops, was headed for Maleme, not Canea. Freyberg concentrated his best forces close to Canea and insisted that Australian troops replace those New Zealanders earmarked for the counter-attack due that night against Maleme airfield. This delayed its start fatally. Shortly before midnight, a Royal Navy force intercepted the flotilla and destroyed much of it. Freyberg went to bed convinced that Crete had been saved. But the two understrength battalions, all that had been allocated for the counter-attack on Maleme, had started so late that they were caught in the open at daybreak on 22 May by General

Wolfram von Richthofen's fighters. Freyberg's son later claimed that his father had acted as he had only to protect the secret of ULTRA.

At Heraklion and Rethymnon the airfields had been saved through prompt and vigorous counter-attacks. But once Student had secured Maleme, he was able to fly in the rest of his mountain troops. The Commonwealth forces, exhausted from continual air attack, pulled back. Freyberg gave the order to retreat south over the White Mountains to the tiny port of Sphakia, whence Royal Navy warships from Alexandria evacuated 15,000 men. Those left behind surrendered on 1 June. The Axis had conquered Crete, but at such a cost that Hitler forbade any further airborne operations.

The Dieppe Raid (1942)

First planned in June 1942 but cancelled on 7 July, the Dieppe raid was remounted at the urging of Vice Admiral Lord Louis Mountbatten, chief of combined operations, and launched as operation JUBILEE on 19 August. The Germans were aware of the threat of cross-Channel raids and of the assembly of landing craft as early as June, but there is no evidence to support persistent rumours that security was compromised.

The plan called for a frontal assault on Dieppe at 05.20 by the 2nd Canadian Infantry Division supported by 58 Churchill tanks. Unfortunately, flank landings at Puys and Pourville timed for half an hour earlier failed to neutralize defences on the two headlands dominating town and seafront. Intelligence, moreover, had missed gun positions in the face of the east headland and anti-armour guns wheeled out after dark at the entrance to streets leading off the esplanade; nor had the immobilizing effect of shingle on tank tracks been anticipated. Consequently, only small parties penetrated Dieppe itself and of the 27 tanks landed only fifteen crossed the sea wall. Meanwhile the troops huddled on the beach were at the mercy of the 302nd Infantry Division's well-directed fire. Naval and air support was utterly inadequate to resolve this impasse: eight small destroyers and a gun-boat lacked the necessary weight of shell, while the RAF's predominantly fighter force was engaged in a major battle of its own.

Of the lessons learnt by JUBILEE at the cost of 3,367 Canadian casualties, 106 aircraft, a destroyer, and numerous landing craft, the most valuable was the urgency of providing overwhelming fire support in the initial stage of a landing. Mountbatten's supporters have claimed that but for JUBILEE, the Allies would have planned the invasion in 1944 to be dependent on the prompt capture of a major port.

The Invasion of Sicily (1943)

A blend of the battle-hardened men of the Eighth Army under General Sir Bernard Montgomery, the profusion of US war *matériel*, and American troops of the Seventh Army under General George S. Patton were considered enough to overwhelm the island garrison and bring the war to mainland Italy. Amphibious ships and landing craft were the resource that defined Allied military strategy in 1943–4, and it took six months to assemble enough for the main component of HUSKY, an operation involving 150,000 men and 3,000 ships.

The two Allied armies were to attack on 10 July, landing on two separate 64 km (40 mile) strips of beach, in a mutually supporting operation. General Dwight D. Eisenhower was the theatre commander and General Sir Harold Alexander at the head of the

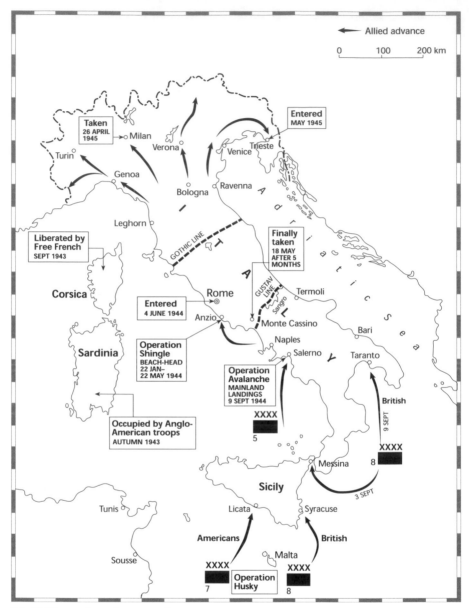

World War II: the Italian campaign

Fifteenth Army Group was the operational commander. The British Eighth Army of one airborne and six infantry divisions, plus one infantry and two armoured brigades, and three Royal Marine Commandos, was to land in the south-east. Its objective was to clear the eastern half of Sicily, including Syracuse and Messina. The US Seventh Army of one armoured, one airborne, four infantry divisions, and one commando was to assault in the south and take the western part of the island, including Palermo. Nearly 4,000 Allied aircraft ensured local air supremacy, although there were 1,500 German and Italian aircraft in the theatre. The Axis could muster only ten Italian divisions of dubious quality and two dependable German formations with which to counter any landings.

Driving winds and poor weather disrupted the first-ever large-scale deployment of Allied airborne forces by parachute and glider. The worst affected were the 144 gliders carrying the British 1st Airborne Brigade: only 54 landed in Sicily and the majority ditched in the Mediterranean, drowning their occupants. The gale also played havoc with the invasion fleet, but the rough seas caused the defenders to relax their watch. They were woken up by naval gunfire support from a bombardment fleet including six battleships, while the few airborne units scattered behind the coastal defences distracted attention and hampered the arrival of reinforcements. The Seventh Army had a rougher reception than the Eighth, but by the end of the first day the Americans held nearly 64 km (40 miles) of beach between Scoglitti and Licata, while the British held a coastal strip from Pozallo to Syracuse, having captured the latter port intact.

Recovering quickly from the initial shock, German forces counter-attacked at Gela and Licata and were repulsed only within sight of the coast, while heavier opposition halted Montgomery around Catania. After much hard fighting, Canadian units reached Enna in the centre of the island on 20 July, and two days later Patton's troops had taken Palermo after a lightning strike across the island. The Seventh Army then turned eastwards, Patton having decided to capture Messina ahead of the slower Montgomery. Italian re-sistance collapsed rapidly and the locals were friendly once the danger of turning their villages into battlefields was past. Nonetheless, the broken landscape favoured the Ger-mans, commanded by the energetic General Hans Hube, who defended a series of stop lines, counter-attacking with armour when the terrain suited. But once his main position at Adrano had been captured, Montgomery advanced towards Messina on either side of Mount Etna. Field Marshal Albert Kesselring, the German commander-in-chief in Italy, was determined not to see another army thrown away and prepared to evacuate his best forces from the island in defiance of Hitler. He concentrated them in the north-east corner and lined both shores of the narrow Straits of Messina with anti-aircraft artillery.

By the time Patton occupied Messina, a few hours ahead of the indignant Montgomery, Kesselring had evacuated 40,000 German and 60,000 Italian troops to the mainland, along with much valuable armour, from under their noses. The success of this German Dunkirk was to have serious repercussions for the Allies in Italy later on. On 17 August, after 38 days' fighting, the whole of Sicily was in Allied hands. The Eighth Army had suffered 9,000 casualties and the Seventh 7,000. The Axis losses were 160,000, including 30,000 Germans.

The Italian Campaign

On 9 September 1943, after the invasion of Sicily, the downfall of Mussolini on 24 July, and the subsequent armistice with Italy, the Allies launched a two-pronged invasion of southern Italy at Taranto and Salerno.

The Salerno Landing (1943)

AVALANCHE involved landing one US and two British divisions of Lieutenant General Mark Clark's US Fifth Army along a 42-km (26-mile) stretch of coast in the Gulf of

Salerno, 64 km (40 miles) south-east of Naples. The aim was threefold: to cut off German forces in the south, capture the port of Naples, and reach the Volturno river.

Field Marshal Kesselring had disarmed Italian troops in the area and manned coastal defences just prior to the invasion and counter-attacked with elements of six divisions, supported by artillery in the surrounding hills. Naval gunfire and reinforcements from the sea alone could not stem the German attack, which was halted with the deployment of US paratroopers and massive air support. By 16 September the British and US forces had linked up and the crisis had passed, with Naples falling on 2 October. On 20 September, 300 British troops had refused orders to move inland. The Salerno mutiny, Britain's only troop rebellion during 1939–45, was defused, but had been caused by the inept management of convalescing soldiers who should have been sent home, but were diverted to unfamiliar units at Salerno instead.

The First Battle of Cassino (1944)

Cassino lies south-east of Rome on Highway 6, the main road to Naples along the Liri valley. The ground rises abruptly to its north, and the abbey of Monte Cassino, founded by St Benedict in 524, dominates the town and the valleys of the Gari and Rapido. In late 1943 town and rivers were stitched into the Gustav Line, the last major obstacle between the Allies and Rome, and there were four battles there between 12 January and 5 June 1944.

In January Lieutenant General Mark Clark, commanding the Fifth Army, planned to break the Gustav Line by attacking on both sides of Cassino and then breaking out down the Liri valley. The French Expeditionary Corps under General Alphonse Juin would attack into the mountains north of Cassino, then the British X Corps would attack across the Garigliano, nearer the coast, and finally the US 36th Division, in the centre, would cross the Gari (wrongly described as the Rapido in most sources) south of the town. The French attack, launched on the night of 11/12 January, gained ground in circumstances which left nobody in doubt as to the qualities of Juin's men, for whom the battle was an opportunity to redeem honour besmirched by 1940. The British seized a wide bridgehead across the Garigliano and beat off counter-attacks before running out of steam. This might have persuaded Clark that his central thrust was too weak, especially as the 36th Division was already bruised. Although some Americans managed to cross the river they could not stay there, and over half the attacking riflemen and company officers were killed or wounded.

It had been hoped that there would already have been good progress on the Cassino front when the Anzio landing began on 22 January. To distract German attention from the beachhead, Clark sent the the US 34th Division into the mountains above Cassino, and launched Juin against the Colle Belvedere, further north. Although some ground was gained, the first battle ended with Lieutenant General Fridolin von Senger und Etterlin, the German corps commander responsible for the sector, in firm control.

The Battle of Anzio (1944)

As early as October 1943 Dwight D. Eisenhower and Sir Harold Alexander, who was

A German armoured column on the move in the Appenine mountains, 24 September 1943.

commanding in Italy, discussed an amphibious operation to outflank the Gustav Line. SHINGLE, the plan for Anzio, was championed by the British premier Churchill, but there was competition for amphibious resources between it and the coming invasion of France, and a dangerous lack of operational clarity.

The landings took place under Major General John P. Lucas on 22 January 1944 and achieved complete surprise, the British 1st Division going ashore north-west of Anzio, the US 3rd Division near Nettuno, to its east, and Anzio being taken by US Rangers. Within 48 hours Lucas had secured a beachhead 11 km (7 miles) deep, but he was unsure what to do with it. Lieutenant General Clark had ordered him to secure a beachhead, and then advance to the Alban hills, but had privately warned him not to stick his neck out. Field Marshal Kesselring did not react by pulling back from Cassino, as the Allies had hoped, but counter-attacked. The beachhead became the scene of vicious fighting, with ground disputed yard by yard and German guns ranging across the whole area. By early April it was clear that fighting had reached a stalemate.

The Second and Third Battles of Cassino (1944)

The second battle was fought by Lieutenant General Freyberg's II New Zealand Corps. The monastery was levelled by heavy bombers on 15 February, despite the misgivings of those who objected on cultural grounds and feared that the Germans would fortify the ruins. Results were disappointing, for both the New Zealand Division in Cassino itself and the 4th Indian Division on the high ground above it: dreadful terrain prevented the attackers from committing more than a fraction of their total force.

The third battle began on 15 March after a massive bombing raid on the town of Cassino. This failed to destroy the morale of the parachutists defending the town, and the New Zealanders barely picked their way into the rubble. The Indians clawed their way up the crags leading to Monastery Hill, taking and holding Castle Hill. Freyberg's men were relieved after ten days of gruelling combat which left all the vital ground in German hands.

The Fourth Battle of Cassino (1944)

General Alexander, advised by his competent chief of staff Lieutenant General John Harding, now recognized that instead of isolated attacks at Cassino he must mount an army group operation against the Gustav Line, bringing divisions from the Eighth Army, on the other side of the Apennines, into the battle. DIADEM began on the night of 11/12 May with the crossing of the Gari south of Cassino. Where one tired division had failed in the first battle, two now attacked with another on hand to exploit success. Further south, the French Corps and II US Corps pushed out of the Garigliano bridgehead in such strength and determination that the defence could not hold. The attack on the high ground around the monastery, entrusted to Lieutenant General Władysław Anders's II Polish Corps, driven, like Juin's men, by the powerful mainspring of national revenge, was making the slow progress dictated by this uncompromising terrain. But Field Marshal Kesselring recognized that Allied penetration to its south made Cassino untenable and ordered a general withdrawal: on 17 May the Poles entered the ruins of the monastery.

Cassino cost the Allies some 45,000 killed and wounded. Although the Germans also lost heavily, they succeeded in disengaging without being cut off by either the Allied southern hook or the breakout from Anzio. Some Germans thought conditions at Cassino even worse than at Stalingrad.

The Anzio force broke out and though Lieutenant General Clark took Rome, he failed to strike through the Velletri gap to reach Valmontone, which would have cut off many of the defenders of Cassino. Anzio aroused lasting controversy. Major General Lucas, relieved of command in February, was not an inspiring commander, but was hamstrung by lack of a clear mission: had he pushed straight for Rome he would have been engulfed. The fighting cost the Allies 7,000 killed and 36,000 wounded, as well as 44,000 sick. Kesselring estimated German losses at 40,000, including 5,000 killed and 4,500 captured.

The Normandy Campaign

The Western Allies had long agreed that continental Europe should be invaded as soon as practicable, and the Soviets vigorously demanded a second front to reduce German pressure in the east. However, the British, with imperial commitments and the painful legacy of World War I, were more cautious than their allies. The raid on Dieppe had failed with heavy casualties, but by illustrating the problems of cross-Channel assault it gave planners an early indication that specialized armoured vehicles and landing craft would be required, but also that overwhelming naval gunfire support would be vital. Lieutenant General Morgan, chief of staff supreme allied commander (designate) (COSSAC), began planning an invasion, and a target date of 1 May 1944 was set.

COSSAC staff considered two main invasion sites: the Pas de Calais, across the Channel at its narrowest point, and Normandy. They decided on the latter. Morgan believed that it would take two weeks to capture Cherbourg, and in the meantime the Channel weather might make it difficult to land supplies: work was begun on two huge floating sectional harbours (Mulberries) which would be towed to France. Essential to success was a long-term method of supplying fuel for the mass of transport and fighting vehicles. The solution was Pluto, Pipe Line Under The Ocean. Major General Percy Hobart commanded the 79th Armoured Division composed of 'funnies', specialist vehicles which would help the attackers get ashore and fight their way through the beach defences. They also included the Duplex Drive (D-D) M4 Sherman tanks, fitted with propellers and capable of amphibious operation when canvas skirts were raised. Their freeboard was, at some 1 m (3 ft), not generous and many sank during the landings, especially when launched too far from shore.

The assault operation required 138 bombarding ships, including 7 battleships, 221 escorts, 287 minesweepers, 2 submarines, 4 minelayers, a seaplane carrier, 495 coastal vessels (motor torpedo boats, gunboats, and launches), 58 other escort ships, 310 landing ships, 1,211 major landing craft, 950 minor landing craft, 531 ferry service landing barges, and 1,125 additional landing craft of various special types. The post-assault support required another 423 naval vessels and 1,260 merchant ships, bringing the total to 7,016 vessels for operation NEPTUNE.

In addition to the naval plan for the invasion (NEPTUNE) and the invasion itself (OVER-LORD), a comprehensive deception plan (FORTITUDE) would seek to persuade the Germans first that the Pas de Calais would be attacked and second that the invasion of Normandy was simply a diversion.

In December 1943 General Dwight D. Eisenhower had been appointed supreme allied commander, with a British deputy, Air Chief Marshal Sir Arthur Tedder. The component

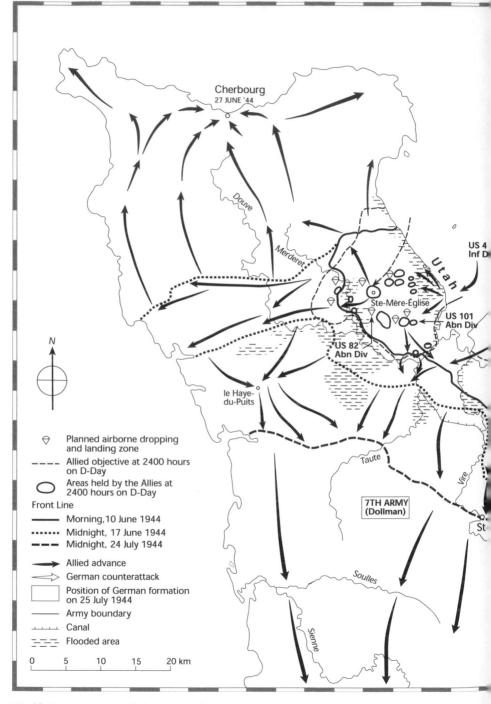

Cherbourg
27 JUNE '44

Douve

Merderet

Utah

US 4
Inf D

Ste-Mère-Église

US 101
Abn Div

US 82
Abn Div

le Haye-
du-Puits

N

Taute

Vire

7TH ARMY
(Dollman)

St

Soulles

Sienne

⊖ Planned airborne dropping
   and landing zone
- - - Allied objective at 2400 hours
   on D-Day
◯ Areas held by the Allies at
   2400 hours on D-Day
Front Line
──── Morning,10 June 1944
•••••• Midnight, 17 June 1944
- - - Midnight, 24 July 1944

➤ Allied advance
⇨ German counterattack
☐ Position of German formation
   on 25 July 1944
──── Army boundary
⊥⊥⊥ Canal
≈≈≈ Flooded area

0   5   10   15   20 km

World War II: D-Day and the Normandy campaign

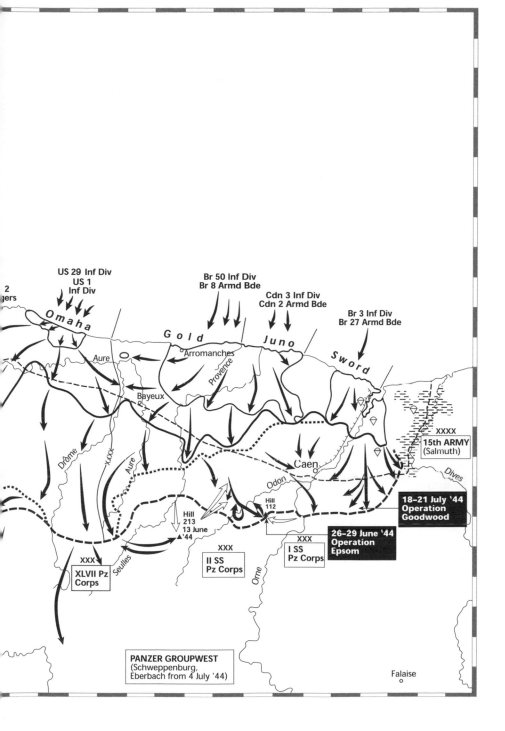

US 29 Inf Div
US 1 Inf Div

Br 50 Inf Div
Br 8 Armd Bde

Cdn 3 Inf Div
Cdn 2 Armd Bde

Br 3 Inf Div
Br 27 Armd Bde

O m a h a

G o l d

J u n o

S w o r d

Arromanches

Provence

Aure

Bayeux

Drôme

Aure

Seulles

Caen

Odon

Dives

XXXX
15th ARMY
(Salmuth)

Hill 213
13 June ▲'44

Hill 112

18–21 July '44
Operation
Goodwood

26–29 June '44
Operation
Epsom

XXX
XLVII Pz
Corps

XXX
II SS
Pz Corps

XXX
I SS
Pz Corps

Orne

PANZER GROUPWEST
(Schweppenburg,
Eberbach from 4 July '44)

Falaise

commanders were all British. Naval forces would be commanded by Admiral Sir Bertram Ramsay, ground forces (Twenty-First Army Group) by General Sir Bernard Montgomery, and air forces by Air Chief Marshal Sir Trafford Leigh-Mallory. Montgomery decided that the COSSAC team had allocated too few troops to the initial attack, and directed that five divisions (from east to west British, Canadian, British, and two American) would form the first wave, their flanks protected by three airborne divisions, the British 6th, commanded by Major General Richard Gale, to the east and the US 82nd All American and 101st Screaming Eagles to the west under Major Generals Matthew Ridgway and Maxwell Taylor respectively. FORTITUDE gained momentum, persuading the Germans that an American army group under Lieutenant General George S. Patton was in south-east England, ready for a descent on the Pas de Calais.

The Germans knew that invasion was likely. Their forces in France and the Low Countries, under Commander-in-Chief West Field Marshal Gerd von Rundstedt, comprised Army Group G, in southern France, and Field Marshal Erwin Rommel's Army Group B. The latter's Seventh Army, 130,000 men strong, held Normandy, with the Fifteenth responsible for the Pas de Calais, Belgium, and the Netherlands. The Germans had been at work on the defences of the Atlantic wall since 1942, and Rommel pushed the work ahead as quickly as he could. He was convinced that the invasion would have to be stopped on the beaches, and that, for Allies and Germans alike, the first day would be the longest. Both Rundstedt and the commander of Panzergruppe West, General Geyr von Schweppenburg, disagreed. The argument was made more complex by the fact that most German armoured divisions in Normandy could not be moved without Adolf Hitler's personal authority. When the invasion came Rommel had only one usable armoured division, 21st Panzer, in the immediate area.

D-Day (1944)

Bad weather compelled Eisenhower to postpone the invasion for 24 hours, and even on 5 June the forecast was uncertain. Early that morning Eisenhower took the brave decision to go ahead on the 6th, which was to become D-Day. Almost 5,000 ships set out, and some 23,000 parachutists and glider troops prepared to board their aircraft. The first blow fell just after midnight on the 6th when a company of 2nd Oxfordshire and Buckinghamshire Light Infantry secured the bridges over the Caen canal and the river Orne just north of Caen. Shortly afterwards the airborne divisions began to arrive, and although they were widely spread, with some men lost in the sea or flooded rivers, their arrival helped confuse German commanders. German response was not helped by the fact that Field Marshal Rommel was on leave in Germany.

The British and Canadian landings on Gold, Juno, and Sword beaches went much as planned, although exploitation inland was somewhat disappointing, and the British 3rd Division, in the east, failed to capture Caen. Although the American landing on Utah beach went well, at Omaha beach the Americans ran into a strong defence and, with most of their amphibious tanks swamped offshore and lacking the specialist armour used in the British sector, they suffered heavily before wresting a toehold. The results of D-Day were

The D-Day landings were not all opposed with the ferocity shown at Omaha beach. Here, at Utah, resistance was trivial and American troops approach in comparative safety.

impressive enough. Over 150,000 Allied soldiers were ashore, and the expected German counter-attack had failed to materialize: even 21st Panzer Division, dangerously close to Sword beach and the British airborne landings, had not been committed until it was too late.

The Battles of Normandy (1944)

Over the days that followed, the Allies linked up their beachheads and, while the Americans swung up the Cotentin peninsula towards Cherbourg, General Montgomery made the first of several attempts to take Caen. The 7th Armoured Division, with desert experience but uneasy in the very different terrain of Normandy, was checked at Villers-Bocage on 12–14 June. Cherbourg fell at the end of June, but the harbour was so thoroughly damaged that it took months to repair. On 24–30 June the British launched EPSOM, another attempt to outflank Caen from the west, and made slow progress in very heavy fighting.

The characteristics of the battle for Normandy, where the intensity of the fighting at times resembled that on the western front in World War I, were already clear. The Allies enjoyed superior resources, and sustained themselves despite a storm which destroyed the American Mulberry and damaged the British. Their air power played havoc with German units on their way to the front and made movement in the battle area risky. But they lacked relevant experience, and sometimes their morale wavered. The *bocage* terrain of western Normandy favoured the resolute defender.

By early July there was growing concern at an invasion which seemed to have stuck fast and cost some 61,700 casualties. Yet German commanders were no more sanguine; they had lost over 80,000 men. Hitler replaced the gloomy Field Marshal Gerd von Rundstedt with Field Marshal Gunther von Kluge, who arrived filled with a confidence which soon evaporated. Rommel was wounded in an air attack on 17 July, and three days later the bomb plot assassination attempt increased the tensions between Hitler and his senior commanders.

Montgomery's role remains controversial. He was to maintain that his master plan involved fixing German armour in the east to allow the Americans to break out in the west, while his critics have suggested that he was in fact more opportunistic. He was under pressure to take decisive action when, on 18 July, he launched three armoured divisions east of Caen in GOODWOOD. The attack was preceded by a strike by Allied heavy bombers, and it may be that the need to secure the support of the strategic bombing force induced Montgomery to oversell the operation to Eisenhower. It cost almost 6,000 casualties and 400 tanks, and produced no breakout. Montgomery argued that this did not matter, for he had attracted German reserves, giving Lieutenant General Omar Bradley, in command of the US First Army, the chance to break out.

On 25 July Bradley mounted COBRA, west of Saint-Lô. Its initial aims were modest, but Lieutenant General Lawton Collins, commanding the assaulting corps, realized that he had achieved a breakthrough and hustled on towards Avranches. It had been planned that when the Americans had sufficient forces in theatre they would activate the US Third Army under General George S. Patton, with Lieutenant General Courtney H. Hodges taking over the First Army while Bradley became commander of the Twelfth Army Group. Patton, ideally suited to fighting a mobile battle, sent some of his troops to Brittany but swung others eastwards. The British and Canadians continued the long slog around Caen, the former taking Mont Pincon and the latter mounting two methodical attacks, operations TOTALISE and TRACTABLE, down the Caen–Falaise road. Hitler insisted on a counter-attack at Mortain with the intention of cutting off Patton, but despite initial progress on 7 August it foundered in the face of Allied air attacks.

The Falaise Gap (1944)

General Patton's turn to the east created the possibility of catching the Germans between the Third Army and the Anglo-Canadian forces pressing down from Caen. The abortive Mortain counter-attack made this outcome more likely by pushing German armour deeper into the pocket. However, determined resistance slowed down the Canadian and Polish advance on Falaise, and on 13 August Bradley ordered Patton not to proceed north of Argentan, fearing accidental collision with the Canadians. Falaise did not fall until the 16th, and in the meantime thousands of Germans streamed through the Argentan–Falaise gap. On 19 August the 1st Polish Armoured Division met the Americans at Chambois, in the neck of the pocket. Polish defence of Mont Ormel, north of Chambois, played an important part in closing the gap, but until the last days it remained possible for determined Germans to get away. Perhaps 10,000 Germans died in the pocket and 50,000 were taken prisoner. Allied aircraft inflicted terrible damage: huge quantities of tanks, half-tracks, and trucks were destroyed or abandoned.

It is easy to criticize the Allies for not closing the pocket more swiftly. However, envelopment on such a scale, carried out by two army groups, demanded a greater degree of operational slickness than the Allies possessed. Paris was liberated on 25 August, and the tide of war rolled away. The cost to the Allies by the end of August was 209,672 men, of whom 36,976 had been killed and 153,475 wounded.

The Battle of Arnhem (1944)

The battle was part of MARKET GARDEN, Montgomery's ambitious two-part operation involving three airborne divisions to secure key bridges in the Netherlands, cross the Rhine, and advance into Germany before the winter of 1944. MARKET involved dropping the 101st (US) Airborne Division to capture two canal bridges at Zon and Veghel, the 82nd (US) Airborne to take bridges over the Maas at Grave and the Rhine at Nijmegen, and the 1st (British) Airborne to capture the Arnhem bridge over the Rhine. While MARKET was taking place, GARDEN called for British XXX Corps to advance 100 km (64 miles) over the bridges and secure the airborne corridor. There remains a highly charged doubt whether Lieutenant General F. A. M. Browning, commanding the Allied airborne corps, was unaware that the 9th and 10th SS Panzer Divisions were refitting in the vicinity of Arnhem, or whether he mentally suppressed ULTRA indications as being inconvenient to the grandiose plan. The same unbalanced (and deeply uncharacteristic) precipitation can be seen in Montgomery's pointed failure even to consult Dutch staff officers, who could have told him that running armour along easily defended causeways was not the manner to advance into the Netherlands.

The choice of the Guards Armoured Division to spearhead the 100 km (64 mile) dash was also misconceived, as dash was not its hallmark. Although it managed to advance and link up with the two US divisions, it failed to reach Arnhem. Last in a far from exhaustive list of failures of planning and preparation, 1st Airborne landed at Arnhem on

17 September 1944 by parachute and glider, on landing zones 11 km (7 miles) distant from their objective, and their radio communications promptly broke down. One battalion (2nd Parachute Battalion) managed to reach the bridge, but was isolated and reduced by German armour. A Polish Parachute Brigade landed on 21 September on the far bank of the Rhine, but was unable to help. Faced with dwindling supplies, heavy casualties, and no prospect of relief from XXX Corps, Major General R. E. Urquhart and 2,700 troops withdrew across the Rhine on the night of 25/6 September, leaving behind nearly 7,600 killed or captured.

The Battle of the Scheldt (1944)

The history of the campaign to clear the Scheldt estuary is the tale of lost opportunities. On 4 September 1944, to both the Germans' and Allies' surprise, the port of Antwerp was taken by the local resistance, preventing the German garrison from destroying the harbour facilities. The Allies badly needed a large working port by late 1944, their logistic tail still stretching back to the artificial port at Arromanches. Montgomery might have concentrated on clearing the Scheldt estuary from Antwerp to the sea, but instead he launched MARKET GARDEN, in the hope of taking a short cut into Germany. The defeat at Arnhem removed any hopes of gaining Rotterdam or Amsterdam as alternative ports and belatedly he ordered Lieutenant General Guy Simonds's First Canadian Army to clear the Scheldt. The estuary mouth was dominated to the north by the garrisoned island of Walcheren, and to the south by a defensive perimeter around Breskens. The 2nd Canadian Division attacked along the north bank from 2 October, and eventually overran the Beveland peninsula, with the help of the 52nd (Scottish) Division, allowing an amphibious assault to be made against Walcheren in early November. On the southern bank, the 3rd Canadian Division attacked towards the coast, taking Breskens on 21 October, and reaching Zeebrugge by 3 November. The reduction of Walcheren by 8 November allowed the Scheldt to be swept of mines and obstacles and by the end of the month the first Allied ships arrived in Antwerp.

The Battle of the Bulge (1944)

The German Ardennes offensive, popularly known as the battle of the Bulge, was a desperate attempt, initiated by Hitler, to reverse the tide of the war in the west. Three German armies were engaged, Sixth SS Panzer, Fifth Panzer, and Seventh Army, under the command of Field Marshal Walther Model in Army Group B. The operation, deceptively code-named WATCH ON THE RHINE, sought to split the Allied armies and recapture the port of Antwerp. It struck Lieutenant General Courtney H. Hodges's First US Army, on the northern edge of General Omar Bradley's Twelfth US Army Group, holding the Ardennes sector thinly at a time when bad weather grounded the otherwise-dominant Allied air forces. The attack achieved tactical surprise, for although ULTRA indicated that the Germans were massing it was assumed that this was for defensive purposes. German special forces, disguised in US uniforms, parachuted behind Allied lines, and achieved disproportionate results by causing US units to distrust each other.

The attack was launched early on 16 December 1944. Some American soldiers, encircled on the snowy uplands, surrendered, and in the north Lieutenant Colonel Jochen

Peiper's battle group of the Sixth SS Panzer Army initially made good progress. In the centre the Fifth Panzer Army encircled Bastogne, containing the 101st Airborne Division and part of the 10th Armoured Division, but the town held out. On 19 December Eisenhower cancelled offensive action elsewhere, ordering Patton to swing his Third Army into the southern flank of the bulge. He also placed US troops in the threatened sector under Montgomery, commander of the British Twenty-First Army Group, to the north, to ensure unity of command. With the Sixth Panzer Army stuck in the north, Hitler switched the main effort to the Fifth Panzer Army in the centre, but although its vanguard reached Foy-Nôtre-Dame, just 5 km (3 miles) from the Meuse, it was hopelessly short of its planned objectives. The weather cleared on 22 December, and German troops, jammed on poor roads and short of fuel, were mercilessly harried from the air.

On New Year's Day the Luftwaffe launched an all-out attack on Allied airfields, and although it inflicted considerable damage it did so at a cost it could not afford. The Allies attempted to cut off the German penetration, with one of Hodges's corps striking south as Patton moved northwards, but the Germans fell back before the pincers closed. Nevertheless, they lost 100,000 men, together with most of the irreplaceable tanks and aircraft they committed. Allied losses were also heavy, but they could make good their losses.

The Battle of the Rhineland (1945)

The name is given to a series of battles fought by the Allied armies to capture terrain up to the west bank of the Rhine river, from 8 February until the crossings of mid-March 1945. In the northern sector Montgomery planned to seize the land ahead by a pincer movement, advancing from the line of the Roer river westwards towards the Rhine. Operation VERITABLE began on 8 February with the most concentrated British–Canadian artillery barrage of the war: 6,000 tonnes of shells were fired in the first 24 hours to support the advance of II Canadian Corps moving south-east, while XVI US Corps of Lieutenant General William H. Simpson's Ninth Army moved north-east to meet it. Lieutenant General Brian Horrocks's British XXX Corps held the front between the two, but the Germans breached local dykes to create large flooded areas, and with foul weather, notoriously difficult terrain, and the stiffening resistance of the German First Parachute Army of Army Group B, the Allied advance was stalled.

To the south, fierce German resistance at Düren and Jülich on the Roer, and the use of floodwater from the Schwammenauel dam, delayed the progress of Simpson's Ninth and Lieutenant General Courtney H. Hodges's First US Armies. By 23 February the water levels had subsided sufficiently for the Americans to resume, and the Canadian–American pincers in the north closed at Geldern on 3 March. By 7 March all troops had come up to the west bank of the Rhine, and were preparing to cross. Elements of the eight German divisions under Field Marshal Walther Model in Army Group B fought in the Rhineland battle, which was characterized by its unfriendly weather and hard terrain, and suffered about 45,000 killed, wounded, or captured, while Allied losses were 15,000.

Early 1945 saw the battle for the Rhineland conclude with another stroke of good fortune when the 9th Armoured Division of the US First Army captured the almost intact Ludendorff railway bridge over the Rhine at Remagen. Before it fell to water and air attacks ten days later, several First Army divisions had made it across. The capture of the bridge resulted in the dismissal of Gerd von Rundstedt as commander-in-chief west and his replacement with Albert Kesselring, but this was an irrelevance. Between 22 and 26

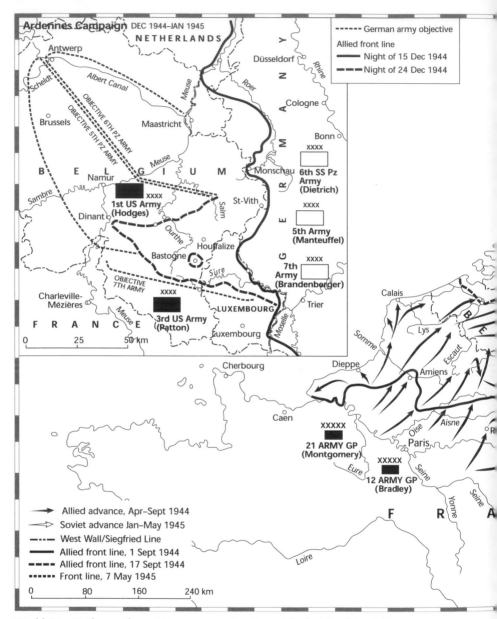

World War II: the north-west Europe campaign. Inset: The battle of the Bulge

March, all the Allied armies crossed the Rhine, involving the British, who had to cross in the north where it was a greater obstacle, in a set-piece assault combining large-scale amphibious and airborne operations.

Eisenhower was concerned that the Germans planned an Alpine redoubt (they did not), and accordingly directed the US armies to strike deep into the mountains of

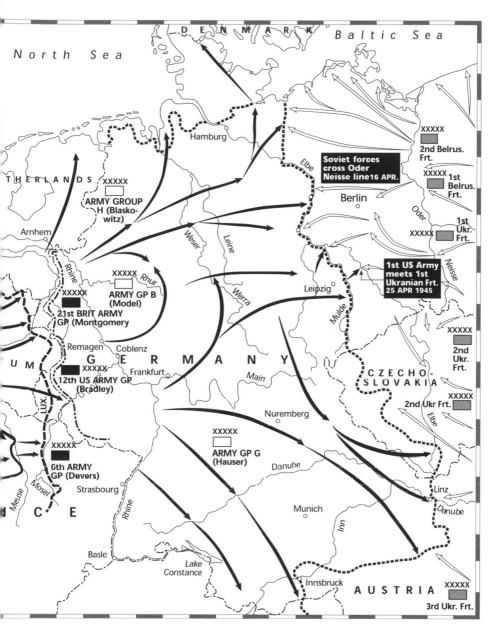

southern Germany and Austria, which they did with comparative ease. He also knew that taking Berlin was going to be very dearly bought. And it was, by the Russians.

By 1 April, Model's Army Group B had been surrounded when the pincers of the US Ninth and First armies closed at Lippstadt. Three hundred thousand men surrendered and their commander shot himself. Hitler also shot himself as the Soviets fought their way into Berlin, a process completed by 2 May. Montgomery's Army Group reached Hamburg on the following day and between 4 and 5 May the surrender of German formations in the west was negotiated, Montgomery taking that of units in north-west Germany, Denmark, and the Netherlands, while Admiral Karl Dönitz surrendered what was left of German forces to Eisenhower at his headquarters in Rheims on 7 May. The campaign and the European war officially ended at midnight on 8 May 1945.

THE EASTERN FRONT

The campaign on the eastern front was the largest land campaign ever fought, unsurpassed in the length of the front, depth of the advance and retreat, duration of continuous fighting, and the size of the contending armies. It was unique, too, in the scale of violence and the number of casualties. It was the last great extensive war of the age of coal, steel, and railways, for weapons of mass destruction have almost certainly ruled out another such massive ground war between great powers. Although a war of machines and of movement, the eastern front was essentially a war between ground forces, albeit between armies with a large motorized component and huge tactical air forces employed as flying artillery.

Operation Barbarossa (1941)

Operation BARBAROSSA, correctly 'case BARBAROSSA', was the code name for Germany's surprise attack on the USSR on 22 June 1941. It was the most ambitious campaign of World War II, planned and prepared to achieve by combat a strategic objective within a single theatre of war and a set time-frame. It was also the centrepiece of a geopolitical vision clearly predicated on genocide.

Hitler's war against the USSR had two facets, a military and an ideological one, since BARBAROSSA was meant to solve Germany's strategic dilemma and at the same time conquer Lebensraum (living space). Hitler succeeded in branding BARBAROSSA a war of annihilation against Bolshevism and Jewry because the army high command and other senior commanders willingly allowed the troops to 'fight the ideological war' alongside the various SS forces. Thus the Nazi concept of extermination could also become a component of operations, rear area security, and exploitation. The brutalization of German soldiers had begun in Poland. The barbarization of warfare itself would begin on Soviet territories.

On 18 December 1940, Hitler had issued Directive No. 21: 'to crush Soviet Russia in one rapid campaign even before the conclusion of the war with England.' The essence of the initial phase of operations was to destroy the bulk of the Red Army in a series of sweeping encirclements west of the rivers Dnieper and Dvina and to prevent the withdrawal of Soviet forces capable of combat into the expanse of Russian space. Then, by means of rapid pursuit, the final Soviet defeat was to be accomplished and the general line Volga–Archangel to be reached within three months. Thus, no preparations were made for winter fighting. The air force's task was both interdiction near the front and direct support of the army on the battlefield. Attacks on the Soviet arms industry in the Urals area were to be left until after the conclusion of mobile warfare. The navy's mission was to prevent Soviet forces from breaking out of the Baltic Sea.

To defeat the Red Army, Germany massed over 3 million men and 152 divisions, including 17 panzer and 13 motorized divisions with a total of 3,350 tanks, 600,000 motor vehicles, and 625,000 horses. They were supported by 7,146 artillery pieces and 1,950 operational aircraft. The Finnish army added 17 divisions and 2 brigades, while Romania's contribution consisted of 14 divisions, 7 brigades, and 1 reinforced panzer regiment. Three army group headquarters were responsible for operations in one of the main sectors: North, led by Field Marshal Wilhelm von Leeb, in the direction of Leningrad; Centre, under Field Marshal Fedor von Bock, toward Smolensk; and Army Group South, Field Marshal Gerd von Rundstedt commanding, toward Kiev. In addition, there was an Army of Norway, an expeditionary force of which was to advance toward Murmansk. These four senior field commands each had one *Luftflotte* (air fleet) allocated to them, commanded by Colonel-General Keller, Field Marshal Kesselring, General Löhr, and Colonel-General Stumpff. The mass of the German offensive power was located north of the Pripet Marshes, with two of the four Panzergruppen assigned to Army Group Centre. Overall control lay with the army high command under Field Marshal Walter von Brauchitsch and the army's chief of staff Colonel-General Franz Halder.

The extraordinary early successes against the numerically superior Red Army achieved by the attacking German forces in BARBAROSSA had a number of explanations: the efficiency and experience of the Wehrmacht, the ability of the Germans to concentrate the bulk of these forces in the east, the exposed position of the enemy forces along the new Soviet western frontier, and the operational and tactical surprise achieved on 22 June 1941. In many respects the Wehrmacht succeeded in its initial objective of destroying known Soviet forces in the western frontier zones. In encirclements extraordinary in military history, the panzer formations of von Bock's Army Group Centre had by the end of the first week of the war trapped the main mass of General Dmitri Pavlov's Western Army Group in the region west of Minsk. Leeb's Army Group North had meanwhile secured crossings over the river Dvina, opening the way into the Baltic region and Leningrad. In mid-July another grand German encirclement was completed by Army Group Centre east of Smolensk. Some historians perceive a critical German mistake in Hitler's decision to secure the flanks in the Ukraine and Leningrad rather than pushing on immediately to Moscow, which was only 350 km (220 miles) to the east. In particular, when Hitler ordered the transfer of General Heinz Guderian's Panzergruppe from Army Group Centre to Army Group South, which had been making a relatively slow advance into the Ukraine, the result was a decisive success in the Kiev encirclement but a missed chance to take the Soviet capital.

The battle of Smolensk (July–September 1941) was thus a protracted affair, and the point when Soviet resistance in the centre began to stiffen. Only in early September did Guderian's group again become available as part of what became the final offensive of the year, TAIFUN, the attack on Moscow.

The Battle of Vyazma-Bryansk (1941)

A vast battle of encirclement immediately preceded the great battle of Moscow. The Soviet Western Front (army group) under Colonel-General Ivan Koniev and the Reserve Front under Marshal Semyon Budenny attempted to prevent the German Army Group Centre breaking through towards Moscow and buy time for the build-up and concentration of reserves. The German attack began on 2 October, forcing back elements of the Nineteenth, Twentieth, Twenty-Fourth, and Thirty-Second Soviet armies and encircling them with elements of two other armies west of Vyazma. The Third and Fourth Panzer armies linked up on 7 October to form the Vyazma pocket. This great battle of encirclement continued until 23 October, with several attempts by the Soviets to break out. In three weeks the Germans netted 700,000 prisoners. However, the onset of the autumn rains and the need to clear the pockets, which kept fighting, slowed the German advance. Meanwhile, General Guderian's Second Panzer Army, swinging up from the south, captured Orel on 3 October and Bryansk on 6 October. The resistance of the main Soviet forces on the Tula, Kalinin, and Mozhaisk defensive lines was equally stubborn, further slowing the German advance. Moscow was put under a 'state of siege' on 19 October and the remnants of the Western and Reserve fronts were combined in one front under Marshal Georgi Zhukov.

The Battle of Moscow (1941–1942)

The defence of Moscow was entrusted to the Western Front (army group), under Colonel-General Koniev until 10 October when he was replaced by Marshal Georgi Zhukov. In mid-November the Germans were 64 km (40 miles) from Moscow, but Soviet resistance was ferocious and the Germans encountered a new weapon, the remarkable Soviet T-34 tank. On 15 November they attempted to encircle the city from Tula in the south and Kalinin in the north, but made slow progress. The onset of a severe winter froze the mud but German equipment was not designed to cope with minus 30 °C.

Stalin's counterstroke was made possible by intelligence from the Sorge ring in Tokyo that the Japanese, sobered by their punishment at Khalkin-Gol, had no intention of attacking in Manchuria. He was therefore able to move armoured divisions west into European Russia and had the patience to wait until they were fully assembled and the freeze came. On 30 November the Soviets had fallen back to their final defence line at kilometre 22—near Moscow's international Sheremetevo airport. There were two Soviet counter-attacks on 4 December and then on 6 December the main counter-attack began with the First Shock Army and Twentieth Army attacking north of Moscow, and the Tenth Army attacking from the south, past Tula. The Soviet reserves, well equipped against the winter cold, struck German forces that were exhausted, paralysed by the bitter cold, and at the limit of their lines of supply. Large areas were still held by partisans behind the German lines, and the Soviet forces tried to link up with them using airborne forces. The Red Army recaptured thousands of villages—crucial shelter in the cold—and the German salients north and south of the city were driven back. Airborne and cavalry corps penetrated the German rear areas, notably IV Airborne Corps on 20 January, near Vyazma. The Red Army pushed the German lines back 150–400 km (93–248 miles). In total, the Germans lost 500,000 men, 1,500 tanks, 2,500 guns, and 15,000 trucks—many of them immobilized by the cold.

Compared with anything the Germans had experienced before, the scale of their losses and the scope of the Soviet counter-offensive were staggering. The Red Army launched the overambitious second phase of its winter campaign in mid-January, attempting to encircle Army Group Centre. The Russians lacked the resources to maintain the offensive.

The Siege of Sevastopol (1941–1942)

By 16 November 1941 the Germans had captured all the Crimea apart from Sevastopol.

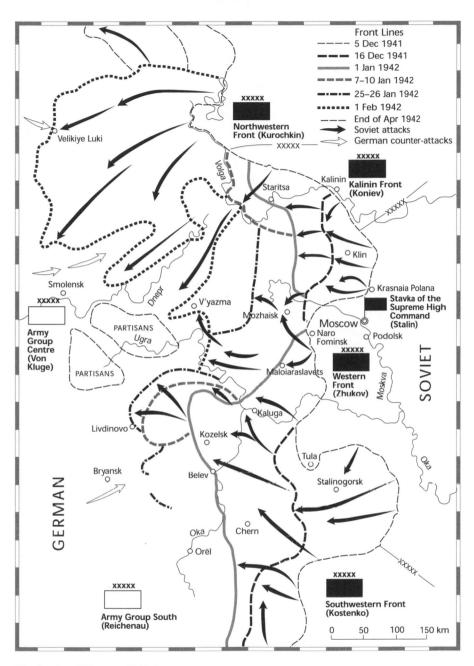

The battle of Moscow, 1941–2

The Eleventh Army and elements of the Third Romanian Army ringed the fortress. Sevastopol was surrounded by forts with armoured emplacements buried deep in concrete and rock. The garrison numbered 106,000. The Germans began to bombard the fortress on 17 December. They brought up the fearsome 31½-inch Gustav Gerät, known as Big Dora, then the largest-calibre gun ever built, to help flatten it. The Red Army and navy attempted to relieve the city with a huge amphibious assault, the Kerch-Feodosiya operation, on 25 December. They captured Feodosiya but were then dislodged.

The assault went in on 7 June 1942 and the Soviets fought on for 27 days. The Germans used toxic smoke to kill them in their underground installations, one of the few times in World War II when chemical weapons were used. Sevastopol fell, after 250 days, on 4 July. The Soviets were to recapture it on 9 May 1944, after a campaign to recapture the whole of the Crimea lasting a month.

The First Battle of Kharkov (1942)

Kharkov, in the Ukraine, had fallen to the Germans relatively easily at the end of 1941, and became one of the 'hedgehogs' in which the Germans held fast during the winter. In May 1942 Soviet forces in the Izyum salient to the south-east and Volchansk to the east launched a concentric attack under Marshal Semyon Timoshenko to recapture the city, but Colonel Gehlen, the new chief of Fremde Heere Ost, the German intelligence organization, predicted it, and it was defeated with the loss of another 250,000 Soviet troops.

Timoshenko's failure at Kharkov cleared the way for the main German effort in 1942. BLAU began on the anniversary of BARBAROSSA, its objectives being the destruction of Soviet reserves and capture of Soviet oil production centres in the Caucasus, sensibly avoiding the strongest part of the Soviet defences, the central sector before Moscow. The Soviets made a long retreat across the Don steppe, avoiding the encirclements of the previous summer. Hitler is often criticized for dividing his forces as a result of his initial success; Army Group A was sent south-west toward the oilfields and Army Group B west toward Stalingrad, with the result that neither could fully complete their tasks. General Friederich Paulus' Sixth Army did reached the outskirts of Stalingrad in early September.

The Battle of Stalingrad (1942–1943)

The battle of Stalingrad entered the realm of legend almost as soon as the guns fell silent in the vast industrial city on the river Volga on 2 February 1943. As the closest and bloodiest battle on the eastern front, it was a German disaster and a Soviet triumph.

As late as 17 November 1942, Paulus tried to take the city, while aware of the weakness of his flanks, mainly defended by Allied troops. General Vasily Chuikov's Sixty-Second Army was successful in holding four shallow bridgeheads on the left bank of the river Volga. Mobile operations had long been replaced by urban fighting in which both sides bled heavily for a few dozen ruined city blocks while Stalin and Red Army commanders planned to counter-attack.

Both the high command and Sixth Army had anticipated a Soviet attack against its

Soviet resistance at Stalingrad was stubborn in the extreme, with house-to-house fighting leading to the destruction of much of the city before the Germans were surrounded and forced to surrender.

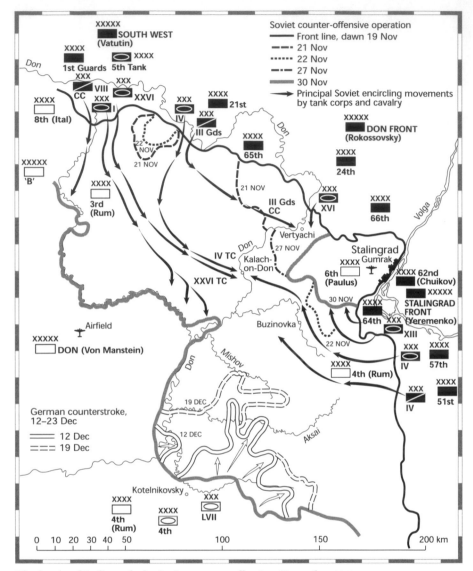

The battle of Stalingrad: the Soviet counter-offensive, November 1942

vulnerable flanks but underestimated an encircling offensive on the massive scale prepared by the Red Army. On 19 November, the South-Western Front (army group) under Colonel-General Nikolai Vatutin began its long-prepared counter-offensive (URANUS), attacking the Third Romanian Army north of Stalingrad. One day later, the Stalingrad Front, under Colonel-General Andrey Eremenko, joined in against the Fourth Romanian and Fourth Panzer Army south of Stalingrad. Soviet superiority was absolute in the main penetration sectors. After the spearheads had linked up at Sovetsky south-east of Kalach on 23 November, Soviet forces established an inner encirclement around the

Sixth Army, one corps of the Fourth Panzer Army, and Romanian remnants totalling 250,000 men, including 195,000 Germans (among them one Croatian infantry regiment), 50,000 Soviet auxiliaries, and 5,000 Romanians.

While Hitler refused to contemplate withdrawing from Stalingrad, Paulus did not possess the logistical strength to break out unassisted. His regrouped Sixth Army lacked fuel, ammunition, and transportation. While the Sixth Army was (inadequately) supplied by the Luftwaffe a relief force was assembled. Although all available transport was concentrated, the airlift hardly ever met the army's needs. In addition, its troops had been exhausted and undernourished before the siege.

Alongside the outer encirclement, the Red Army did everything to disrupt envisaged German relief operations. It succeeded in allowing only one thrust from Kotel'nikovskij (100 km/62 miles). It began on 12 December (WINTERGEWITTER). While LVII Panzer Corps struggled forward to link up with the Sixth Army, the South-Western Front continued its winter campaign (LITTLE SATURN) and penetrated deep into the rear of Army Group Don. When LVII Panzer Corps had given its best, Paulus was too short of motor fuel, ammunition, and rations to implement the breakout (DONNERSCHLAG). The Sixth Army's leaders knew by the end of December that it was doomed.

The end began when the Don Front under Colonel-General Konstantin Rokossovsky executed RING on 10 January, after Paulus had rejected an offer to capitulate. Seven days later, the Stalingrad pocket was reduced to half its size and the Sixth Army had lost its last major airfield. On 22 January, Paulus asked Hitler in vain for permission to cease fire. By 26 January, the Sixth Army was confined to two small pockets in Stalingrad. Paulus was unwilling to put a formal end to the fighting although the remnants of the 297th Infantry Division had already surrendered. On 31 January he surrendered himself, despite his last-minute promotion to field marshal, but refused to order the northern pocket to do the same. It fought until 2 February. According to recent estimates 60,000 Germans died in Stalingrad and 110,000 went into Soviet captivity, of whom only 5,000 returned home, including the dishonoured Paulus.

The exposed southern part of the front was rolled up, Rostov was recaptured by the Red Army, and General Ewald von Kleist's Army Group A was only with difficulty extracted from the Caucasus. Although the Wehrmacht had to give up all the ground captured in 1942, and even some of the positions held since the winter of 1941/2, it was able to stabilize the situation after the Stalingrad defeat. There was even a final German victory in the east, when Kharkov was recaptured in February–March 1943. But the overall outlook was poor.

The Battle of Kursk (1943)

The greatest tank battle in history, but also an important air battle, took place between 5 and 23 July 1943. Fighting in early 1943 had left a huge salient sticking out into German-held territory round Kursk in Ukraine. Hitler had once postponed ZITADELLE, the plan to cut out the salient, but on 18 June 1943 decided to go ahead in order to achieve a crushing victory over the Red Army which had so humiliated the Wehrmacht at Stalingrad. The Germans concentrated 70 per cent of their tanks and 65 per cent of their aircraft from the entire eastern front. The German forces totalled 900,000 men, 2,700 tanks and assault guns, and 1,800 aircraft. The Germans had been seeking an answer to the successful Soviet T-34, and produced the Panther, which first appeared in May 1943. It had a 75 mm gun and thick

frontal armour, but was unreliable. The Soviets, meanwhile, had begun up-gunning the T-34 from 76 mm to 85 mm. The Germans also had the massive Tiger tank with an 88 mm gun and 100 mm of armour and the Ferdinand assault gun on a Tiger chassis. It was in some ways to be a ritualistic contest, between heavy, armoured German knights and fast-moving Soviets. But more important, the Soviets knew the Germans were coming and built a huge defensive network 240–320 km (150–200 miles) deep. There were five to six defensive 'belts,' each 3–5 km (2–3 miles) deep. Most of the engineering effort went into the first 30 km (20 miles)—the 'tactical zone', with field defences, mines, and anti-tank guns.

The German plan envisaged the Ninth Army under Field Marshal Walter Model with five corps attacking the salient from the north, southwards from Orel, and General Hermann Hoth's Fourth Panzer Army, also with five corps, from the south, around Belgorod. The Soviet *Lucy* spy ring discovered the rough timing of the attack: 3 to 6 July. Battlefield intelligence refined this to 02.00 on 5 July. The Soviet artillery therefore fired the biggest artillery 'counter-preparation'—smashing up enemy forces as they are concentrating for the attack—in the history of war.

At 05.00 Hoth's panzers, already shaken, pressed forward in wedge formations into a waiting arc of fire. Many of the Panthers broke down. The heavy Ferdinands and Tigers pressed on, to be met by *Pakfronts*, whole batteries of anti-tank guns which would blast a single tank, then move to the next. By 10 July the southern pincer had stalled, not having penetrated the 30 km (20 mile) tactical zone. The same happened in the north, where the Germans only penetrated 13 km (8 miles). Now the Germans had stalled, the Soviet tank armies were committed. Hoth's Fourth Panzer tried to penetrate the Soviet defences near the village of Prokhorovka. They collided with Marshal Pavel Rotmistrov's Fifth Guards Tank Army. In the general area there were 1,200–400 tanks, but only 850 (600 Soviet and 250 German) actually met on the Prokhorovka field. Among them the Germans had 100 Tigers. On 12 July, under a sky full of thunderclouds, the titans clashed, the Soviets under orders to close with the Tigers to negate the latter's advantage in range. The outcome was a stand-off, although General Guderian recalled he had 'never received such an overwhelming impression of Soviet strength and numbers as on that day'. Soon, T-34s were streaming 'like rats over the battlefield'.

The Germans lost 400 tanks and 10,000 men. The Soviets lost more, but they could afford them. In the entire battle the Red Army claimed to have killed or captured 500,000 Germans and destroyed 1,500 tanks. The Germans claimed to have destroyed 1,800 tanks on the south face alone. Through an inferno of blazing armoured vehicles and scorched and shattered bodies surrounded by shell-cases and stale bread, the Soviet counter-attack—the BELGOROD–KHARKOV operation—began. In the air, and on the ground, the fundamental balance of forces had shifted in favour of the USSR. It had been Germany's last chance to win the war.

The battle of Kursk showed the Soviets could fight successfully in the summer, and after it the Germans no longer could, losing the strategic initiative irrevocably, something underlined by the simultaneous Allied landing in Sicily. The Soviet counter-offensives that followed removed, in turn, German salients around Orel (KUTUZOV) and Belgorod–

The battle of Kursk. Soviet T-34 tanks and supporting infantry attack at Prokhorovka.

Kharkov (RUMIANTSEV). By the end of the autumn of 1943 the Red Army had reached the line of the Dnieper river and crossed it at a number of points.

The traditional Soviet view sees a third period of the war in the east from January 1944 to May 1945, and this does form a coherent period. The Soviets now combined abundant resources of *matériel* with a mature command system and military structure. Using concentrated mobile forces, especially the Guards Tank Armies, and backing them with massed artillery and tactical air power, they finally achieved those 'deep operations' which had been the focus of Soviet strategic thought in the 1930s. Soviet propagandists spoke of the '10 Stalinist crushing blows' of 1944. The first of these was the recapture of the 'right bank' Ukraine west of the Dnieper in December 1943–April 1944, followed by the recapture of the Crimea in April–May. At about the same time, in January–March, at the other end of the front, the German stranglehold around Leningrad was finally broken. Shortly after D-Day in Normandy came two more major offensives. The first, the Vyborg-Petrozavodsk operation north-west of Leningrad (June–August 1944), forced the Finns to sign an armistice. Much more important in the overall course of the war was BAGRATION in Belorussia.

Operation Bagration (1944)

The Belorussian operation by the Red Army between 23 June and 29 August 1944 was the largest of the war, resulting in the destruction of German Army Group Centre under Field Marshal Ernest Busch and the reconquest of what is now Belarus. It was timed to begin on the third anniversary of the German invasion on 22 June (in fact it was a day late). Four fronts (army groups) were involved: First Baltic (Colonel-General Ivan Bagramyan), Third Belorussian (Colonel-General I. D. Chernyakovsky), Second Belorussian (Colonel-General G. F. Zakharov), and first Belorussian (Colonel-General Konstantin Rokossovsky), totalling 1.4 million men. The Germans were in deeply echeloned defensive positions 250–70 km (155–68 miles) deep, with 1.2 million. The Soviets attacked simultaneously in six places along a 1,100-km (683-mile) front, pushing west 550–600 km (340–70 miles). Minsk was recaptured on 3 July, and by 29 August the Red Army was close to Warsaw and well into East Prussia.

BAGRATION was shortly followed by breakouts further south, the Lvov–Sandomierz operation (July–August 1944), in what had been south-east Poland, and the Jassy–Kishinev operation (August 1944), which captured Moldavia (in Bessarabia), led Romania to change sides, and opened the road to the Balkans.

The Warsaw Uprising (1944)

The uprising was a tragic attempt by the Polish Home Army (Armija Krajowa) to overthrow the German occupation as the Red Army closed on Warsaw. By 28 July 1944 citizens of Warsaw could hear the sounds of the battle between the Wehrmacht and the Red Army. The Soviets were concerned about a German counter-attack and ordered their troops onto the defensive on 1 August.

The Home Army was sponsored by the British and the Polish government in exile in London, but the British turned down requests for active assistance from RAF aircraft and the Polish Parachute Brigade because Warsaw was beyond normal aircraft range and lay within the Soviet sphere. The USSR had its own plans and government-in-waiting, Rada

Narodowa, and sponsored a different Polish army, the Armija Ludowa, which was unified with the Polish army that had been formed in the USSR. Nonetheless, the charge that the Soviets sat back and waited for the Germans to crush the uprising is baseless; there were four German armoured divisions between them and the city and Marshal Konstantin Rokossovsky, commanding the Soviet First Belorussian Front, needed to regroup before continuing the offensive. The lamentable fact is that the uprising was intended to present the advancing Soviets with a fait accompli and was launched without prior consultation with either London or Moscow. It should also be noted that the Home Army did little to support the equally heroic and doomed uprising of the Jews in the Warsaw Ghetto in April 1943.

On 1 August Home Army underground units opened fire inside Warsaw, beginning two months of bitter fighting. The lull in Soviet operations permitted the Germans to send in overwhelming force, backed up by *Einsatzgruppen* extermination squads, and even if the Soviets had cooperated with earlier British efforts to airdrop supplies, it would not have made much difference. The Soviets themselves dropped supplies in the second half of September, but much of these fell into German hands. By 24 September the Germans had forced the isolated Polish units into small pockets and escape through the sewers was the only option. Fifteen thousand fighters of the 30,000–40,000-strong Home Army were dead, and 120,000–200,000 civilians were killed. On 2 October the fighting stopped, the remaining Poles were rounded up for slavery or extermination, and the Germans began razing Warsaw to the ground.

In the autumn of 1944 the Red Army began the campaign for the 'liberation' of east central Europe that would indirectly have such a telling effect on post-war international relations. Having already occupied Romania the Red Army quickly invaded Bulgaria (an Axis member but not an active anti-Soviet belligerent) in September 1944. The Belgrade operation (September–October 1944) took the Red Army into Yugoslavia, and the Debrecen and Budapest operations (October 1944–February 1945) into Hungary.

By 1945 the Third Reich was on its last legs, under siege from east and west. The most striking Soviet success of this period was the Vistula–Oder Operation (January–February 1945) in which Marshal Georgi Zhukov and Marshal Ivan Koniev took the Red Army from the middle of Poland to the approaches to Berlin. The flanks of this operation were secured by hard fighting in East Prussia and Lower Silesia.

The Battle of Berlin (1945)

As it was only at the Yalta conference from 4 to 11 February that the wartime Allies finally agreed post-war zones of occupation and since the demarcation line between the Soviet forces and their Western Allies was the river Elbe, well west of Berlin, there was no need for Stalin to rush for Berlin. The Soviet forces which had advanced with breathtaking speed through Poland were exhausted and running out of fuel. A pause was needed— especially as resistance on German soil proved tougher than expected. Besides, the Red Army was fully occupied moving through Hungary, Slovakia, and Austria. It was nearly two months before Stalin assembled his Main Planning Conference, on 1 April, and decided to take Berlin.

The Red Army had about two million troops available for the assault, with 6,000 tanks and self-propelled (SP) guns and 40,000 artillery pieces against 750,000 German troops

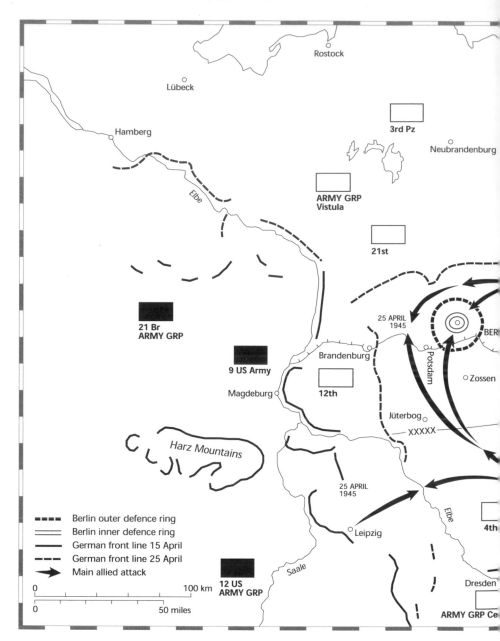

Rostock

Lübeck

Hamberg

Elbe

3rd Pz

Neubrandenburg

ARMY GRP
Vistula

21st

21 Br
ARMY GRP

9 US Army

Brandenburg

Magdeburg

12th

25 APRIL
1945

Potsdam

BER

Zossen

Harz Mountains

Jüterbog

XXXXX

25 APRIL
1945

Elbe

4th

Berlin outer defence ring

Berlin inner defence ring

German front line 15 April

German front line 25 April

Main allied attack

Leipzig

0

100 km

12 US
ARMY GRP

Saale

Dresden

0

50 miles

ARMY GRP Ce

with about 1,500 tanks and assault guns. Berlin lay in the path of Marshal Georgi Zhukov and the first Belorussian Front (army group), with Colonel General Ivan Koniev and the first Ukrainian to the south. Stalin capitalized on their rivalry by scrubbing out the front boundary line 64 km (40 miles) east of the German capital. From there on in the two commanders raced each other to the kill and many thousands of casualties from friendly fire resulted.

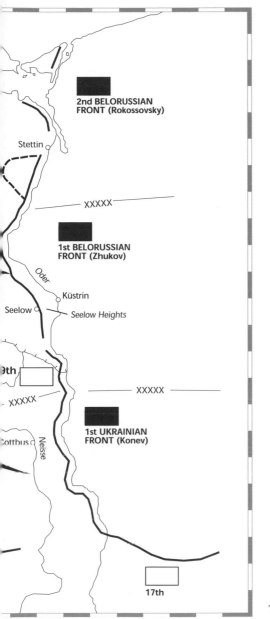

The Soviet conquest of Berlin, 1945

Zhukov used a huge, elaborate scale model of the city to brief his commanders, but in spite of abundant air photography, he failed to identify the main line of German resistance and his attack stalled before the Seelow Heights. Impatient, he launched his two reserve tank armies (First and Second Guards Tank), in defiance of instructions from Stavka, the supreme war council. Stalin was furious but Zhukov won the race. On 23 April Stalin drew the boundary line 150 metres (490 feet) west of the Reichstag, leaving

Koniev, advancing from the south, on the other side. The Red Army broke into the centre of Berlin on the 26th. By 30 April, having fought through the zoo, the Soviet 150th Division of LXXIX Rifle Corps, Eighth Guards Army, first Belorussian Front, was poised to attack the Reichstag—'target number 105'. Two sergeants raised the red flag on the second floor at 14.25 and from the roof at 22.50, although the Germans fought on. That night, the Soviets learned of Hitler's suicide. Negotiations continued until the middle of 1 May when Stalingrad veteran General Vassily Chuikov, commanding Eighth Guards, exasperated, ordered artillery fire to be resumed. Early on 2 May General Weidling, commander of the Berlin garrison, drafted an order for Berlin to give in. At 15.00 on 2 May, Soviet artillery finally ceased fire.

Arguments will continue about the relative importance of the eastern front in the overall history of World War II. The Soviets certainly paid the heaviest price in lives and territory, but that does not in itself make their role decisive. They did engage, in the middle part of World War II, much the greater part of mobile German ground forces, and they inflicted huge losses on those forces. At the same time the operations of the Americans and British would not have been decisive without the immense contribution of the eastern front.

NORTH AFRICAN CAMPAIGNS

It is arguable that the North African theatre, in its constant changes of fortune, was unlike any other during World War II. Both sides prolonged their campaigns there unintentionally, due to the demands of other theatres which were considered more important by their political masters—thus the British diverted forces to the Far East and Greece at crucial moments, as did the Germans to Russia. For both sides also, the campaign stressed the tensions of coalition warfare. The British effort from the start involved its whole empire, with South Africans, Indians, New Zealanders, and Australians fighting under British command, later joined by Free French and, after operation TORCH in November 1942, Americans. The Germans had to contend with the wildly variable Italian army, and a highly political command structure based in Italy. As the Allied and Axis forces in North Africa relied on air cover to protect their Mediterranean shipping convoys and ground troops in the desert, at a strategic level joint cooperation was vital. The Allies eventually mastered this, but the Axis failed effectively to integrate an air campaign to support movement on the ground or across the Mediterranean.

With the Italian invasion from Libya eastwards into British-protected Egypt on 13 September 1940, the desert war began. The Italians halted at Sidi Barani after three days, establishing a series of colonial-type fortified camps which were too far apart to provide mutual assistance. Major General Richard O' Connor's tiny Western Desert force of two divisions from Mersa Matruh counter-attacked on 9 December, and within two months— greatly to his surprise—pushed the Italians out of Egypt and across Cyrenaica, destroying 10 Italian divisions and taking 130,000 prisoners, for a British loss of 2,000 killed and wounded. Mussolini appealed to Hitler for help and a relatively unknown lieutenant general was dispatched with two divisions to North Africa. General Erwin Rommel's arrival in Tripoli on 12 February 1941 altered the course of the desert war. Without waiting to build up his forces, he attacked on 24 March, and over the next 30 days drove the British from El Agheila right back across Cyrenaica and into Egypt at the Halfaya Pass. The port of Benghazi fell on 4 April, but Rommel was unable to take Tobruk, which remained isolated 160 km (100 miles) behind the front. Tobruk was a deep-water port which had been taken by Australian troops from the Italians on 22 January 1941, possession of which would have shortened German supply lines. Its continued resistance assumed a symbolic significance for the British when the war elsewhere was going appallingly, and German propaganda chief Dr Joseph Goebbels called the men of the 9th Australian Division who were holding it 'rats'. The name was adopted by the British army at large and they proudly became the Desert Rats. Rommel had actually been forced to pause before Tobruk due to petrol and other logistical shortages: such problems dogged the rest of his war in North Africa, and dominated the whole campaign over the waterless desert wastes for both sides.

General Sir Archibald Wavell mounted the unsuccessful operation BATTLEAXE to relieve Tobruk in June, but by the time the British launched their next offensive, their commanders had changed. Richard O'Connor, commanding the Western Desert force, had been captured in April and was replaced by Lieutenant General Sir Alan Cunningham (whose admiral brother commanded the RN Mediterranean Fleet), whilst an impatient Churchill sacked the unfortunate Middle East commander Wavell (who had also to contend with the abortive operations in Greece and Crete), replacing him with General Sir Claude Auchinleck. With both sides reinforced, Cunningham's renamed Eighth Army struck back at Rommel's Afrika Korps on 18 November 1941 in operation CRUSADER. The British outnumbered Rommel in CRUSADER, but individual German units within the Italo-German army were better led, and possessed much greater initiative and resourcefulness, with the result that the campaign subsided into a series of inconclusive battles between the Egyptian frontier and Tobruk. Whilst Rommel withdrew west all the way back to El Agheila, Cunningham was replaced by Lieutenant General Neil Ritchie.

With the arrival of fresh forces in Tripoli, Rommel immediately counter-attacked on 21 January 1942, retook Benghazi on the 29th, and in three weeks had rolled Ritchie's Eighth Army back east to Gazala, close to Tobruk. The British southern flank at Bir Hacheim was held by a Free French brigade under Major General J. P. Koenig, which had fought its way up from Chad, and provided the first evidence that de Gaulle's Free French units could play a role in the war.

The Battle of Gazala (1942)

During a four-month lull both sides considered further offensives. Rommel hoped to take Tobruk and go on to Egypt. The British wished to advance into Cyrenaica to establish airfields to cover Mediterranean convoys. General Sir Claude Auchinleck had been forced to send troops to the Far East and believed that defensive strategy was more realistic, but Churchill demanded an attack. Lieutenant General Neil Ritchie's Eighth Army held the Gazala Line in a series of 'boxes', held by infantry protected by wire and minefields, with its armour to the rear.

On 26 May Rommel led his armoured divisions around the southern end of the line and did serious damage to dispersed British armour. However, the new Grant tank was an unpleasant surprise, and German tank losses were heavy. Worse, the Free French garrison of Bir Hacheim held out. Unable to roll the line up, Rommel needed to break through it to get supplies to his armour, fighting hard to its east. He was urged to break off the battle, but penetrated the minefield in the nick of time.

The British failed to counter-attack Rommel's bridgehead until his anti-armour screen was ready, and the Germans emerged victors from very bitter fighting in the Cauldron. Bir Hacheim had to be abandoned, and Rommel then forced the British out of the Knightsbridge box, behind the Gazala Line, making the whole position untenable. Tobruk fell on 21 June, and Rommel crossed the Egyptian frontier two days later. Auchinleck flew up to take personal command, but could not rally survivors until they reached the Alamein position on 1 July. Gazala marked the nadir of British fortunes. Although they were numerically superior in men and tanks, hesitant command and immature tactical doctrine led the British to lose a battle they had been within measurable distance of winning. Churchill took the blow badly, whilst Rommel was rewarded with a field marshal's baton.

By this stage, Eighth Army morale was suspect, especially as regards the relationship between infantry and tank units, whilst reinforcements were being diverted to the Far East, and the logistical tail through the Mediterranean was under severe German and Italian air and U-boat attack. But Rommel, too, had outrun his lines of supply, and was surviving only on what had been captured in Benghazi and Tobruk. Auchinleck took the opportunity to remove Ritchie and assume command of the Eighth Army himself. However, he was still forced to retreat before Rommel, first at Mersa Matruh on 28 June, and thence on 7 July to a fortified line on the Alam Halfa ridge, between the railway station at Alamein and the Qattara depression 48 km (30 miles) to the south. The series of fierce battles between the armies' arrival at Alam Halfa and 22 July proved the exhaustion of both forces and Rommel's inability to advance further without substantial reinforcement. Consequently both sides paused, but now the British were able reinforce quicker, whilst Auchinleck was replaced by General Sir Harold Alexander, and Lieutenant General William Gott was nominated to take over the Eighth Army. The latter's death when his plane was brought down resulted in Lieutenant General Bernard Montgomery assuming command of the Eighth Army on 13 August.

The Battle of El Alamein (1942)

Lieutenant General Montgomery set about turning the Eighth Army into a confident, capable, aggressive, and successful force. The turning point for the Eighth Army was undoubtedly the battle of Alam Halfa (30 August–7 September 1942), sometimes hailed as the first battle of Alamein. Montgomery's operational competence was displayed, as was his sense of caution and his reluctance to commit his forces unless conditions were overwhelmingly in his favour. Its attack blunted, the Afrika Korps withdrew to regroup; but Montgomery refused to counter-attack and pursue. Rommel then departed for Germany with a catalogue of ailments, the result of exhaustion. Montgomery, firmly in command of a confident force which had tasted victory, waited for his moment.

After much deliberation and disagreement among the Allies, it had finally been agreed that the 'Germany first' strategy should begin in autumn 1942 with an attack against Axis forces in the Mediterranean. The outcome would be the Anglo-American landings in the western Mediterranean. Against this strategic background, Montgomery's moment arrived on 23 October 1942, when he launched the Eighth Army's 230,000 men and 1,030 tanks against Rommel's 100,000 men and 500 tanks. By 4 November 1942, the German–Italian army had been routed. Days later, the TORCH landings took place in Morocco and Algeria, and, with the counter-offensive at Stalingrad on 19 November, World War II changed its course.

Montgomery executed his attack on Rommel (who was still on sick leave in Germany when the battle began) in three phases. In the first, the 'Break-In', XXX Corps (Lieutenant General Sir Oliver Leese) attacked the Axis defence in its centre, heavily fortified and defended by minefields; XIII Corps (Lieutenant General Brian Horrocks) attacked in the south. Neither XXX nor XIII Corps were able to break through to exploit the more open country to the rear of the Axis position. Montgomery's second phase—the 'Dog-Fight'—therefore took place in the midst of the Axis position. Between 26 and 31 October Axis fortifications were steadily, and characteristically for Montgomery, reduced by attrition. Axis counter-attacks were repulsed with the use of air power. The final phase—the 'Break-Out'—took place between 1 and 4 November. The reinforced New Zealand Division drilled through the weakened Axis defensive position, making it possible for X Corps, which had been in reserve, to break out into the Axis rear. Counter-attacking constantly, the Afrika Korps was nevertheless unable to wrong-foot Montgomery and resist the torrent. Those German and Italian divisions which were mobile fell into a headlong withdrawal, leaving infantry divisions to surrender. On 23 January 1943, the Eighth Army reached Tripoli.

Second Alamein proved Montgomery's ability as a field commander, justified his elaborate and time-consuming logistic and deception plans, and was an important psychological blow both to Rommel (who quickly resumed command on 25 October), and to Berlin. As Alexandria lay only 97 km (60 miles) east of Alamein, Egypt and the Suez Canal had been in grave danger, but Montgomery's victory lifted this threat for good, and restored Eighth Army morale just when needed.

Although the British lost almost as many tanks as Panzer Army Africa, Rommel could not replace the losses he sustained at Alamein, and the TORCH landings at Casablanca, Oran, and Algiers in French North Africa to his rear (which followed Montgomery's victory by a mere four days) altered completely the nature of the campaign. By November 1942 Hitler was preoccupied exclusively with the struggle for Stalingrad which was nearing a climax, and the 'stand-and-fight' order issued to Rommel immediately after Alamein demonstrated Berlin's complete lack of understanding of the situation, or the nature of desert war. Rommel began his retreat on 4 November 1942 anyway. Thereafter his withdrawal westwards was swift, and Montgomery was slow to pursue. Nevertheless by 17 December the Eighth Army had reached El Agheila, whence Rommel had set out 21 months previously, in March 1941. The Axis supply base of Tripoli fell on 23 January 1943, and, although the port was partially wrecked, it started taking shipping within a week. Montgomery's logistics remained a nightmare, though, all the way into Tunisia, which he entered on 4 February, two days after Stalingrad fell.

A few days after Alamein an Allied invasion force under Lieutenant General Dwight D. Eisenhower landed in French North Africa. There was some fighting with the French before Admiral François Darlan, a senior minister in Marshal Pétain's Vichy government, who happened to be in Algiers, ordered a ceasefire. Having secured Oran, Algiers, and Casablanca, the Allied First Army advanced eastwards, taking Bone on 12 November before being stopped at Mejez el Bab, just 48 km (30 miles) south-west of Tunis. Hitler had reacted swiftly to the invasion, sending his troops into the Unoccupied Zone of France and reinforcing his troops in North Africa with what was to become General Jürgen von Arnim's Fifth Panzer Army.

Arnim, anxious to prevent the Allies from cutting him off from Rommel, who was withdrawing before Montgomery, stopped the First Army in hard-fought battles at Tebourba and Longstop Hill, and then counter-attacked in January 1943, knocking it off balance.

The Battle of the Kasserine Pass (1943)

In February 1941, Rommel, who was facing Montgomery, decided to launch a pre-emptive attack against an Allied threat to his communications with Arnim, further north. He sent one column through Sidi bou Zid to the Kasserine Pass and another further south. The Germans attacked in the best blitzkrieg style, their armour supported by aircraft. The US 1st Armoured Division was caught flat footed, its piecemeal counter-attacks roughly handled. On 18 February Rommel broke through the Kasserine Pass and pressed northwards to the Western Dorsal Range, threatening the supply base at Tebessa. Eisenhower rushed reinforcements into the sector, Allied units steadied to their task, a thrust by Arnim failed to materialize, and the attackers ran out of steam. Rommel then swung back to meet Montgomery.

The Allied reverse was in part a consequence of American inexperience. More culpably, it was the result of overextension and poor coordination. It produced a command shake-up, with Major General George S. Patton taking over the US II Corps from Major General Lloyd Fredendall, and General Sir Harold Alexander assuming command of the Eighteenth Army Group.

On 23 February Rommel was given command of Army Group Africa: his old German-Italian Panzer Army was retitled the First Italian Army under General Giovanni Messe. Rommel was still very dangerous, and planned to use all three of his armoured divisions against Montgomery, who was now approaching the Mareth Line, a pre-war French defensive system, which had been designed to prevent the Italians moving from Libya into south-eastern Tunisia. On 6 March Rommel made an unsuccessful jab at Medenine, just east of the line, and was flown home, a sick man, three days later. Although Montgomery's frontal attack on the Mareth Line failed, he outflanked it from the south, and Messe fell back on Wadi Akarit.

By now Arnim's position was worsening daily as the Allied sea and air blockade throttled him. While the Eighth Army took Wadi Akarit and advanced northwards to Sousse and Enfidaville, the First Army fought its way towards Bizerta and Tunis. Arnim's men fought hard to the end, but Bizerta and Tunis were both captured on 7 May and the last Axis troops surrendered on 13 May. The Allies took 238,000 prisoners, and had at last won the campaign in North Africa.

German tanks of the Afrika Korps move towards Mersa Brega, March 1941.

THE PACIFIC AND FAR EASTERN THEATRE

In 1931 the Japanese army in Manchuria seized the whole province. Border incidents with China were provoked until in 1937 full-scale war broke out, which led to the Japanese conquest of much of northern China by 1941. The Japanese experience against the USSR was very different.

The Battle of Khalkin-Gol (1939)

The battle of Khalkin-Gol (Nomonhan) was an exemplary encirclement by Soviet forces of Japanese troops within a defined and disputed area, leading to a decisive Soviet victory which protected the USSR from a two-front war after the German invasion in 1941. It was also a formative experience for General Georgi Zhukov, later the pre-eminent Soviet commander in World War II.

The boundary dispute over Khalkin-Gol (Halha river) was 200 years old. On 28 May 1939 a Japanese force tried to encircle a Soviet-Mongolian force in the disputed area. The Japanese then pushed forward not only to the river, which they claimed as the border, but beyond it. On 2 June Zhukov was summoned to see Marshal Kliment Voroshilov and ordered to Mongolia. Zhukov decided to launch an attack with LVII Special Corps, later renamed the First Army Group, to destroy the Japanese. It had to be decisive, even spectacular, in order to work. Stalin approved the plan, and Zhukov reported directly to him.

The area was 650 km (404 miles) from the nearest railhead. A conveyor belt of trucks brought supplies forward, including materials to build defences. This was an important part of Zhukov's deception, to convince the Japanese that the Soviets had no intention of attacking. Zhukov built up a force of 65,000 Soviet and Mongolian troops against 28,000 Japanese and Manchukuoan (from the puppet state the Japanese had created in Manchuria). Soviet troops began pressing forward on both flanks on 19 August. The battle followed what would become a classic pattern of Soviet encirclement: establishing an outer front of mobile forces (tank and mechanized brigades) while an inner front, largely infantry, worked to destroy the trapped enemy. The Japanese divisional commander and 400 survivors just managed to escape. On 3 September the Japanese emperor, aware of the crisis in Europe as World War II began, ordered the incident to be resolved. The USSR admitted 18,500 casualties in the battle, and claimed to have inflicted 61,000; the Japanese admitted 18,000.

French defeat in Europe in 1940 permitted the Japanese to move into Indochina without firing a shot. The USA was slow to react to Japanese expansion, while the European colonial powers did almost nothing to obstruct it from fear of provoking a Pacific war they could not afford. But by 1940 US President Franklin D. Roosevelt felt strong enough to do more than merely provide aid to China, and began an economic campaign against Japan. In July oil and scrap-metal exports were restricted and, following Japan's occupation of Indochina, a tighter oil embargo was imposed.

Chinese troops use the Great Wall as their route to advance against the Japanese.

World War II: the Pacific theatre

The oil factor prompted Japanese military leaders to plan a 'southward advance' to seize the oil and other resources of the Dutch Indies and British Malaya. After the failure of diplomatic negotiations with the USA in the autumn of 1941, the emperor finally approved the plan to seize the southern area on 1 December 1941. Admiral Isoroku

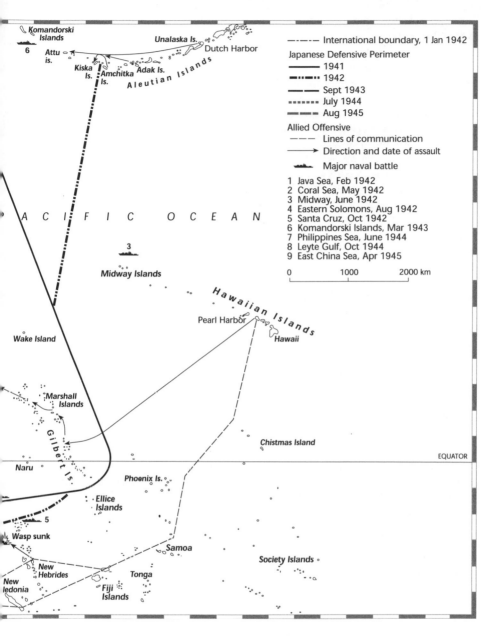

Komandorski Islands
6 Attu is.
Unalaska Is.
Dutch Harbor
Kiska Is. Amchitka Is. Adak Is.
Aleutian Islands

International boundary, 1 Jan 1942
Japanese Defensive Perimeter
————— 1941
—·■—·■·· 1942
————— Sept 1943
········ July 1944
———— Aug 1945
Allied Offensive
— — — Lines of communication
————▶ Direction and date of assault
⚓ Major naval battle

1 Java Sea, Feb 1942
2 Coral Sea, May 1942
3 Midway, June 1942
4 Eastern Solomons, Aug 1942
5 Santa Cruz, Oct 1942
6 Komandorski Islands, Mar 1943
7 Philippines Sea, June 1944
8 Leyte Gulf, Oct 1944
9 East China Sea, Apr 1945

P A C I F I C   O C E A N

3
Midway Islands

Hawaiian Islands
Pearl Harbor
Hawaii

0   1000   2000 km

Wake Island

Marshall Islands

Gilbert Is.

Chistmas Island

EQUATOR

Naru

Phoenix Is.

Ellice Islands

5
Wasp sunk

Samoa

Society Islands

New Hebrides
Tonga
New Caledonia
Fiji Islands

Yamamoto, commander-in-chief of the Combined Fleet, knew the economic power of the USA and was not sanguine about the army-driven policy, but devised a plan whereby naval aircraft flown from a powerful group of aircraft carriers would neutralize the American Pacific Fleet while the southward advance was completed.

Pearl Harbor (1941)

The attack on Pearl Harbor of 7 December 1941 was at one level simply a repeat of the Sunday surprise attack with which the Japanese navy opened the Russo-Japanese War. A task force under Vice Admiral Nagumo Chuichi, which included six aircraft carriers and two battleships, sailed from Japan on 26 November and from 400 km (250 miles) north of the island launched some 350 aircraft before dawn. Surprise was complete, 8 battleships and assorted other warships were sunk or disabled, and 186 aircraft were destroyed, mostly on the ground. The Japanese lost 29 aircraft and 6 submarines, 5 of them ineffectual midgets. However, the attack did not find the US fleet carriers in port and Nagumo showed the fear of land-based aircraft that was to be fatal at Midway seven months later, and withdrew without sending in a third strike to destroy crucial oil storage facilities.

The episode remains deeply controversial. Although Vice Admiral Husband E. Kimmel and Lieutenant General Walter C. Short, the senior US naval and military commanders in Hawaii, were unwise in allowing normal peacetime routine to prevail at a time of tension (and both had to resign in consequence), they were not provided with intelligence deriving from intercepted radio messages, which would have altered their view of the risk.

Nagumo thought that all he had done was 'to waken a sleeping giant, and to fill her with a terrible resolve'. His point was well made: except for the battleships *Arizona* and *Oklahoma* and the target vessel *Utah* all the US vessels were returned to service, while of the Japanese only the destroyer *Ushio* survived the war.

As Admiral Yamamoto had predicted, the Japanese ran wild for the first six months. The southward advance proved unstoppable against weak or poorly prepared defences.

The Fall of Hong Kong (1941)

In December 1941 the colony of Hong Kong island and its associated British-held territories were garrisoned by Major General Christopher Maltby's six British-Indian and Canadian battalions and six companies of local volunteers, with six medium batteries and an assortment of coast defence guns. He was supported by a tiny flotilla and five aircraft. It was recognized that sustained defence of Hong Kong was impossible, for half its water came from the mainland: Maltby was ordered to hold 'as long as possible'.

Maltby divided his force into the Mainland Brigade (Brigadier Wallis) and the Island Brigade (Brigadier Lawson) with three battalions apiece. With too few men to hold the Sham Chun river, the border with China, Wallis defended the Gindrinkers Line, running across the neck of the Kowloon peninsula. Although some defences had been constructed before 1938, and coast-defence guns on Stonecutters Island could provide supporting fire, the line was not ideal. There was a gap which obliged Wallis to commit his one reserve company, and it was so close to the sea that there was no room for another line behind.

Early on 8 December 1942 Japanese air attack destroyed all the British aircraft, and six battalions of the 38th Division began to cross the Sham Chun. A British covering force with light armour delayed them briefly, but they were up on the Gindrinkers Line late on 9 December. In the early hours of 10 December the commander of the Japanese 228th

The attack on Pearl Harbor. A rescue launch approaches the blazing USS *West Virginia*.

Regiment, acting without his divisional commander's approval, attacked and took the Shing Mun redoubt which dominated the ground in his sector. Wallis had no reserve available, and the local battalion commander was also unable to counter-attack. Wallis pulled back about 1.5 km (1 mile) on his left to compensate for loss of the redoubt, and was soon clear that the Japanese were so close to embarkation points that there was no alternative to evacuation, which was completed by early on 13 December.

Maltby reorganized his command into East Brigade (Wallis) and West Brigade (Lawson) with a two-battalion Fortress Reserve. An attempted crossing was repulsed on 15 December, but late on the 18th Japanese crossed Victoria Harbour and advanced inland. Lawson was killed defending the crucial Wong Nei Chong gap in the centre of the island, and there was some confusion as East Brigade withdrew prior to launching a counter-attack which was repulsed on the 20th. Despite some courageous local actions Maltby's position was impossible, and the governor, Sir Mark Young, authorized surrender which was completed on 26 December.

The Malaya and Singapore Campaign

The British had built a naval base at Singapore to counter the threat of Japanese expansionism. Heavy guns were put into position on Singapore island to defend it against attack from the sea. In the 1930s there was recognition that Singapore and Malaya could best be defended from the air, and new airfields were built. By 1938 it was accepted that the defence of Singapore must involve that of Malaya and its airfields, but with the outbreak of war in Europe, aircraft and warships which might have been sent were needed elsewhere.

In October 1940 Air Chief Marshal Sir Robert Brooke-Popham was recalled from retirement to become commander-in-chief Far East: he was 62 and lacked recent operational experience and knowledge of the area. Each service had its own commander: Lieutenant General Arthur Percival arrived as general officer commanding Malaya in May 1941. Brooke-Popham had demanded more resources, but was told by Churchill in January 1941 that 'The political situation in the Far East does not seem to require, and the strength of our air force by no means permits, the maintenance of such large forces in the Far East at this time.'

When Japan entered the war in December 1941 Malaya was defended by the two under-strength divisions, 9th and 11th, of Lieutenant General Sir Lewis Heath's III Indian Corps. Major General Frank Simmons, general officer commanding Singapore Fortress, was responsible for the defence of Singapore and the southern tip of Johore, and his force included the leading brigade of the 8th Australian Division under Major General Henry Gordon Bennett. The RAF had only 158 first-line aircraft, mostly old and vulnerable. The Japanese invasion was well prepared, with landings at Singora and Patani in Thailand and Khota Bharu in Malaya.

The pattern of the campaign emerged quickly. The Japanese soon gained air superiority, and three divisions under Lieutenant General Tomoyuki Yamashita moved rapidly southwards, attacking along the axis of main roads but hooking into the jungle to outflank the defenders and establish road blocks behind them. The British lost successive battles at Jitra (11 December), Gurun (15 December), Kampar (2 January 1942), and Slim River (7 January). Kuala Lumpur fell on 11 January.

In October 1941 the British decided that the brand-new battleship *Prince of Wales* and the equally new aircraft carrier *Indomitable* would join the old battlecruiser *Repulse* in the

Indian Ocean. The carrier was damaged during working-up trials, but the other vessels, known as Force Z, under the command of Admiral Sir Tom Phillips, reached Singapore. On the evening of 8 December Phillips put to sea in an effort to engage the Japanese landings, and on the 10th was attacked by aircraft based in Indochina: both his capital ships were sunk by torpedo bombers, and he was among over 800 men lost.

Disasters on land and sea encouraged the Allies to establish a unified American-British-Dutch-Australian (ABDA) Command, with the British General Sir Archibald Wavell at its head. Wavell visited Malaya, revised Lieutenant General Percival's plans, and warned him to prepare defences in case he had to withdraw to Singapore. The commitment of the Australian division could not prevent the fall of Johore, and on 31 January the causeway linking Singapore to the mainland was blown.

Percival was ordered by Churchill not to contemplate giving up until 'after protracted fighting among the ruins of Singapore city', but his position was already difficult. Singapore's population was swollen by refugees, and two-fifths of the city's water had come in pipes from the mainland. Early on 9 February the Japanese landed on the north-west shore, and made good progress, rapidly reaching the reservoirs in the island's centre. The newly arrived 18th Division, committed to battle without preparation, could do little to stem the flow, and after consulting his senior commanders Percival surrendered on 15 February. Yamashita was desperately short of ammunition, and in no position to fight a protracted battle.

Churchill was right to call it 'the worst disaster and largest capitulation in British military history'. Of the 140,000 British and Commonwealth engaged, some 9,000 were killed and about 130,000 captured. The Japanese committed 55,000 men and lost 3,500 killed. The real origins of the catastrophe lay in a British pre-war defence policy which failed to balance commitments with resources.

US forces in the Philippines were quickly cornered and finally surrendered on 6 May, while the Dutch East Indies, the Solomon Islands, and most of New Guinea were in Japanese hands by March. British, Dutch, and US naval and air forces in the theatre had been destroyed, but in April 1942 a US bomber attack on Tokyo was mounted as a gesture of revenge and defiance by a group of Mitchell B-25s under Colonel James Doolittle. They were flown from the carriers *Hornet* and *Enterprise* and the aircraft continued to land in China. The damage inflicted was minimal, many of the aircrew fell into Japanese hands, and the carriers found themselves back in Pearl Harbor when they were badly needed in the Coral Sea.

The Battle of the Coral Sea (1942)

Admiral Chester Nimitz was aware, through signals intelligence, that the Japanese planned to seize Port Moresby on the southern coast of New Guinea and to establish airfields that would allow them to bomb targets in Australia. An invasion force was to sail from New Britain by way of the Jomard Passage into the Coral Sea between their destination and Australia, covered by a striking force which would sail east of the Solomon Islands. This they did, turning west on 7 May to seek the American task forces which included the carriers *Lexington* and *Yorktown*. On 8 May the western Coral Sea was clear and sunlit while cloud obscured the Japanese fleet to the east. Reconnaissance aircraft of both sides scanned the ocean for their enemies.

At 08.30 the Americans found the Japanese, and Dauntless dive-bombers and Devastator torpedo bombers were sent to attack, covered by Wildcat fighters. The fleet carrier *Shokaku* was hit by bombs and with difficulty kept afloat. In the absence of the Wildcats the Japanese attack on the American ships met little effective resistance. *Lexington* was hit by two torpedoes and *Yorktown* was bombed; the former eventually had to be sunk but the latter was able to remain operational. When the action was broken off at dusk neither fleet had seen the other; the first sea battle conducted entirely by aircraft was over and the Japanese had been forced to abandon their invasion.

Admiral *Isoroku Yamamoto* had been ordered to secure the ocean perimeter, an operation he combined with a plan to lure what was left of the American Pacific Fleet into a battle of annihilation. The plan was in jeopardy. The Pacific theatre became a chiefly American responsibility, as British Commonwealth forces struggled to contain Japanese pressure through Burma towards India. Though President Roosevelt favoured priority for the European theatre following German declaration of war on 11 December 1941, the Anglophobe US navy chief Admiral Ernest King (and much of American opinion) favoured emphasis on the Pacific. Forces were rushed to the southern Pacific to hold the remaining islands and to protect Australia, but the quantity of material and trained men available left a thin shield until American rearmament reached higher levels in 1943.

The Battle of Midway (1942)

On 2 June 1942 the Japanese combined fleet under the direction of Admiral Yamamoto on the super-battleship *Yamato* was committed to an elaborate ocean-wide operation with three objectives. The first was to seize an outer perimeter including the undefended Aleutian Islands in the north and the well-garrisoned atoll of Midway, with its important airbase, in order to prevent a repetition of the raid on Tokyo by B-25 bombers. The second was thereby to disperse what was left of the US Pacific Fleet after Pearl Harbor and the battle of the Coral Sea. The third was to draw the remaining US carriers towards Midway to counter the attack by four large carriers under Vice Admiral Nagumo, while the main battle fleet sailed to the north to cut them off.

US naval intelligence was achieving considerable success against the Japanese naval code then in use and Admiral Chester Nimitz was well informed of his opponent's intentions, but not of the full danger he faced. Of his three remaining fleet carriers, *Hornet* and *Enterprise* were intact, but the *Yorktown* had been severely damaged. She was made battleworthy in 48 hours and sailed to form the heart of one battle group under Rear Admiral Frank Fletcher, while *Hornet* and *Enterprise* under Rear Admiral Raymond Spruance formed the other.

The invasion force making for Midway was ineffectually attacked on 3 June, and Midway was heavily bombed on the following day. Nagumo was preparing for a second attack on Midway when the Americans found him. Their torpedo bombers were massacred and scored no hits, but the result was to pull down the Japanese carriers' fighter cover, and the US dive-bombers had the further good fortune to catch the carriers with their decks loaded with fully armed and fuelled bombers awaiting launch against the US carriers. *Akagi*, *Kaga*, and *Soryu* were set on fire from stem to stern within minutes at around 10.30, all to be sunk later by their escorts. *Hiryu*, the sole survivor, got off two strikes, both of which found and crippled *Yorktown* (which eventually sank only after being torpedoed by a Japanese submarine while under tow) but she was herself found and set ablaze at 17.00. The US navy lost 150 aircraft and 300 men. The Japanese lost their entire front line of naval aviators, 250 aircraft, and their crews, as well as the carriers that had been running wild in the south Pacific for six months. Yamamoto ordered a withdrawal and the combined fleet never regained the strategic initiative. Yamamoto did not play his battleship trump card when it might still have been decisive.

While the USA devoted the bulk of its army to the war in Europe, the Pacific was by far the main theatre for the navy and US Marines, while General Douglas MacArthur was successful in his public and private lobbying to ensure that the army also got enough resources to compete. The strategy was to assault (or bypass) key island strongholds while unrestricted submarine warfare gnawed away at Japanese trade and military supply lines.

The Battle for Guadalcanal (1942–1943)

The British possession of Guadalcanal is one of the largest of the southern group of Solomon Islands, and its occupation in early 1942 marked the limit of Japanese expansion in the south-west Pacific. The southern Solomons dominate New Guinea and provided a springboard for an invasion of Australia; therefore their possession was vital for both sides. Just as the Japanese, with invasion plans in mind, started to move powerful forces into the area, a force of US Marines landed on Guadalcanal on 7 August 1942, seizing the adjacent harbour of Tulagi and the strategically valuable airfield the Japanese had constructed. In the fierce fighting that followed the Marines were introduced to the all-or-nothing 'banzai' charge and to the fact that the Japanese were prepared to fight to the last man. The battle, which raged until February 1943, was decided by five sea battles fought in the vicinity, which began with US and Allied disasters, but ended with the Japanese loss of two battleships. The 'Tokyo Express' down 'The Slot', as the channel leading to Guadalcanal was called, came regularly by night (to negate US air superiority) to shell the airfield (Henderson field) and to land reinforcements. Defending the airfield perimeter, US Marines were locked in a bitter struggle with an enemy better trained and equipped to cope with the malaria-ridden jungle. Eventually US forces built up to an overwhelming 50,000 troops on the island, and the remaining Japanese were evacuated with one last run of the Tokyo Express.

During 1944 the US advance northwards from New Guinea and the Solomon Islands and westwards across the Pacific from the Marshall and Gilbert and Ellice Islands was speeded up in order to secure bases from which American long-range bombers, and in particular the new B-29 Superfortress, could attack the Japanese home islands. In June 1944 the US navy was in a position to attack and seize the Mariana Islands, including Saipan, from which sustained air attack could be conducted. Japanese leaders were determined to hold on to what they saw as the critical area of the Pacific theatre. Vice Admiral Jisaburo Ozawa gathered a force of 9 aircraft carriers and 450 aircraft, but was greatly outnumbered by the 15 carriers and 902 aircraft available to the US task force. In what became known as the Great Marianas Turkey Shoot US aircraft destroyed the Japanese carrier force and all but 35 Japanese aircraft. The battle of the Philippines Sea was an overwhelming US victory and paved the way for the successful occupation of Saipan by 10 July.

The Battle for Guam (1944)

The largest, most populous, and southernmost of the Marianas island chain, with an excellent harbour and an important source of fresh water, Guam had been occupied immediately after Pearl Harbor by Japanese forces who quickly overwhelmed the 500 defenders. When it came to be reinvaded by 55,000 Marines of III US Amphibious Corps on 20 July 1944, the Japanese defenders put up a stiff fight for three weeks, but over 10,000 (out of 19,000) were killed. The island is about 48 km (30 miles) long and 6.3–13 km (4–8 miles) wide, and covered with dense jungle, which made the going heavy, and gave the defenders an immense advantage. Major General Roy Geiger's solution was an extended naval and air bombardment which dislocated the defenders and bought time to clear away some of the beach obstacles. Once occupied, the island was then turned into a huge air and naval base, and squadrons of B-29 Superfortresses were stationed there to attack the Japanese mainland. Some defenders resisted for long afterwards, the last surrendering only in 1972.

On every island Japanese soldiers refused to surrender, which made conquest a longer and more costly process than the balance of material forces suggested. In savage fighting almost all the 27,000 Japanese troops on Saipan were killed.

Not to be outdone, MacArthur was making a virtue of necessity by 'island-hopping' around areas of Japanese strength, and used political and sentimental arguments to insist on the strategically irrelevant invasion of the Philippines. In October the largest task force of the Pacific war sailed for the island of Leyte to begin the reconquest of the archipelago. The Japanese navy calculated that a triple-pronged counter-attack making use of the channels between the islands and the remains of their land-based air power might offer a last chance of success, but they simply lacked the strength to make their brilliant conception work. The battle of Leyte Gulf was the largest naval engagement in history and despite luring away Vice Admiral William Halsey's main battle fleet, there were enough ships left to withstand the Japanese attack, and US submarine and air dominance was decisive. The Japanese lost 28 warships to 6 and were finished.

The Battle of Iwo Jima (1945)

One of the most intense battles of World War II was fought for an island from which it would be possible to fly fighter escorts for bomber attacks on mainland Japan. Japanese commander Lieutenant General Tadamichi Kuribayashi negated US firepower by sheltering his 22,000 men in 1,500 bunkers linked by 26 km (16 miles) of tunnels, enabling them to strike in areas believed to be secure. He turned the whole 21-square-km (8-square-mile) island into a meat grinder. US Marine Corps casualties between 19 February and 25 March were 26,000. The defenders swore there would be 'no Japanese survivors' and 99 per cent of them kept their word. Aerial kamikaze attacks also sank an escort carrier and damaged several other ships.

A photograph which has achieved iconic status: the raising of the flag on Iwo Jima. Joe Rosenthal's picture of the second flag-raising on Mount Suribachi is the model for the US Marine Corps memorial at Arlington Cemetery.

The emblematic event of the battle was the raising of the US flag atop extinct volcano Mount Suribachi on 23 February 1945, the subject of the most famous battle photograph of all time by Associated Press photographer Joe Rosenthal and the model for the US Marine Corps memorial at Arlington National Cemetery.

The conquest of the Mariana Islands allowed US bombers to be deployed for a concerted attack on the Japanese war economy. The Twenty-First Bomber Group was transferred to Saipan from where operations were launched from November 1944. The Japanese war economy was already crippled by the submarine campaign, but the American joint chiefs ordered the air force to attack Japanese aircraft and shipping industries, and to undertake urban area bombing as in Europe. From March 1945 General Curtis LeMay undertook the firebombing of vulnerable Japanese cities, and between May and August a schedule of 58 cities was drawn up for destruction from the air. As has since become their habit, American air leaders argued that bombing alone would decide the issue, ignoring the fact that without the US navy they would not even have got within range.

Nonetheless preparations began for a massive amphibious assault on Japan, codenamed OLYMPIC, for which the US navy allocated 90 aircraft carriers and 14,000 combat aircraft, larger than the force deployed for the Normandy campaign. The Japanese military prepared for a last-ditch defence of the motherland. It was the fear of massive casualties from the conquest of the home islands that encouraged the American government to launch attacks with atomic bombs.

The Bombings of Hiroshima and Nagasaki (1945)

The atomic bombing of the Japanese cities of Hiroshima and Nagasaki in August 1945 represents arguably the most important and most sinister development in warfare in the twentieth century. On 16 July 1945 the first atomic bomb was tested at a site called Trinity in New Mexico. The blast that resulted was the release of energy equivalent to 20 kilotonnes of TNT.

Hiroshima became the target of the first weapon at 08.15 on 6 August 1945. The all-clear had in fact sounded from an initial alert when the bomb was dropped. It was carried by a B-29 Superfortress called Enola Gay, and exploded about 550 m (1800 yards) over the city producing the equivalent of 15 kilotons of energy. Between 130,000 and 200,000 people died, were injured, or disappeared. The Japanese government attempted to play down the impact and significance of this ominous development, which was followed a few days later by a second atomic bombing. This weapon had been destined for Kokura on the southern Japanese island of Kyushu, but cloud cover forced the crew to attack their secondary target of the shipyards of Nagasaki. The Nagasaki bomb was of about 20 kilotonnes but did less damage because of the local topography. It exploded above Urakami to the north of the port.

The injuries and destruction from the two bombs resulted from three factors: the intense blast; thermal radiation causing burns and producing fires; and nuclear radiation, which caused death and injury from damaged tissues. Each of the three effects was found on victims within 1.5 km (1 mile) from the epicentre, but the first two factors caused most deaths.

Even though more people died in the conventional bombing of Tokyo (including 85,000 on 10 March alone), the atomic bombings were significant because they caused death on a huge scale from one bomb dropped by one plane. In purely military terms the bombs proved decisive in persuading the Japanese government to think the unthinkable and accept defeat.

The Manchurian Campaign (1945)

In the final campaign of the war the Soviet Far Eastern Command destroyed the million-strong Japanese Kwantung Army in the Japanese puppet state of Manchukuo between 9 August and 2 September. The campaign began the night before the dropping of the second atomic bomb on Japan on 9 August, which has led some historians to question its importance. However, on 9 August a Japanese theatre command with 3 army groups ('area armies'), 1 million men, 5,000 guns, 1,100 tanks, and 1,800 aircraft was still intact, and it fought on until the end of the month. The Soviet operation was considered by Cold War military analysts to be the prototype for a future Soviet theatre strategic operation in, for example, Western Europe. The theatre was the size of Europe and the terrain very varied, including the Gobi Desert, the Greater and Lesser Khingan mountain ranges, melted permafrost, and swamp.

Three months after defeating the Germans in Europe, the Red Army was at its most powerful. In firepower, mobility, communications, support, and even battle experience (their veteran troops mostly having died in the Pacific campaign) the Japanese were no match for the three Soviet fronts (army groups) gathered round Manchuria: First and Second Far Eastern on the Pacific and the Transbaikal Front in Mongolia. Units which had experience against German defences in East Prussia were drafted in to deal with similar defences near Vladivostok. The Second Far Eastern Front, with most of the lower-quality formations, stood mainly on the defensive north of the Amur river. An independent force, equating to an army, in the Gobi Desert was Issa Pliev's Soviet–Mongolian cavalry mechanized group. This secured the right (south-western) flank and moved to threaten Peking (Beijing).

The Japanese had seriously misjudged how far the Soviet army had come in conducting 'deep operations'. They believed any Soviet offensive would have to halt for resupply after 400 km (250 miles) and planned to use this breathing space to marshal their forces for a defensive battle on the central Manchurian plain. In fact, the Soviets and Mongolians penetrated much deeper without halting. They made extensive use of airborne forces to seize airfields and communications centres ahead of the main advancing columns.

The Transbaikal Front advanced through the mountains to the central plain covering an astonishing 900 km (560 miles) in eleven days—virtually unopposed because the Japanese had not thought the Soviet-Mongolian forces would be able to advance through the mountains because of resupply problems. As the Soviet columns bit deeply into Manchuria the Kwantung army, following an order from Tokyo, surrendered at Khabarovsk. Soviet forces also advanced south from Kamchatka and northern Sakhalin to occcupy southern Sakhalin and the Kurile islands. Soviet and Japanese troops continued to fight until the day before Japan's formal capitulation on 2 September.

By August 1945 Japan was in ruins, and the political conflict between hard-line militarists and civilian capitulationists was resolved by the emperor, who made his first ever broadcast to his people on 15 August, announcing in one of history's greater understatements that the war had 'not necessarily developed in a manner favourable to Japan'. The Japanese surrendered to General MacArthur on board to US battleship *Missouri* in Tokyo Bay.

The War in Burma

At the outbreak of the war Burma (Myanmar) was an agricultural country, exporting rice and teak, with an oilfield at Yenangyaung on the Irrawaddy and deposits of wolfram and rubies. Shut in by hills to north and east, Burma included jungle, a central plain around its second city Mandalay, alluvial deltas, and coastal swamps. It was watered by four rivers, from the east the Salween, forming the border with Thailand; the Sittang; and the mighty Irrawaddy, whose tributary, the Chindwin, marked the border with India.

There was a vigorous nationalist movement, some of whose members were in contact with the Japanese. Japanese interest in Burma focused on the Burma road, which ran from Lashio in Burma to Kunming in China, and formed a source of supply to their enemies the Chinese. The British were badly overextended in the Far East, and Lieutenant General Sir Thomas Hutton, army commander in Burma, disposed of two inexperienced divisions, 17th Indian and 2nd Burma. In January 1942 the Japanese took the airfields in Tenasserim, in the far south, using them to provide air cover for their offensive. Moulmein fell, and the withdrawal of the 17th Indian Division was disrupted when the Sittang bridge was blown on 23 February, with much of the division still on the far bank. General Wavell, British commander in the theatre, agreed with London's suggestion that Lieutenant General Harold Alexander should replace Hutton, and the commander of the 17th Indian Division—brave, but tired and sick—was also relieved. An extra infantry brigade and 7th Armoured Brigade were shipped in.

None of this could stop the two confident and aggressive Japanese divisions. Rangoon fell, and the withdrawal of its garrison and elements of 17th Indian Division was only possible when the Japanese fortuitously removed a roadblock at Taukkyan, just north of the city. Lieutenant General William Slim arrived to command the force, now called Burcorps, and Chinese forces, coordinated by the Anglophobe US Lieutenant General Joseph Stilwell, intervened to assist the British. Yet there was no stopping the retreat. The oil wells at Yenangyaung were blown in mid-April, and a month later Slim's survivors crossed the Chindwin after the longest retreat in British military history. It had cost them 13,000 casualties compared with only 4,000 Japanese. Tens of thousands of civilians had also made the appalling trek: some 500,000 reached safety in India, but perhaps 50,000 perished.

Wavell, aware of the psychological impact of the loss of Burma—coming so soon after the fall of Malaya and Singapore—was determined to retake it. His first attempt, launched towards Akyab in the Arakan in December 1942, was an ignominious failure which highlighted poor British and Indian tactics and the low quality of many troops. But in February–May 1943 a weak brigade under Brigadier Orde Wingate, fighting in self-contained columns, crossed the Chindwin to strike at the Japanese lines of communication. The material damage done by the Chindits (from the Burmese word for the mythical beast that guards pagodas) was far less important than the demonstration that Europeans could win in jungle warefare. This first Chindit expedition gave a powerful fillip to British morale, but it also encouraged the Japanese commander in northern Burma, Lieutenant General Renya Mutaguchi, to launch an offensive of his own. The

Motorized Brigade advance on Meiktila in Operation CAPITAL.

World War II: the Burma campaign

Japanese had raised the Indian National Army (INA) from captured Indian troops who rallied to the call of the nationalist leader Subhas Chandra Bose, and Mutaguchi hoped to use a successful attack to launch the INA into India. In the meantime, the Allies restructured their own command, with Admiral Lord Louis Mountbatten heading South-East Asia Command and Slim's force being designated the Fourteenth Army. In January 1944 Mutaguchi received authority to launch his attack, U-GO. Slim knew that an offensive was coming, and decided to break it before mounting his own attack.

The Japanese began by attacking up into the Arakan to clear the left flank of their main thrust towards Imphal. This operation (HA-GO) went badly wrong. After an initial setback the British defended themselves doggedly on the ground, and quickly gained superiority in the air. The XV Corps administrative area—the 'Admin Box'—was supplied by air when the Japanese encircled it. Slim wrote that the moral effect of this victory was 'immense'. Mutaguchi's main assault, launched in March, followed the classical Japanese pattern of encirclement.

The Battle of Imphal (1944)

In 1944 Imphal was the capital of Manipur state, India's eastern province. A scattering of villages rather than a real town, it lies in a plain 30 km (20 miles) long by 30 broad, with hills all around. It formed the main British base in the area, held by IV Corps of General Slim's Fourteenth Army. The corps commander, Lieutenant General Geoffrey Scoones, expected to be attacked, and planned to draw in his outlying troops and supply a defensive box around Imphal by air. However, the difficult country and poor communications made his task difficult. Lieutenant General Renya Mutaguchi's Japanese Fourteenth Army attacked in March 1944, sending a division against Imphal from the south while two others hooked around to cut Scoones's communications with his railhead at Dimapur. One took most of the little hill station of Kohima, which became the scene of some of the war's fiercest fighting.

The British held Imphal, greatly assisted by command of the air and artillery superiority. Mutaguchi's logistic plan relied on captured British supplies, and when these were not forthcoming his men starved. The offensive was called off by Lieutenant General Kawabe of the Burma Area Army in July. The Japanese suffered 55,000 casualties at Imphal, the British 12,500.

The Battle of Kohima (1944)

The hill station of Kohima stood on the road connecting the main British forward base of Imphal with the railhead at Dimapur, 74 km (46 miles) to the north. Its garrison, commanded by Colonel H. U. Richards, consisted of 2,500 men, about 1,000 of them non-combatants, with Lieutenant Colonel Laverty's 4th Royal West Kents as its most effective unit. The British were expecting Imphal, 130 km (80 miles) to the south, to be attacked, and although they thought that the Japanese would hook northwards to cut the road at Kohima they judged that only a regiment would be given the task. Lieutenant General Kotoku Sato's 31st Division, after a difficult march across country, attacked it on 3 April, greatly outnumbering the defenders.

For the next fortnight the Japanese mounted attacks on the string of defended localities running along the road. They took GPT (General Purpose Transport) Ridge early on, gaining control of the water supply, and pushed the garrison back into a small area around the district commissioner's bungalow and the FSD (Field Supply Depot) area to its south. The fighting was some of the worst in the war, with wounded being hit again as they lay on stretchers, and the smell of unburied bodies polluting the position.

Kohima was relieved on 20 April, but fighting went on in the area for another two months. Overall casualties there amounted to 4,000 British and almost 6,000 Japanese. The British memorial at Kohima bears the poignant words:

> When you go home
> Tell them of us, and say:
> For your tomorrow,
> We gave our today.

U-GO was cancelled in early July: it had cost the Japanese some 60,000 casualties. The Japanese offensive coincided with THURSDAY, the second Chindit expedition, in which Orde Wingate, promoted to major general, commanded a much larger force, most of which was flown in by glider. Wingate was killed when his aircraft crashed, but his columns established strongholds which became centres of fierce battles. There was some friction between Wingate's successor and Lieutenant General Joseph Stilwell, whose men were attacking towards Myitkyina, an operation which involved Merrill's Marauders, the only US ground troops to serve in Burma. The operation came to an end in August. It had had less overall impact than the first expedition, but the remarkable endurance displayed by so many of those involved deserves recognition. No less remarkable were the achievements of Force 136, widely deployed across the whole theatre, working with indigenous support to carry out sabotage.

CAPITAL, the Allied offensive, began in early December 1944. It comprised a Chinese advance on the left and a thrust into the Arakan on the right while, in the centre, Slim pressed south. Rangoon was to be taken by an amphibious landing, DRACULA.

The Battles of Mandalay and Meiktila (1945)

General Slim had two corps available for his attack, Lieutenant General Sir Frank Messervy's IV and Lieutenant General Sir Montague Stopford's XXXIII. Divisions were shifted between them as the battle developed, but each usually comprised at least two infantry divisions and a tank brigade. Slim's opponent, Lieutanant General Kimura Heitara of the Burma Area Army, had been ordered to hold southern Burma, and to interfere as much as he could with Allied links with China. His three armies were under-strength, and he was badly outclassed in the air. He hoped to hold a line from Lashio to Mandalay and on down the Irrawaddy south of Mandalay.

Slim sought to defeat the Japanese, not merely to capture ground, and sent XXXIII Corps against Mandalay while IV headed south and then swung eastwards to Meiktila. The Japanese 15th Division had been ordered to hold Mandalay to the last man, and both Fort Dufferin and Mandalay Hill, to its north, were splendid defensive positions. But the 19th Indian Division, well handled by Major General Thomas (Pete) Rees, duly crossed the Irrawaddy and took the town in early March 1945 while Stopford's other divisions encircled the city. IV Corps, meanwhile, crossed the Irrawaddy opposite Meiktila, and pushed its armour out of a bridgehead seized on 17 February. Meiktila was first invested, and then assaulted, by Major General D. T. Cowan's 17th Indian Division. Fierce fighting followed, and when the Japanese fell back at the end of March they were intercepted by 20th Indian Division and suffered heavily.

Slim failed to encircle the bulk of Japanese forces holding Mandalay and Meiktila, and the balance of casualties did not seem to tell heavily in his favour. However, only 2,600 of his 18,000 casualties were killed, while the Japanese lost 6,500 dead from total casualties of 13,000. They also lost most of their tanks and guns, and were in no position to resist Slim's subsequent breakout towards Rangoon which the Japanese abandoned as the Allies approached. Most succeeded in escaping to the south-west. The Japanese command formally surrendered on 28 August 1945, on orders from Tokyo, though it proved difficult to notify survivors.

THE BATTLE OF THE ATLANTIC

The dominance of the Atlantic Ocean was one of the pivotal campaigns of World War II, for upon its success depended Britain's capacity to survive militarily and to join the USA in the eventual invasion of occupied Europe. The Germans realized this from the start, but placed their initial hopes in the effects of surface raiders and individual warships like the *Graf Spee* and the *Bismarck*.

The Surface War

On 21 August 1939 the pocket battleship *Admiral Graf Spee* sailed from Wilhelmshaven for the south Atlantic where, off Africa, she sank nine Allied merchant ships. A hunt was mounted by 22 British warships organized in eight groups, one of which, under Commodore Henry Harwood and consisting of the cruisers HMS *Exeter*, HMS *Achilles*, and HMS *Ajax*, was stationed off the river Plate esturary in South America. On 13 December the German ship was brought to action, but her 11-inch guns were matched against lighter guns, 9-inch the heaviest, of the British. The damaged *Graf Spee* entered the harbour of Montevideo and, anticipating the gathering of yet larger forces against her, Captain Hans Langsdorff scuttled her.

In the north Atlantic the battlecruisers *Scharnhorst* and *Gneisenau* were loose in 1941 and sank twenty-two ships before sheltering in Brest. They broke out in February 1942 and regained their home port. The most serious chase took place in May 1941 when the battleship *Bismarck* and the heavy cruiser *Prinz Eugen* put to sea heading for the Denmark Strait between Iceland and Greenland where they would be a serious threat to British supply lines from North America. They were seen by British cruisers on 23 May and the battlecruiser HMS *Hood* and the battleship HMS *Prince of Wales* attacked. A German shell entered the magazine of *Hood* and she blew up with the loss of all but three of her crew. On 24 May a Swordfish biplane flown off the carrier HMS *Victorious* managed to damage *Bismarck* and the two German ships turned for Brest. On 26 May an aircraft of the RAF Coastal Command located *Bismarck* and torpedo attacks flown from HMS *Ark Royal* eventually damaged her steering gear, allowing the British to bring her under fire and finally sink her with torpedoes. Of her crew of 2,222 only 115 survived. *Prinz Eugen* took shelter in Brest. Thereafter the surface war became a contest off Norway as convoys attempted to supply Russia and German surface vessels opposed them.

The Submarine War

In fact it was the U-boat that turned out to represent the most dangerous threat, under the calculating direction of Admiral Karl Dönitz. The campaign against the U-boat ran throughout the war, but was at its most intense from 1940 to 1943, a period which culminated in the decisive convoy battles of March 1943.

Dönitz organized his boats in wolf-packs which were brought into action when one of a line of U-boats standing sentinel across the shipping lanes sent a signal to its headquarters. The pack would then attack at night, operating on the surface and penetrating the convoy to do as much damage as possible within a short time. The British tried to counter these tactics with aerial observation, flying out of Iceland and Northern Ireland.

On 9 May 1941 Convoy OB318 was attacked by a pack including *U-110* which sank two ships, but which was attacked by three British destroyers. Before she sank the captain of HMS *Bulldog* sent a boarding party which brought back maps, documents and an Enigma coding/decoding machine. Until February 1942 the British were able to read German signal traffic but then the machines were modified. HMS *Petard* captured a new machine from *U-559* in November.

The campaign against the U-boats intensified with the entry of the USA into the war in December 1941 which increased the air cover possible over the Atlantic. Convoys were accompanied by auxiliary aircraft carriers and long-range aircraft such as, as it was known under different designations, the B-24 or PB4Y or Liberator, which joined the battle in August 1942 as Allied losses were reaching their peak. New radar and the acoustic torpedo added to the Allies' effectiveness. In March 1943 yet another modification of Enigma halted the flow of radio intelligence but Allied activity also increased, inflicting unsustainable losses on the German boats. The wolf-packs were withdrawn halfway through the year and while sinkings continued, their scale declined to logistically tolerable levels.

The help provided by ULTRA special intelligence made possible by the capture of Enigma machines, the role of anti-submarine aircraft operating from carriers or from land bases, and the Allied powers' ability to build merchantmen, escorts, and aircraft faster than the Germans could sink them or build U-boats, were all vital to the Allied campaign. Nor should the importance of the Allied strategic bombing campaign, their ship-repair industry, and the eventual efficiency of their docking and land transportation systems be forgotten.

Statistics on this campaign are hard to agree, but in all about 83,000 Allied sailors (naval and civilian) and airmen, approximately 12 million tonnes of merchant shipping, about 90 allied warships, and 1,700 Coastal Command aircraft were lost during the campaign. In the whole war, the Germans lost 784 U-boats, and 28,000 out of their 41,000 submariners, two-thirds in the battle of the Atlantic. Although the campaign was won, the costs were high and the late appearance of dangerous and advanced German U-boats like the Type XXI and the Type XXIII showed that the submarine threat had been managed rather than completely defeated.

7 The Americas

War did not come to the Americas with the arrival of Europeans in 1492. But horses, iron, and gunpowder did, and they not only enabled the Spanish to win an empire in central and south America, but helped other European powers to secure themselves elsewhere. English and French settlements in North America were established later, and were initially tiny by comparison with Spanish domains. Yet they were eventually to be extended by military conquest to become the mightiest nation in history.

Christopher Columbus astonished Caribbean peoples with a demonstration of gunpowder weapons and a crossbow with iron-tipped arrows. The next time such weapons appeared they were used in earnest. The conquistadors, often from the tough frontier provinces of Extremadura and Andalusia, were a product of the militarization of Spanish society during the *Reconquista* (the long process in which the Christians drove the Muslims out of the Iberian peninsular), and the fall of the last Moorish kingdom in 1492 left them eager for employment. They found it in the New World, where many motives—personal ambition, religious zeal, and desire to seize specie with which Spanish monarchs could finance wars against rival Catholics or heretic Protestants—saw them carve out the world's first overseas empire. The best known are Hernán Cortés, who wrested Mexico from the Aztecs, and Francisco Pizarro, who overthrew the Incas in Peru, but there were many others. Gonzalo de Quesada was a lawyer who secured what is now Colombia, and the Dominican friar Bartolomé de Las Casas helped pacify Cuba and part of what became Guatemala.

Not all were soldiers, and some succeeded with diplomacy where force had failed. However, without arms there would have been no conquest. The Spaniards' use of modern weapons, coupled with their Machiavellian approach to negotiation and alliance-making, enabled them to beat warriors equipped with obsidian edged clubs, bronze-headed maces, and swords crafted from hard wood. They regarded war as a bloody means of seizing power, giving them an advantage over the Aztecs, who fought to take captives for subsequent sacrifice. Iron and its purest form, steel, also gave the Spaniards a defensive advantage, for their helmets and body armour deflected blows. When the Incas besieged Cuzco with some 200,000 men in 1536 only one of the 190 Spanish defenders was injured: he had failed to don his helmet. There were occasional Spanish reverses. In 1520 they were ejected from the Aztec island-capital of Tenochtitlán with the loss of 450 men and ten times as many of their Indian allies. But they returned to take revenge, first securing the causeways linking Tenochtitlán with the mainland, then bombarding it with cannon mounted on warships on the lake, and finally storming it building by building in a three-month assault which left the city devastated.

Similar technological imbalances enabled Europeans to win elsewhere: in 1644 when 140 Dutch soldiers attacked an Indian village near Greenwich, Connecticut, they killed up to 700 of its occupants for the loss of fifteen men wounded. In North America fighting was sometimes ritualized before the Europeans arrived. One English captain wrote that: 'they might fight seven years and not kill seven men ... This fight is more for pastime than to conquer and subdue enemies.' In contrast, colonists saw war as a matter of survival, and struck remorselessly at enemy warriors, Indians (as they were called at the time), non-combatants, and economic resources alike. Settlers in North America were sometimes caught at a disadvantage: in 1644 Indians of the Tidewater confederation killed almost 500 colonists on the first morning of their attack. However, disease worked in the conquerors' favour in both North and South America, for indigenous populations were ravaged by diseases like smallpox, measles, and typhoid, against which they had no natural resistance and whose catastrophic impact on leadership structures helped the interlopers divide and rule.

It proved impossible to stop the seepage of technology into indigenous groups, and steel weapons, firearms, and horses were coupled to traditional tactics of raids and ambushes to delay European expansion. But it would never be possible for local peoples to recoup their losses, for Europeans' dominance of the sea enabled them to move heavy guns along the littoral, and just as the technology of field warfare had been exported to the New World, so too the techniques of fortification enabled Europeans to construct defences which could not be taken without access to the doctrine and equipment of siegecraft.

Penetration of the North American hinterland was hindered as much by rivalry between colonial powers as by local resistance, and settler populations grew so slowly that appetite for fresh land was initially restrained. Traders and settlers of rival powers often clashed before the start of European wars that spilled over into America, and squabbled after the conclusion of peace in Europe. Between 1689 and 1763 there was almost uninterrupted conflict in North America, with the British, along the Atlantic seaboard, and the French, in what is now eastern Canada, as the principal protagonists. Both sides used a mixture of European regulars, local militias, and Indian allies.

The clash with the longest-lasting results began in North America in 1754 as the French and Indian War, and was then subsumed into the wider Seven Years War. Things started badly for the British, with Major General Edward Braddock's defeat on the Monogahala river (1755). But then the British threw all their weight into the war, blockading French ports to restrict the flow of reinforcements, and using the Royal Navy to move troops first to Louisbourg (1758) and then to Quebec (1759). Further inland, French forts at Ticonderoga and Crown Point had already fallen, and in 1760 Montreal, capital of New France, surrendered. The Peace of Paris, which ended the war, left Canada in British hands.

One war helped create another. In the wake of its victory, the British government sought to ensure that the cost of defending its North American colonies was borne by the colonists, and many British officers had a low regard for militiamen and Indian allies, and favoured regulars for the task. In 1763 the British closed the area west of the Appalachians to further settlement, hoping to quell Indian fears of encroachment and, in due course, to make money out of regulating expansion. This affronted those colonists who saw virgin land as theirs by right. Many shared that mistrust of regular soldiers which was a feature of contemporary Europe, and some went further, arguing that colonial legislatures should have more say over taxation. The British government might have avoided breakdown had it pursued a consistent policy, but it did not. Its supporters—loyalists to the British and Tories to their opponents—struggled on without effective support, and radical politicians moved into the vacuum. Although war did not break out until 'the shot heard round the world' rang out across Lexington Common on 19 April 1775, the battle lines were already drawn. In most colonies royal governors had lost control of the militias, and it was the patriots who made the running.

In few wars is the difference between popular myth and historical reality more marked. The War of American Independence was not won by sharpshooters in buckskin and lost by brutal bumpkins in red coats. On the one side was a power which enjoyed almost unfettered command of strategic communications, generally controlled more conventionally trained manpower, but faced a clash of strategic priorities as what started as a struggle in North America became a world war, and enjoyed no unanimous domestic support. Just as they could not protect loyalists before the war broke out, so the inability of the British to control the hinterland enabled local supporters to be terrorized, for there was brutality on both sides.

On the other was a new nation, which declared its independence in 1776. Recognizing that militia could never win the war on its own, it formed the Continental Army, which owed much to the British in terms of organization and tactics, and whose commander, George Washington, had held the king's commission as a militia colonel. It saw that external support was essential to success: this would prevent the British from concentrating on America and would enable arms to be secured abroad. Washington may not rank as a great tactician (though he deserves praise for beating German regulars at Trenton in the bitter winter of 1776), but he had a better understanding of the real nature of the war than his opponents. They opined that 'a few bloody noses' might give them North America. He recognized that he could survive defeat in pitched battles provided his army did not wholly disintegrate, and that time would work in his favour. Even the loss of New York and Philadelphia was not fatal, for the British could mint no strategic currency from tactical victory.

In 1777 a British plan to send an army down from Canada to join another advancing up the Hudson valley failed when John Burgoyne was forced to surrender at Saratoga. This brought France into the war, although its entry was not immediately decisive. There was little movement in the north for the rest of the war. Instead, the British shifted their grip to the south, where they first took Savannah and then, in May 1780, Charleston. Charles Cornwallis trounced Horatio Gates at Camden, but strengthening local resistance, encouraged by British excesses, saw Patrick Ferguson routed by 'over the mountain men' at King's Mountain, while Banastre Tarleton, with a few regulars and his own American Legion, was crushed at Cowpens. Cornwallis went on to beat Major General Nathanael Greene at Guilford Court House, and then marched up into Virginia. Greene was subsequently defeated at both Hobkirk's Hill and Eutaw Springs, and has the distinction of being a great general who never won a battle. But that was not the point. The British paid more for these victories than they could afford and control of the south—the ability to make their writ run in small towns and farming communities—slipped from their hands.

Cornwallis, meanwhile, withdrew to Yorktown, with his back to the sea, so that he could be reinforced or evacuated. But Admiral de Grasse arrived from the West Indies with a powerful French fleet, and the British botched an attempt to break through. The battle of the Chesapeake Capes was insignificant by the standards of eighteenth-century naval warfare, but it proved decisive. Cornwallis was assailed by French and American regulars and bombarded by French heavy guns which had been landed at Rhode Island and then whisked down by sea. When he surrendered in October 1781 only 8,000 British troops marched into captivity. It was not the size of the defeat that proved decisive, but its impact on British determination, and although it took two years to conclude the Treaty of Paris after Yorktown the British were in no mood to continue.

The fledgling United States fumbled to devise a military organization that would neither overburden its finances with a large standing army nor dispense with the militia, often unreliable but entrenched in the national psyche. The dual army that emerged, regulars backed by citizen soldiers, has survived to this day. In 1812 frustration at British interference with maritime trade and fear of a fresh incursion from Canada encouraged President James Madison to take his country into a war that was welcomed by few on either side. This ill-starred conflict had three theatres. In the north, there was inconclusive fighting along the Canadian border. In the centre, a British force was landed by sea and entered Washington, where it burned the White House and the Capitol. It moved on to attack Baltimore, where a fruitless bombardment encouraged the lawyer Francis Scott Key to scribble down what became 'The Star Spangled Banner'. In the south, Wellington's brother-in-law Edward Pakenham was defeated and killed at New Orleans in January 1815. Cruelly, the war had already ended, on terms that represented a return to the status quo, but news had not reached America.

Over the next half-century or so there were two distinct developments in the Americas. In South America a series of risings, in which veterans of the Napoleonic wars played a major part, saw Spanish and Portuguese colonies achieve independence. President James Monroe not only recognized the new republics, but affirmed in 1823 'that the American continents ... are henceforth not to be considered as subjects for future colonisation by any European power'. The process created the states of modern South America. There were sometimes clashes between them, often more bloody than their causes suggested. In the 1860s Paraguay fought a destructive war against its neighbours, and as late as 1933–5 the Chaco War between Bolivia and Paraguay cost perhaps 100,000 lives.

In the north there was westward expansion at the expense of the Indians, in which accelerating military technology generally gave soldiers and settlers the advantage, though not without setbacks, of which George Custer's defeat at Little Bighorn (1876) was the most spectacular. In 1846 the process brought the United States into conflict with Mexico, a recently independent Spanish colony, over Texas, part of Mexico but in fact in revolt. The Americans won a war on two fronts, beating the Mexicans and their supporters in California and what became New Mexico, and sending an expeditionary force by way of Vera Cruz to seize Mexico City.

The war established the Rio Grande as the south-west frontier of the USA. It weakened Mexico, which, racked by internal dissention and unable to sustain its foreign loans, suspended payment in 1861. The affronted British, Spanish, and French governments sent troops, and the French stayed on, establishing the Habsburg Archduke Maximilian as emperor. The venture ended in tragedy: soon after French troops were withdrawn in 1867 Maximilian was overthrown and executed.

European intervention would have been difficult had the USA not had preoccupations of its own. In 1861 tension between its northern and southern states, in which the issue of slavery was fundamental, flared into war. There was a general belief that it would be short. Some argued that the North's larger population and its superiority in railways and economic resources would give it easy victory. Conversely, many southerners believed that the North could not impose its will upon a population fighting to preserve its way of life.

The war became an exercise in the decisive application of overwhelming force, thanks to the imposition of naval blockade on the South, and President Abraham Lincoln's ability to hold the North together, and his persistence in waging war despite setbacks occasioned by the fighting quality of the Confederate soldier and the skill of commanders like Robert E. Lee and Thomas J. (Stonewall) Jackson. Lincoln was handicapped by incompetent senior officers, many of them appointed because of their political connections, and it was not until Ulysses S. Grant was made general-in-chief in March 1864 that the Union was at last able to implement the strategy of bulldozing towards Richmond, the Confederate capital, and Atlanta, in the Confederacy's heartland. Clear numerical superiority, buttressed by a powerful economy, enabled Grant to meet Lincoln's remit of 'holding on with bulldog grip, and chew and choke as much as possible'. Although Grant lost over twice as many men as Lee in his Wilderness campaign of 1864, at its conclusion the Confederates were fixed in northern Virginia, condemned to an attritional contest whose stakes they could not afford.

It remains the costliest war in American history, with 620,000 military dead, two-thirds victims of disease. Battlefield deaths reflected the fact that the Napoleonic tactics favoured at the start were especially costly when combined with the muzzle-loading Minié rifle, and the growing use of field fortifications was a response to increases in the range and accuracy of infantry fire. Railways were crucial, and here the North enjoyed a decisive advantage. In September 1863 23,000 Union soldiers, with baggage, horses, and artillery, were carried 1,900 km (1,200 miles) in twelve days: their arrival tilted the balance on the western theatre. The South, at a grave material disadvantage, did not help matters by failing to manage its threadbare logistics effectively.

The war's technology was transitional: the Franco-Prussian War, fought soon afterwards, saw both sides equipped with breech-loading rifles and one with breech-loading artillery. Yet even this intermediate weaponry was heavy with portent. In March 1862 the CSS *Virginia* fought the USS *Monitor* in Hampton Roads, in the world's first battle between ironclad warships, and in February 1864 the Confederate submarine *Hunley* sank the USS *Housatonic*, though *Hunley* herself was lost. The Confederacy's few commerce-raiders inflicted disproportionate damage: the CSS *Shenandoah* disposed of almost the entire northern whaling fleet in the Barents Sea in 1865.

With the Civil War over, the US Army returned to its pre-war preoccupation with the frontier, corralling Indians into reservations and fighting them if they left. Many officers felt uneasy about it. 'We took away their country and their means of support, broke up their mode of living, their habits of life, introduced disease and decay amongst them and it was for this and against this that they made war,' declared Major General Philip H. Sheridan. In a series of wars between from the 1860s to 1890 the US army crushed the Indians of the Great Plains, as well as the Commanche and Apache of the south-west, in a process that had reduced the Indian population, once reckoned in the millions, to a remnant of 250,000.

Thereafter the United States exported its military might. In 1898 President McKinley told Spain that it must grant independence to its remaining New World colony, Cuba, then in revolt. When Spain stalled, the USA declared war. The Americans defeated the Spaniards at sea, in the battles of Manila Bay in the Philippines and Santiago Bay off Cuba, and on land, where Santiago capitulated after American victories at El Caney and San Juan Hill. The USA emerged with the Philippines, Guam, and Puerto Rico, as well as a protectorate over Cuba. It improved the shining hour by seizing Hawaii, Samoa, and Wake Island. As Allan Millett and Peter Maslowski wrote: 'A nation born more than a century earlier in a reaction to imperial domination had become an imperial power, joining the maelstrom of international politics.'

THE FRENCH AND INDIAN WAR

The French and Indian War (1754–63) was precursor and part of the worldwide Seven Years War. Smouldering rivalry for dominance of the Ohio valley burst into flames in May 1754, when an expedition under George Washington ambushed an alleged French 'embassy' that was stalking him. Later captured by the brother of the slain emissary, Washington was released after signing a confession to the 'murder'.

In 1755, newly arrived with regular army reinforcements, Major General Edward Braddock prepared to advance from Virginia on Fort Duquesne in the Ohio valley in western Pennsylvania, pausing only to alienate potential Indian allies and the colonial militia by his arrogance.

The Battle of Monongahela River (1755)

In the battle of Monongahela river some 224 French troops accompanied by approximately 600 Indian warriors enveloped the front of the British column of 1,400 regulars and 700 colonials. The British were marching when ambushed. It is taken as a classic example of the unwisdom of employing European tactics in the forests of North America, but it was really a failure of scouting and intelligence, for Braddock's firepower might have proved decisive if sensibly deployed. In the crossfire over 400 men, including Braddock, were killed and a similar number wounded. Washington rallied the survivors and, although still outnumbering the French, they retreated to Fort Cumberland in Maryland. The defeat encouraged previously neutral and even well-disposed Indians to drive in the frontier of settlement by 240 km (150 miles), killing hundreds.

Thus, long before the formal declaration of hostilities in 1756, the conflict in North America was already a full-scale war. The presence or absence of Indian allies defined the earlier engagements, in which the French generally prevailed. Defending his use of atrocity-prone Indians, the French governor boasted that thanks to them 100 British died for every Frenchman. Not counted by either side, Indian casualties are unknown.

British success during this time was limited to the capture of Nova Scotia (called Acadia by the French) and the deportation of the French settlers, who became the Cajuns of Louisiana. The New York militia with Mohawk allies won a rare victory at Lake George, and Fort William Henry was built on the spot, only to be taken (as depicted in *The Last of the Mohicans*) and razed after the 1756 arrival of General Louis-Joseph, marquis de Montcalm to command French forces. Before that, he seized New York's western outpost at Fort Oswego, and with it British hopes of controlling Lake Ontario. To forestall their move towards an overt alliance with the French, desperate colonial officials concluded treaties with the Iroquois confederation and the Delaware in 1756–8, which gave up ceded lands and promised an end to British expansion into their territory.

Recognizing the shortcomings of the regular army, the British encouraged the development of light infantry units and tactics better suited to frontier warfare. The outstanding practitioner was Robert Rogers, commissioned in 1755 by the governor of

Massachusetts to 'distress the French and their allies' by every means possible. But although his Rangers and a similar regiment raised by his brother were later to be incorporated into the regular army, the lessons taught by this war were never fully accepted by the British army. Contempt for colonials and parsimony towards Indian allies prevailed through the American independence war to the War of 1812.

The Siege of Louisbourg (1758)

Situated on Cape Breton Island, the fortress of Louisbourg protected access to French Canada via the great waterway of the St Lawrence river. It was the most formidable fortification in North America, but it had fallen once before, in 1745, to a combined British operation. In July 1758, a British force of 11,600 under Lieutenant General Jeffrey Amherst was able to capture it again after a sustained land and naval bombardment. The French garrison surrendered and 5,600 prisoners and 239 guns were taken. Its fall cut communications between France and the hitherto successful French forces in the interior.

Oswego and Duquesne followed in quick succession, closing the St Lawrence lifeline to France and the French Lake Ontario route west of the Alleghenies. Finally even the staunchly anti-British Seneca tribe abandoned the French in 1759, which contributed to the fall of Forts Niagara and Ticonderoga in July.

The Battle of Quebec (1759)

In June 1759 a convoy of ships carrying 8,500 British troops headed down the St Lawrence and set up a base of operations on the Île d'Orléans, opposite Quebec. To the east the banks of the river were heavily defended against a landing, but scouting revealed a cove on the banks of the St Lawrence west of the city, below the dominant Plains of Abraham, that could be used for an amphibious assault. On 13 September, the British commander Major General James Wolfe led a force of 1,700 to seize this vital point and scramble up the cliffs. Once on the high ground above the city the British mustered 5,000 men and the French, preceded by swarms of Indian and French-Canadian sharpshooters, deployed to meet them. A brisk firefight ensued, in which both Wolfe and the French commander General Montcalm were mortally wounded. Wolfe expired knowing that victory was in his grasp: the city surrendered on 17 September 1759, the beginning of a run of victories that temporarily secured North America for the British crown.

Although the French counter-attacked in May 1760, bottling up the British garrison, it was sustained by the navy until relieved when militia columns advanced from the south, combining to take Montreal in September. Some French resistance continued, but the rest of the war in North America was mainly against Indian guerrilla outbreaks.

The biggest of these was in the south where the Cherokee, in return for promises from the governor of South Carolina to defend their homelands against the pro-French Choctaw and the opportunistic Creek, sent warriors north to assist in the 1758 attack on Fort Duquesne. The forts built to 'protect' the Cherokee homeland proved to be a Trojan horse, and simmering discontent erupted into an uprising which took four years and two armies to subdue. The Treaty of Paris in February 1763 formally ended French participation in the war, but within months the Ottawa chief Pontiac's rebellion gave renewed significance to the conflict's Indian element. Inspired by a Delaware prophet, the uprising began with a botched attack on Fort Detroit in May 1763 and continued with the killing of some 2,000 settlers. Amherst, apart from the innovative device of giving the besiegers of Fort Pitt smallpox-infected blankets, had no answer and was replaced by Lieutenant General Thomas Gage. The uprising slowly collapsed and Pontiac signed a peace treaty at Oswego in July 1766.

THE WAR OF AMERICAN INDEPENDENCE

With the Treaty of Paris in 1763, British fortunes in North America reached their zenith. Threat of French intervention had been removed from the American colonies, which enjoyed considerable wealth and freedom from external interference. The war had cost huge sums of money, and it was felt by London that the colonists should pay for the garrison of 8,000 British soldiers. Various taxes were imposed and in 1773 the Boston Tea Party saw British-monopolized tea thrown into the harbour in a gesture of contempt. As a result, Boston harbour was closed to shipping, and generous trade concessions were given to the newly integrated French Canadians in Quebec.

The Actions of Lexington and Concord (1755)

On receipt of peremptory orders from London on 19 April 1775 the governor of Massachusetts, Lieutenant General Gage, reluctantly sent 700 soldiers from Charlestown to seize militia stores in Concord, followed by a support column from of Boston. An earlier expedition to Salem had retreated in the face of threatening Minutemen (militia who undertook to be ready 'at a minute's warning') and Gage knew that his orders made a showdown inevitable.

Signal lamps and mounted couriers, including the night ride of Paul Revere, gave warning. Militiamen made a demonstration on Lexington Green, but were dispersed with small loss by the redcoats, evidently out of their officers' control. By the time the column arrived at Concord, the stores had been removed or destroyed, and Minutemen defended the North Bridge, the first time any British soldiers were killed. In imminent danger of being cut off, the column retreated under heavy sniping. Order broke down in the face of tactics for which the troops were unprepared and the rout continued until they came under the guns of the support brigade. For the remainder of the retreat the redcoats gave as good as they got, but lost 273 men in exchange for no more than 95 rebel casualties.

The conflict quickly escalated and militia began to entrench themselves around Boston Harbour, overlooking the British garrison. In June Gage's replacement, Sir William Howe, launched a successful frontal assault against the American earthworks on Breed's Hill and Bunker Hill, which cost the British over 1,000 casualties, 40 per cent of the attacking force, and was a serious blow to their pride, morale, and capability for offensive operations.

In June 1775, the Continental Congress appointed George Washington as its commander-in-chief. In autumn 1775, the British found themselves under pressure on all fronts. The Boston garrison was hemmed in, and patriots had also seized the forts at Crown Point and Ticonderoga, threatening the Canadian urban centres of Montreal and

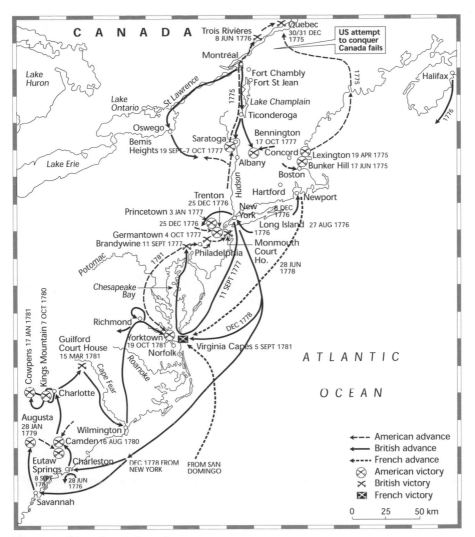

The War of American Independence

Quebec. In the southern colonies Sir Henry Clinton attempted a *coup de main* in May at Charleston, but was repulsed, losing a ship and many men in an artillery duel with batteries at Fort Moultrie. Meanwhile, Howe had brought 9,000 reinforcements from Britain to Boston, but his supply ships failed to arrive, and by early spring of 1776, when his opponents occupied the Dorchester Heights, overlooking the town, his situation began to look desperate. He had no choice but to evacuate Boston, and this he did, making for Halifax, Nova Scotia, in March.

British strategy now came to centre on the Hudson and the Canada–New York axis, in an effort to advance from Canada to capture New York, splitting Pennsylvania and the southern colonies from New England and New York. But the British proceeded slowly

and lacked unifying direction, confused as they were by contradictory instructions, arriving with a time lag of three months from London. Meanwhile Howe's army was starving in Nova Scotia, where it was delayed until June 1776 waiting for provisions. Once victualled, the fleet set out for Staten Island, where it deposited the army. In August the brigade of Guards arrived, accompanied by a Hessian force and Clinton's refugees from Charleston. Howe felt ready to launch his offensive. He was ably supported by his brother Richard, Lord Howe, commanding the fleet, and had a force of 25,000 troops, many of them first-rate. After a token resistance, American forces abandoned New York. Howe took the city and a month later captured Fort Washington. The American cause now seemed to be in serious trouble. However, Washington crossed the Delaware, surprising a Hessian detachment at Trenton on 26 December 1776. This developed into a general engagement between Lord Cornwallis and Washington on New Year's Eve, and the Americans were bundled back to Princeton where the British were checked, and in consequence abandoned New Jersey.

Lieutenant General John Burgoyne was appointed to command the Canadian offensive. He was a flamboyant leader, but he was also headstrong, and this proved to be his undoing. Howe, meanwhile, was concentrating on a push towards Philadelphia, the congressional capital, and it was unclear how the two commanders would coordinate their operations. In the event Howe did not land at the mouth of the Delaware, but sailed instead to the head of Chesapeake Bay, ending up no nearer to Philadelphia than where he had started from. After a month at sea, his army was in bad shape, whereas Washington was ready and waiting. Nevertheless at Brandywine Creek on 11 September 1777, the Americans proved unable to resist a bayonet charge, combined with a subtle flanking manoeuvre. However, the British were worn out by their march and a hard fight, and could only look on as the Americans recoiled in panic. By 25 September, Howe had occupied Philadelphia. On 4 October Washington launched another surprise attack, at Germantown, but a running battle proved inconclusive. The year 1777 ended with Howe penned up at Philadelphia.

In late June 1777, Burgoyne, setting out from Canada with 9,500 men, captured Ticonderoga, and pressed southwards to Hubbardton and to Fort Edward on the Hudson in an abortive attempt to link up with Clinton's forces marching north from New York. This strategy was an attempt to split the economic base of New England from the seat of the rebel Congress in Philadelphia, along the axis of the Hudson. It was a bold plan that took no account of the terrain or local conditions.

The Battle of Saratoga (1777)

Saratoga, one of the key battles of the war, consisted of two main engagements: Freeman's Farm on 29 September, and a British assault on Bemis Heights on 7 October. Lieutenant General Burgoyne, marching down the trackless wastes of the Hudson valley, found his way barred by American forces at Bemis Heights. On 19 September there was a sharp battle at Freeman's Farm, in front of the American position, which the British won on points, though with heavy loss: the action gave combatants on both sides heightened respect for their opponents. The British withdrew to construct a fortified camp and await

The battle of Concord. The British retreat under fire.

developments. When prospects of relief by Sir Henry Clinton faded, Burgoyne ordered a major assault on Bemis Heights on 7 October, but was repulsed, and the American follow-up lapped round the British redoubts. On the 17th, surrounded and outnumbered, Burgoyne capitulated. Only 1,500 of his remaining men were to survive a captivity that lasted until 1782. Burgoyne was released on parole, and returned to London to attempt to vindicate himself.

Despite this signal victory, the congressional forces remained in disarray. Horatio Gates and George Washington feuded with Congress, and the Continental Army endured great hardship during a severe winter at Valley Forge outside British-occupied Philadelphia. But France now resolved to enter the war on the side of the colonists. The war had changed from insurrection to a world war which would engulf the West Indies, Europe, and India. To prevent a separate peace treaty, France recognized the USA in December 1777. Spain joined the war as France's ally in June 1779. As the conflict dragged on, the Dutch took up arms on behalf of the Americans, and eventually in 1780 Denmark, Sweden, Russia, Prussia, Austria, Portugal, and the Two Sicilies formed the League of Armed Neutrality against British attempts to seize and search shipping suspected of supplying the Americans. By the spring of 1778, Lord North, the British premier, found himself not only fighting a world war, but faced with domestic opposition which regarded American war aims as eminently reasonable.

In the winter of 1777–8, Sir William Howe remained supine in Philadelphia until replaced by Clinton in May. Clinton promptly withdrew to New York, where he planned to disperse his forces to the West Indies, Florida, and Halifax, retaining New York as a base for naval and amphibious operations. In contrast, the French alliance had strengthened patriot morale, and Washington felt confident enough to launch an assault on Clinton's rearguard at Monmouth, as the British retreated to New York. The Americans under Charles Lee launched an attack with 4,000 disciplined regulars, but were repulsed, as Clinton executed a masterly withdrawal. Washington himself had to intervene to prevent the flight of his army in the face of counter-attacks.

French support gained the Americans little in 1779 and in February 1780 Clinton landed 8,000 troops in the southern theatre, first laying siege to Charleston, which surrendered with 5,000 men in May. Opposition in South Carolina crumbled, making way for a strike to the north, where Major General Jean-Baptiste-Donatien Rochambeau, with a sizeable French force, was threatening New York. Clinton returned northwards, nominating Lord Cornwallis as his successor in the south, and Congress, for its part, renewed the effort against the British there. Horatio Gates, the victor of Saratoga, was sent south but at Camden, on 16 August 1780, the Americans suffered one of the worst defeats of the war: Gates himself fled. As Cornwallis moved into North Carolina in September 1780, his capable subordinate Lieutenant Colonel Patrick Ferguson, inventor of an early breech-loading rifle, was killed at King's Mountain. This provided a major boost to American morale, and the British retired to Winnsborough under continuous attack.

Cornwallis was reinforced in January 1781, and could draw on a force of 4,000 tough and disciplined local supporters—'Tories'—and regulars. For their part, the Americans were invigorated by the appointment of Nathanael Greene as commander in the south, assisted by Light Horse Harry Lee and the veteran Pennsylvania commander Daniel Morgan. Cornwallis was forced to protect his extended posts from Greene's pinprick attacks. The controversial Banastre Tarleton, commander of the loyalist American

Legion, attacked Morgan at Cowpens on 17 January and was almost annihilated in the process. Cornwallis swiftly turned on the Americans, but Greene retired into the marshes of North Carolina, followed by the British who were plagued by sickness, desertion, and lack of supplies. Cornwallis's army was so weary that he was obliged to withdraw towards Hillsboro, pausing at Guilford Courthouse. Seeing Greene close at hand, Cornwallis seized the opportunity to attack. Despite a magnificent victory, won by his formidable but threadbare infantry, Cornwallis could not exploit his advantage, and marched down the Cape Fear river to Wilmington for much-needed rest.

In 1781 Clinton prepared an expedition to the Chesapeake in support of Cornwallis, to be commanded by Benedict Arnold, patriot hero of Saratoga but now a British general. The British landed, occupied Portsmouth, and resisted all attempts to dislodge them. The patriot cause seemed in peril: the French were horrified by the apparent weakness of their allies, and inflation and profiteering were turning the population against the patriot cause. In May 1781 Cornwallis and Arnold united their forces near Richmond. Clinton instructed Cornwallis to fortify Yorktown on Chesapeake Bay to command the sea approaches. Rochambeau appealed to Admiral de Grasse, naval commander in the West Indies, to bring his fleet to the Chesapeake, while Washington, leaving only a screen facing Clinton in New York, moved 7,000 French and American regulars to Yorktown to reinforce the outnumbered marquis de Lafayette. They were soon to be reinforced by Grasse with 24 ships of the line and 4,000 more troops.

The Battle of the Chesapeake Capes (1781)

On 15 August General Rochambeau heard that Admiral de Grasse was on his way, and ten days later persuaded Vice Admiral de Barras to sail south from Rhode Island with eight warships and siege guns. Samuel Hood, following Grasse from the West Indies, travelled faster that his quarry and unwittingly overtook him. When Hood reached New York he found that the French were not there. The horrified British at once guessed what had happened, and Rear Admiral Samuel Graves immediately took nineteen ships of the line south. When Grasse emerged to fight him it became clear that the French had stripped the West India station to produce 24 ships of the line, and the British were at a numerical disadvantage, worsened by the fact that many of Graves's ships had been on the North American station for years and urgently required refit.

On 5 September the rival fleets fought an inconclusive engagement, marred for the British by confused signalling and friction between Graves and Hood. Graves remained in contact with de Grasse over the next few days, but he made no effort to get into Chesapeake Bay, and favourable winds allowed Grasse to return safely. On his arrival he found that Barras's flotilla had arrived, and its presence gave him a clear edge. Graves returned to New York: one of his ships was in such atrocious condition that it had to be burned at sea. Samuel Graves performed less badly than his critics (notably Hood) were to maintain, but this was one of those moments when 'the Nelson touch' might have changed history.

The Siege of Yorktown (1781)

Graves's withdrawal left 6,000 British facing 16,000 French and continental troops when the siege began on 28 September 1781. The following day Lord Cornwallis withdrew from his outer works, and by 9 October he was under heavy and continuous fire, and attempted an evacuation across the York river to Gloucester, but was foiled by bad weather. On 17 October, the fourth anniversary of the fall of Saratoga, the attackers unleashed a massive bombardment and Cornwallis asked for terms. With only 3,000 men fit for duty and artillery ammunition exhausted, he surrendered on 19 October.

The British had failed to prevent Washington's move to Virginia or to intercept the French fleet. Admiral de Grasse, George Washington, and General Rochambeau had coordinated their efforts in a way hitherto unimaginable. The campaign was a masterpiece that only served to highlight the weakness of the British command. When news of the surrender reached London, Lord North cried out 'Oh God! It is all over,' and the way was clear for the Treaty of Paris (1783) recognizing American independence.

The war had old and new aspects. Although both sides made wide use of light troops, the Americans, like the British, placed heavy reliance on regular infantry fighting in line, and the contribution of the Continental Army—shaped by European drillmasters—was at least as important as that of Daniel Morgan's riflemen or the 'over the mountain men' who beat Patrick Ferguson at King's Mountain. Conversely, there were times when the British and their Hessian allies were actually more flexible than the Americans. British commanders wrestled with significant disadvantages. They remained dependent on sea transport to bring supplies and reinforcements from Britain, and their field army was constantly eroded by the need to garrison bases embedded in an often hostile population.

LATIN AMERICAN WARS

The Battle of Carabobo (1821)

Carabobo was one of the most important battles of the Latin American wars of independence, which decided the fate of the northern Spanish settlements. In 1820 a new liberal government in Madrid had ordered royalist Governor Morillo to conclude an armistice with Simón Bolívar, who had gained control of Colombia in 1819. Bolívar broke the agreement and marched east to Maracaibo at the head of a numerically superior army, which included a contingent of Irish and British volunteers, some of them veterans of the Peninsular War, and General Páez's *llaneros*, excellent Venezuelan plains light horsemen. There does not appear to have been much tactical skill displayed and the royalist army under General de la Torre was overwhelmed. Bolívar proclaimed the republic of Gran Colombia, encompassing today's Venezuela (his homeland), Colombia, Panama, and Ecuador—the last of which he had not yet conquered.

The Siege of the Alamo (1836)

The fall of the Alamo is the most celebrated episode in the Texas war of independence. The name 'cottonwood tree' was given to the walled compound of the secularized Franciscan frontier mission of San Antonio de Valero outside San Antonio de Bexar, the principal centre for Spanish settlement in Texas. In 1813, Spanish Governor Saucedo and his officers were killed after they had surrendered by Mexican rebels and Anglo adventurers, who were treated likewise by a Spanish expedition including then-Lieutenant

Santa Anna. In 1835, General Cos, the brother-in-law of Santa Anna, now president, sur-rendered the Alamo after a siege of 56 days. The scattered, mostly Anglo rebel forces were destroyed in detail when Santa Anna counter-attacked the following year, giving no quarter. A garrison of less than 200 with eighteen pieces of artillery under the command of Jim Bowie and William Travis and including the legendary David Crockett held the Alamo from 23 February to 6 March. All were killed during and after the final assault in which they inflicted more than twice their number of casualties. 'Remember the Alamo' was the battle-cry of the Texans at San Jacinto on 26 April, where Santa Anna was captured and the independence of Texas won.

The Mexican War (1846–1848)

The first successful international war of USA 'manifest destiny' imperialism was provoked by President James K. Polk with a border dispute used as a pretext to seize the New Mexico territory (all of today's south-western states) and California. Mexico had not accepted the independence of Texas, still less its claim to the strip between the Nueces river and the Rio Grande. Following American annexation of Texas in early 1845, a US army of 'observation' under General Zachary Taylor moved from Louisiana to the Nueces strip. In May 1846, 3,700 Mexicans attacked Taylor's 2,300. Repulsed at Palo Alto and defeated at Resaca de la Palma, they fell back behind the Rio Grande. The USA declared war on the 13th.

In a murky episode which could well have defined the course of the war, Polk's agents encouraged the return to Mexico of exiled dictator Santa Anna in August 1846. He agreed to a face-saving formula whereby the USA would occupy Saltillo, Tampico, and Vera Cruz, after which he would sell the territories Polk wanted for the $30 million earlier refused by the Mexican government.

The New Mexico and California territories fell early to a small expedition under Major General Stephen W. Kearny. To his rear a revolt of Pueblo Indians and unreconciled Mexicans was crushed in January 1847, while Colonel Alexander Doniphan with 600–700 Missouri volunteers overawed the powerful Navajo. The latter then rode into Mexico over appalling terrain, defeating a more numerous and entrenched enemy outside Chi-huahua, after which he rode east to join the main army with captured guns in tow.

On the Rio Grande front, the Mexican commander ignored Santa Anna's order to fall back on Saltillo and fortified Monterrey. Taylor successfully assaulted the town in Sep-tember, but permitted the defenders to retreat on terms including an undertaking that US forces would not advance for eight weeks. Taylor was convinced that an invasion from the north to Mexico City was not viable and underlined his conviction by delay. His army suffered most of the 9,000 desertions during the war and lost at least as many more who refused re-enlistment or were sent home because of indiscipline.

Probably aware of this and informed that part of Taylor's army was being withdrawn for a seaborne expedition to Vera Cruz, Santa Anna attacked in February 1847 with 15,000 men. At Buena Vista, south of Saltillo, he drove back Taylor's 5,000 by sheer weight of numbers and would probably have prevailed the next day, but chose to retreat. Thereafter the theatre subsided into guerrilla warfare.

The US navy duly captured Tampico and army commander General Winfield Scott led the expedition to Vera Cruz, landing where Santa Anna had recommended in March 1847. The port fell to bombardment twenty days later. At Cerro Gordo in mid-April, a strong position designed by Santa Anna to keep the Americans in the lowland yellow-fever belt was outflanked with minimal casualties. No further organized resistance was encountered until the Americans approached Mexico City, where on 20 August Santa Anna's forces were defeated at the battles of Contreras and Churubusco, the latter featuring fanatical resistance by Irish deserters and volunteers organized in the San Patricio regiment. Last-ditch resistance was overcome at Molino del Rey on 8 September and at the fort of Chapultepec five days later, whose defenders included a group of military cadets, the *niños heróicos* of Mexican folklore.

In these later battles fewer than 11,000 Americans overcame 30,000 defenders, inflicting 7,000 casualties and capturing a further 3,000, for a loss of only 3,100 killed, wounded, and missing. Overall, US forces suffered 5,800 battle casualties and 11,500 deaths by disease, 22 per cent of all involved. The duke of Wellington, no less, said the Vera Cruz campaign showed Scott to be the greatest soldier living.

THE FRENCH MEXICAN EXPEDITION

The Mexican expedition was the French attempt to counter Protestant Anglo-Saxon influence in the Americas and included the battles the anniversaries of which are still celebrated by Mexico and the French Foreign Legion. Racked by civil wars, Mexico suspended payment on its international loans in 1861 and in retaliation a joint Anglo-Spanish-French force seized Vera Cruz. The others withdrew when they realized that Napoleon III had wider plans. Although much of Benito Juárez's army was tied up by conservative forces elsewhere, the first French advance towards Mexico City was stopped at the Puebla pass on 5 May 1862, where about 5,000 men commanded by General Ignacio Zaragoza repelled a rash attack by an elite force of 6,500. This was the first Mexican victory over a foreign enemy since independence.

The Battle of Camerone (1863)

In April 1863 the 3rd Company of the French Foreign Legion's 1st battalion, commanded by the one-handed Captain Danjou, was escorting a bullion convoy through the Mexican countryside when it was surrounded by a greatly superior Mexican force in a farm near the village of Camarón (from the Spanish *camarón*, shrimp). Danjou refused to surrender and was killed, and his men followed his example until only a handful were left. Their ammunition gone, they made a last bayonet charge in which all were killed or wounded. Danjou's wooden hand was recovered and takes pride of place when the Legion celebrates Camerone day on 30 April each year.

Napoleon III dispatched 30,000 reinforcements under Marshal Élie-Frédéric Forey, who besieged a Mexican army of 20,000–25,000 men at Puebla. After it capitulated on 17 May, large-unit resistance ended and Forey marched into the capital on 10 June. He directed an assembly of conservative and clerical 'Notables' to issue an invitation to the Habsburg Archduke Maximilian, Napoleon III's candidate, to become emperor of Mexico. He then returned to France, leaving General François Achille Bazaine with the thankless task of pacifying a people with a long tradition of guerrilla warfare.

Maximilian was duly installed in mid-1865 while Bazaine's troops chased Benito Juárez in the north and Porfirio Díaz in the south. The French controlled the cities, but in the countryside their authority was limited to where they stood. In anticipation of this, from 1863 they countenanced the operations of a ruthless irregular force of mercenaries under Major Charles-Louis Dupin and attempted to recruit bandit gangs. These added little to military effectiveness and greatly to the suffering of the Mexican people.

The original pact between Napoleon III and Maximilian specified that 10,000 European troops were to remain as the nucleus of a new Mexican army, and consideration was given to transferring the Foreign Legion. But the occupation proved costly and with the end of the American Civil War it became a serious liability, underlined when Juárez took refuge against the border beneath the protection of an 'army of observation' under the aggressive Major General Philip H. Sheridan. In February 1866 Napoleon III agreed to withdraw his troops by November 1867, but the growing threat from Prussia advanced the date and in March 1867 an embittered Bazaine embarked his 29,000 men for return to France, destroying supplies to deny them to Maximilian. The hapless Habsburg felt honour bound to make a last stand at Querétaro with a small Austrian contingent and an unreliable Mexican conscript army. Betrayed, he and his two remaining Mexican generals were shot on 14 June 1867.

THE AMERICAN CIVIL WAR

The war was detonated by the refusal of the southern, slave states to accept the decision of the 1860 presidential election, which had seen the first Republican candidate, Abraham Lincoln, sweep the northern states but gain not a single electoral vote in the South. From December 1860 to February 1861 seven states in the Deep South passed ordinances of secession, occupied federal installations, and called out their militias. These states set up the Confederacy with a pro-slavery constitution headed by President Jefferson Davis, and this new government located its capital initially at Montgomery, Alabama. The rebel government was eager to remove the two remaining federal outposts on their territory, at Pensacola in Florida and at Fort Sumter in Charleston harbour. After a stand-off lasting four months, the Confederacy bombarded the latter on 12–13 April 1861.

President Lincoln responded by issuing a proclamation calling for 75,000 volunteers for three months to suppress a rebellion against federal authority. Virtually all participants believed that the conflict would be short. However, four important states of the Upper South, Virginia, Tennessee, North Carolina, and Arkansas, seceded rather than cooperate in the 'coercion' of their sister slave states. They added not only to the Confederacy's population and territory but also to its sparse industrial resources as well as placing Virginia and Tennessee in the front line.

A widespread belief in a short war was buttressed in the North by an awareness of a great disparity in resources. Should secession be limited to eleven states then the northern states could mobilize four million fighting men to the Confederacy's 1,100,000. The industrial disparity was even greater. The states of Massachusetts and Pennsylvania alone produced more manufactured goods than the entire Confederacy. The South could produce sufficient food to feed itself but lacked the means to transport it. In 1860 only 14,500 km (9,000 miles) of the American total of 50,000 km (31,000 miles) of railway track

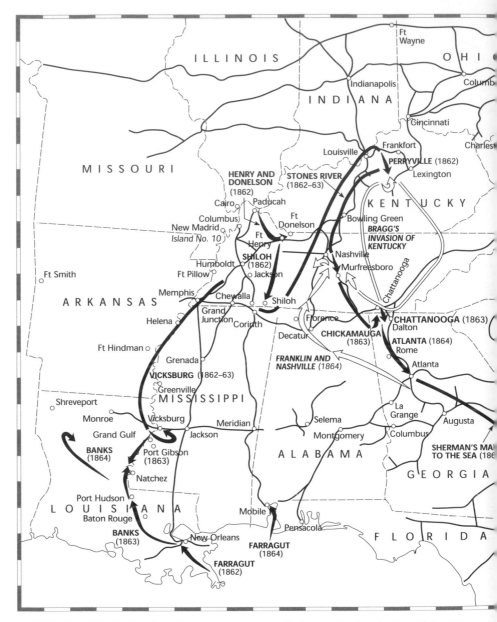

could be found in the South, and southern engineers had completed only nine of the 470 locomotives built before 1860. Nonetheless, Lincoln's main problem was in mobilizing and organizing the great resources available to him for waging war.

In the North the 75,000 volunteers were soon supplemented, and by 1 July 1861 300,000 men had been raised, the majority for three years. Jefferson Davis had succeeded in raising 200,000 Confederate volunteers by August 1861. These hosts on both sides were difficult to command. The men believed that they were civilians in uniform and enjoyed

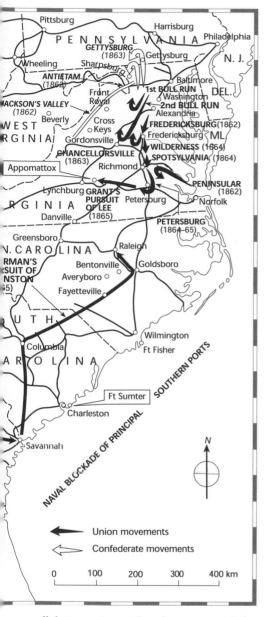

The American Civil War

all their previous rights; they were not deferential to their officers, who were often elected. Many incompetents had to be weeded out. Armies on both sides were subject to political influences, but especially those Union forces that were encamped near Washington, known by the summer as the Army of the Potomac.

Political pressure helped shape the first campaign. The elderly general-in-chief Winfield Scott preferred to launch a well-prepared campaign in the Mississippi basin relying on the economic strangulation of the South. This concept was strategically sensible but was

unacceptable to public opinion because it would work slowly. The power of the press and propaganda was notable throughout the conflict. In the spring of 1861 the Confederacy decided to move its capital to Richmond, Virginia, a mere 160 km (100 miles) from Washington. A clamour developed that the federal army should move 'on to Richmond'.

The First Battle of Bull Run (1861)

Manassas Railway Junction was crucial for communications across northern Virginia to the Shenandoah valley and only 40 km (25 miles) from Washington. It was near here that the Union suffered its first defeat. Irvin McDowell took the offensive in July 1861 knowing his 35,000 men were 'green'. But so were the Confederates, who were widely dispersed with 22,000 under Pierre Beauregard close to Washington and 9,500 under Joseph E. Johnston 80 km (50 miles) away in the Shenandoah. Beauregard fell back on the Bull Run river, but his left was outflanked and fell back in disorder after fierce resistance. Leading the Shenandoah reinforcements from the railhead at Manassas Junction, T. J. Jackson formed on the reverse slope of Henry House Hill and halted the rout, earning the name of Stonewall. Enfiladed by aggressively handled Union artillery, his position was salvaged by a spontaneous infantry charge. Union forces massed against him were outflanked in turn and dissolved in panic. Washington would almost certainly have fallen to a determined pursuit.

George B. McClellan was appointed to command the Army of the Potomac and began an energetic programme of consolidation, reorganization, and training. In November he replaced Winfield Scott as general-in-chief and became overburdened by his dual role. The first lull in the eastern theatre ensued, but this brought immense political dissatisfaction with the war's conduct and culminated in the creation of the Congressional Joint Committee on the Conduct of the War on 20 December 1861. This was highly critical of McClellan's conciliatory policy, which stressed that the war aimed at the restoration of the Union and not the destruction of slavery.

By the spring of 1862 the federal government had made rapid progress in suppressing the Confederacy. A series of successful amphibious operations on the littoral of the Carolinas was followed by the seizure of New Orleans on 24–25 April 1862. An early Confederate victory at Wilson's Creek, Missouri, in August 1861 was followed by crushing Union victory at Pea Ridge, Arkansas, 6–8 March 1862, which made incursions into the south-west possible. In Tennessee, Ulysses S. Grant seized Forts Henry and Donelson, which led to the fall of Nashville on 25 February 1862.

The Battle of Shiloh (1862)

Following the loss of the Tennessee–Kentucky line, Confederate commander Albert Sidney Johnston concentrated 45,000 men at the Mississippi–Tennessee border. Ulysses S. Grant advanced by river with 48,000 while Don Carlos Buell with 18,000 marched from Nashville to join him. On 6 April Johnston surprised William T. Sherman and drove his corps and the rest of the Union army back on Pittsburg Landing. Next day, with his own

---

The camp of the Tennessee Colored Battery at Johnsonville.

divisions concentrated and reinforced by Buell, Grant broke an attack under the fallen Johnston's successor Pierre Beauregard and reclaimed the field. There were 13,050 Union casualties to the Confederates' 10,700.

No general emerged with credit. Grant and Sherman were caught unprepared, while Johnston was persuaded by Beauregard and Braxton Bragg to weaken his envelopment of the Union right and to pound it up the middle. Thereafter he exercised little control and died leading a regiment. Bragg wasted momentum with frontal assaults on the Union rearguard, until others took the initiative and deployed massed artillery. Beauregard failed to regroup for either attack or defence the following day. This success enabled the overall commander in the west, Henry W. Halleck, to concentrate 130,000 men and occupy Memphis, gaining control of the vital Tennessee river.

But appearances were deceptive and the war was actually taking the form that would prevail for a further three years. There were three central theatres of operations: first, in western Tennessee and Mississippi, where the Union attempted to complete its stranglehold of the Mississippi basin; second, eastern Tennessee and Kentucky, focused around the railway junction of Chattanooga; and third, northern Virginia between the Rappahannock and Potomac rivers. As strategic movement over such huge distances was dependent on the railway, railway junctions assumed an enormous importance in all three theatres. The eastern theatre was the most sensitive politically and also bore more on the attention of the great European powers. Great Britain and France sympathized with the Confederacy, the former having awarded the Confederacy belligerent rights in 1861; France was supporting a puppet government in Mexico; but neither would enter the war until the Confederacy could demonstrate that it could win independence by its own exertions; so far there was scant evidence for that.

In April 1862 George B. McClellan set out on his 'grand campaign'—an amphibious operation up the peninsula between the James and York rivers, occupying Yorktown and the Confederate capital at Richmond. He was relieved of his duties and replaced by Halleck. Lincoln had disliked McClellan's plan, preferring a direct advance towards Manassas Junction and thence on Richmond from the north.

The Seven Days Battles (1862)

In this series of battles 60,000 Confederates newly under Robert E. Lee drove the Unionists away from their position of imminent threat to Richmond and back against the James river, from where they were eventually evacuated. Convinced he was outnumbered, George B. McClellan with 100,000 men crawled up the Jamestown peninsula, hoping to combine with an advance by Irvin McDowell from the North. After repulsing a Confederate attack at Seven Pines (31 May–1 June), he did little while Lee replaced the incapacitated Joseph Johnston and recalled T. J. Jackson's army from the Shenandoah valley. A dangerous Union probe at Oak Grove (25 June) nearly disrupted Lee's plans, and his first attack at Mechanicsville (26 June) was a draw, but McClellan began to retreat, hurried on his way at Gaines' Mill (27 June). The Union army again held its own at Savage's Station (29 June) and White Oak/Glendale (30 June), and severely mauled Lee's final frontal assault at Malvern Hill (1 July). Including Seven Pines, McClellan had inflicted nearly 27,000 casualties in exchange for less than 21,000 of his own more numerous and better equipped army. But he was mastered by his fears and Lee's relentless aggressiveness, and his promising campaign came to nothing.

Lee's Army of Northern Virginia had succeeded in driving McClellan back to Harrison's Landing, but failed to secure the ultimate objective, the destruction of the Army of the Potomac.

The Second Battle of Bull Run (1862)

Here President Lincoln learned that he had no talent for directing armies. Having recalled Irvin McDowell when his advance on Richmond might have helped George B. McClellan in the Seven Days battles, and Nathaniel P. Banks when he might have made a difference in the Shenandoah, he put them both under the command of John Pope and ordered him to advance before McClellan could return from the Jamestown peninsula. Uncannily echoing the first battle, throughout 29 August Pope battered a strong position held by T. J. Jackson's corps, which was reduced to throwing rocks. Oblivious to James Longstreet coming up on his left, he continued the attack the next day and was shattered by a Confederate counter-offensive that came very close to enveloping his whole army. Pope was sent to chase Indians in Minnesota and McClellan regained command. Thereupon Robert E. Lee crossed over into Maryland, determined to seek an outright Confederate victory at the earliest opportunity.

The Battle of Antietam (1862)

Underestimating how quickly McClellan would revitalize the Army of the Potomac, Robert E. Lee scattered his army in drives on the federal arsenal at Harper's Ferry and towards Harrisburg, the capital of Pennsylvania. Despite fortuitous capture of a copy of Lee's disposition of forces, McClellan failed to exploit the opportunity, permitting the Confederates to beat a fighting retreat and regroup along a ridgeline around the town of Sharpsburg, with their backs to the Potomac river, faced by more than twice their number.

Through the early morning of 17 September first Major General Joseph Hooker, then Major General Joseph Mansfield's corps, and then Major General John Sedgwick's division of Major General Edwin V. Sumner's corps advanced against Jackson's corps on the Confederate left flank. There were 10,000 combined casualties including Hooker and Mansfield, mostly incurred over an 8-hectare (20-acre) cornfield which changed hands fifteen times. This drew in troops from D. H. Hill's corps at the Confederate centre, where first Major General French's and then Major General Israel Richardson's divisions of Sumner's corps struck at the aptly named Bloody Lane through late morning. Richardson died achieving a breakthrough, but McClellan refused to commit his reserve and Lee was able to restore the hinge of his position.

The most flagrant of all the wasted Union opportunities was the simultaneous failure of Major General Ambrose E. Burnside to cross Antietam creek against the Confederate right, threatening Lee's line of retreat and the direction from which desperately awaited reinforcements had to advance from Harper's Ferry. With a brute obstinacy which prefigured the massacre into which he was to send his army at Fredericksburg three months later, he permitted a brigade of Georgia sharpshooters to hold up his 12,000 men throughout the morning by persistently attacking across a narrow bridge, when the creek was easily fordable. After the opposite bank was gained, he paused for two hours before resuming an advance that drove the remains of the Confederate right under Lieutenant General James Longstreet back around Sharpsburg, but McClellan again held back his reserve of 20,000 men. The last minute arrival of Lieutenant General Ambrose P. Hill with 3,000 men after marching 27 km (17 miles) in eight hours from Harper's Ferry took Burnside in the flank and he fell back.

Stunned by the carnage, the two sides devoted the next day to dealing with their casualties: over 12,000 Unionists and nearly 11,000 Confederates, one out of every four men engaged. Despite the arrival of two fresh divisions, McClellan took no further offensive action and permitted Lee's army to retreat from Maryland unhindered, an inaction which precipitated his dismissal as army commander by an exasperated President Lincoln.

Missed opportunity though it was, the battle aborted Confederate hopes for early British recognition and gave Lincoln the opportunity to issue the Emancipation Proclamation, making recognition of the Confederacy by the premier abolitionist world power impossible.

The Maryland adventure, in any case, was only one wing of a Confederate counter-offensive. General Braxton Bragg, Confederate commander in Tennessee, moved into Kentucky, but on 8 October Don Carlos Buell caught up with him at Perryville, and repulsed his attacks; only one-third of the Union army was engaged but Bragg escaped through the Cumberland Gap. The civil war now entered a period of stalemate, and increasingly the Union resorted to an attritional strategy to bring the Confederacy down. McClellan, the chief spokesman for limited war, had been removed on 8 November. But Lincoln's chief problem was in finding a general who could match Lee's operational skills and wear away the Confederacy's lighter, more mobile armies.

The Battle of Fredericksburg (1862)

Major General Burnside planned a swift crossing of the Rappahannock at Fredericksburg to outflank Robert E. Lee, but a three-week delay in the arrival of pontoons to bridge the river permitted the Confederates to fortify the ridge overlooking the town. It took a further two days to establish crossings in the teeth of deadly sniping by Brigadier General William Barksdale's Mississippians, but finally throughout 13 December Major General Sumner's Grand Division launched nine completely unsuccessful attacks in the open against a stone wall and a sunken road held by James Longstreet's corps, covered by fire from Confederate artillery on the commanding Marye's Heights.

Better progress was made on the Union left by Major General William B. Franklin's Grand Division where, despite galling fire from flanking horse artillery under Major John Pelham—a rare event in this war—Major General George G. Meade's division penetrated a weak spot in A. P. Hill's division of T. J. Jackson's corps. Unsupported and counter-attacked by Jubal Early's division, Meade was thrown back and suffered 40 per cent casualties. Union losses were 12,500 against fewer than 5,000 for the Confederates.

The Battle of Chancellorsville (1863)

The battle of Chancellorsville is notable for one of the most daring displays of generalship in history. Between 1 and 4 May, faced with a well-conceived but poorly coordinated attack by greatly superior Union forces, Robert E. Lee divided his army twice and drove them back to their start line. Union commander Joseph Hooker sought to fix him at Fredericksburg with John Sedgwick's corps, while crossing upstream with his main force. The key element, a massed cavalry raid against Confederate communications with Richmond, was not pursued with vigour, depriving Hooker of reconnaissance while utterly failing to distract Lee, who was well served by his own cavalry. Leaving a thin force under Jubal Early to contain Sedgwick, he marched against the main Union force.

The next day he kept Union attention to the front with 15,000 men, while T. J. Jackson with 30,000 executed a flank march designed to look like a retreat, drawing Major General Daniel Sickles's corps in pursuit. With Union forces extended towards his supposed line of retreat, Jackson enveloped their right wing and drove it for miles. Although he was mortally wounded by friendly fire, the flank attack continued under Major General James E. B. (Jeb) Stuart the next day, joining up with Lee. Concussed after Confederate artillery found the range of his command post, Hooker retreated into a tight perimeter covering his river crossing.

Sedgwick belatedly took the heights above Fredericksburg and marched towards the guns, causing Lee to turn from a third day of assault on Hooker to deal with the threat to his rear. Both Hooker and Sedgwick were well placed to defeat further attacks on them by an exhausted Confederate army, but their will was broken and they withdrew across the river. Union casualties were 17,000, which they could afford, against the Confederates' 13,500, including the incomparable Jackson, which they could not.

These defeats almost brought Lincoln's administration to its knees. A defensive success at Murfreesboro (Stone's River, 31 December 1862–2 January 1863) in central Tennessee seemed a greater triumph than it actually was. It was also becoming clear that battles could no longer be won in a single day and demanded nerve and stamina not only from the fighting troops but also from commanders.

The spring of 1863 placed the Confederacy on the horns of a strategic dilemma. Ulysses S. Grant was inching closer to the crucial Mississippi communications centre at Vicksburg. Yet the brilliant victory at Chancellorsville offered an opportunity to renew the campaign north of the Potomac. President Jefferson Davis had already sent a recuperated Johnston to take charge of the west, but he was cautious and acted without confidence. Lee's view prevailed and he invaded Pennsylvania.

The Battle of Gettysburg (1863)

The three-day engagement at Gettysburg marked the turning point of the war. Robert E. Lee for once commanded near parity of numbers, with 75,500 men against 85,500. After Union cavalry unexpectedly mauled Major General Stuart at Brandy Station on 9 June, he took half his corps on a raid around the Union army. It has been argued that by depriving himself of his 'eyes', Lee stumbled into an unwanted battle, but in fact he was eager for a decision, and Stuart's raid was an unsuccessful diversion, like Major General Hooker's failed cavalry ploy at Chancellorsville. The battle itself began with a chance 1 July encounter between elements of the corps under A. P. Hill and a federal cavalry division, which sucked in both armies. The Unionists were driven through Gettysburg, falling back into a shallow 'U' with their right curled around Culp's and Cemetery hills, and their centre and left stretching along Cemetery Ridge towards the Round Top hills. Major General George G. Meade, the newly appointed Union commander, decided to hold this ground.

Corps commanders on both sides performed poorly, none more so than Daniel Sickles, who advanced the Union left into the open on 2 July, to be driven back in disorder. But at least partly because of this, James Longstreet in turn failed to perform the outflanking manoeuvre Lee entrusted to him, which could have rolled up the whole Union line. By the time the Confederates regrouped to assault the earlier unguarded Little Round Top, Union commanders had rushed just enough reinforcements to hold it. Meanwhile Lieutenant General Richard S. Ewell displayed none of his predecessor T. J. Jackson's dash and only attacked Culp's and Cemetery hills late in the day. It is likely that they would have fallen earlier.

The third day has given rise to more controversy than most others in military history. Lee, who was ill, continued to show none of his customary sureness of touch and judged himself responsible for what followed, but others blame Longstreet instead. Both views discount the unexpectedly steadfast performance of the Union army. Convinced that defeats and frequent changes in commander must have shaken enemy morale, and believing that the attacks on their flanks must have weakened their centre, Lee ordered a reluctant Longstreet to launch a frontal assault against Cemetery Ridge. After a two-hour bombardment that served mainly to warn where the blow would land, Major General George E. Pickett's and Brigadier General J. J. Pettigrew's divisions advanced unsupported and with exemplary discipline over an open kilometre (0.5 mile), to be beaten back by Major General Winfield S. Hancock's reinforced II Corps.

Hindsight supports Longstreet's view that after the second day Lee should have forced Meade to attack him by getting between him and Washington. Gettysburg was not a crushing defeat, because the Unionists were unable to mount a vigorous pursuit, but the Confederates lost about 40 per cent of those engaged against only 25 per cent of their opponents, and never regained the strategic initiative.

As for operations in the west, Ulysses S. Grant slipped south of Vicksburg and crossed to the east bank of the Mississippi river. In an object lesson in calculated audacity, he advanced towards Jackson, Mississippi, and then turned west, defeating the Confederates at Champion's Hill before investing Vicksburg on 19 May. The city surrendered on 4 July 1863 thus cutting off the Confederate Trans-Mississippi from Richmond and permitting untrammelled Union passage of the Mississippi river. A third success for Union arms was recorded when William S. Rosecrans occupied most of east Tennessee in August 1863 in a series of sweeping turning movements that drove Braxton Bragg back into Georgia with his army intact. The Union needed to deliver a knockout blow. Despite Union successes, Confederate armies fought on, Richmond was inviolate, and the heartland in the Deep South remained untouched. The capacity of the Confederacy to strike back was revealed in the autumn of 1863 when Bragg defeated Rosecrans's Army of the Cumberland at Chickamauga (19–20 September) and moved to besiege Chattanooga. His opportunity was thrown away by what amounted to a virtual mutiny of the general officers of the Confederate Army of Tennessee. In the meantime, Grant was given command at Chattanooga, and first concentrated overwhelming Union forces before defeating the Confederates who occupied the high ground south and east of the town. This success led to his promotion (as lieutenant general) to general-in-chief of the Union armies, and he moved to Washington to take command in March 1864.

Although it had been tried before, Grant was determined to unleash a simultaneous concentric advance on all fronts that would prevent a Confederate concentration at key points. However, the terrain favoured the tactical defence in the two major theatres, Virginia and Georgia, and the war had demonstrated that the defensive was growing in potency. This was an infantryman's war. Soldiers were equipped with rifled muskets which fired the 18 mm Minié bullet to a range of about 900 m (3,000 feet), a significant improvement on the Napoleonic musket. Consequently, soldiers of both sides increasingly resorted to entrenchments by 1863; but as the rifle-musket was generally fired standing up, these consisted of shallow rifle pits, perhaps 1–1.2 m (3–4 feet) deep with a breastwork several feet high placed in front. Cavalry was reduced to intelligence gathering and screening, and, as a result, often fought its own separate, mounted engagements away from the main battlefield. Artillery was in transition: it still had to be 'pointed' by direct fire at the enemy. Although devastating against attacking infantry, it as yet lacked explosive power to destroy even shallow entrenchments. In short, Grant's dynamic strategy faced severe tactical obstacles, but he was remorseless in pursuit of his objective.

The 1864 campaign consisted of two attritional thrusts on geographical objectives, Atlanta and Richmond. The two overall Union commanders, General Ulysses S. Grant and General William T. Sherman, sought to destroy the two Confederate armies in front of them before either could fall back into Richmond or Atlanta's defences. The main difference between them was that Lee fought Grant for the initiative whereas Joseph E. Johnston did not contest this with Sherman. The result in Virginia, where two well-matched adversaries were determined to fight it out, was a ferocious series of battles, Wilderness (4–6 May), Spotsylvania (8–21 May), followed by the bloody Union repulse at Cold Harbor on 3 June. The Confederates inflicted casualties equal to their own strength, but Grant recovered from this setback to cross the James river and on 15 June advance on Petersburg, Richmond's communications centre on the Appomattox river. Lee arrived in the nick of time. The siege that he had always feared was the result of his tenacious defence. Sherman, who now commanded the Military Division of the West, was determined to apply pressure on Johnston so that he could not send reinforcements to aid Lee. The strategic coordination of Union armies over such great distances was facilitated by the use of the telegraph. Outflanking his opponent's position on the Rocky Face Ridge, Sherman almost cut the Army of Tennessee off from its communications. Johnston considered launching a counter-attack at Cassville but refrained, and withdrew through the Allatoona Pass behind the Etowah river. Sherman moved into the woods around his left, and was blocked at New Hope Church. Sherman tried to force the Confederate lines at Kennesaw Mountain but was repulsed on 27 June with 3,000 casualties. Yet Sherman inched towards Atlanta and by 9 July was only 6.5 km (4 miles) from its centre. Johnston was replaced by the impulsive Lieutenant General John B. Hood. He launched a series of disastrous counter-attacks, which failed to prevent Sherman from extending his tentacles south of Atlanta, and the city was evacuated on 1 September 1864. This tremendous success guaranteed Lincoln's re-election in November, and offered Sherman the chance to cut the Confederacy in two by marching towards the Atlantic coast.

The event which made this possible was the rash decision by Hood to attack towards Chattanooga, thus evacuating the critical theatre of operations. Sherman was eventually able to advance towards Savannah with impunity. Neither Grant nor Lincoln was keen on this alternative, but Sherman reassured them by sending George H. Thomas and the Army of the Cumberland to Nashville to defend his rear. There on 15–16 December 1864 Thomas crushed Hood's army. Sherman's prime targets in his famous marches were Confederate war-making resources and morale. Property rather than the people themselves were the victims of his depredations but his attacks were aimed just as much at the civil will as at the morale of Confederate soldiers. In January 1865 he moved through South Carolina and thence into North Carolina, determined to link up with Grant.

The final Confederate collapse was precipitate. A much enfeebled Army of Northern Virginia was besieged in Richmond. Lee's efforts the previous summer to distract attention by sending a small force under Jubal Early up the Shenandoah valley towards Washington brought an awful retribution on this beautiful rural area. Confederate troops were driven back and the new Union commander, Major General Philip H. Sheridan, was ordered by Grant to destroy all provisions and crops, a duty which he executed with zeal. Denied the foodstuffs of the Shenandoah, the fall of Richmond was just a matter of time. Sheridan rejoined Grant and shattered Lee's right flank at Five Forks (31 March 1865), causing the evacuation of Richmond on 1–2 April. Grant pursued the remnants of the Confederate army and forced their capitulation at Appomattox Court House on 9 April 1865. Remaining Confederate troops in North Carolina surrendered to Sherman at Durham Station on 26 April, although small detachments in the Trans-Mississippi did not surrender until May.

The Civil War had cost 620,000 American soldiers' lives (360,000 Union and 260,000 Confederate), although two-thirds of these were victims of disease not bullets. The civil war pointed to the great importance in modern war of organization, especially in the related spheres of logistics, communications, and transportation. Further, as the North was dragged into an attritional conflict, so the deployment of numbers and quantities of equipment became more important than operational skill. Consequently, victory in the Civil War went to the side with the largest population, the most durable financial system, and the greatest industrial capacity.

THE PLAINS INDIANS WARS

These wars were uprisings from the 1860s to the 1880s by the 'hostile' tribes of the Great Plains horse and buffalo cultural area, excluding the Apache of the south-west and the Utes and others of far west and mountain zones. They were subdued by a strategy of exterminating the buffalo and winter campaigning devised by General William T. Sherman. The main hostiles with their approximate ranges stated in terms of modern US states were:

- *Northern Cheyenne/Arapaho*: Algonquian-speaking tribes in Wyoming and Montana;
- *Southern Cheyenne/Arapaho*: in Colorado, Kansas, Oklahoma, and Texas;
- *Comanche*: Uto-Aztecan speaking people, from Kansas to Mexico inclusive;
- *Kiowa*: Kiowa-Tanoan speakers in Kansas, Oklahoma, and Texas;
- *Kiowa-Apache*: Athapascan speakers in Texas and New Mexico;
- *Santee Sioux* (Mdewkanton, Sisseton, *et al.*): Siouan speakers in Minnesota and Wisconsin;
- *Teton Sioux* (Brulé, Hunkpapa, Mineconjou, Oglala, Sans Arc): spread over the Dakotas, Wyoming, and Montana.

The Canada border-area hostile Algonquian-speaking Blackfoot tribe is included among the Teton Sioux. Because of tribal enmity or prudent calculation, many of the Caddoan Arikara and Pawnee, the Siouan Crow and Osage, and the Uto-Aztecan Shoshoni allied with the whites against the hostiles—when, that is, they were not raiding on their own account amid the swirling confusion of a frontier war where the autumn hostiles could be the winter reservation Indians and be back out on the warpath in the spring.

Like the Yankton/Yanktonai Sioux, the Santee grudgingly accepted 'concentration' in 1858. In August 1862, a corrupt Indian agent of the government denied them treaty supplies and one of his soon-to-die confederates suggested they eat grass. Led by the previously accommodationist Mdewkanton Little Crow, the Santee went on an orgy of raiding that spread into Wisconsin until defeated at Wood Lake on 23 September. Two thousand surrendered and 303 were condemned to death by courts martial, but President Lincoln reviewed the sentences and reduced the number to 38. The Sisseton and some Teton Sioux were chased into Dakota, where the last battle took place at Killdeer Mountain in July 1863.

For the southern hostiles, the moment when resisting the whites finally took absolute precedence over fighting each other came with the massacre of Black Kettle's trusting Cheyenne at Sand Creek. The Cheyenne-Arapaho War of 1864–5, Hancock's Campaign of 1867, and Sheridan's Campaign of 1868–9 were basically one long spasm of related uprisings. In the first, raids by the Cheyenne and Arapaho joined by some Teton Sioux ravaged Colorado until battles at the North Platte and Powder rivers in late 1865 bought a year's relative tranquillity. When raiding revived in 1867, General Winfield S. Hancock drove them out of Colorado, to spread terror through western Kansas.

Although he signed the Treaty of Medicine Lodge in 1867 and withdrew to a reservation in Indian Territory (now Oklahoma), the hapless Black Kettle could not control the elite Dog Soldiers of his own tribe, who joined a Kiowa and Comanche uprising the next year, once again provoked by withheld supplies. In September, 50 troopers held off 600 Oglala and Dog Soldiers at Beecher's Island in Kansas, killing their leader Roman Nose. On 27 November, Black Kettle and 102 others, mostly old men, women, and children, were killed in Sheridan's Campaign when George Custer attacked their camp at Washita River. On Christmas Day, Dog Soldiers and Kiowa were defeated at nearby Soldier Spring. After a further defeat in July 1869 when fighting alongside the Northern Cheyenne at Summit Springs in north-east Colorado, surviving Dog Soldiers surrendered.

The Kiowa rebelled again in May 1871. Satanta and other leaders were captured and condemned to death, but their sentences were commuted—unwisely, because they led the Kiowa war faction to join the Comanche again in the Red River War of 1874, which tore up the Texas panhandle. After defeats at Adobe Walls and Palo Duro Canyon, Satanta surrendered to Colonel Nelson A. Miles in October. Sporadic raiding continued, but the southern Plains Indians wars are considered to have ended when the feared half-breed Comanche Quanah Parker surrendered in June 1875.

Their northern brethren, particularly the Teton Sioux, gave the overstretched US army even more trouble. Always ready to join the uprisings of others to the east and to the south, under remarkable leaders such as Spotted Tail of the Brulé, his nephew Crazy Horse and Red Cloud of the Oglala, and Sitting Bull of the Hunkpapa, the defeats they inflicted on the regular army were unique in the Plains wars saga. In 1854, after the Brulé wiped out a 30-man punitive column under Lieutenant John L. Grattan near Fort Laramie, the ensuing punishment persuaded Spotted Tail to become an advocate of negotiation. The same pattern of winning prestige in battle first and then accepting the inevitable was followed by Red Cloud after his successful 1866–8 war against the Bozeman Trail in Wyoming. Sent to build three forts through the heart of the Teton's range in 1866, the army encountered fierce resistance. On 21 December a party of Oglala led by Crazy Horse lured to destruction an 80-man column out of Fort Kearny under Lieutenant Colonel William J. Fetterman, who had boasted he could ride through the whole Sioux nation with precisely that number. In the face of constant harassment, the Trail was abandoned by the Fort Laramie Treaty of April 1867.

The northern Plains Indians' last stand was provoked by a treaty-violating ultimatum to surrender their sacred Black Hills (*Paha Sapa*), where an expedition under Custer discovered gold in 1874. In June 1876, driven by converging army columns, a unique concentration of Sioux and Cheyenne/Arapaho in southern Montana first repulsed a 1,000-man column under Major General George Crook at the Rosebud on 17 June and then destroyed Custer's command at Little Bighorn.

The Battle of Little Bighorn (1876)

On 25 June Lieutenant Colonel George Custer sent part of his 7th Cavalry under Major Marcus A. Reno to 'beat' the hostiles out of their encampment, while, led by Crow scouts, he hooked around to drive off their pony herd and envelop them, a standard Indian-fighting tactic. He was outmanoeuvred and his detachment of 215 men was annihilated between an anvil led by the Hunkpapa Lakota Gall that cut off his retreat and a head-on mounted hammer led by the Oglala Crazy Horse. The rest of the regiment lost a further 100 men when Reno was forced back upon the reserve elements under Captain Frederick W. Benteen in the hills along Custer's line of advance, where they were besieged for 36 hours. Coming nine days before the centenary of the USA, the battle immediately assumed mythic status and it is probably the most written-about skirmish in military history.

The Plains Indian concentration dispersed and the ensuing winter campaign broke the back of their resistance, with battles at Slim Buttes and Wolf Mountain. One by one the war bands surrendered or followed Sitting Bull to refuge in Canada. The last battle was Colonel Nelson A. Miles's destruction of the Mineconjou at Muddy Creek in May 1877 after their chief Lame Deer had died trying to kill him in a personal gunfight.

The Plains Indians wars effectively ended within a year of the Indians' greatest victory at Little Bighorn, which finally goaded Washington into providing the resources necessary to crush them. There were two subsequent clashes. In 1878 the Northern Cheyenne, desperate to return, were almost exterminated, an act which aroused pity and an unusual concession to their wishes. The pathetic and inevitably doomed Ghost Dance revival was drowned in blood at Wounded Knee in December 1890.

THE SPANISH-AMERICAN WAR

This war was an imperialist conflict of 1898 in which the USA extended its formal authority over the Caribbean and across the Pacific, achieved on the back of long-standing insurgencies in Cuba and the Philippines. The American establishment wanted to establish hegemony and to acquire naval bases in both places, but President William McKinley shrank from embarking upon the necessary war. It was forced upon him by popular clamour whipped up by the press and by Spanish intransigence.

American public opinion strongly sympathized with the nationalist guerrillas in Cuba, particularly after the Spanish military governor introduced a system of concentration camps (the origin of the term) in which as many as 100,000 died. The flashpoint was the publication on 9 February 1898 of a dispatch by the Spanish ambassador in Washington which spoke contemptuously of McKinley, followed six days later by the sinking of the battleship *Maine* in Havana harbour. Post-war investigation showed that it sank from an internal explosion, but at the time an American enquiry blamed it on a mine. Popular agitation led to a US ultimatum and Spain declared war on 23 April.

Already possessed of a two-to-one advantage in warship tonnage, the US navy spent over $30 million acquiring 131 new vessels and doubling its manpower between March and August. By contrast, the Spanish possessed neither the means to add significantly to their fleet, nor the diplomatic clout to obtain coal in foreign ports for the ships they had. Their armoured cruisers were designed as ocean-going raiders and certainly not to engage their more heavily armoured and gunned American counterparts, built for coastal defence. They were to be sacrificed by the Madrid government, which incorrectly calculated that it could survive a heroic defeat.

In a classic demonstration of 'mission creep', Commodore George Dewey of the Pacific squadron based in Hong Kong set out to neutralize the obsolete Spanish naval presence in Manila and ended by adding the Philippines to the US empire. During the morning of 1 May, he sank or disabled the outgunned enemy squadron at Cavite. The Spanish admiral could have run to maintain some kind of 'fleet in being', or could have anchored under the heavy guns of nearby Manila. He chose instead 'heroic defeat'.

There were about 26,000 Spanish regulars and 15,000 local militia facing about 30,000 insurgents throughout the archipelago. With the exception of the 12,000 Manila garrison, the rest soon fell to the insurgents. That this was due mainly to Spanish defeatism is illustrated by the tiny outpost at Baler, which held out beyond the end of the war to June 1899. Once 11,000 American ground forces had landed, Manila surrendered on 13 August after symbolic resistance. By conspiring with the Spanish governor to bring this about while excluding the rebels, who had done most of the fighting, the American commanders set in motion the second Philippines insurrection.

There were 70,000 Spanish 'effectives' in Cuba (27,000 more were in hospital) with perhaps 30,000 local militia. These were also scattered around the island and pressure from the insurgents made concentration of forces impossible. Havana was strongly held, but the poorly provisioned garrison at Santiago numbered less than 12,000. What made it the prize of the campaign was the arrival there on 19 May of the Spanish Atlantic squadron under Admiral Pascual Cervera, who believed he had nowhere else to go. This was fortunate, because it took the blockading fleet under Rear Admiral William Sampson ten days to locate him. An unsuccessful attempt was made to sink a blockship in the narrow mouth of the harbour on 3 June, and US Marines seized Guantánamo Bay to provide a sheltered anchorage in mid-month, but a decision awaited the arrival of the expeditionary force under General William Shafter.

After a rushed and chaotic embarkation at Tampa, followed by landings on open beaches at Daiquirí and Siboney, where it proved impossible to bring heavy equipment ashore, some 17,000 US troops were available for the battles around Santiago. Much of the fighting was done by a spearhead formed by highly motivated dragoon units, including the African-American troops of the 9th and 10th regiments and the Rough Riders, the 1st US Volunteer Cavalry, at Las Guásimas on 24 June and at El Caney, Kettle Hill, and neighbouring San Juan Hill on 1 July. Shafter failed to follow up, but the positions won were sufficiently menacing to force Cervera to steam out of Santiago harbour to annihilation on 3 July.

Pausing to satisfy 'honour' and to obtain repatriation at American expense, the Spanish commander surrendered the whole province and 23,000 men on 17 July at a ceremony from which the leader of the Cuban insurgents, hitherto working in close concert with the Americans, was excluded. Further operations in Cuba and those of army commander Major General Nelson A. Miles in Puerto Rico ended with the suspension of hostilities on 12 August. By the Treaty of Paris, the USA annexed Puerto Rico, Guam, and the Philippines, paying $20 million compensation for the latter, and Cuba exchanged Spanish rule for an independence subject to US intervention.

In a war that ended in bitter mutual recrimination among American commanders ashore and afloat, the popular hero was the Rough Riders' dynamic Theodore Roosevelt. US combat casualties were 385 killed (2,061 more died of disease) and 1,662 wounded.

THE FALKLANDS WAR (1982)

The Falkland Islands (Malvinas in Spanish) lie approximately 800 km (500 miles) east of southern Argentina. From 1833 they were in British hands, although sovereignty was claimed by Argentina on the basis of previous Spanish occupation. In 1982 East and West Falkland had a population of only 1,800. The climate was temperate but windy, the terrain a mixture of downland, rocky hills, and peat bogs. The capital, Port Stanley, had a small airport, but was not unlike a Scots fishing village. Outside Stanley people lived in sheep-farming settlements. Further east lay the Falklands dependencies, South Georgia, and the South Sandwich Islands.

The 150th anniversary of British occupation came when the Argentine military was looking for an external adventure to rally national support after a deeply shaming 'dirty war' in which thousands of people suspected of subversive activities had been tortured and 'disappeared'. British policy had long been one of appeasement, trying to get the islanders to accept some kind of sovereignty-sharing with the mainland. The final signal may have been the announcement that the symbolically armed ice patrol vessel HMS *Endurance* was to be withdrawn. On 2 April 1982, special forces overwhelmed both the 50-man garrison of Royal Marines at Port Stanley after a sharp firefight, and a detachment on South Georgia.

On 31 March Margaret Thatcher's government received warning that invasion was imminent, and an early meeting suggested that while nothing could be done to prevent it, the navy could send a 'retrieval force' rapidly. The decision to mount operation CORPORATE was taken early and owed much to the prime minister's determination. It was controlled from the navy's headquarters at Northwood near London by Admiral Sir Henry Fieldhouse and his staff. The idea of swift retrieval was soon replaced by one of deliberate attack, and a task force was assembled, incorporating the old aircraft carrier HMS *Hermes* and the new HMS *Invincible* equipped with Sea Harriers and helicopters, other warships, Royal Fleet Auxiliaries, and chartered merchantmen. The landing forces, under Major General Jeremy Moore, would eventually comprise the 3rd Commando Brigade (Brigadier Julian Thompson), with three battalion-sized Marine Commandos and the 2nd and 3rd battalions of the Parachute Regiment under its command, and the 5th

---

The Falklands War. The flight deck of HMS *Hermes*.

Infantry Brigade (Brigadier M. J. A. Wilson), with the 2nd Battalion Scots Guards, 1st Battalion Welsh Guards, and 7th Gurkha Rifles. Special forces included the Special Boat Service and the 22nd SAS Regiment, and the Royal Artillery furnished both field and air defence artillery.

The Argentine garrison was reinforced to comprise two brigades under Brigadier General Menendez, the islands' military governor. The British used Ascension Island just south of the equator as a forward base, and on 18 April the main task group (Rear Admiral John (Sandy) Woodward) sailed from it. On 12 April, with two nuclear submarines in the theatre, Britain announced a Maritime Exclusion Zone around the Falklands. South Georgia was recaptured by Royal Marines and special forces on 24–25 April, and on 1 May a Vulcan based at Ascension Island (refuelled several times en route) bombed Stanley airport, inflicting little damage but demonstrating the RAF's long reach. On the same day aircraft from Woodward's task group attacked ground targets, while his ships came under attack from Argentine aircraft. On 2 May the old Argentine cruiser *General Belgrano* was torpedoed by the submarine HMS *Conqueror* south of the Falklands, after which the Argentine navy did not venture out of coastal waters.

On 4 May the Argentine air force sank HMS *Sheffield* with an Exocet missile, and when the British landed around San Carlos on 21 May it mounted repeated attacks on warships in Falkland Sound. HMS *Ardent* and *Antelope* were sunk and other vessels damaged. On 25 May HMS *Coventry*, on radar picket to the north of West Falkland, was also sunk. Ship casualties would have been higher if bombs had burst on impact, and British prospects would have been poor if troopships rather than warships had been lost. As it was, the sinking of *Atlantic Conveyor* on 25 May was to make land operations difficult: all but one of the heavy-lift Chinook helicopters she carried were lost.

The beachhead at San Carlos, which included the old meat plant at Ajax Bay whose buildings housed the field hospital, had been secured by the 3rd Commando Brigade, and its commander had been ordered to await the arrival of Moore and the 5th Brigade. Pressure from London in the wake of naval losses provoked a change of plan, and it was decided to send 45 Commando and 3 Para eastwards on foot, while 2 Para jabbed south to the settlement of Goose Green. On 28–29 May 2 Para took Goose Green from a superior force in a vicious battle which left its commanding officer, Lieutenant Colonel H. Jones, among the dead. The loss of Goose Green struck a powerful blow at Argentine confidence, for Menendez had just reinforced it.

The 45 Commando and 3 Para completed their gruelling march across East Falkland to invest Stanley and the 5th Brigade landed at San Carlos. The two Guards battalions were moved by sea to Bluff Cove, on the east coast, and suffered severe casualties when the RFA (Royal Fleet Auxiliary) vessels *Sir Galahad* and *Sir Tristram* were hit by aircraft. With the bulk of his forces now investing Stanley, Moore planned attacks on the high ground around it. On the night of 11–12 June 3 Para took Mount Longdon, 45 Commando Two Sisters, and 42 Commando (flown forward by helicopter) Mount Harriet. On 13–14 June the Scots Guards took Tumbledown Mountain while 2 Para stormed Wireless Ridge. The defence began to collapse: the attackers followed crowds of demoralized men into Stanley and Menendez surrendered.

The war cost the lives of 255 British servicemen and Falklanders: well over 700 Argentines were killed (368 of them on the *Belgrano*), and the junta fell soon afterwards.

8 Asia and the Middle East

From classical times there was an interplay between Asia and Europe. For centuries this was because great pulses of nomadic movement originating on the Asian steppe sent successive waves of invaders rolling both east and west, and more recently it was because the relative military weakness of Asia abetted European colonization. These processes make simple geographical definitions impossible. In the sixth and seventh centuries, for instance, a wave of expansionism took the Arabs along the coast of North Africa into Spain and, by way of frequent raids rather than settled occupation, into France too. The Crusades saw European military techniques exported to the Middle East, and at the height of Ottoman power Turkey was a major player in European affairs.

Just as currents of invasion ran in two directions, so too did the flow of technology. A primitive stirrup appeared in Siberia in the first century AD, and stirrups were in use in China in the 5th century and Japan and Korea a century later. Europeans may have first encountered the stirrup on Hunnish saddles, or perhaps coming from the Middle East by way of the Iberian peninsula. It was used by European horsemen from the seventh and eighth centuries, and without it there could have been no armoured knight. Gunpowder originated in China, as a pyrotechnic rather than a propellant, before 1000 AD, and it was known in the Muslim world before it eventually arrived in Europe in the thirteenth century.

Yet soon the current surged the other way. The Persian ruler Shah Abbas I (1587–1629) borrowed western technology to help recover territory lost to the Ottomans. Over 500 brass cannon were cast in Persia during his reign, and he employed Europeans to train gunners and musketeers. The first European cannon (*folang zhi*, or Frankish gun) had reached China in the fifteenth century, and by the nineteenth century Asia became a net importer of western military technology. Japanese victory in the Russo-Japanese War showed just how successful the Japanese were in their adaptation, and one of the most striking factors at the beginning of World War II was the quality of some Japanese weapons, like the Zero fighter and the 'long lance' torpedo.

It is easy to overemphasize the technological edge enjoyed by Europeans who established themselves in Asia from the 1600s. As late as the 1840s, for example, British artillery could find itself outmatched by that of the Sikhs. Dominance of the sea was, however, fundamental in the establishment of European enclaves in Asia, and as the nineteenth century wore on burgeoning military technology gave Europeans a decisive advantage. There were still moments when a local adversary might outclass his European opponents by means of a judicious military purchase: the honours of the battle of Maiwand (1880) were carried off by the Afghans' German-supplied artillery which outshot British guns that day.

Tides of invasion shaped Asia and the Middle East just as rivers crease a landscape. The late Roman empire was battered not only by invaders from the north, like the Goths and the Vandals, but by the Huns, steppe nomads who drifted westwards after raiding into the Persian empire in 35 AD and whose ruler Attila (d. AD 435) controlled a state centred on the eastern Danube. They were kin to the Hsiung-nu, tribesmen who provided a constant threat to China during and after the later Han dynasty (around AD 100 to 300). The horse archer, plying his powerful composite bow from the saddle, was the distinctive steppe warrior. He came from a society which practised 'extensive' economy, moving livestock (and with it his whole itinerant community) between seasonal pastures, as opposed to the 'intensive' economy of settled agricultural folk. Steppe societies had both a regional imperative, for land was crucial to their pattern of seasonal migration, and family and clan structures. But they were not narrowly territorial like farmers, traders, or city-dwellers, and were far less amenable to rigid control by a ruling class. They were reviled as 'barbarians' in China and the west alike, and were sometimes wholly terrifying in their sudden and rapacious descent. But, equally, they could change and adapt, often beginning the process by serving as irregular troops for settled states, whose authority they then usurped.

In China, several dynasties were created by steppe warriors from beyond the Great Wall: the Jurchids founded the Chin dynasty (1115–1206) and the Mongols eventually established the Yuan dynasty (1279–1367). The Manchus invaded in the early seventeenth century and established a dynasty of their own, overcoming the north relatively easily but spending 30 years to take the south. It speaks volumes for China's ability to assimilate its conquerors that the greatest of the Manchus, the Qianlong emperor (1736–95), looked and behaved like the long-established, highly cultured ruler of a mighty kingdom, not the descendant of a band of warrior horsemen.

However, a series of famines encouraged revolt, and the Taiping Rebellion (1851–4), instigated by a non-Manchu candidate who had failed the civil service exam, was the most bloody civil war in history and, in terms of overall loss of life, ranks second only to the Second World War. Chinese military weakness enabled Britain, France, Russia, and latterly Japan to inflict a series of defeats on China, and to impose the 'unequal treaties' which caused lasting resentment. The Manchus were replaced by a republic in 1911, and it is ironic that the last Manchu emperor was revived by the Japanese to 'rule' their puppet state of Manchukuo, on the Mongolian steppe where the Manchus had once originated.

The Middle East, North Africa, and eastern Europe were also scoured by nomadic torrents. Between 1219 and 1223 the Mongol ruler Genghis Khan defeated the monarch of what now comprises Iran, Afghanistan, Turkmenistan, and Uzbekistan, sacking the cities of Bokhara, Samarkand, and Herat. From 1235 his successors began to invade the Russian principalities. They then pushed deep into Europe, and in April 1241 beat Duke Henry of Silesia at Leignitz and King Bela of Hungary on the river Sajo. The Mongols got as far as Wiener Neustadt, and might well have remained in Europe had a series of political crises in the Mongol empire not drawn them back to the steppe.

The Turks originated in nomads from the area of the Altai mountains in what is now Mongolia. One group, the Seljuks, entered the Middle East in the tenth century, and eventually assumed the role of protectors of the Abbasid caliphs of Baghdad. In 1055 their leader Tugrul Beg was recognized as sultan, or temporal ruler, and there was soon tension between the Seljuks, who, in the way of such conquerors, rapidly became more settled, and the Turcoman tribes on the fringes of their empire. The Seljuks created a regular army from slaves taken from the steppes north of the Black Sea, and later from the Caucasus. These Mamelukes at first helped the Seljuks divert the Turcomans, and in 1260, under their leader Baybars, established a state of their own in Egypt.

The Seljuks, meanwhile, raided into Anatolia, part of the Byzantine empire, and in 1071 their sultan Alp Arslan defeated the Emperor Romanus Diogenes at Manzikert, north of Lake Van. The battle breached the Byzantine frontier defences and left Anatolia ripe for infiltration by the Turcomans. Some of these accepted Seljuk authority, and amongst those that set up states of their own were followers of one of Tugrul's descendants, who established the empire of Rhum, which soon included much of Anatolia. The authority of the main Seljuk line declined, because of the emergence of a capable caliph, the impact of the Crusades, the constant pressure of Turcoman nomads, and latterly the attacks of the Mongols, who brought the Seljuks of Rhum under their control in 1242 and then took Baghdad, killing the last Abbasid caliph, in 1258. But in 1260 Mongol advance in the Middle East was checked decisively by the Mamelukes at the battle of Ain Jalut, and it was the Mamelukes who put an end to crusader occupation of the Holy Land by taking Acre in 1291.

Osman Bey, founder of the Ottoman dynasty, was born in north-eastern Anatolia in about 1258, and by his death in 1324 he had established a state, which gained real weight when his son Orhan took the Byzantine city of Bursa in 1326. The Ottomans capitalized on a disputed succession to the Byzantine throne by supporting one claimant, but, having pushed on into Thrace, they declined to leave and, under Murad I (1360–89), struck deep into the Balkans, beating the Serbians and their allies in the resonant battle of Kosovo Polje (1389). Sultan Bayezit I earned the nickname *Yilderim* (thunderbolt) by hurtling between Anatolia and Europe: in 1396 he destroyed a crusading army at Nicopolis on the Danube, and went on to besiege Constantinople. But he was himself beaten by Timur just east of Ankara in 1402, and died in captivity. The Tartars went on to ravage Anatolia, but under Mehmet I (1413–20) and Murad II (1421–51) the Ottoman empire was restored, though it was left to Mehmet II (1451–81) to take Constantinople in 1453.

From Constantinople the Ottomans ruled an empire which stretched deep into Europe. In 1683 Ottoman domains included not only Thrace, Hungary and the Balkans, the Crimea and some of the lands to its west, but Anatolia, the whole of the Middle East and what is now Iraq, as well as Egypt and a narrow strip of territory along the coast of North Africa. That year Mehmet IV's grand vizier was repulsed from the gates of Vienna, and thereafter the empire declined. The process saw some local rulers establish their independence, and states on the empire's fringes, notably Russia and Austria, made steady encroachments. This long process was not simply the result of wars, but the decline of Turkish power created instability which itself provoked conflict. Indeed, Count Otto von Bismarck had predicted that 'some damned foolish thing in the Balkans' would eventually cause a major European war, and he was right, for it was the assassination of the Archduke Franz Ferdinand in Sarajevo, once a Turkish town, that lit the fuse which blew the old world apart in 1914.

Just as the Ottomans had begun as nomads and became a settled imperial power, so too nomads became rulers of India. In 1398 the Mongol Timur (Timur-i-Lank, Timur the Lame, hence Tamburlane) swept into India, beating the sultan of Delhi at the first battle of Panipat. His descendant Babur repeated the process in 1525, winning second Panipat the following year, and going on to lay the foundations of the Mughal empire. By the time Emperor Aurangzeb died in 1707 this included not only India as far south as Mysore, but Afghanistan as well. There too there was the familiar pattern of expansion and decline, although the whole process was much more rapid than it was in the case of Turkey. The empire was already beginning to tilt out of control under Aurangzeb, with local rivals, of whom the Marathas were the most serious, challenging the emperor's central authority, and Europeans, drawn to India by trade, establishing themselves in coastal enclaves.

Eventually the British emerged as the dominant European power in India, first working alongside the Mughals and eventually supplanting them altogether. Battles like Plassey (1757) and Buxar (1764) saw the British tighten their grip on Bengal, while Wandiwash (1760) dashed French hopes in India. Even at the zenith of their power the British did not rule all India directly, but controlled much of it through local princes. However, they had defeated their most serious rivals, in Mysore, the Deccan, and the Punjab, in pitched battles which decided the fate of the subcontinent. In the nineteenth century the British were preoccupied with Afghanistan, fearing a Russian invasion across India's north-west frontier. They fought three Afghan wars, the first two of which saw British reverses on the retreat from Kabul (1842) and at Maiwand (1880), but ended with Afghanistan in the hands of rulers who could be expected to defend their independence as fiercely against the Russians as against the British.

Geography set Japan apart from the pattern of invasion that characterized so much of Asian history. In the first centuries AD Japanese troops took part in dynastic wars between the kingdoms that then constituted Korea, but the major preoccupation of the Yamato state, which had established the basis of centralized power by the seventh century, was in ensuring its control of Japan. The Gempei wars of 1180–5 were a contest between two samurai clans, the Taira and the Minamoto. They left the Minamoto as Japan's most powerful family, controlling the state through the emperor, with Yoritomo, whose younger brother had won the decisive naval battle of Dan no Ura in 1185, as the first shogun, or military dictator, of Japan. The Gempei wars were also important in establishing the codes of samurai behaviour which were to last until the Meiji restoration of 1868 saw the shogunate abolished and witnessed a return to imperial rule. The samurai left not with a whimper, but a bang, and the Satsuma rebellion of 1877 saw them beaten by conscript infantry, organized on western models and using western technology. Their spirit was revived in World War II, when kamikaze pilots (named after the 'divine wind' that had destroyed an invading Mongol fleet in 1281) showed that, for the true warrior, death could still be lighter than a feather.

Although Japanese society was shut off from the rest of the world, there were nevertheless reflections of developments elsewhere. The samurai, with their emphasis on courage and courtly behaviour, had something in common with the European knight, and their use of *mon*, family badges, struck a chord with heraldry in Europe. Cannon arrived in Japan in the sixteenth century, and at the battle of Nagashino in 1575 the mounted samurai of the Takeda clan, charging with a determination that had won them the day in the past, were met by 3,000 arquebusiers whose fire broke their attack. The arrival of firearms had an effect on fortification in Japan which superficially resembled the development of 'artillery fortification' in the west. Stone-clad walls, following the contours of hillsides, protected lofty keeps, and sharply angled protrusions from curtain walls looked not unlike European bastions. Yet there were far fewer cannon in Japan than in Europe, and so Japanese fortresses rarely had to face sustained battering by heavy artillery. However, the stone plinths on which Japanese castles stood were enormously strong: when Hiroshima was struck by an atomic bomb in 1945 the superstructure of its castle was blown away, but its plinth was unscathed. There can be few better examples of the durability of the old in the face of the new.

ISLAMIC WARS

After the death of the Prophet Muhammad, Abu Bakr was chosen as successor (*khalifa*, from which comes the word caliph) and enforced his authority through the 'wars of the *ridda*' which eventually secured the whole of Arabia, the Sasanian lands, which ran from modern Syria to the borders of India, and the Egyptian and Syrian provinces of the Byzantine empire.

The Battle of Ajnadain (634)

Ajnadain was probably the first major engagement between the Byzantine forces defending Syria and Palestine, and the Arabs expanding northwards from the peninsula at the start of the Islamic conquests. Accounts differ on details of the battle, which took place, possibly, on 30 July 634 between Jerusalem and Gaza, including the identity of the Arabs' leader. As many as 20,000 Arabs defeated a similar number of Byzantines. Ajnadain marked the start of a confrontation which ended in the battle of the Yarmuk.

The Battle of the Yarmuk (636)

This was the key battle in the early Islamic conquests. In an attempt to stem the escalating Arab invasion of Syria and Palestine the Byzantines assembled an army of at least 100,000 in August–September 636. It encountered a much smaller Arab force on the Yarmuk river in eastern Palestine. Accounts differ on detail, but all agree that the Byzantine force was driven into an angle between the Yarmuk and a tributary and destroyed. As a result, Syria came under effective Arab control.

There were, however, considerable tensions between three groups of the victorious Arabs: the original Companions of the Prophet and their followers, the men of Madina, and, finally, the leading Meccan families. An open rift appeared in the time of the third caliph, Uthman, who had been chosen by members of Quraysh, Muhammad's tribe. He appointed members of his own clan as governors and this provoked both the sons of the Companions and the Prophet's wife 'A'isha. When Uthman was assassinated he was succeed by 'Ali ibn Abi Talib, of Quraysh, but not universally supported. Uthman's family opposed him in Syria, as did 'A'isha and her followers in Basra.

The Battle of the Camel (656)

With 'A'isha occupying Basra with some 30,000 men, 'Ali ibn Abi Talib and his 20,000 followers made camp at Rabaza, still hoping to avoid war and the shedding of Muslim blood. By 4 December 656 the two armies faced each other in the valley of the Lion near Khuraiba. 'A'isha mounted her camel, which gave the battle its name, and the fighting began. Eventually 'Ali realized that as long as 'A'isha dominated the field high on her mount, her army, although suffering terrible casualties, would fight on. He ordered one of his men to cut the legs off the beast. The order was carried out (though we may suspect that the hamstringing of a single leg, often inflicted on mounts by foot soldiers ducking in low with sword or dagger, would have been the fate actually suffered by the luckless beast) and the camel collapsed. Resistance collapsed with it and the victory was 'Ali's at a cost of, it is said, a mere 1,000 men. 'A'isha's army, on the other hand, lost half its strength.

The Syrian challenge had yet to be confronted and 'Ali's forces met those of Mu'awiya at Siffin on the upper Euphrates. Arbitration took over from conflict, but some of 'Ali's followers objected to human will replacing that of God and 'Ali's strength grew weaker until he was killed in 661, permitting Mu'awiya to become caliph and the centre of power to shift to Damascus. The character of what was becoming the Islamic empire grew more secular and its spread extended from the Atlantic coast of Morocco to the valley of the Oxus by the end of the seventh century.

The Battle of Karbala' (680)

Karbala' lies to the south of modern Baghdad in Iraq, and was the site of an engagement between the forces of the Umayyad Arab Caliph Yazid I and Husayn, son of the former Caliph 'Ali and grandson of the Prophet Muhammad. The Umayyads had come to power on 'Ali's assassination and the abdication of his elder son Hasan (661), but Husayn seems to have felt that he had a right to the throne through hereditary succession and, as his later partisans, the Shi'a, were to maintain, through divine designation. Husayn refused allegiance to Yazid in 680 and raised a revolt with some 50 supporters. The actual battle, on 10 October, seems to have been merely a series of skirmishes, but Husayn was killed. The event had a disproportionate significance, since Husayn's fate aroused widespread sympathy among many Muslims. He was subsequently made into a martyr by the Shi'a, to be mourned as the central, suffering figure in the *ta'ziyas* or Shi'ite 'Passion Plays' of recent times, with his richly endowed tomb at Karbala' becoming the major pilgrimage goal for Shi'ites.

The Battle of Manzikert (1071)

A hinge event in Middle Eastern history was the battle fought near Manzikert (Malazgird) some 40 km (25 miles) north of Lake Van in what is now eastern Turkey. The most valuable account is that of the Byzantine historian Attaliates who was an eyewitness, but the battle is also mentioned in Armenian, Syriac, Islamic, and western European sources. In the battle the Byzantine emperor Romanus IV Diogenes, campaigning on his eastern borders to counter the Seljuk Turk threat, met a depleted army under Sultan Alp Arslan. Few details of the actual battle are known. The Byzantine rearguard left the battlefield at nightfall and the Seljuk army was able to lure it into ambushes. The terrain favoured the Seljuk mounted archers and the Byzantine army was racked with internal dissension. Although Romanus' army was superior in numbers, its composition was heterogeneous, containing many foreign mercenary contingents. The ultimate humiliation was the capture of Romanus himself. The sources agree that he was honourably treated by Alp Arslan and released after a few days. Byzantine prestige was seriously damaged by this defeat. The disaster at Manzikert has been seen as a convenient point from which to date the decline of the eastern Byzantine empire and eventually the Turkification of Anatolia.

The battle has also been viewed as one of the mainsprings of European involvement in the Levant in the Crusades.

The Battles of Tarain (1191–1192)

Also known as the battles of Taraori, the battles of Tarain were a series of engagements, the last of which resulted in a decisive Muslim victory which opened all of northern India to Muslim conquest. Sent forth by his elder brother Ghiyas al-Din to extend their Ghur territories, Muizz al-Din Muhammad was soon drawn to the vast wealth of India. He proclaimed a jihad against the Hindus and his initial campaigns met with considerable success, capturing Sind in 1182 and Lahore and the Punjab in 1186.

He was checked for the first time on the plain of Tarain, about 100 km (60 miles) north of Delhi, in 1191. The Hindu Rajputs, seeing the common threat Muhammad posed, for once managed to unite and put a vastly superior force into the field. Led by Prithviraja, king of Delhi, and supported by Jai Chand of Kanoaj, the Rajput coalition soundly defeated Muhammad who was fortunate to escape the battlefield with his life.

Muhammad returned to the plains of Tarain with a new army the following year. Once again he was heavily outnumbered, his 12,000 men facing an alleged 100,000 Hindus. Muhammad conducted a masterly mobile battle against the largely static defenders. Employing flexible Turkish tactics to which the Hindus had no adequate response, his cavalry harried the Rajput flanks and showered their ranks with arrows while eschewing the hand-to-hand combat at which the Rajputs excelled. The Hindus were unable to chase the elusive cavalry without dangerously exposing themselves and thus were forced to endure the attrition of the Muslim arrows. When Muhammad finally judged his enemy sufficiently worn down, he charged their centre and routed them. Prithviraja died in the mêlée. The battle proved decisive and Delhi was captured in 1192–3. The whole of northern India fell to the Muslims within twenty years.

The Battles of Panipat (1399, 1526, 1556, 1761)

Panipat is a town, still with a fort and a wall with fifteen gates, in the Haryana province of northern India, in the Ganges–Jumna basin to the north of Delhi. It lies in a corridor, between the southern foothills of the Himalayas and deserts of Rajasthan, through which the Ganges and Jumna flow, one much used by invaders from Afghanistan and hence of strategic significance. It was the site of four battles, all decisive for the fate of Muslim India.

The first came in 1399, when Timur defeated the sultan of Delhi with great slaughter, and sacked the city. The second was in 1526 when the Turco-Mongol adventurer Babur was invited into Hindustan from Kandahar by dissident members of the Delhi sultan Ibrahim Lodi's family. In a battle on 20 April, Babur's troops were heavily outnumbered, but he managed to gain a decisive victory, end the 75-year rule of the Lodi dynasty, and lay the initial foundations for Mughal rule, although this was only consolidated a generation later by his grandson Akbar the Great. The victory has been attributed to Babur's use of some primitive cannon, lashed together with bull's hide and placed at intervals along a wagon line, and he also had musketeers using matchlocks.

The third battle was on 5 November 1556, when Bayram Khan, on behalf of the newly acceded Akbar, defeated the usurping Hindu minister Hemu, who had assumed the regal title of Raja Vikramaditya. He was then able finally to vanquish the last ruler of the preceding line of Suri sultans and consolidate Mughal power in India.

The fourth battle was fought on 14 January 1761 when the Afghan ruler of Kabul, Ahmad Shah Durrani, entered northern India for the fourth time in an attempt to oust the Hindu, fiercely anti-Muslim Marathas from the Punjab and north-western India, and thereby to preserve the shrinking authority of the Mughal emperors, now essentially reduced to the area round Delhi (which the Marathas had in fact recently occupied). The Afghans crushed Sardashiv Rao, uncle of the peshwa of the Marathas, inflicting great losses. Although Ahmad Shah returned to Afghanistan and Maratha power revived, being only reduced by the East India Company in the early nineteenth century, the battle had important and lasting consequences in the rise of a Muslim state in Mysore under Haydar Ali, while the British in Bengal were granted a respite to consolidate their power *pour mieux sauter*.

JAPANESE WARS

Oda Nobunaga (1534–82) is one of the pivotal figures in Japanese history. He was only 15 when his father died, and rose to national prominence with his stunning victory of Okehazama in 1560, when he defeated the powerful army of Imagawa Yoshimoto. In 1564 he defeated the Saitō family and made his capital at Gifu. Campaigns against the Asai and Asakura followed, including the battle of Anegawa in 1570. In 1571 he destroyed the temples of Mount Hiei, ending for ever the influence of the *sōhei* (warrior monks). Other religious rivals caused him more problems. His campaign against the Ikkō-ikki at Nagashima and Ishiyama Honganji lasted a decade.

The Battle of Nagashino (1575)

Oda Nobunaga had to raise the siege of Nagashino castle, imposed by the army of Takeda Katsuyori, son of the late Shingen. The Takeda army that laid siege to Nagashino castle consisted of 15,000 men, of whom 12,000 took part in the subsequent battle. They were therefore well outnumbered by the Oda and Tokugawa Ieyasu force of 38,000 which advanced to meet them, whose positions looked across the plain of Shidarahara towards the castle. About 100 m (328 feet) in front flowed the little Rengogawa, which acted as a forward defence for the positions Oda Nobunaga had chosen.

Oda Nobunaga also had the advantage of a unit of 3,000 matchlock musketeers (*ashigaru*), but realized that they would need some form of physical protection, so his army built a palisade halfway between the forested edge of the hills and the river. It was a loose fence of stakes, staggered over three alternate layers, and with many gaps to allow a counter-attack. Nobunaga's plan was for the matchlock men to fire rolling volleys as the Takeda cavalry approached. For the majority of the Takeda troops, their first sight of the enemy came when they moved out of the woods to the east of Shidarahara. From this point it was 200 m (650 feet) at its narrowest to the Oda/Tokugawa line, and at its broadest only 400 m (1,300 feet). There were three matchlock men in the Oda lines for every four Takeda mounted samurai charging at them, but Takeda Katsuyori hoped that his horsemen would be upon the *ashigaru* as they tried to reload, to be followed within seconds by the Takeda foot soldiers.

At 06.00 on 28 June 1575, Takeda Katsuyori ordered the advance. The three vanguards of the Takeda cavalry under Yamagata Masakage, Nait, and Baba swept down from the hills on to the narrow fields. Horses and men carefully negotiated the shallow riverbed, to pick up speed again as they mounted the far bank. At this point, with the horsemen within 50 m (160 feet) of the fence, the volley firing began. All along the line horsemen in the vanguards, and the attendant foot soldiers who had advanced with them, were falling in heaps. The samurai, with their shorter spears, took the fight to the Takeda in small group actions. The battle lasted until mid-afternoon, when the Takeda began to retreat, and were pursued. Takeda Katsuyori left behind him on the battlefield 10,000 dead, a casualty rate of 67 per cent. Out of 97 named samurai leaders of the Takeda at Nagashino, 54 were killed and two badly wounded. Eight of the veteran 'Twenty-Four Generals' of the Takeda were killed.

It took a further seven years for Oda Nobunaga to destroy the Takeda family. In 1576 he built Azuchi castle, and towards the end of his career conducted successful campaigns in Ise and Iga provinces. As a ruler he was tolerant towards the spread of Christianity in Japan and encouraged foreign trade. In 1582 he was murdered in a surprise night attack on the Honnōji temple in Kyoto by his general Akechi Mitsuhide When Imagawa Yoshimoto had, in the 1550s, invaded Nobunaga's territories Tokugawa Ieyasu (1542–1616) played a distinguished role in the capture of the fortress of Marune, and in 1560 Ieyasu allied himself to Oda Nobunaga and fought loyally at Azukizaka (1564) against the Ikkō-ikki sectarians. Ieyasu took part in the battle of the Anegawa (1570), when his army took much of the brunt of the fighting. He was defeated by Takeda Shingen at Mikata ga hara (1572), but avoided the loss of Hamamatsu castle by a tactical withdrawal and a night attack. He also accompanied Nobunaga in the relief of Nagashino castle in 1575. The death of Nobunaga placed Ieyasu against Toyotomi Hideyoshi, but through adroit political skills Ieyasu avoided the fate of other rivals, and their major conflict at Nagakute (1584) ended in stalemate.

Following the defeat of the Hōjō in 1590, Ieyasu received their territories and transferred his capital to Edo (Tokyo). As his army had avoided service in Korea he was in a strong position when Hideyoshi died, and challenged the Toyotomi family for the succession against a powerful alliance under Ishida Mitsunari.

The Battle of Sekigahara (1600)

Ieyasu's Eastern Army and Ishida's Western Army met in what was one of the most decisive battles in Japanese history. Ishida had carried out a night march to Sekigahara. His plans were that the main body would hold the Tokugawa in the centre while others would attack them in the rear. Early in the morning of 21 October the Western Army was fully in position. In the centre were the divisions under Ukita Hideie and Konishi Yukinaga. To the left of them was Ishida Mitsunari himself. On the right wing, straddling the Nakasendō road, were various contingents including Kobayakawa Hideaki.

By daybreak the Eastern Army had advanced along the Nakasendō to meet them on as wide a front as the narrow valley would allow them. There was a thick fog which persisted until about 08.00, when the fighting started. The central divisions were the first to engage, the first shots of the battle probably being fired by Ukita's troops at those of Ii Naomasa of the Eastern Army. Ukita was successful in driving the easterners back, but they rallied and the fight swayed one way and then the other. All the main divisions were now engaged, and Ishida thought the moment opportune to light the signal fire that would bring Kobayakawa down from Matsuoyama. But Kobayakawa turned traitor and assaulted the flank of Ōtani. Ieyasu then ordered a general attack along the line, and further contingents of the Western Army changed sides.

In the meantime Kobayakawa's men swept through the defeated Ōtani troops, round the rear of Ukita, and attacked Konishi from behind. The Western Army began to break up. Only the army of the Shimazu clan was left intact. Putting himself at the head of 80 survivors Shimazu Yoshihiro succeeded in cutting his way through the Eastern Army. Unfortunately this route took them south-west of Mount Nangu where Ishida's reserve troops were stationed. Some had already decided to join Ieyasu, others were wavering, unsure what to make of the noise they could hear and the garbled reports they were receiving. The battle was already lost, so the very contingents who might have been able to reverse Ishida's defeat turned and marched away from Sekigahara. Ieyasu's victory enabled him to become shogun in 1603, establishing the Tokugawa dynasty.

He finally vanquished the Toyotomi heir, Hideyori, with the long and bitter siege of Osaka castle in 1614–15. He died peacefully in bed, having established a dynasty that would last until 1868, two and a half centuries.

EUROPEANS IN INDIA

While the Seven Years War (1756–63) was rearranging Europe, France and Britain were involved in conflicts in the Americas and in the east. In the Indian subcontinent France's position was undermined by a series of British successes. Victory by Robert Clive in the small-scale but decisive battle of Plassey (from which he took his title when raised to the peerage) gave Britain, or rather its East India Company (EIC), control of Bengal.

The Battle of Plassey (1757)

Following the attack by the independent Mughal nawab (governor) of Bengal, Siraj al-Dawla, on the British settlements in Bengal in the summer of 1856, a force commanded by Colonel Robert Clive was sent from Madras. In March 1757 Clive forced the submission of the French settlement at Chandernagore and then marched against Siraj al-Dawla's forces, having first suborned his principal commanders, who remained inactive during the battle which took place on 23 June 1757 on the banks of the Bhagirathi river. Clive was very heavily outnumbered and outgunned, but the battle resolved itself into an artillery duel which the nawab lost when his powder was soaked by rain. Clive's total casualties numbered only 63.

Subsequent successes at Wandiwash (January 1760) and Pondicherry (January 1761) weakened the French position on the Carnatic coast in the south-east.

The Maratha Wars

The three Maratha Wars were fought between 1775 and 1818 involving the English East India Company and the confederacy of chiefs in western and northern India was the Maratha wars. Maratha power had begun as a Hindu challenge to Mughal domination of India during the seventeenth century and by the latter part of the eighteenth century had become the dominant force in northern and western India and the principal rival of the EIC. The Maratha confederacy consisted of the fiefs of many semi-independent chiefs, of whom the most prominent were Holkar, Sindhia, the bhonsla of Berar (Nagpur), and the gaekwar of Baroda, grouped under the leadership of the peshwa in Poona (Pune).

The first Anglo-Maratha war (1778–82) arose out of the interference of the EIC's Bombay government in Maratha affairs in the hope of obtaining some territorial advantage following Panipat. The EIC achieved little and peace was made at Salbai (May 1782) in which the EIC relinquished all gains since 1776.

The second Anglo-Maratha war began when the governor general, then Lord Wellesley, saw an opportunity to establish British control over the Maratha confederacy by a treaty with the peshwa (Bassein, 1802). In the war that followed there were four theatres of operations. In Orissa operations against the bhonsla gave Britain territory which enabled the Bombay and Madras presidencies to link up. In Gujerat Broach was seized from Sindhia. But the main operations were in central India where the governor general's brother Major General Arthur Wellesley (later the duke of Wellington) defeated the forces of Sindhia and the bhonsla.

The Battle of Assaye (1803)

Arthur Wellesley, who had divided his forces, was greatly outnumbered (c.40,000 to 7,000) and outgunned (100 to 22) and was very inferior in cavalry when on 23 September 1803 he unexpectedly came upon the Marathas encamped on the opposite side of the Kaitna river near the village of Assaye in central India (modern Maharashtra). Wellesley decided it was too dangerous to retire or to wait for the rest of his forces and that he should attack. Relying on his army's superior mobility and his own considerable powers of decision, he found a ford, crossed the river, and attacked the Marathas' left flank, winning a close and bloody battle (Wellesley himself lost two horses) in which he incurred over 1,800 casualties, mostly from the fire of the disciplined Maratha artillery. Wellesley captured 100 guns. He was too weakened to pursue the Maratha at once but on 29 November caught and defeated them at Argaum. Many years later, in response to an enquiry as to his greatest military achievement, he answered 'Assaye'.

In northern India the commander-in-chief, Lord Lake, attacked the French-trained forces of Sindhia in the Ganges–Jumna Doab and was victorious at Delhi and Laswari.

By the end of 1803 these victories and conquests were consolidated in peace treaties with Sindhia and the bhonsla. Holkar was not included and in 1804 war commenced against his forces in Hindustan and the Deccan. The EIC forces were not successful and peace was made in 1805.

In the following years the Maratha territories increasingly became a refuge for plundering bands of irregular cavalry known as Pathans and Pindaris. British indignation at the activities of the bands eventually boiled over and in 1816 Governor General Lord

Hastings set in motion an extensive plan to bring them under control. This plan involved allying with some of the Marathas and the Rajput states beyond the Jamna and launching military operations against the Pathans and Pindaris from the north and the south. Inevitably the war spread and the main Maratha chiefs were drawn in and duly defeated: the peshwa at Kirkee (6 November 1817), the bhonsla at Sitabaldi (27 November 1817), and Holkar at Mahidpur (21 December 1817); the first were two brilliant defensive actions and the last an expensive charge straight at the enemy guns. The danger from the Pathans and Pindaris was eliminated by a mixture of military action and conciliation. By the conclusion of hostilities in 1818 Britain was paramount throughout India as far as the borders of the Punjab and Sind.

THE SIKH WARS

Under Ranjit Singh (1780–1839) several of the various Sikh communities were united and formed the basis of the Lahore state which also embraced Hindus and Muslims. The expansion of the state towards British India was checked in 1809 on the river Sutlej but the state was extended to include Kashmir (1819) and Peshawar (1834). Britain was content to leave the Lahore state as a valuable buffer on its north-west frontier, insulating British India from the Muslim peoples of central Asia, but the Punjab fell into increasing disorder after the death of Ranjit Singh and there was evidence of mutinous conduct in the Sikh regiments which were run by their own councils (*panchayats*). Fears became reality in December 1845 when Sikh forces crossed the Sutlej and invaded East India Company-protected territory.

The Sikh army was the most formidable military opponent Britain encountered in India. Trained by French and other European mercenaries, it included *c*.50,000 well-drilled infantry, 10,000 disciplined artillerymen, and 6,000 regular cavalry as well as irregular formations. Because of previous fears of provoking just such an attack, EIC forces were comparatively unprepared, but Sir Hugh Gough marched rapidly to the relief of the garrisons on the Sutlej and encountered an advanced Sikh force at Mudki on 18 December, where he fought a bloody, confused, and indecisive battle. The advanced party retired on Firuzshah where they joined the main Sikh force. There a second battle took place on 21 December. As at Mudki, Gough attacked when there was insufficient daylight and when fighting was broken off he feared defeat on the morrow, when Sikh reinforcements were expected. Instead the Sikh army abandoned the field and the reinforcements did likewise when they learned of this. Gough was left in possession of the field and 73 captured guns. His casualties were severe—2,415 out of 16,000 engaged—and were especially heavy among his British regiments, which had borne the brunt of the superior Sikh artillery. Consequently he elected to wait for reinforcements, especially of heavy guns. In the meantime Sir Harry Smith carried out a series of skilful manoeuvres to protect British garrisons along the Sutlej, collect scattered forces, and defeat the Sikhs at Aliwal (28 January 1846).

The Battle of Sobraon (1846)

The final and decisive battle of the war was fought on 10 February 1846 on the eastern bank of the river Sutlej. The Sikhs were in entrenched positions with their backs to the river. After a heavy exchange of artillery fire and a general assault which the Sikhs fiercely opposed, Sir Hugh Gough's infantry breached the Sikh left. The bridge of boats securing the Sikh retreat collapsed, turning defeat into rout. Losses on both sides were severe, the Sikhs suffering between 8,000 and 10,000 dead and the British 2,300. As a result of the defeat the threat from the Sikhs was contained, but not yet eliminated. The Sikhs then sued for peace.

The resulting East India Company-controlled regency in Lahore was inherently unstable and culminated in an uprising at Multan in August 1848. The EIC was drawn into operations against Multan and into a formal siege which lasted from October into January 1849. The Army of the Punjab was formed under Gough who crossed the Sutlej on 9 November but proceeded cautiously, waiting for reinforcements. There followed a period of manoeuvre, punctuated by an indecisive cavalry engagement at Ramnuggur, before Gough encountered the main Sikh force at Chillianwala (13 January 1849). The Sikhs had some 30,000 men and 62 guns against the 12,000 Gough managed to put into the field. A struggle in jungly terrain ensued in which Gough suffered 2,331 casualties and once more the excellent Sikh artillery pounded the British infantry. Both sides pulled back, and when battle was rejoined at Gujerat near the river Chenab, Gough's newly arrived artillery silenced the Sikh guns and a complete victory was obtained. The Sikhs surrendered at Rawalpindi on 14 March and the Punjab was formally annexed. Sikhs subsequently became and remain important elements in the Indian army.

THE ANGLO-AFGHAN WARS

The steady advance of the Russian empire into central Asia and the equally relentless advance north-westwards of the British dominion in India in the first half of the nineteenth century forced Afghanistan—the kingdom of Kabul—into the uneasy position of a buffer state between the two. Emir Dost Muhammad, despairing of British support, prepared to listen to the Russians, and a Russian envoy, Vitkevich, arrived in Kabul on 19 December 1837 while the British envoy, Alexander Burnes, was still there.

Convinced that the emir was now pro-Russian, the governor general of India, Lord Auckland, decided to replace Dost Muhammad with a former ruler, Shah Shuja. The Sikhs were persuaded to enter a Tripartite Treaty for this purpose and in December 1838 the British Army of the Indus assembled at Ferozepore in the Punjab to escort Shah Shuja to Kabul. The force reached Kabul on 7 August 1839, having stormed the immensely powerful fortress of Ghazni en route. Shah Shuja was installed as emir and Dost Muhammad fled, eventually surrendering in November 1840 and being exiled to Calcutta.

It soon became clear that Shah Shuja lacked popular support. The storm burst in November 1841 when Burnes was murdered by a mob. The British attempted to negotiate a peaceful withdrawal with Muhammad Akbar Khan, Dost Muhammad's son and leader of the insurgents round Kabul. Akbar offered to allow the British force at Kabul to retire in peace. It was a trap and when the British began their retreat on 6 January 1842 they came under immediate attack from Akbar's tribesmen. Under constant attack and enfeebled by the bitterly cold weather, the army and its followers were gradually destroyed in the passes leading to India and only a handful escaped. At Jalalabad

a garrison under Brigadier Robert Sale hung on under constant siege and in the south Major General William Nott maintained his position at Kandahar.

When news of the outbreak reached India preparations were made to assemble a relief force under Major General George Pollock at Peshawar. Pollock took his time in cementing morale among his troops and in careful preparation. He began his advance on Kabul on 5 April 1842, and, picketing the heights as he went, relieved Jalalabad a few days later. There 'the Army of Retribution' remained for some months while the new governor general, Lord Ellenborough, tried to decide what to do. Finally, Nott at Kandahar was given permission to retire via Kabul if he wished. Pollock seized the opportunity to advance to Kabul to meet Nott and the two armies were united there on 17 September 1842. Pollock succeeded in rescuing the British captives still in Afghan hands and after blowing up the Kabul bazaar as an act of retribution the combined forces reached Peshawar on 6 November. A grand review was held at Ferozepore and the first Anglo-Afghan War was at an end. Shah Shuja having been murdered the preceding March, Dost Muhammad was released from captivity and resumed his throne.

In 1876 a new Conservative administration under Benjamin Disraeli decided that the expansion and consolidation of Russia in central Asia, which had brought its southern border into direct contact with Afghanistan, constituted a real threat to India. Attempts to persuade the emir, Sher Ali, to enter into an alliance and to accept a resident British envoy failed and Viceroy Lytton became convinced that Sher Ali had become pro-Russian rather than simply neutral.

In the summer of 1878, at the height of the Near Eastern crisis, Sher Ali was pressured into receiving a Russian mission but refused to receive a parallel British embassy. That gave Lytton the excuse he needed and three British columns invaded Afghanistan in November 1878, defeating the Afghans in the Khyber Pass at Ali Masjid and in the Kurram valley at Peiwar Kotal; in the south, Kandahar was occupied virtually without a fight. Sher Ali fled, dying in February 1879, and his successor, his eldest son Yakub Khan, sued for peace, which was signed at Gandamak in May 1879. It provided *inter alia* for a British envoy to reside at Kabul. In September 1879 the envoy, Sir Louis Cavagnari, was murdered in Kabul with his escort. The only readily available striking force was the column under Lieutenant General Sir Frederick Roberts at Kurram and in October he occupied Kabul after a victory at Charasia. Yakub Khan was deposed and exiled to India on suspicion of involvement in Cavagnari's death and Roberts proceeded to execute some scores of Afghans suspected of being involved in the envoy's murder. Two months after seizing Kabul a popular uprising forced Roberts to abandon Kabul and retire into his base at Sherpur where he was besieged for three weeks. On 23 December 1879 he defeated a major attack, trouncing his besiegers and reoccupying Kabul.

In May 1880 Sir Donald Stewart marched from Kandahar to Kabul, defeating an Afghan attack at Ahmed Khel en route, and took over the overall command from Roberts. In the summer of 1880 Abdurrahman Khan, a nephew of Sher Ali long exiled in Russia, entered Afghanistan. The British accepted him as emir of Kabul and of whatever he could control, except for Kandahar. At this moment Sher Ali's younger son Ayub Khan, the governor of Herat, decided to make his own bid for the throne.

The 10th Bengal Lancers in the Jugdulluk Pass, December 1879.

The Battle of Maiwand (1880)

In June 1880 Ayub Khan left Herat with a small army. A British brigade was dispatched from Kandahar to intercept him and the two forces met on 27 July 1880, near the village of Maiwand some 70 km (45 miles) west of Kandahar. The British force under Brigadier General George Burrows was outnumbered but trusted to the firepower of the Martini-Henry rifle. But Burrows reckoned without the superiority of the modern Afghan artillery, which outranged his own, and the fervour of the *ghazis* who made up part of the Afghan force. After a prolonged firefight the *ghazis* pressed in to close quarters, and his force was overwhelmed, with its single British battalion, the 66th Foot, losing both its colours. Nearly 1,000 of his men were killed, with most of the wounded butchered where they lay. The survivors, amounting to some 1,500, retreated in confusion to Kandahar and with the rest of the garrison were besieged there by Ayub Khan until relieved by Roberts in his famous Kabul to Kandahar march of August 1880. Roberts then defeated Ayub outside Kandahar on 1 September 1880.

Kabul had been evacuated by the British in August 1880 and the cabinet after much debate decided to give up Kandahar, finally evacuating Afghanistan in May 1881. Abdurrahman died in 1901, having successfully united Afghanistan and restored good relations with the British.

THE RUSSO-JAPANESE WAR

The 1904–5 war between Russia and Japan was most important militarily as a full dress rehearsal for World War I. It was a war of extended fronts and protracted battles, leading to the emergence of the concept of the operational level of war, trench warfare, the use of machine guns, mortars, grenades, land and sea mines, submarines, barbed wire (sometimes electrified), indirect artillery fire, radio transmission, and even electronic warfare (jamming). Foreign observers from the USA, UK, France, and Germany were present on both sides and their detailed and perceptive reports help make it the best-documented war up to that time.

In 1898 Russia leased the Kwantung peninsula from Japan, set up its naval base at Port Arthur, and in autumn 1900 went on to occupy the whole of Manchuria. In 1902 the Japanese concluded an agreement with Britain and began preparing for war. Russia's ability to influence events in the region was dependent on the trans-Siberian railway, begun in 1891. By 1896 the western section, through Irkutsk to Lake Baikal and from its eastern shore to Sretensk near the Amur river, was built. However, the Russians then decided to cut straight across Manchuria from Chita, 480 km (300 miles) east of Baikal, via Harbin to Vladivostok—the Chinese Eastern railway. The occupation of Manchuria upset the Japanese even more, so the line by which the Russian troops would have to be supplied was itself a cause of the war, and it was single track, with lightweight rails and badly laid.

The sinking of a Japanese ship seen through the eyes of a Japanese artist.

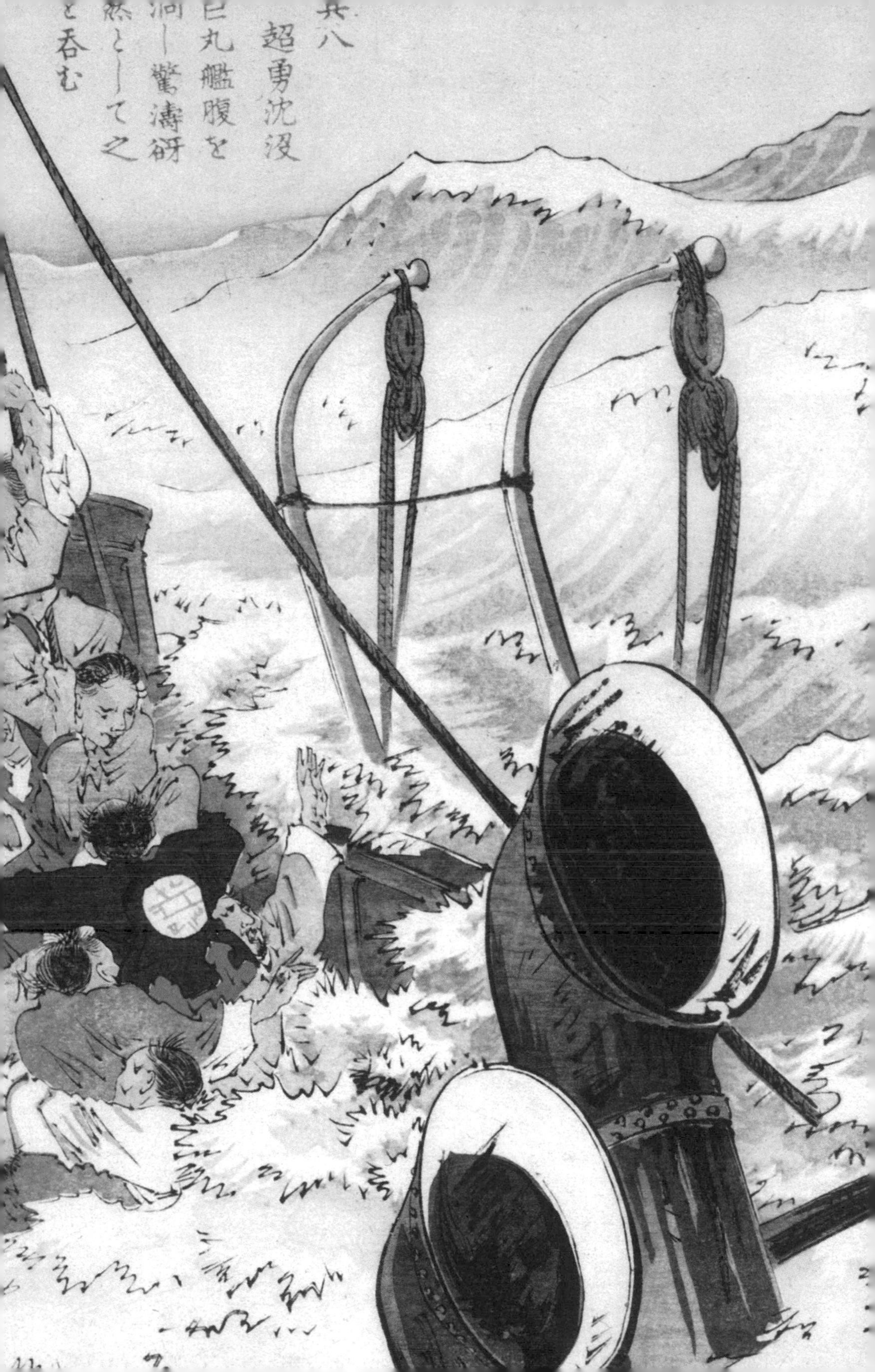

廿八　超勇沈没
巨丸艦腹を洞し驚濤硏然として之を呑む

Legend:
- ⇨ Japanese movements
- → Russian movements
- ▬ Russian positions
- ▪▪▪ Japanese position

RUSSIAN BORDER 500
MILES (800 KM)
MOSCOW 3,500 MILES
(5,600 KM)

Harbin

Russian submarines carried by railway from west

CHINESE EASTERN RAILWAY

C H I N A

R U S S I A N

E M P I R E

Vladivostok

Sypingai

1st, 2nd, 3rd Russian Armies
29 MAR–5 SEPT 1905

M A N C H U R I A

29 MAR–5 SEPT 1905

Russian withdrawal up railway, leaving Port Arthur isolated

San-de-pu

⑩ Mukden

1st, 2nd, 3rd, 4th, and 5th Japanese Armies

POSITION BEFORE MUKDEN

⑨ ⑦

Liao-Yang ⑥

Valu

1 Attack by Japanese torpedo boats on Russian
  Pacific Squadron, 8–9 Feb 1904
2 Battle of the Ya-lu, 1 May 1904
3 Battle of Tszynchkou, 26 May 1904
4 Battle of Wafangkou (Telissu), 14–15 June1904
5 Battle of Tashichao (Yingkou), 23–24 July 1904
6 Battle of Liao-Yang, 24 Aug–3 Sept 1904
7 Battle of Shah Ho, 5–17 Oct
8 Defence of Port Arthur, 9 Feb 1904–2 Jan 1905
9 Battle of San-de-pu (Lushun), 25–28 Jan 1905
10 Battle of Mukden (Shen-Yang),
   19 Feb–10 Mar 1905
11 Naval battle of Tsushima, 27–28 May 1905

Tashichao
⑤ 1st Feng Cheng
4th   ②
Lagushan

Wafangkou
(Telissu) ④ 2nd
Bytszyvo
Dalny ③   **XXXX 2nd (Oko)** APR 1904

⑧ ①   **XXXX (Nogi) 3rd** MAY–JUN 1904
Port Arthur

TOGO

K O R E A

XXXX 1st (Kuroki)

Nampo

S e a o f

J a p a n

Chemulpo (Inchon) Seoul

IA APR–NOV 1904

Advance Guard IA

JAN 1904

XXXX ELMS 4th (Nodzu) MAY 1904

Y e l l o w   S e a

Area of Sea
Battle of
Tsushima
27–28 MAY
1905

Pusan

Note :
All dates are new style
(Gregorian calendar). At
the time the Russians were
using the old style (Julian)
calendar, 13 days behind.

Tsushima Is ⑪ Shimonoseki

0   100   200   300   400 km

6 FEB 1904 Squadron FROM BALTIC

2nd Pacific Sasebo J A P A N

The Russo-Japanese War

At the outbreak of war Russia had the world's largest standing army—1,350,000 men—
but most of it was in Europe. In the Far East Russia had two corps totalling 98,000 men,
plus 24,000 local troops and 198 guns, scattered across Manchuria, the Pacific coast, and
the trans-Baikal region. The Russian Far Eastern Fleet comprised 63 warships including 7
battleships and 11 cruisers, mostly obsolete. Japan, much nearer to the theatre of war, had
an army of 375,000 on mobilization, with 1,140 guns and 147 machine guns, and 80
warships including 6 battleships and 20 cruisers. The Russian army in the west—8,000 km

(5,000 miles) away—was re-equipped with the 76 mm M-1900 and M-1902 field guns, described by foreign observers as 'really excellent' and 'the most powerful field gun in the world' respectively. However, most of the fortress artillery in Port Arthur was antiquated. Russia was not ready for war with Japan in the Far East, and the Japanese knew it. The Russian plan, sensibly enough, was to delay the Japanese while they built up their own strength in the Liao-Yang area, bringing forces south from the Chinese Eastern railway at the top of the T at Harbin.

Neither were the Russian command arrangements ideal. The commander of the Manchurian Army, General Aleksei Kuropatkin, a highly academic general and former war minister, was appointed in February 1904, but as such he was junior to the commander-in-chief Far East, Admiral Yevgeni Alekseyiev, which led to friction. Kuropatkin was made commander-in-chief in October 1904, but after the battle of Mukden in 1905 he was demoted to command the First Army.

On 6 February 1904 Japan cut off diplomatic relations with Russia and two days later launched a surprise attack before declaring war—a technique repeated in 1941. On the night of 8/9 February Japanese torpedo boats attacked the Russian squadron in Port Arthur and the following day sank two Russian warships at Inchon, Korea. In spite of heavy losses, the Port Arthur squadron remained a threat and was blockaded, permitting the Japanese to transport its armies to the peninsula. These deployed for a land offensive under Marshal Iwao Oyama and at the end of April General Kuroki's 45,000-strong Japanese First Army, which had advanced north through Korea, met the Russians at the river Yalu.

The Battle of the Yalu (1904)

On 1 May 1904 a 34,000-strong Japanese force with 128 guns and 18 machine guns met the eastern detachment of the Russian Manchurian Army (19,000 men with 62 guns and 8 machine guns) on the Yalu (correctly Yalu-tsyan, Amnokkan) river on the border with Manchuria. The Russians held the western river bank but the Japanese, helped by superior firepower, got across the river and the 12th Japanese Division outflanked the Russians from the north. The Russians failed to bring up their reserves in time, and were splintered by the Japanese. Russian casualties in the battle and subsequent pursuit were 2,200–3,000, 21 guns, and all their machine guns. Japanese losses were reckoned at 1,000.

The Russians withdrew, the first of many withdrawals under General Kuropatkin's probably overcautious command. On 5 May General Oku's Second Army, with 35,000 men, landed on the Liao-dun peninsula, cutting Port Arthur off from the Russian Manchurian Army. After an unsuccessful attempt by the Russian I Siberian Corps to re-establish communications at the battle of Wafangkou (Telissu) on 14–15 June, the Japanese laid siege to the fortress, shipping in the new Third Army under General Marasuke Nogi with 60,000 men and 400 guns. The Second Army meanwhile tried to push the Russians north up the railway line, in the battle of Tashichao (23–4 July). The Russians fought the Japanese off but General Kuropatkin nevertheless ordered a withdrawal north. Here, from 24 August to 3 September the great battle of Liao-Yang took place. Once again the Russians, dug in on a wide front, and exploiting the emerging supremacy of the defensive, held the Japanese but again Kuropatkin ordered withdrawal. On 6 September the Russians pulled back to the Shah-ho, where Kuropatkin intended to build up his strength further and then counter-attack. By this time the

Manchurian Army was 214,000 strong with 758 guns against total Japanese forces of 170,000 with 648 guns. Kuropatkin, who still believed in the possibility of a decisive battle, decided the time was now right to go over to the offensive. However, the encounter engagement on the Shah-ho proved indecisive and a continuous front 60 km (37 miles) wide developed, just as it would in World War I, giving rise to a positional battle from 5 to 17 October.

After the Shah-ho battle there was a lull in the fighting. In January 1905 the Russians launched a raid under General P. Mishchenko, round the left (western) flank of the Japanese to cut the railway supplying their troops in the front line north of Liao-Yang. This force of 7,500 Cossacks cut the line in several places—a classic 'strategic' cavalry raid and prototype of the Soviet operational manoeuvre group.

Realizing that the Russians were gaining strength, Oyama decided to reduce Port Arthur, which had been blockaded since February and under land attack since May, in the shortest possible time and switched his main effort to achieving this, increasing the besieging force from 70,000 to 100,000. Two attempts by Russian squadrons to break in from the sea, on 23 June and 10 August, failed. The 50,000 Russians, well dug in, repelled numerous land assaults, using, among other things, trench mortars and hand grenades, but on 2 January 1905 the commander, General Anatoli Stoessel, surrendered the fortress. The Russians claim to have inflicted 60,000 casualties on the Japanese in its defence. The siege of Port Arthur was certainly not taken to suggest that fortresses were obsolete but, on the contrary, that they could hold up huge armies for periods of time unacceptable to the enemy.

Following a Russian attempt to outflank the Japanese at San-de-pu from 25 to 28 January 1905, the final land battle took place at Mukden (also called Shen-yan).

The Battle of Mukden (1905)

The fall of Port Arthur enabled Marshal Oyama to redeploy General Nogi's besieging Third Army and, with the creation of a new Fifth Army under General Kamura, the Japanese concentrated five to attack General Kuropatkin's three. The Russian forces totalled 293,000 men with 1,494 guns, and 56 machine guns: the Japanese had 270,000 men, 1,062 guns, and 200 machine guns. The Japanese attacked on 19 February 1905 attempting to envelop and destroy the Russian force, but failed in the face of artillery, machine guns, and barbed wire. The Russians lost 89,000 men and the Japanese 71,000 on a continuous front 155 km (95 miles) wide with fighting to a depth of 80 km (50 miles), in a battle lasting nineteen days until 10 March. The Russians then withdrew to prepared positions at Sypingai 175 km (110 miles) to the north. It was the shape of wars to come. Both commanders tried, in Napoleonic fashion, to destroy the other army. Both failed.

From the middle of March active military operations ceased on land. The main Russian forces, meanwhile, had been supplied and reinforced along the trans-Siberian and Chinese Eastern railways—a distance of 6,400 km (4,000 miles) from European Russia and 8,700 km (5,400 miles) from their main bases, most of it single track. Down this single line the Russians carried vast quantities of munitions, barbed wire, and all the requisites for a fully modern war. They even brought submarines, built in St Petersburg, by rail, to Vladivostok, where they launched them into the Pacific.

Although Russian strength was still growing, there had been a revolution in European Russia, starting with the massacre of peaceful protesters in St Petersburg on 22 January

1905. Protest spread rapidly to the army and fleet. Kuropatkin blamed the 1905 revolution for his failure.

Japanese control of the sea was a major problem for the Russians and in October 1904 and February 1905 Russian squadrons were sent from the Baltic Fleet round Europe, Africa, and Asia to the Far East to form the Second Pacific Squadron.

The Battle of Tsushima (1905)

On 27 May 1905, after half circumnavigating the world, the Russian fleet was surprised by the Japanese in the Straits of Tsushima between Korea and Japan. Vice Admiral Zinovi Rozhdestvenski commanded the Russian force. His eight battleships, nine cruisers (only one of them armoured), three coast defence monitors, and an assortment of other ships ran into Admiral Heihachiro Togo's four battleships and 24 cruisers, eight of them armoured. The Russians had 228 guns to the Japanese 910 but their strength in big guns— 8 to 12 inch—was almost equal, with 54 Russian to 60 Japanese. At 07.00 on 27 May the Russians spotted a Japanese cruiser. At 13.15 the Russians encountered the main Japanese fleet trying to cross their bows, and at 13.49 they opened fire at a range of 38 cables (more than 6,400 metres (7,000 yards)). In the battle that followed the Russians lost all eight battleships and their armoured cruiser, and one of the monitors, plus a number of other ships. The cruiser *Aurora* made it to Manila, but only one cruiser and two torpedo boats reached Vladivostok. The Russian fleet had been utterly destroyed.

This was one setback too many. As the 1905 protests at home gathered strength, the Russians sued for peace. The Russo-Japanese War is sometimes cited as an example of the backwardness of the Russian armed forces, and this is true of the navy, but the foreign observers who were there with the Russian army were impressed by its performance and equipment, and particularly its artillery and the way it utilized indirect fire—the first time these techniques were generally used in war. It could have won, had the home front not collapsed behind it.

THE KOREAN WAR

In 1945, the Japanese colony of Korea was divided 'temporarily' between the USSR and the USA along the line of the 38th Parallel of latitude. Josef Stalin, the leader of the USSR, established a satellite state under Kim Il-sung in North Korea, while in the south the Republic of Korea (ROK) was formed under an autocratic right-wing coalition, elected under UN supervision. Its president was Syngman Rhee. On 9 February 1950, perceiving that US support for the ROK was declining, Stalin at last assented to an invasion of the south and the new ruler of China Mao Tse-tung (Mao Ze-dong) concurred.

With complete surprise, the offensive was opened on 25 June 1950. It was a Sunday; many of those in the southern defence lines were away on weekend leave and the ROK army took US forces with them in headlong retreat. Although the attack was immediately condemned by a majority of UN members, it was only the fact that the USSR was boycotting the Security Council that permitted the passage of a UN resolution authorizing the formation of a multinational force to combat the aggression. General Douglas Mac-Arthur was appointed commander-in-chief. Two US divisions were rushed to Korea from

Japan under strong air and sea cover, but these were unfit, untrained occupation troops who were roughly handled by the hardy and well-drilled North Korean People's Army (NKPA). Eventually five divisions were fed into the peninsula as they arrived, mostly US but including a British-led Commonwealth brigade. Formed as the Eighth Army under the US Lieutenant General Walton H. Walker, these troops along with the ROK army remnants held a perimeter around Pusan, the principal southern port.

Meanwhile MacArthur was building up a reserve corps in Japan consisting of the 1st Marine and 7th Infantry divisions and launched them in an amphibious landing at the port of Inchon on the west coast of the peninsula, 320 km (200 miles) behind the battle front.

The Landing at Inchon (correctly Inch'on) (1950)

The landing offered surprise, on which MacArthur relied, while the national capital Seoul lay nearby on the main road and railway routes. But access to the port basin lay through channels where the tide fell 10 m (32 feet) twice daily. This factor and the distance from the Japanese bases prompted the US chiefs of staff to advise a less ambitious plan, but MacArthur insisted on his audacious one. The fleet carrying X Corps under Lieutenant General Edward Almond sailed early in September, despite delays imposed by successive typhoons. Meanwhile, the USAF continued to attack the NKPA around Pusan.

The US navy had surveyed the Inchon approaches by night, and had posted a small observation team to watch the port area from an offshore islet. At high risk, the team leader ignited the seaward light there on 14 September. US naval and Marine Corps aircraft supported the landings in complement to American and British naval gunfire. Inchon exuded smoke as the assault began at 06.15 on 15 September. The Marines' assault echelon had three hours to offload before tidefall threatened to beach their ships.

Absolute surprise was achieved and the landing forces secured the harbour defences and a third of the town by midnight. A relieved MacArthur, who had suffered an hour of doubt following an early misreport of failure, informed Washington that 'the whole operation is proceeding on schedule'. By 20 September, 50,000 troops were ashore fighting for Seoul and meanwhile, preceded by an intense air and land bombardment, the UN and South Korean forces at Pusan shattered the NKPA and began to drive northwards. On 26 September, a divisional column joined elements of X Corps close to Seoul. By then, NKPA remnants were joining guerrilla bands in the south or filtering northwards across the 38th Parallel, incapable of forming a comprehensive line at any point. MacArthur was at the peak of his reputation but the complete success of the operation fed his hubris and led to the adoption of an overambitious strategy which carried him into a defeat.

Apprehensive of such a landing, Mao had earlier reinforced the Fourth Field Army (in fact an army group) in north-east China with two divisions. Now anticipating the destruction of the NKPA, he discussed countermeasures with Stalin. On the 27th, the American I Corps linked up with the 7th Infantry Division near Seoul. MacArthur asked Washington for instructions: was he to stand on the 38th Parallel or cross it in pursuit?

While US President Harry S. Truman considered this, Chinese prime minister Chou En-lai (Zhou En-lai) gave warning through Indian diplomatic channels that 'if the American authorities decided to cross … China will be forced to act accordingly'. The British chiefs of staff took this to mean Chinese military intervention. The US and British governments, in close consultation, disagreed; likewise a majority in the UN. Against the protests of the communist bloc in the UN, where the USSR had resumed its place, the decision was taken to occupy North Korea as a preliminary to uniting North and South following democratic elections.

China was not bluffing. As the UN and ROK armies advanced, General P'eng Te-huai marched 130,000 soldiers of the Fourth Field Army into Korea, a host represented as 'volunteers' to establish the pretence that China remained aloof from the struggle. Stalin had promised them air cover, but withheld it as the march began. P'eng responded by restricting all movement to the winter nights. This simple stratagem paid a high dividend.

Crossing the Yalu river into north-west Korea, his veterans emerged from the darkness on 26 October, unexpected because undetected by the UN air force, to encircle and penetrate the UN and ROK formations approaching them. Usually fighting at night, sometimes in snowstorms, P'eng's light infantry bore in, shifting their axes of attack frequently, until on 6 November they had swept so far afield that it became essential to draw them back, laden with plunder from the retreating UN forces, to regroup.

The governments of the UN alliance were stunned by this setback so soon after the defeat of the NKPA. Seeking at least to stabilize the battlefield, a truce was suggested as a preliminary to reaching an accommodation with their foes. When, at MacArthur's insistence, his troops, rebalanced and reinforced, advanced again on 24 November, Walker deployed eight UN and four ROK divisions. They were assailed almost at once by 30 of the Chinese. Despite considerable supporting firepower, the Eighth and ROK armies were still unable to withstand the close actions forced upon them selectively by P'eng's forces across the front from coast to coast. General Walker decided to break contact while he maintained some measure of control. He withdrew his line 240 km (150 miles) south below the Han, abandoning Seoul. Edward Almond's X Corps in the northeast began a closely contested withdrawal to the coast. Many in the UN Command believed that they would be driven out of Korea altogether.

The UN forces moved in trucks. The Chinese marched. When the latter again closed on the UN and ROK positions in January 1951, they were suffering from exposure in temperatures often more than 20 °C below freezing at night, lacking proper clothing and supplies. P'eng asked for a pause but Mao urged him on. Lieutenant General Matthew Ridgway, replacing Walker who had been killed in an accident, brought his subordinate commanders to order. The Eighth Army was to stand and fight. As the Chinese ardour waned, the spirits of the Eighth Army waxed. They held the line and, encouraged, counter-attacked. Now P'eng was forced to withdraw. By mid-April 1951, Ridgway's line commanded the 38th Parallel.

As the winter ended, P'eng was preparing to strike again. Forty assault divisions were available to him. The march to contact began on 21 April, directing principal thrusts across the Imjin and Kap'yong rivers, areas held by chance by the 29th British and 27th Commonwealth brigades. Both held firm while the UN line 'rolled' back unbroken, drawing out the enemy. Sustaining high casualties, running short of supplies due to widespread air attack, P'eng's 40 assault divisions were unable to maintain their momentum. They drew off never to engage in a strategic offensive again. Manoeuvre was succeeded by costly but localized trench warfare, using the tactics of World War I, employing the weapons of World War II. Seven American, one British Commonwealth, and eleven ROK divisions held the line, together with battalions and a brigade from fourteen other nations. It scarcely moved for the remaining two years of the war.

A ceasefire might have been agreed in 1951 but for American and British

Commonwealth insistence that no prisoner of war would be returned against his will, a condition that affected only the Chinese and North Koreans. The UN prisoners and ROK prisoners had been treated so shamefully by their communist captors that all but a handful opted for repatriation.

American air commanders sought during the stalemate to win the war by bombing the enemy into submission. The full effect of their offensive was limited by UN rules forbidding attacks on targets in China or any use of atomic weapons. But in North Korea the capacity to survive exceeded the bombers' capability for destruction. UN naval forces maintained their domination of the sea flanks in all seasons but lacked the means to break the massed ranks of the Chinese and NKPA remnant.

Fortunately a common factor militated for peace: the costs of war. Hostilities ceased on 27 July 1953, some three years after they began. The victory won in Korea, albeit qualified, encouraged a powerful section of American opinion to believe that the USA could win any war of its choice in Asia.

THE FRENCH INDOCHINA CAMPAIGN

In French Indochina, guerrilla resistance to the Japanese by the Vietminh in World War II had become organized and united under the leadership of Ho Chi Minh, and perforce had to be defeated if French authority was to be restored.

At this time more than 80 per cent of Indochina was forested, much of it dense and humid jungle. The problems for any force attempting to carry on a campaign in such terrain are obvious, and these difficulties were exacerbated by the peculiar weather patterns which prevail in the region. The south-west monsoon limited the campaigning season to October to mid-May. During the remainder of the year it was almost impossible to move troops because the smallest logistical problems would be magnified by the torrential rains which swept across the country. The political context of the war is also essential to an overall understanding of its shape and outcome. The Vietminh, under the operational direction of General Vo Nguyen Giap, began with significantly inferior resources, but after 1949 were able to draw wholehearted support from newly communist China's leader, Mao Tse-tung. By contrast the French government received only slight support from the USA and was also indecisive, bureaucratic, and largely half-hearted about the campaign in Indochina.

The Vietminh had great sympathy among the population, but little strength in 1946, and were soon pushed back into their stronghold, the Vietbac, which is an almost impenetrable region of steep valleys and caves near the Chinese border. In 1947 General Jean Valluy, the French commander, having taken time to marshal his resources, attacked this area. Operation LEA, as it was known, met with initial success, but the plan became bogged down in the difficult terrain. French units were isolated, and the Vietminh leadership was able to adapt to circumstances much more rapidly than the French. In the end the French managed to extricate themselves from an increasingly dangerous situation, while the Vietminh remained intact and with soaring morale.

The next two years of the French campaign were marked by small battles and French indecision. Valluy was replaced by General Roger Blaizot in 1948, and Blaizot was, in turn, replaced by General Marcel Charpentier a year later. Charpentier took over just before Giap's first major offensive in 1950 and was outgeneralled. After some vicious fighting shortly before the monsoon, the resumption of campaigning in the early winter months saw the Vietminh capture the key supply base at Dong Khe. Charpentier counter-attacked by sending two columns, which were ambushed and defeated in detail by an enemy with intimate knowledge of the terrain.

General Jean de Lattre de Tassigny, Charpentier's successor, enjoyed rather more success against Giap's second offensive in 1951. French forces repulsed the Vietminh at Vinh Yen, Mao Khe, and during the Day river battles. De Lattre built up the Vietnamese National Army to provide support for the French, and used these troops to man the de Lattre Line, a series of forts and bases. This freed French troops for an offensive at Hoa Binh in November 1951, but Vietminh counter-attacks forced a withdrawal from that position three months later. Illness forced de Lattre to return to France in late 1951 and his replacement General Raoul Salan carried on the pattern of limited offensives and counter-offensives, winning a victory at a pitched battle at Na San in November 1952. Giap enjoyed some degree of success in the Black river campaign of 1952, and his Laotian campaign a year later was thwarted only because his troops advanced so far so quickly that they outran the limited Vietminh logistical capacities.

The success of the Laotian campaign opened the way for a final Vietnamese victory. General Henri Navarre became the latest French commander, and began to plan a major battle to give the French a strong bargaining chip in ongoing peace negotiations. When this set-piece battle began, however, it was on Giap's terms.

The Battle of Dien Bien Phu (1954)

The valley of Dien Bien Phu may have been the militarily significant route between Tonkin and Laos alleged at the time, but it was undoubtedly important in the opium trade, revenues from which were vital to the cash-starved French forces. The mistaken calculation by General Navarre was that at best his elite airborne forces and French Foreign Legionnaires, 15,000 men strong, could turn the valley into a killing ground, at worst they would draw in disproportionate Vietminh forces, granting him greater freedom of manocuvre elsewhere. The French were therefore airdropped into the valley in November 1953 to build a series of strong points, not all within supporting distance of each other, around the 1 km (0.62 mile) airstrip upon which the fortress was to depend for supplies. In a further fatal miscalculation the hills commanding the valley were only lightly held, in the belief that French artillery could deny them to the enemy.

Giap accepted the provocative invitation without hesitation, deploying a force of 50,000. In a heroic logistical feat employing mainly bicycles (the secret weapon of the Vietnam wars), he secretly surrounded the position with artillery in dugouts, some tunnelled through from the far side of the hills. The siege began on 13 March 1954. From the opening barrage the airstrip and French artillery were neutralized, while anti-aircraft fire was to force supply planes to make drops from a height that precluded accuracy. Many of the defenders, aware that they were doomed, became internal deserters and left the fighting mostly to the Paras under Colonel Pierre Langlais and Marcel Bigeard, who took over direction of the battle from the nominal commander Colonel Christian de Castries. The siege proceeded in Vauban style, with the attackers sapping towards the French strong points, all incongruously given girls' names. Following a massive bombardment, outer strong points Béatrice and Isabelle were overrun on 13–14 March,

The core positions of Éliane, Dominique, Claudine, and Huguette were closely invested and finally overwhelmed on 7 May, 12,000 French officers and men surrendering. The French delegation at the peace conference in Geneva was compelled to capitulate. Giap later admitted that his troops suffered severe morale problems during the protracted preparations, but the victory was to give them an aura of invincibility that carried them through the next war.

THE VIETNAM WAR

The signing of the 1954 Geneva agreements divided Vietnam along the 17th Parallel, but did not halt the continuation of the Vietminh's effort to free Vietnam from foreign domination. Relative calm descended on Vietnam. In Hanoi, the Vietminh, who had come under the control of the Vietnamese Lao Dong (Communist) Party by the time of the French defeat, consolidated their power under Ho Chi Minh, collectivized agriculture in the north (which sparked a bloodily suppressed peasant uprising in 1956), and debated how to gain control of South Vietnam. In Saigon Bao Dai, the French-backed emperor, was deposed in a referendum by the US-supported Ngo Dinh Diem in late 1955. Diem, a Catholic in a predominantly Buddhist country, was a committed anti-communist. Bolstered by increasing economic and covert aid from the USA, Diem launched an anti-communist sweep of South Vietnam. By the late 1950s, the hard-pressed Vietminh cadres who had remained in the South, derisively dubbed Vietcong by Diem, appealed to Hanoi for reinforcement.

In May 1959 Hanoi decided to support 'armed revolution' against Saigon: 4,500 'regroupees' (a southern communist cadre who had come to the North after the Geneva accords) began to stream down the Ho Chi Minh Trail between North and South Vietnam to help form Vietcong units. In December 1960, Hanoi announced the creation of the National Liberation Front (NLF), a collection of southern groups opposing the Diem regime, to bolster the contention that the revolt against Saigon was an indigenous movement.

This reversed the military situation and by the early 1960s Saigon was under enormous pressure. In November 1960, Diem narrowly avoided being overthrown in a military coup. In 1959 the Vietcong killed about 1,200 government representatives, in 1961 this had risen to 4,000. Vietcong units also began inflicting a string of defeats on the Army, Republic of Vietnam (ARVN). Diem now relied increasingly on his brother Ngo Dinh Nhu to eliminate political opposition.

The Ngos overstepped the bounds of US patience in 1963 when they forcefully suppressed a series of Buddhist protests. The administration of US president John F. Kennedy had come to perceive Diem and his brother Nhu as obstructionists. The US diplomatic mission in Saigon gave tacit approval to, if it did not actually orchestrate, a November 1963 *coup d'état* that resulted in the assassination of Ngo Dinh Diem and Ngo Dinh Nhu.

Saigon was rocked by a series of military coups and Hanoi quickly capitalized on this opportunity: by the end of 1964, Vietcong units had been organized into division-size formations and entire PAVN (People's Army of Viet Nam) regiments had infiltrated into South Vietnam. As Vietcong/PAVN activity spread, more US personnel became

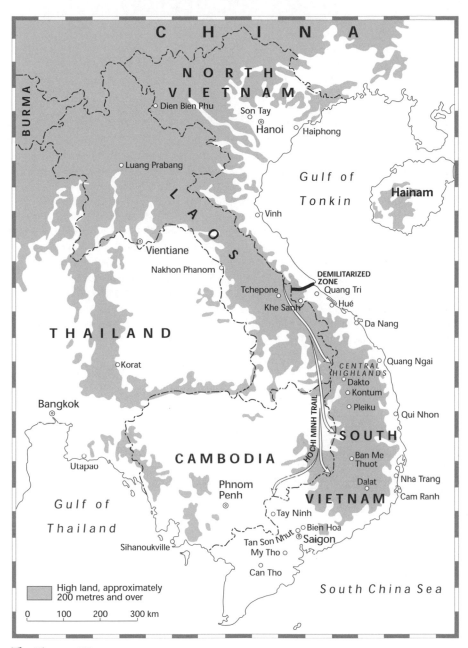

The Vietnam War

casualties in the conflict. On 3 February 1964, the Vietcong attacked the US advisers' compound in Kontum City. In May, the USS *Card* was sunk by Vietcong commandos in a Saigon harbour. In November, the Vietcong attacked the US airbase at Bien Hoa and on 24 December they claimed credit for a bombing at the Brinks Hotel in Saigon.

A controversial incident in the Gulf of Tonkin had a profound impact. Early in the morning of 2 August 1964, the US destroyer *Maddox*, while patrolling along North Vietnamese territorial waters, was attacked by three North Vietnamese torpedo boats. The *Maddox* returned fire and was quickly supported by aircraft from the USS *Ticonderoga*. During the night of 4 August, the *Maddox*, now joined by the destroyer *C. Turner Joy*, initially reported a renewed attack, although officers at the scene quickly determined that the North Vietnamese vessels were nowhere to be found and that inexperienced crewmen had simply responded to sonar and radar anomalies. The administration of President Lyndon B. Johnson, uninterested in validating initial reports and indifferent to the probability that Hanoi might have been responding to South Vietnamese attacks, ordered retaliatory air strikes against the torpedo-boat base at Vinh. The Johnson administration also gained congressional approval in the Gulf of Tonkin Resolution, which provided the administration with carte blanche to take military action in South-East Asia.

By 1965, the nature of the war was changing. The conflict became a deadlock between the USA and North Vietnam, which was backed by its Soviet and Chinese allies. Hanoi hoped that the USA would not resist a PAVN invasion of South Vietnam; while Washington hoped that Ho Chi Minh and his followers would be deterred by a demonstration of US military might. The 7 February 1965 Vietcong attack on the US airbase at Pleiku prompted US retaliatory air raids against North Vietnam; on 13 February President Johnson ordered a 'program of measured and limited air action' against North Vietnam, which came to be known as ROLLING THUNDER.

To protect the US airbase at Da Nang from Vietcong retaliation for US air strikes, the Johnson administration dispatched two battalions of US Marines to guard the base. More US troops soon followed, initially to protect other US installations, but US military commanders viewed this initial 'enclave' strategy as ineffective. On 27 June 1965, General William Westmoreland, commander of the US Military Assistance Command, Vietnam (MACV), ordered the first US offensive ground operation of the war. The 'Big-Unit war' had begun.

As US troops streamed into the country, Westmoreland faced his first major challenge: preventing the collapse of South Vietnam and a successful PAVN occupation of the northern sections of the country. In November 1965, the battle was joined in the Ia Drang valley in the Western Highlands, a hard-won victory for the US 1st Cavalry Division. As US troop strength grew, Westmoreland went on the offensive. Launching a series of large-scale Search and Destroy operations, US and allied forces targeted Vietcong operating bases. Vietcong and PAVN units often managed to evade allied forces by fading into Cambodian and Laotian sanctuaries, but continuous attacks took their toll, especially on Vietcong forward-supply bases.

By mid-1967, the war had reached a turning point and officers at MACV began to proclaim 'light at the end of the tunnel'. US attrition objectives were being achieved: Vietcong and PAVN units were apparently losing more forces in South Vietnam than could be replaced through recruitment or infiltration. Policy-makers in Hanoi also came to the conclusion that the war was stalemated and that battlefield trends were not in their favour. In response, they called for a 'Tong Cong Kich, Tong Khai Nghia' (General

Offensive, General Uprising). Known in the USA as the Tet offensive, because it occurred during the celebration of the Chinese lunar New Year, the countrywide attacks were intended to spark an insurrection among South Vietnamese civilians and military forces.

The Tet Offensive (1968)

Early on 31 January 1968, North Vietnamese and Vietcong forces attacked 27 of South Vietnam's 44 provincial capitals and scores of villages. Timed to take advantage of a truce declared for the New Year celebrations, it utterly failed to prompt an uprising, although government supporters were methodically massacred in a telling use of terrorism. With the exception of the battles of Saigon and Hué, US and South Vietnamese forces quickly defeated the attacks and Vietcong units indigenous to South Vietnam were indeed decimated.

At Khe Sanh, the US Marines, supported by thousands of air sorties, stood firm and inflicted enormous casualties on PAVN. But the Tet offensive was a brilliant political success for Hanoi. Believing that progress was being made in the war, the Johnson administration and the US public were shocked by the scope and intensity of the offensive. On 31 March 1968, Lyndon B. Johnson announced that he would not seek re-election as his administration reassessed its policies. becoming increasingly determined to devise an exit strategy that would not simply abandon South Vietnam to PAVN. US and North Vietnamese negotiators began meeting in Paris in May 1968, but their talks made little progress. On the battlefield, the administration of President Richard M. Nixon implemented a policy, called 'Vietnamization', to bolster ARVN. The USA began turning the war over to ARVN while gradually withdrawing US combat troops from South Vietnam.

Vietnamization came none too soon. In America domestic opposition to the war mounted, reaching a peak in May 1970 following a US-ARVN raid into Cambodia. The raid sparked nationwide student protests and tragedy at Kent State University when four students were shot and killed by the Ohio National Guard. In South Vietnam, morale among US troops plummeted as soldiers became preoccupied by the prospect of becoming the last casualty in a war that was winding down. By 1971, over 7,000 troops in Vietnam faced charges related to heroin (out of a force that numbered about 225,000), insubordination, and fragging incidents (attacks against officers and NCOs), and courts martial soared. Vietnamization continued, but ARVN remained incapable of holding its own against PAVN: in spring 1971, ARVN launched Lam Son 719, a raid into Laos to destroy PAVN base areas, but was saved from disaster only by the massive use of US air power. In the spring of 1972, during the so-called Easter Offensive, Saigon was again saved from disaster by a massive US air effort. Although PAVN, which by now resembled a conventional military force complete with armoured vehicles and ample large-calibre artillery, suffered devastating casualties, it succeeded in bringing western portions of South Vietnam under complete communist control.

By late 1972, Hanoi and Washington, moved along by secret negotiations conducted by US secretary of state Henry Kissinger and Le Duc Tho, were near agreement on a negotiated end to the fighting in South Vietnam, but objections by both South and North Vietnam threatened to frustrate their efforts. Nixon initiated LINEBACKER II, also known as the Christmas Bombing. Although aircraft loses were significant, the USA dropped over 20,000 tons of bombs on the North between 18 and 29 December 1972, causing enormous damage and completely exhausting North Vietnam's air defences. This surge in military-diplomatic pressure finally produced agreement: ceasefire accords were formally signed in Paris on 27 January 1973. The Paris agreement turned out to be a short-lived truce. Saigon forces collapsed in the face of an eight-week offensive launched by PAVN in March 1975.

THE ARAB-ISRAELI WARS

The first Arab–Israeli War formally began on 15 May 1948 when the League of Arab States announced its 'intervention' against the state of Israel which David Ben Gurion had proclaimed hours before. It ended with an armistice agreement between Egypt and Israel, signed at Rhodes on 24 January 1949, which was followed by others with Lebanon, Syria, and Jordan. The war had enabled Israel to sustain its independence. For the Palestinian Arabs it had been a disaster. Not only had their country ceased to exist, but over 750,000 were refugees. Defeat also set the scene for the Arab revolutions of the 1950s, particularly that which brought Gamal Abd al Nasser (correctly Nasir), a veteran of the war, to power in Egypt. In November 1956 British and French troops made an ill-advised attempt to seize the Suez Canal, recently nationalized by Nasser. The attack was presaged by a collusive Israeli invasion of Sinai on the pretext of dealing with guerrilla bases there. The most significant development of the next decade was the revival of Palestinian activism, chiefly directed by the Movement for the Liberation of Palestine (Fatah), led by Yasser Arafat. Its raids, which began in 1965, measurably increased Arab–Israeli tension. Israel's relations with Syria also worsened as Israeli settlements came under intermittent bombardment from the Golan Heights.

The Six-Day War (1967)

The immediate crisis which provoked the 1967 war was a warning, incorrect as it turned out, to Nasser from the USSR that Israel was about to mount an attack on Syria. In an attempt to take the pressure off his Syrian ally, on 14 May the Egyptian leader deployed two armoured divisions in the Sinai desert. There is no evidence that at this stage he wanted war but when the Israelis countered this with a tank brigade it was clear that danger might be at hand. On 16 May, Nasser further escalated the situation by ordering the United Nations Emergency Force to concentrate in the Gaza Strip and on 21 May he announced a blockade of the Strait of Tiran. This ran counter to assurances he had given in 1957 and was done in knowledge that Israel had insisted such a move would constitute a *casus belli*. On 5 June Israel launched devastating air strikes against the Egyptian and other Arab air forces. Directed by air force commander General Mordechai Hod, it proved to be one of the most daring, and decisive, blows in the history of air power. In a matter of hours the Egyptian air force alone lost 309 of its 340 operational aircraft. Hod and his pilots had won the war for Israel.

The genius behind the land campaign was chief of staff Yitzhak Rabin. His plan was for a three-pronged offensive in Sinai by armoured and mechanized forces led by Generals Israel Tal, Avraham Joffe, and Ariel Sharon. Facing them the Egyptian commander General Abd el Mohsen Mortagui had five infantry and two armoured divisions with over 1,000 tanks, but robbed of air support he had no hope of victory. As the extent of the Egyptians' plight started to emerge, he was further confounded by contradictory orders issuing from Field Marshal Amer's headquarters. On 8 June, Israeli forces reached the

Suez Canal, having destroyed the Egyptian forces in the Sinai for a loss of some 300 killed. By then, the focus had switched elsewhere. On 5 June, out of a sense of Arab solidarity, King Hussein of Jordan entered the war. At his disposal he had a well-trained force of eight infantry and two armoured brigades, as well as some Iraqi support, but, like the Egyptians, no air support. Israeli forces in the central sector were largely reservists of the Jerusalem brigade but once Jordan's intentions became clear these were reinforced by Colonel Mordechai Gur's 55th Parachute Brigade, diverted from the Sinai front. While Israeli aircraft disrupted communications between the Arab Legion in Jerusalem and its headquarters, Gur's paratroopers attacked the Old City from the north. After intense fighting, on 7 June his men entered the Old City. Their arrival at the Western Wall was, for Israelis, the emotional pinnacle of the war. With the collapse of the Jerusalem sector, the Jordanians had no hope of holding the remainder of the West Bank. The territory, with its key cities of Nablus, Ramalah, Bethlehem, and Hebron, fell to the Israelis. With the Gaza Strip captured from the Egyptians, Israel now controlled all of pre-1948 Palestine. Having secured their southern and central fronts, the Israeli command now resolved to remove the threat from the Golan Heights.

The First Battle of the Golan Heights (1967)

The high plateau of the Golan Heights stretches 72 km (45 miles) south from Mount Hermon, is up to 24 km (15 miles) wide, and dominates Israel's northern frontier with Lebanon, Syria, and Jordan, as well as the river Jordan—and therefore Israel's water supply. The Israeli Defence Forces (IDF) opened the Six Day War with a pre-emptive assault on the Heights on 9 June 1967. Airborne forces delivered by helicopter subdued key Syrian garrisons, while armoured bulldozers preceded mechanized columns up steep mountain tracks. Attacking with seven brigades under Major General David Elazar, within a day the IDF bundled the Soviet-trained Syrian forces off the Golan, inflicting losses of 7,500 killed and wounded with 100 tanks and 200 guns destroyed, for a loss of just over 400 Israeli soldiers.

All that clouded Israel's victory was the attack on 8 June on the USS *Liberty*, a surveillance vessel off Gaza, with the death of 34 American sailors. The explanation that it had been a case of mistaken identity was not accepted in Washington. Otherwise, Israel had secured one of the decisive victories of recent history, but with extensive Arab territories under its control it was one which held the seeds of future conflict, should a diplomatic solution fail. Fail it did. The period after the 1967 war saw the reorganization of the Palestine Liberation Organization (PLO) under the chairmanship of Yasser Arafat, and the beginning of armed Palestinian actions against Israel and Israelis at home and overseas.

The Second Battle of the Golan Heights (1973)

In the October 1973 Yom Kippur (Day of Atonement) War, five Syrian divisions attempted to retrieve the Heights in an attack coinciding with an Egyptian strike in Sinai. The two armoured brigades of IDF defenders possessed only 180 Centurions and M-60s against the Syrian armoured forces' 1,300 tanks, including Soviet T-55s and T-62s, with APCs (armoured personnel carriers) in close support, while concentrations of SAMs (surface to air missiles) kept the Israeli air force at bay. Achieving total surprise, Syrian

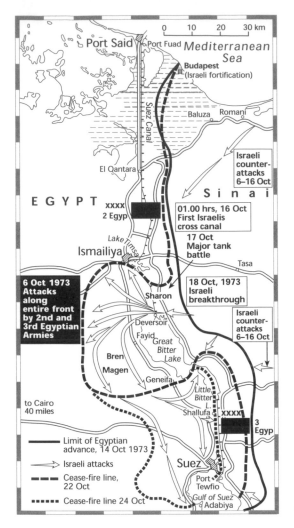

The Yom Kippur War, 1973

tanks assaulted the Golan on 6 October but continuous fighting—which stretched the endurance of both sides' tank crews to the limit—resulted in an epic Israeli victory just four days later. The Israelis stood their ground, sustaining 90 per cent casualties and the loss of all their armour, but 7th Armoured Brigade had destroyed over 500 Syrian vehicles in the northern sector before its destruction and 188th inflicted similar damage in the south. Their sacrifices bought time for three reserve armoured formations to be mobilized and rushed to the area.

Forty-eight hours of solid fighting saw Syrian units across the Heights, at terrible cost, and approaching the Upper Jordan. There they were halted by the timely arrival of the IDF reserves, but further heavy fighting was required to stabilize the front. The reservists managed to surround and destroy massed Syrian armour in the Hushniya pocket, and on 10 October Israel went over to the offensive, pushing the demoralized Syrian forces back beyond their start line. Moroccan, Jordanian, and Iraqi forces tried in vain to stem the IDF

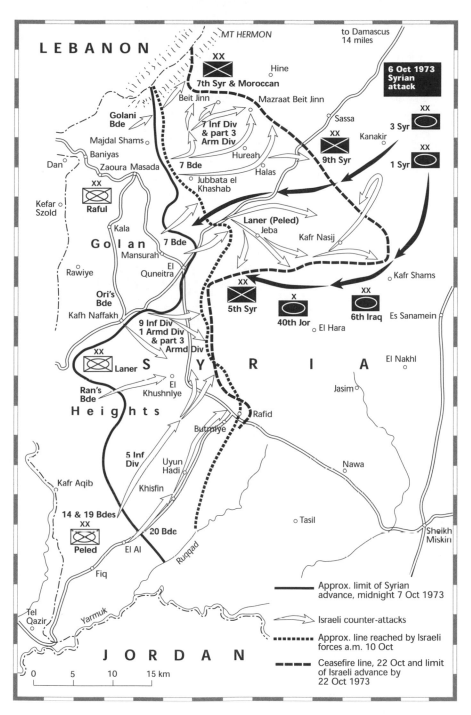

LEBANON

MT HERMON

to Damascus
14 miles

6 Oct 1973
Syrian
attack

Hine

XX
7th Syr & Moroccan

Beit Jinn

Mazraat Beit Jinn

Sassa

XX
3 Syr

Golani
Bde

7 Inf Div
& part 3
Arm Div

Kanakir

XX
1 Syr

Majdal Shams

Baniyas

Hureah

XX
9th Syr

Dan

Zaoura Masada

7 Bde

Halas

Kefar
Szold

XX
Raful

Jubbata el
Khashab

Kala

Laner (Peled)

G o l a n

7 Bde

Jeba

Kafr Nasij

Mansurah

Rawiye

El
Quneitra

Kafr Shams

Ori's
Bde

XX
5th Syr

XX
6th Iraq

Es Sanamein

Kafh Naffakh

9 Inf Div
1 Armd Div
& part 3
Armd Div

X
40th Jor

El Hara

El Nakhl

XX
Laner   S   Y   R   I   A

Ran's
Bde

El
Khushnlye

Jasim

H e i g h t s

Rafid

Butmiye

5 Inf
Div

Uyun
Hadi

Nawa

Kafr Aqib

Khisfin

14 & 19 Bdes

XX
Peled

20 Bde

El Al

Tasil

Sheikh
Miskin

Fiq

Ruqqad

Tel
Qazir

Yarmuk

J O R D A N

0   5   10   15 km

——— Approx. limit of Syrian
advance, midnight 7 Oct 1973

Israeli counter-attacks

········· Approx. line reached by Israeli
forces a.m. 10 Oct

- - - - Ceasefire line, 22 Oct and limit
of Israeli advance by
22 Oct 1973

counter-attack, and by the time of the UN-sponsored ceasefire (on 22 October) over 1,300 wrecked or abandoned Arab armoured vehicles choked the Golan Heights, while 10,000 of the attackers had been killed, wounded, or captured. The Israelis lost 250 tanks and 3,000 casualties, but the victory had been a very close-run affair. These battles affirmed the strategic importance of the Heights.

Meanwhile, the Egyptian Second and Third armies crossed the Suez Canal with textbook precision and broke through the poorly held Bar-Lev Line. Heavy fighting on 8 and 9 October, in which the Egyptians operated from behind concentrated missile batteries, resulted in the virtual destruction of the Israeli 190th Armoured Brigade. The 9th proved pivotal. An Egyptian armoured assault was broken up, and the Israelis persuaded US president Richard M. Nixon to send replacements, allowing Israel to commit its reserves. On 16 October, with the American resupply operation in full swing, an Israeli force under General Sharon crossed the canal just north of the Great Bitter Lake, opening a gap between the Second and Third armies. By the time a ceasefire, largely brokered by US secretary of state Henry Kissinger, took effect on 27 October, the Egyptian Third Army and the city of Suez had been encircled.

The war helped create the conditions for the Camp David Agreements of 1978 and the subsequent Egyptian–Israeli peace treaty. But the basic quarrel between Israel and the Palestinians was far from resolved.

THE FIRST GULF WAR (1991)

The first Gulf War was a limited war in which a US-led coalition enjoying overwhelming technological superiority defeated the armed forces of Iraq in a six-week air campaign crowned with a 100-hour land campaign, with minimal coalition casualties. However, the coalition forces failed to destroy the Republican Guard, mainstay of the Iraqi dictator Saddam Hussein, who, the USA thought, remained a threat primarily because of his continued development of nuclear, chemical, and biological weapons, leading to repeated aftershocks in the form of US and allied air strikes throughout the 1990s and renewed war in 2003.

The proximate cause was the Rumaila oilfield straddling the Iraq–Kuwait border. In mid-July 1990 Saddam claimed, not entirely unreasonably, that Kuwait had stolen oil from this field by diagonal drilling and refused to pay back loans received from Kuwait to fund the recent Iran–Iraq War. He massed armour on the frontier and after being told by the US ambassador that the USA did not wish to become involved in the dispute, at 01.00 local time on 2 August the Iraqi columns invaded.

Minds were concentrated and US president George Bush denounced the invasion, alarmed that the Iraqis would carry on into Saudi Arabia and thus control half the world's oil reserves. The UN condemned the invasion in Resolution 660, demanding immediate and unconditional withdrawal and on 7 August the USA announced it was sending forces in a joint operation with Egypt and Saudi Arabia: OPERATION DESERT SHIELD. The following day the UK announced it would send forces too, in OPERATION GRANBY.

On 29 November 1990 the Security Council adopted Resolution 678, authorizing the US-led coalition to use 'all necessary means' against Iraq to liberate Kuwait if it did not withdraw by 15 January 1991. Instead, the Iraqis reinforced their positions along the southern Kuwaiti border and by 8 January had an estimated 36 to 38 divisions, each nominally 15,000 strong but actually considerably less. The coalition eventually had about 700,000 troops in the theatre, with the main ground contributions coming from the USA and important contingents from the UK, France, Egypt, Syria, and Saudi Arabia, under the operational command of US General Norman H. Schwarzkopf. The maintenance of the coalition, in which Arab states were arrayed with infidels against another Arab state, was pivotal. It was therefore imperative to ensure that Israel—a target for Iraqi missile attacks—should stay out of the war. The Iraqis were known to have the means to deliver their chemical and biological weapons (CBW) with their al-Hussein missiles, which had a range of 600 km (370 miles), double that of the original Soviet Scud missiles on which they were based.

At 02.38 local time on 17 January DESERT STORM began when US Apache helicopters began attacking Iraqi air defence sites near the border to clear a corridor through which a massive air armada then passed, beginning a 43-day air campaign involving 100,000 sorties. The F-117A Stealth light bomber was very successful in striking key targets in heavily defended Baghdad, as were sea-launched cruise missiles. Early targets were the Iraqi air defences, electrical power, and command and control facilities, also suspected nuclear and chemical and biological warfare facilities. Although precision-guided munitions got all the publicity thanks to the excellent TV pictures they sent back, the bulk of the ordnance delivered was conventional bombs. As the campaign continued, the allies switched to Iraqi ground forces although the elite Republican Guard was less badly damaged than the poorer-quality infantry in the forward positions. Schwarzkopf later explained that this was because of his strong concern to avoid his ground troops being held up and drenched with CBW (chemical and biological weapons).

Schwarzkopf formulated a classic military plan of encirclement. While the Iraqis were to have their attention fixed to the south and on the coast by the US Marines, his main effort would be to the west of the main Iraqi forward defences, swinging round behind them and straight for the Republican Guard.

After several days of probing and artillery raids, the main ground attack began on 24 February with direct attacks into Kuwait from the south by the US Marines and two Saudi task forces. The next day, the outflanking forces swung into action, the main force being the US VII Corps including the 1st British Armoured Division, while the XVIII Airborne Corps including the French 6th Light Daguet Division swung even wider to protect the left flank. The VII Corps hit its breach area with 60 batteries of artillery and multiple launch rocket systems, delivering more explosive power than the Hiroshima atomic bomb. Although Iraq was expected to use CBW, Saddam refrained for fear of retaliation. Late on 25 February he gave the order to withdraw from Kuwait, but the bulk of Iraqi armour was trapped between the allies closing in from the south and west, and the marshes to the east and north.

TV pictures of the comprehensively incinerated Iraqi column that had been attempting to flee Kuwait City raised fears of public revulsion and President Bush called a halt after only 100 hours of land campaign. At 08.00 local time the guns fell silent, and Saddam was to be left with most of the Republican Guard and the freedom to use attack helicopters to crush the rebellions among the Sunni in the south and the Kurds in the north that the coalition had encouraged. Post-war, the extent and sophistication of his weapons development programmes came as a shock. Nonetheless, Kuwait's territorial integrity was restored and most of Saddam's larger fangs were pulled.

THE SECOND GULF WAR (2003)

lthough Iraq had been defeated in the first Gulf War of 1991, the coalition's reluctance to press on and unseat Saddam Hussein enabled him to proclaim it a victory. In its aftermath he pursued a policy of confrontation, obstructing UN inspectors searching for weapons of mass destruction, and testing the resolve of the USA over scores of issues, major and minor. Two years later, when the deaths of eighteen American soldiers in Somalia seemed to have affected US resolve, he once again threatened Kuwait, and although his troops withdrew without crossing the border the incident was typical of the brinkmanship at which he excelled. In 1999, after UN inspectors were barred from Baath party headquarters (and, perhaps coincidentally, at the moment that President Clinton was impeached for lying about the Monica Lewinsky affair), the Americans mounted operation DESERT FOX, a limited air strike against Saddam's Republican Guard.

By 2000 Saddam seemed to be edging ahead in the game of cat and mouse. Although he had failed to shoot down aircraft patrolling the no-fly zones in both northern and southern Iraq, he had some reason to believe that the UN-imposed sanctions against his country, increasingly linked, in the public's mind, to pictures of ill-equipped hospitals and sick children, would be lifted. However the terrorist attack on the World Trade Center on 11 September 2001 encouraged President George W. Bush to mount a comprehensive attack on those he believed responsible, and he began by removing the Taliban regime in Afghanistan. He attempted to build a coalition for military action against Iraq. Here both President Bush and Prime Minister Blair were influenced by the fact that Iraq had certainly used chemical weapons in the past, and its reluctance to cooperate with UN inspectors suggested that it still had something to hide. Some analysts have gone further, sensing an 'undertow' of feeling in Washington that the USA needed to show determination in confronting its enemies, and that 'a short swift military campaign' would serve as a warning to others. The extent to which the war was prompted primarily by a concern about WMD (weapons of mass destruction) or reflected American desire to inflict punishment for 9/11 and further its wider interests in the Middle East remains open to question.

While the USA and Britain continued, with very limited success, to seek international support for military action, the Americans began to deploy. The operation was the re-sponsibility of the Florida-based US Central Command (CENTCOM) under General Tommy Franks, and Lieutenant General David McKiernan was combined force land component commander in the theatre of war. McKiernan disposed of the US V Corps (its strength generally three divisions, with the 3rd Infantry Division in the lead), which was to move west of the Euphrates and take Baghdad, and 1 Marine Expeditionary Force (a Marine division and a smaller Marine task force), advancing up the central axis and then crossing the Tigris to attack Baghdad from the east. 1 MEF had the 1st British Armoured Division (a hybrid formation with the 7th Armoured Brigade, 16th Air Assault Brigade, and 3rd Commando Brigade) under its command, and the British were to be used to secure the port of Umm Qasr and Iraq's second city, Basra, as well as to act as a reserve for the US Marines.

US, British, and Australian special forces were busy long before the war proper started, helping mobilize the Kurds and preventing Iraqis from torching oilfields. In the first Gulf War the air campaign preceded the ground attack by 38 days, but in 2003 the ground and air wars began simultaneously. The much-televised 'shock and awe' attacks on Bagdhad had less psychological impact than had been expected: since precision-guided weapons were used in a largely successful attempt to minimize collateral damage, most ordinary Iraqis knew that they were perfectly safe. The Iraqi military, however, was in a far worse state than it had been in the first Gulf War, riddled with desertion and short of spares and proper training. Even the Republican Guard (some 60,000 men in all) was scarcely a modern force: capable of mounting fierce resistance, it was simply not up to the manoeuvre operations of which the campaign was to consist.

The offensive began on the evening of 20 March, with Apache helicopters destroying outposts in the path of V Corps and the 1st Marine Division, and air strikes reaching across the whole length and breadth of Iraq. Some Iraqi units fought hard, but others surrendered when it became evident what they were up against. However, irregular 'Saddam fedayeen' proved persistent and troublesome, attacking exhausted soldiers driving up the deeply rutted roads as the advance swept on. On 25 March the leading elements of V Corps took the Euphrates bridge near Najaf, damaged but usable, and on the same day the Marines secured the bridges over the Tigris at Nasiriyah, though not without hard fighting. The British had established a loose cordon round Basra, and on 26–7 March emphatically defeated a tank attack on their lines. However, a vicious storm blew for three days, grounding most close air support and restricting movement. McKiernan decided on an operational pause to secure his lines of communication so that supplies could flow freely in a battle for Baghdad, and to gain better information on Iraqi dispositions.

The press, in a characteristic mid-war wobble, suspected that the advance had run out of steam, but was soon proved wrong. On 6–7 April the British secured Basra and were widely welcomed by the Shi'a population, which had been treated brutally by Saddam In the north, US special forces and airborne troops, working alongside the Kurdish Pesh-merga, eventually secured Mosul. But the advance of V Corps and the Marines was even more remarkable: a combination of precision attacks from helicopters and fixed-wing air-craft, with some state of the art ground/air manoeuvre by the 101st Airborne Division, helped attract Iraqi attention away from V Corps penetrating the Karbala gap, approaching Baghdad airport (despite the steadfast denial of Saddam's spin doctor, 'Comical Ali'), and on the night of 7–8 April much of central Baghdad was in American hands. The Marines swung into Baghdad from the east, and the city fell with none of the last-ditch *Götterdammerung* so gloomily prophesied by many commentators.

The brief campaign was the ultimate pay-off for the doctrinal and psychological regeneration of the US armed forces since Vietnam, and probably represents the high point of the 'manoeuvre warfare' so enthusiastically taught in western staff colleges. Yet if it was a triumph at the tactical and operational levels, the sheer scale of coalition victory ('catastrophic success' was a widely used phrase) immediately raised strategic doubts. Iraq was not a modern state, subject to decapitation, the replacement of one government by another: 'regime change' was easy to talk about but hard to achieve. Coalition forces stayed on, increasingly the targets of attack by a wide spectrum of insurgent groups including former regime loyalists, foreign fighters, resentful Sunni, unemployed young-sters, and tribal militia. At the time of writing it is clear that the question is not whether the coalition will withdraw, but when. However, it is impossible to say how long it will take the soldiers and policemen of the new Iraq to be ready to bear the burden of running a heterogeneous state with no real basis of democratic governance.

9 Africa

In at least one sense Africa is indeed the dark continent, for written sources for its history are limited. Records for Egypt go back to at least 3000 BC, there are royal chronicles and church documents from Ethiopia from the first century AD, and Arab traders began to leave accounts of West Africa from the eighth century AD. But elsewhere there is little of the historian's raw material, although both archaeology and oral history, the latter often astonishingly rich, offer tantalizing clues.

In Egypt, profiting from the annual flooding of the Nile, civilization began in perhaps 5000 BC and had reached a high level of sophistication by 2000 BC. The Sahara desert hindered the transmission of Egyptian culture to the west, and relatively little of it made its way south to Nubia and Ethiopia. Towards the end of the second millennium BC Phoenician traders from the Middle East established the city of Carthage in what is now Tunisia. But the Carthaginians, like the Egyptians, found the deserts to their south an insuperable barrier. After they broke the power of Carthage in the Punic wars, the Romans colonized North Africa. It was a good deal less dry than it is today, and produced both grain and olive oil.

The decline of the Roman empire left no successor state powerful enough to resist invasion, and North Africa was first overrun by the Vandals, striking down from Spain, in the fifth century BC, was next occupied by the Arabs in the seventh century AD, providing a springboard for the invasion of the Iberian peninsula, and eventually became part of the Ottoman empire. In the process Islam largely supplanted Christianity in much of Egypt. Arab traders, eager for gold and slaves, took Islam with them into West Africa, and it also made its way, albeit with more difficulty, from Egypt to the Sudan.

The development of sub-Saharan Africa hinged upon the discovery of iron. Copper was a valuable metal, used for decoration and display, but in much of Africa there was no Bronze Age, and it impossible to say quite when or where iron-smelting originated. It was certainly being carried out by Bantu-speaking peoples in the Great Lakes region of East Africa not long before the birth of Christ. Iron implements helped the Bantu till soil which resisted stone-using farmers, and gave them a clear advantage when their expeditions brought them into contact with hostile tribes.

The use of warhorses spread south, probably from Mameluke Egypt, and cavalry played an important role on the West African savannah. In tropical Africa horses, like Europeans, found it hard to survive the climate, and further south they had little military impact until the nineteenth century. Some African rulers had imperial ambitions, and several used European technology and mercenaries to implement them: Shaykh Umar established a substantial state in the western Sudan, the caliph of Sokoto ruled northern Nigeria, and there were smaller states contending for power in East Africa. One mighty kingdom required no European help. A process called the *mfecane* (crushing) saw two Nguni chiefs, Dingiswayo and Zwide, gain control of what is now KwaZulu Natal. Shaka, illegitimate son of a minor Zulu chief, was Dingiswayo's most enterprising lieutenant, and when Dingiswayo was killed he took control of what remained of his realm, defeated Zwide, and established the Zulu kingdom, its strength resting on disciplined warriors organized in age-regiments, trained to use their spears not for throwing but for stabbing.

The real empires were destined to be European, not African. Portuguese mariners first landed in West Africa in the mid-fifteenth century, and the reach of their trading spread steadily inland. The development of sugar plantations, first on the island of São Tomé and latterly in the Americas, encouraged the slave trade, and slaves were soon not simply captives taken in war, but men, women, and children seized by Arab slave traders and sold to Europeans. Most of them endured the horrors of the 'middle passage' on their way to the New World, and as Philip Curtin has observed: 'One of the ironies of African history is the fact that maritime contact, which ended Africa's long isolation and brought all coasts of the continent into contact with the intercommunicating part of the world, should have led so rapidly to a situation in which Africa's main export was its people.'

The Portuguese established bases on the coast of East Africa in the early sixteenth century, and the Dutch made a permanent settlement at the Cape in 1652. By 1795 this had expanded into a substantial colony, and it finally became British as part of the post-Waterloo settlement. North Africa had long been independent of Turkish control, and its tiny and unstable states were bases for Barbary pirates, who for centuries had preyed on maritime commerce and raided coastal settlements as far afield as the south-west of England. Both European powers and the newly independent USA were determined to stamp them out. In 1801–5 the Americans beat the pasha of Tripoli, first bombarding his harbour and then sending a force ashore in an episode that put the words 'to the shores of Tripoli' into the US Marine Corps hymn. The French had trading interests in Algiers, and in 1827 its ruler struck their consul round the face with a fly-whisk, beginning a process which saw the French invade in 1830, take Algiers, occupy the country by 1857, and complete its pacification by 1881. French rule was extended into Tunisia after a border incident in 1881, and in 1907 the French moved into Morocco, though they did not wholly complete its conquest until 1934.

By this time what had started as coastal encroachment and gradual penetration of the interior for economic reasons, allied to attempts by missionaries to spread Christianity, had become 'the scramble for Africa' with European powers carving out empires of their own. The French, beginning in North Africa, annexed huge tracts of west and equatorial Africa, and Madagascar too. The fate of the West African kingdom of Dahomey in 1892–4 was typical of the process. Although the warlike Fon had obtained repeating rifles and modern artillery from German traders, they were overwhelmed by a methodical French advance which avoided the obvious overland route but struck at the Fon capital of Aboumey via the Ouémé river.

Things were more complex for the British. They secured the Cape in 1814, but their rule, followed as it was by the abolition of slavery, grated on the Dutch-speaking population, and in 1834 many Afrikaners began the Great Trek, moving across the Orange and Vaal rivers and on towards the Limpopo. The process inevitably brought them into conflict with local peoples, and in 1838 a voortrekker column repulsed a Zulu attack at Blood river. Britain annexed Natal in 1843, and in 1879 defeated the Zulus, though not without suffering a major reverse at Isandhlwana. Many voortrekkers had settled in the two Boer republics of the Orange Free State and the Transvaal. The discovery of diamonds at Kimberley in the northern Cape in 1867, followed by the beginning of gold mining in the Witwatersrand in 1886, created a demand for cheap labour, filled by migrant black workers. It also drew in non-Afrikaner whites (known as Uitlanders, foreigners) and so paved the way for two wars between Britain and the Boers. Further north, the British had already secured Rhodesia, and went on to seize Uganda and British East Africa too.

British and French forces had fought in Egypt during the French Revolutionary wars, with French victory over the Mamelukes at the battle of the Pyramids (1798) being followed by Nelson's destruction of the French fleet in the Nile estuary (1798) and eventual British victory at Alexandria (1801). Although Egypt lurched on, part of the Ottoman empire but in practice self-governing, in 1879 the disastrous state of its public finances encouraged Britain and France to intervene. A popular revolt, led by an Egyptian army officer, Urabi Pasha, resulted first in the bombardment of Alexandria by a British fleet (1882) and then by the defeat of Urabi by Garnet Wolseley at Tel-el-Kebir. Britain occupied Egypt, though a veneer of local rule was preserved, and in doing so assumed responsibility for the Sudan, where a rebellion led by Muhammad Ahmad, known as the Mahdi, was running strongly. Although the British intervened, they did so too late and with too few good troops. Khartoum, capital of the Sudan, held by an Egyptian force under Major General Charles Gordon, was taken by the dervishes in 1884. A relief expedition, sent down the Nile, failed to reach him in time. It was not until 1896 that the British began the systematic reconquest of the Sudan, and Kitchener's victory at Omdurman (1898) demonstrated, more clearly than any other battle, the impotence of native valour in the face of imported technology. France and Britain came close to clashing when expeditions met at Fashoda on the White Nile, south of Omdurman, in 1898, but a face-saving compromise resulted in French withdrawal.

By 1914 the scramble was complete. In addition to the huge tracts of Africa governed by the British and the French, the Spanish held a slice of Morocco, and the Rio de Oro to its south; the Portuguese, Guinea, Angola, and Mozambique; the Belgians, the Congo; and the Italians, Eritrea and Italian Somaliland (the British and French enjoyed smaller portions) and Libya. The Germans, late arrivals at the table, had swallowed German South West Africa and German East Africa, as well as Togoland, sandwiched between British-ruled Nigeria and the Gold Coast. Both the republic of Liberia and the empire of Ethiopia were still independent. At the battle of Adowa in 1896 the Ethiopians had inflicted a shattering defeat on an Italian army moving in from Eritrea, and although the Italians recognized Ethiopian independence at the time, the incident rankled, and encouraged Italy to invade again, this time with the help of aircraft and mustard gas, in 1935.

Technology had played a significant part in the process, especially during the second half of the nineteenth century, when firepower was transformed by a series of innovations which made it difficult for indigenous people to compete on the battlefield. Although there were times, as the British and Italians discovered at Isandhlwana and Adowa, when the effects of modern weapons and military organizations were overestimated, Omdurman was a more typical example of what happened when European and African armies met. Yet these 'European' armies were usually only part European. Most colonial powers maintained locally recruited soldiers, and could scarcely have held their empires without them. Some could be very good indeed, and not just when fighting on familiar ground. The performance of the French Expeditionary Corps in Italy in 1944 highlighted the fighting quality of its fine North African troops, and the British army in Burma included men from both East and West Africa.

Not all technology was purely military. Tropical Africa was notoriously lethal to Europeans: until about 1850 their death rate rarely sank below 250 per 1,000 per annum, and could be much higher. Although the development of effective anti-malaria drugs would not come till World War II, daily doses of quinine (often taken in the 'tonic water' that mixed well so with gin) provided a measure of protection. Anti-mosquito campaigns reduced the impact of both malaria and yellow fever, and growing emphasis on sanitation and hygiene helped blunt the impact of many other diseases. Despite this, however, death rates in most African campaigns show the microbe doing far more damage than spear, bullet, or panga. Some 8,000 British soldiers were killed in the second Boer War, but another 13,000 died of disease, and even in 1914–18 the British East African Expeditionary Force lost 10,000 killed in battle and 6,000 to disease. For the force's African and Indian camp followers the figure is even more shocking: just 376 were killed in action, while over 42,000 perished from disease.

The assertion of African independence took place during the second half of the twentieth century. Sometimes there was a peaceful transfer of power, but often there were lengthy guerrilla wars. By now modern small arms were readily available to insurgents, partly because the Soviet Union and its client states were eager to help anti-western elements. Although colonial powers, with aircraft and armoured vehicles, generally enjoyed military superiority it was hard for them to bring it to bear decisively, and just as difficult for them to sustain domestic resolve in the face of long and apparently indecisive conflicts. There was no African equivalent of the battle of Dien Bien Phu (1954) where a French force was beaten on ground of its own choosing by its Vietnamese opponents. Even the regime which unilaterally declared independence in Rhodesia in 1965 had the best of most military engagements against black guerrillas, and staggered on until 1979 in the face of external pressure and diminishing support from South Africa.

The legacy of these conflicts was baneful. Many newly independent nations were awash with cheap weapons, prone to military takeovers, and all too likely to become 'failed states', in which the breakdown of governmental authority is accompanied by civil war, disease, and famine. Western intervention can become part of the problem, rather than its solution: in the early 1990s the Americans learnt painful lessons from a well-intentioned incursion into Somalia. The British were more successful in Sierra Leone a decade later, but a mixture of the legacy of colonial rule, faltering economies, tribal and ethnic fissures, endemic corruption, agrarian change, urbanization, and the impact of AIDS makes it hard to predict Africa's future with optimism.

THE FRENCH CONQUEST OF ALGERIA

In 1827 the dey of Algiers struck the French consul round the face with a fly-whisk. The government of Charles X scented an opportunity to gain domestic popularity by foreign adventure, and in June 1830 a French expeditionary force landed at Sidi Ferruch, marched on Algiers, and took it a week later. This success did little for Charles X, who abdicated on 2 August.

In 1832 Abd al-Qadir, emir of Mascara, had opposed an advance into the interior, raising the tribes around his capital and proclaiming holy war. Beaten at Oran, he concluded a treaty with the French which enabled him to gain ascendancy over the western tribes. In 1836 General Thomas Bugeaud was sent to command in Algeria, and the success of the French campaign owed much to his efforts. A French assault on Constantine was beaten off, and the following year the city fell only after a week of bitter house-to-house fighting and the death of General Denys Damrémont, the French commander.

Abd al-Qadir made terms with Bugeaud in 1837. This left him virtual king of the unconquered portion of Algeria, and in 1839 he again attacked the French, this time with Moroccan support. His household was captured in 1843. On 14 August 1844 Bugeaud defeated Abd al-Qadir's Moroccan allies at the Isly river, west of Oujda (Morocco), though the emir himself did not capitulate until 1847.

Bugeaud lightened the equipment of his troops, forming 'flying columns' which pushed deep into the hinterland under able subordinates like Louis Cavaignac, Nicolas Changarnier, and Juchault de Lamoricière. If resistance to invasion was weakened by factionalism, it was nonetheless determined. It was a vicious war, and French methods could be brutal. *Razzia* (raids) and pillage were standard tactics, and Aimable Pélissier, one of the heroes of the conquest, asphyxiated some 600 civilians who had taken refuge in a cave. Yet Bugeaud was as much pacifier as conqueror. He used public works to help reconcile the tribes he had beaten, and the raising of local units, forerunners of French African troops like spahis and zouaves, helped provide warlike men with a martial outlet. White colonists, many of them ex-soldiers, moved in behind the fighting: there were 109,000 of them by 1847. The whole of Algeria was not physically occupied until 1857, and complete pacification was not achieved before 1881.

ABYSSINIAN WARS

The British Expedition to Abyssinia (Ethiopia) (1867–1868)

Emperor Tewodros (Theodore) II, a modernizer, wanted close relations with Britain, which was reluctant to involve itself in his conflict with Egypt, then invading his country. He responded by imprisoning a British consul and several other Europeans. The British dispatched 13,000 well-equipped United Kingdom and Indian troops from Bombay, led by Sir Robert Napier. The advance force landed at Annesley Bay, on 21 October 1867, and the main body on 2 January 1868. With the cooperation of the local ruler of Tegray, it proceeded inland, across 400 km (250 miles) of mountainous country, toward the emperor's fortress of Maqdala (Magdala). At the decisive battle of Aroge (Arogee), on 10 April, the British, using cannon, breech-loading rifles, and rockets, inflicted immense casualties on Tewodros's poorly equipped forces. Tewodros then released his European prisoners, and sued, unsuccessfully, for peace. British forces thereupon stormed Maqdala on 13 April and Tewodros committed suicide. British troops looted his capital before they left the country.

The Battle of Adowa (1896)

The Italians, who had seized the Red Sea port of Massawa in 1885, had been steadily penetrating inland, when they signed a friendship treaty, at Wechalue in 1889, with Menilek, king of Shewa. By it they recognized him as emperor, while he recognized their presence in the north, where they established their colony of Eritrea in 1890. The treaty had two texts, one in Amharic and the other in Italian. The former stated that Menilek *could* use Italian good offices in his correspondence with other powers; the latter, that he *must*. This the Italians used to claim a protectorate. After long negotiations, during which he imported many firearms, largely from France, Menilek denounced the treaty in February 1893.

The Italians then advanced into Tegray, but were defeated by Menilek at the mountain of Amba Alagi in December 1895 and fell back on Adowa. There the two armies confronted each other, reluctant to attack first. On 25 February 1896 the Italian premier, Francesco Crispi, telegraphed the Italian commander, General Oreste Baratieri, that Italy was ready for any sacrifice. The Italians had 17,000 soldiers (1,650 Italians, the remainder Eritreans). Menilek had about 100,000 men, mostly with modern weapons. Baratieri attempted a surprise attack, on 1 March, but his plans were disclosed by double agents, and his maps were faulty. The Ethiopians, in one day, crushed the three Italian contingents separately. Italy lost 43 per cent of its fighting force. Three out of five commanders were killed, a fourth was captured. Menilek's victory, despite heavy losses, was so complete that Italy recognized Ethiopia's full independence.

The Italian Invasion of 1935-1936

This invasion was effected with the aid of poison gas, and created great popular indignation internationally. The conflict had its roots in the Italian 'Duce' Benito Mussolini's ambition to avenge Adowa. He and his aide Emilio De Bono decided, in 1933, to invade Abyssinia 'no later than 1936'. The pretext was the Wal Wal incident of December 1934, when Ethiopian forces clashed with Italian colonial troops, which had infiltrated 100 km (60 miles) into Ethiopian territory. Mussolini used the ensuing period of negotiations to build up his armies in Italian Eritrea and Somalia. They eventually numbered 200,000 men. Britain and France, which together controlled the remainder of the coastline around Abyssinia, imposed an arms embargo on both parties. This fell more heavily on Abyssinia, which imported arms, than on Italy, which manufactured them.

Mussolini's armies finally attacked, from the north and south, without any declaration of war, on 3 October 1935. They enjoyed vast superiority in weapons, and total control of the air. The League of Nations declared Italy guilty of aggression, but imposed only ineffective economic sanctions. The Italian advance, from Eritrea under De Bono, was initially slow, and that from Somalia under General Rodolfo Graziani relatively unimportant. Mussolini accordingly dismissed De Bono, in November, and replaced him by General Pietro Badoglio, a career soldier, whom he authorized to use chemical weapons. The Italians, who employed heavy aerial bombardments and used mustard gas extensively, then advanced rapidly. They defeated Emperor Haile Selassie's chiefs early in 1936, and the monarch's own army at Mai Chew, at the end of March 1936, and entered Addis Ababa on 5 May. The emperor had left for Europe three days earlier.

EGYPTIAN AND SUDANESE CAMPAIGNS

A popular revolt against the foreign domination of Egypt, led by an Egyptian army officer, Urabi Pasha, resulted in Europeans being murdered in Alexandria and to the bombardment of the city by a British fleet on 11 July 1882. The subsequent dispatch of an army under General Sir Garnet Wolseley resulted in the defeat of the Egyptian army at Tel-el-Kebir on 13 September 1882 and to the British occupation of the country.

In occupying Egypt Britain automatically assumed responsibility for the vast Egyptian Sudan. There, a revolt led by a religious leader, Muhammad Ahmad, self-styled the Mahdi, had started in 1881. By the end of 1882 his forces (popularly if inaccurately known as dervishes) had occupied a major part of the Sudan. A large Egyptian army, under Colonel William Hicks, sent to defeat the Mahdi, was itself annihilated on 5 November 1883—the day before another Egyptian force was destroyed outside Suakin on the Red Sea and the British consul killed. To retrieve the situation at Suakin a hastily assembled force under Major General Gerald Graham was dispatched there and defeated the dervish forces under Osman Digna at El Teb and Tamai after severe fighting in March 1884. Graham's force was then withdrawn and the town remained under siege.

The British government now decided to evacuate the Sudan, with the exception of Suakin, and Major General Charles Gordon was sent to superintend the evacuation of the Egyptian garrisons. Against his instructions, he elected to stay and defend the capital, Khartoum, which came under siege from the Mahdi in May 1884. In October 1884 the government dispatched the Gordon relief expedition under Wolseley, who advanced slowly up the Nile. In the face of increasingly desperate appeals for help from Gordon, Wolseley sent a flying column across the desert. After a desperate fight at Abu Klea on 17 January 1885, a small party embarked at Metemmeh on two steamers and reached Khartoum on 28 January, to find that the city had fallen and Gordon been killed two days earlier. Wolseley was forced to retreat and the Sudan was abandoned to the Mahdi. To salvage something from the debacle Graham was again sent to Suakin with a large, carefully prepared force, in February 1885, with orders to smash Osman Digna and to build a railway to Berber, on the Nile, with a view to the subsequent reconquest of the Sudan. Graham defeated Osman at Hashin and Tofrek in March and succeeded in laying nearly 80 km (50 miles) of the 400 km (250 miles) of track required to reach Berber but in May 1885 the force was withdrawn. Suakin was retained but remained under siege.

Wolseley's withdrawal left Egypt open to a Mahdist invasion, which came in December 1885 and was defeated at Ginnis. In July 1889 a second, major invasion was launched but was decisively defeated by Major General Francis Grenfell at Tushki on 3 August 1889. At Suakin Osman continued to plague the garrison until he was decisively defeated at Tokar in February 1891. In 1896 the British government decided the time was ripe to start the reconquest of the Sudan, using the reorganized and retrained Egyptian army, led by its commander-in-chief, General Sir Herbert Kitchener. Building a railway as he went, he moved methodically forward, inflicting severe defeats at Firket and Hafir in June and September 1896. By the end of September 1896, he was roughly halfway to Khartoum.

The second phase of the reconquest started in January 1897. The railway was steadily pushed southwards, the dervishes outmanoeuvred and defeated at Abu Hamed on 7 August 1897, and Berbert on the Nile, only some 400 km (250 miles) from Khartoum, occupied.

For the final phase starting in January 1898 Kitchener was reinforced with two brigades of British troops. A large dervish army under the Emir Mahmud had entrenched itself at the confluence of the Nile and Atbara rivers but it was attacked and routed on 8 June 1898.

Italian soldiers march through Addis Ababa.

The Battle of Omdurman (1898)

General Kitchener was now only some 320 km (200 miles) from Omdurman, the dervish capital opposite Khartoum. The final advance began at the end of August. Kitchener now had an immensely powerful force, including a cavalry brigade, four Egyptian, and two British infantry brigades, supported by numerous modern field artillery guns, 20 maxim machine guns, and some 25,000 men; ten gunboats gave fire support from the Nile. Against this, Khalifa Abdullah, the Mahdi's successor, could muster some 60,000 men, ill equipped by comparison and lacking in artillery.

By 1 September Kitchener was encamped on the Nile, 10 km (6 miles) from Omdurman. A night attack, in which Kitchener's technological advantage would have been largely nullified, would seem to have offered the khalifa his best chance of success but he elected to fight in daylight. Kitchener was no tactician and in the battle next day he had some moments of concern, but the khalifa was unable to coordinate the actions of his various forces and in the pitiless fire of repeating rifles, machine guns, and high explosive his troops were massacred. Hand-to-hand fighting occurred only when the 21st Lancers, including the young Winston Churchill, charged into a substantial force of enraged Mahdists concealed in a wadi and were roughly handled. The Mahdist losses were estimated at 11,000 killed and 16,000 wounded; British casualties were 48 killed and 382 wounded. Omdurman was occupied the same day but the khalifa, with other leaders, escaped and was not rounded up and killed until November 1899.

THE ZULU WAR

By the 1870s the Zulu army under paramount chief Cetchewayo numbered 50,000 warriors, posing a significant threat to settlers if provoked. This brought the Zulus into conflict with the British of Cape Colony, who had annexed neighbouring Natal in 1843 and the Transvaal Republic in 1877, and thus acquired the Zulu/Boer problem. On 11 December 1878 the British presented Cetchewayo with an ultimatum, giving him a month to disband his army and end the military structure of Zulu society. Meanwhile an army of 16,800 British regular forces and local volunteers (including the Natal Native Contingent or NNC) assembled in Natal under Lieutenant General Lord Chelmsford. The contest would be chiefly one of charging spear-armed, disciplined Zulu foot warriors against British infantry with breach-loading rifles.

Chelmsford divided his force into columns to converge on the Zulu capital of Ulundi: Number 1 Column of 5,000 troops along the coast under Colonel Charles Pearson, Number 4 Column of 2,250 troops under Colonel Evelyn Wood from the north, and Number 3 Column of 4,700 troops in the centre under Colonel Richard Glyn with Chelmsford himself, supported by Number 2 Column of 1,500 NNC under Colonel Anthony Durnford.

On 12 January the invasion began with Chelmsford's main force crossing into Zululand at the ford of Rorke's Drift. The Zulu army commenced its preparations for war on 17 January. Pearson's column won an early victory against 6,000 Zulus at Nyezane Drift on 22 January.

The Battle of Isandhlwana (1879)

The principal Zulu force had reached the Ngwebeni valley by the evening of 21 January, concealed by the Nyoni heights from the Number 3 Column which had encamped at Isandhlwana Hill the day before. Meanwhile the local chief, Matshana, decoyed a British detachment under Major J. G. Dartnell and Commandant R. Lonsdale to a position from which they felt obliged to send for reinforcements.

Chelmsford controversially divided his own force, going south with Glyn at 04.30 hours on 22 January. The remaining 1,700 troops, largely of the 24th Regiment, were encamped below Isandhlwana mountain under Lieutenant Colonel Henry Pulleine, reinforced by 500 NNC mounted troops under Durnford. They were attacked by half the Zulu army under Chiefs Ntshingwayo and Mavumengwana soon after noon. The Zulu advanced fast in their usual crescent formation and came under considerable fire from rifles and field guns. The latter they avoided by throwing themselves down every time the gun-crew drew back preparatory to firing, but the Martini-Henry rifles caused fearful casualties. The attackers' superior numbers threatened the flanks of the defenders and an attempt was made to fall back to camp. A final assault by the Zulu overwhelmed the British and few escaped. The British loss numbered 52 officers, 727 white troops, and 471 black. The Zulu killed exceeded 1,000 men and their lack of medical skill to deal with gunshot wounds meant that, in the coming days, few wounded would recover. The price of victory was heavy.

This costly reverse provoked considerable buck-passing. Chelmsford's supporters argued that Durnford, the senior officer in camp, although recently arrived and not the column's formal commander, was to blame. Recent studies seem to exonerate both Durnford and Pulleine, and to suggest that Chelmsford had made a fundamental error by dividing his force before he had located the enemy. A new examination of the 24th's conduct points to neither a failure in its ammunition supply nor a collapse in morale: simply a battle won by a large body of very brave men over a much smaller one in circumstances where technical advantage was not conclusive.

About 4,000 Zulus under Chief Dabulamanzi carried on to Rorke's Drift on the same day. The garrison of 140 men under two lieutenants held out for two days before the Zulus retired. Eleven Victoria Crosses were awarded for Rorke's Drift, a record for a single British battle.

With his campaign in ruins Chelmsford fell back and General Sir Garnet Wolseley was sent out to replace him. The Zulu, who had suffered heavy losses, did not invade Natal, although they did surround Pearson's column at Eshowe. On 2 April a relief force for Pearson under Chelmsford was attacked by the Zulu at Gingindlovu. Fighting from a wagon-laager, British firepower inflicted a heavy defeat on the Zulus. Wood's attack on the Zulu stronghold at Hlobane mountain on 28 March was also a failure. He fell back to a wagon-laagered position at Khambula ridge, where next day he also fought off a major Zulu attack.

After reinforcements arrived, Chelmsford's second invasion of Zululand began on 31 May. The 1st Division of 7,500 troops under Major General Henry Crealock advanced along the coast, Wood's force of 8,000 troops became the Flying Column, and the centre column became 2nd Division of 8,000 troops under Major General Frederick Marshall, again accompanied by Chelmsford. Zulu resistance had weakened; Cetchewayo accepted

that defeat was inevitable and tried to negotiate peace. On 1 June the prince imperial, heir to the deposed Napoleon III of France, serving as a British officer, was killed in a skirmish. Linking up with Wood, Chelmsford continued his advance to the Zulu capital. The battle of Ulundi on 4 July pitted Chelmsford's 5,300 troops (including 900 mounted men) against 20,000 Zulus, in a British victory climaxed by a cavalry charge. Chelmsford deliberately did not entrench or laager, determined to show that his troops could face Zulus in the open. He then withdrew from Ulundi and resigned his command on 8 July. Wolseley, frustrated at not arriving in time to command at Ulundi, saw the war to a conclusion with the pursuit and capture of Cetchewayo on 20 August. He was deposed as paramount chief and Zululand was annexed to British authority at Ulundi on 1 September. The British were so impressed by the courage of their opponents that, most unusually, they erected a memorial to them at Ulundi along with their own.

THE BOER WARS

The first Boer War arose from rivalry between Britain's claim to be the paramount power in southern Africa and the desire of the Boers (descendants of Dutch who had settled in the Cape) for autonomy. Britain recognized the independence of the two Boer republics, the Orange Free State and the Transvaal Republic, in 1852 and 1854 respectively, expecting to annex both peacefully in due course. In January 1877, the bankrupt Transvaal was indeed peacefully annexed by Britain.

In 1880 Major General Sir George Colley became governor of Natal (also responsible for the Transvaal). The Transvaal Boers under Paul Kruger petitioned London for the restoration of their independence, and when this was refused they declared a republic once more on 16 December. The Orange Free State remained neutral throughout the war. Under the 'commando' military system the Transvaal fielded about 7,000 irregular mounted riflemen with no artillery, against about half that number of British regulars plus local volunteers.

The fighting began with the wiping out of a British column on 20 December at Bronkhorstspruit, south of Pretoria, in an ambush led by General Piet Joubert. Most of the 1,800 British troops in the Transvaal were scattered in small forts, all of which were attacked or besieged but none captured. The government in London sent reinforcements while simultaneously negotiating for a settlement, and failed to provide Colley with clear orders. He in turn advanced with about 1,000 regulars and local volunteers into the pass at Laing's Nek, the frontier between Natal and the Transvaal. Colley failed to open this route with a frontal attack on twice his number of Boers on 28 January 1881. In this action the 58th Regiment (which soon became the 2nd Battalion, Northamptonshire Regiment) became the last British battalion to carry its colours into battle. Then followed the failure of an attack by the Boers on a supply column with 300 men at the battle of Ingogo river on 8 February.

The 24th Foot at Isandhlwana; a detail from the painting by C. E. Fripp which, apart from the addition of the Regimental Colour, is reasonably accurate.

The Battle of Majuba Hill (1881)

On 26 February, Sir George Colley led 595 men in a night march to capture Majuba Hill, which dominated Laing's Nek below. His line of communication was secured as he advanced and 405 men reached the dished summit of the hill in darkness. The arrival of day showed they had not secured the entire top of the hill and the line was thinned as the 92nd Highlanders spread out to do so and set a small, five-man party on Gordon's Knoll, a feature dominating the northern part of the hill. Colley and his staff failed to reinforce them. Under heavy Boer covering fire, Joubert sent 180 men in small parties up onto the hill. First, at about 12.45, they took the Knoll from which their fire supported their comrades in taking the northern side of the hill. From there their superior marksmanship caused a British rout, only the Highlanders holding their ground. Colley was killed, and his force suffered casualties of 85 killed, 119 wounded, and 35 missing or taken prisoner. Boer losses were one killed and six wounded.

Now London sent significant reinforcements under Lord Roberts, while authorizing Colley's replacement, Major General Evelyn Wood, to negotiate an armistice. This was agreed on 21 March, before Roberts's force reached Cape Town. Peace was concluded by the Pretoria Convention in August, restoring independence to the Transvaal with a nod to British sovereignty. Even that was removed in the further London Convention of 1884, at which the Transvaal changed its name to the South African Republic.

During the 1880s and 1890s the autonomy, trade, and traditional way of life of the Boer republics were threatened by the prosperity of Cape Colony and Natal, the creation of British Rhodesia in the north, the flood of substantially British foreign workers into Transvaal gold mines, and pressure from empire-builders who sought to overturn the settlement of the first Boer War and create a federated South Africa under the Union flag. Late in 1895 Cecil Rhodes sponsored a raid led by Dr Leander Starr Jameson to stir Uitlanders against Boer rule and prompt British intervention. This was suppressed by the Transvaal authorities, but it provoked the Boer republics to prepare for war, and firmed imperial resolve to eclipse Boer power.

The republics had no armies but relied on commandos, led by elected officers. These forces were stiffened by armed police and professional artillery regiments with the most modern guns. Boer strategy was to strike swiftly before British reinforcements could arrive, to rouse rebellion in the Cape, and to win a negotiated peace. In October 1899 fast-moving commandos totalling perhaps 40,000 men invested British border garrisons at Mafeking and Kimberley and invaded Natal, locking up a British force at Ladysmith early in November. A civil as well as imperial war got under way as many Cape Colonists took up arms on the Boer side, thousands of Uitlanders formed volunteer regiments to fight beside British regulars, and small contingents from Canada and Australasia arrived to join in the fighting. By the end of September 1900 some 40,000 'colonial' troops were under British command.

Having spread their commandos thinly, the Boer offensive soon ran out of steam. But the arrival of a British army corps under General Sir Redvers Buller did not bring the speedy victory many expected. The failure of forces in the field to withdraw as ordered overextended the limited strength of Buller's Army Corps; he had thirteen cavalry regiments, eight companies of mounted infantry, 49 battalions of infantry, and 29 batteries of artillery. The cavalry was unsuited to the conditions, and the strident demands of Cecil

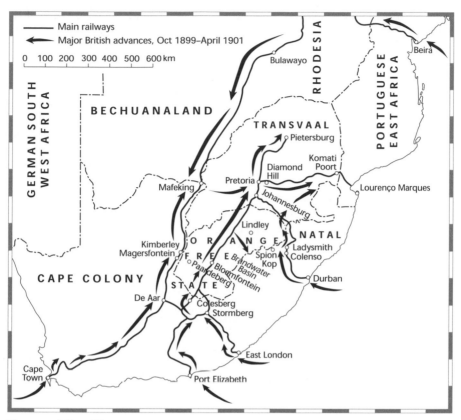

The second Boer War

Rhodes to be liberated from Kimberley contributed to the decision to divide the force in three. During 'black week' the army's three components failed in their attacks. Lieutenant General Sir William Gatacre attempted a 16-km (10-mile) night march to Stormberg in eastern Cape Colony (10 December), but was forced to retire losing 28 dead, 51 wounded, and 634 taken prisoner. Lieutenant General Lord Methuen advanced to the relief of Kimberley, engaging the Boers at Belmont, Graspan, and Modder river during six days in November 1899. On each occasion the Boers withdrew, having delayed the British, and in the last of these actions General Joos De la Rey deployed his riflemen in trenches to fire across level ground, thus exploiting the flat trajectory of the Mauser rifles with which the Boers were newly equipped. The tactic held the British for the greater part of a day.

The Battle of Magersfontein (1899)

The last major obstacle on Lord Methuen's road to Kimberley was the range of hills at Magersfontein where the Boers had dug trenches and built gun positions looking south over the open veldt. Under the command of Assistant Commandant General Piet Cronjé, some 8,500 Boers and five 75 mm Krupp field guns occupied the new line on 4 December.

Methuen had about 12,000 men, a 4.7-inch naval gun, six 5-inch howitzers, and 24 field guns, 15- and 12-pounders. Given the exposed approach to the Boer lines, he decided to move forward by night. Major General Andrew Wauchope led the Highland Brigade forward on 11 December soon after midnight, in the rain, in 'mass of quarter columns'; that is, a deep line about 38 m (120 feet) wide. At about 04.00, in clearing weather, the Highlanders began to deploy left and right, but the defenders heard them and opened fire at a range of some 365 metres (400 yards). The Mauser's flat trajectory made taking aim almost superfluous and an attempted bayonet charge was halted by sheer weight of fire. As day dawned efforts to reinforce the Highlanders were stopped in similar fashion. The British field guns were galled by rifle fire, but luckily their recoil edged them back behind a low hillock, from which shelter they were able to maintain their fire. Continued fighting gave neither side advantage by the end of the day, when a spontaneous truce permitted the retrieval of the wounded. Methuen was forced to pull back to the Modder river, having suffered 239 men killed (202 were Highlanders), 663 wounded (496 of them Highlanders), and 75 made prisoner. The Boer losses, as close as can be calculated, were 87 killed, 149 wounded, and 18 taken prisoner.

The Battle of Colenso (1899)

Sir Redvers Buller was himself in command of the force advancing to the relief of Ladysmith in Natal. His way was barred by the Tugela river and the hills beyond it which were in the hands of the Boers under Commandant General Louis Botha with ten 75 mm guns and a 5-inch howitzer installed in stone-built emplacements. The terrain had been mapped in somewhat primitive fashion and although the line of the river was clear, detail of hills and streams was obscure. A field survey under fire yielded an improved map, but crucially two streams feeding the Tugela west of Colenso were shown as one, entering the river west of the large meander known as 'The Loop'. There were in fact two streams, one entering to the east, but the terrain impeded accurate observation.

The assault on 15 December 1899 was intended to keep the Boers busy in the centre, at Colenso village, and on the right, while on the left Major General Fitzroy Hart's Irish Brigade crossed a drift (ford) west of the Loop and fell on the Boer right, held by their own Irish Brigade. Unfortunately, marching with the unmapped stream on his right led Hart into the Loop itself where fire from three sides halted him: it speaks volumes for the courage of his men that some actually managed to cross the river. On the other flank British artillery had advanced beyond the supporting infantry and was badly shot up. But in the process they revealed the Boer presence south of the river on Hlangwani mountain, and so prevented a surprise counter-attack which would have done terrible damage. Botha said that Colonel C. J. Long, the much-criticized commander of the British artillery, had in fact 'saved the British Army that day'. Buller had the courage to call off the attack before more damage was done, but attempts to retrieve Long's guns cost the life of Lord Roberts's only son Freddie. British losses amounted to 171 killed and 638 wounded with 197 taken prisoner.

The uproar in London led to the appointment of Field Marshal Lord Roberts to take command. Buller was demoted to commanding only in Natal. The need to relieve Ladysmith persisted and Buller's next attempt was made to the west in order to cross the Tugela by Potgieter's Drift and head for the besieged town.

The Battle of Spion Kop (1900)

In January 1900 Sir Redvers Buller received reinforcements: Lieutenant General Sir Charles Warren and the 5th Division. This fresh formation made slow progress, taking ten days to complete the approach march. When he found that the pass west of Spion Kop (Look-out Hill) was, by now, well defended Buller decided to seize Spion Kop and use it as a base for covering fire for the attack on the pass. At 23.00 on 23 January Major General Sir Edward Woodgate led four battalions up the steep hillside and by 04.00 he had control of the summit. Botha declared it must be retaken.

Daylight revealed that the so-called summit was near the edge of a shallow, stony dish, which terminated abruptly in steep slopes, and actually offered poor fields of fire. The Boers found it a gunner's dream and began a steady shellfire. The British were compelled to hang on under this searching bombardment, and many of those who stood up became easy targets for riflemen on nearby hills and, as Boers worked their way forward, around the rim of the feature too. Woodgate was killed and the devolution of command was muddled, with Lieutenant Colonel A. W. Thorneycroft, though not the senior officer in the area, being ordered to take command on the hill. The young Winston Churchill, present as an officer in a volunteer regiment, served as a messenger.

Boer artillery was not effectively challenged by British guns, and Buller, watching the battle from his command post on Mount Alice, failed to grip a situation which might still have slid either way. As darkness fell, both sides thought they had lost the battle and pulled back from the Kop: Churchill delivered a message from Warren to Thorneycroft telling him to hold on, only to hear that he had already issued orders for withdrawal. The dawn of the next day saw the earliest risers, the Boers, reoccupy the undefended summit. British dead numbered 383 and 1,054 were wounded, caused mostly by shellfire. Boer losses were about half of that.

British losses could not be made good with Indian or African troops. Boers and Britons were alike in pretending this was a white man's war. In fact they did not hesitate to arm the black 'scouts' when it suited them. But more British regulars sailed for South Africa and white citizens around the empire roused themselves for the first time to share in the burden of an imperial war. Lord Roberts arrived with Lord Kitchener as his chief of staff on 10 January 1900 to deploy over 180,000 men, the majority in line of supply posts, against elusive Boer resistance.

Roberts reached Modder River Station on 10 February with 60,000 troops. His cavalry commander, Lieutenant General John French, led a mounted force around the Boers' eastern flank. Kimberley was relieved on 15 February after French brushed aside Boer resistance in a 'charge' (more accurately an advance at the gallop in extended order) at Klip Drift. The cost in cavalry mounts was high; out of 5,000 horses that set off only 1,500 remained fit for service afterwards. Piet Cronjé moved west on the same day, hampered by the 400 wagons needed to transport the families of his men along with military supplies. They were surrounded near Paardeberg between pursuing British and the remnants of French's cavalry and a siege developed from 18 February. Roberts was indisposed, and Kitchener took command, mounting a controversial attack which failed. Roberts arrived on 19 February, and Cronjé surrendered with some 4,000 people on 27 February, the anniversary of Majuba.

Roberts's problems included vast distances, shortage of all-important fodder, and typhoid (enteric) fever amongst his troops. They were exacerbated by Kitchener's

reorganization of the transport system in mid-campaign which Roberts approved. However, the British outnumbered their adversaries and were able, time and again, to outflank them to enter Bloemfontein (13 March), Johannesburg (31 May), and Pretoria (5 June). After small detachments liberated Mafeking (17 May), there were ecstatic street celebrations across the white empire.

The Battle of the Tugela Heights (1900)

In Natal, meanwhile, Sir Redvers Buller's men had been in action at Vaalkranz on 5 February and had broken off the fight when it became apparent his artillery was unable to provide adequate counter-battery fire. By the third week of February the Boers had some 5,000 men in the hills north of Colenso and a half-dozen or so 75 mm field guns and possibly other ordnance. Buller disposed of about 25,000 men and 70 guns, but still had to cross the Tugela river and assault the heights beyond to open the way to Ladysmith.

On 21 February, with artillery covering it from hills south of the river, the 10th Brigade crossed and began an attack on what became known as Wynne's Hill, which the 11th Brigade took the next day. On 23 February Fitzroy Hart's 5th (Irish) Brigade assaulted Hart's Hill, further west, but the attackers gaining the top of it had 140 m (450 feet) of flat ground before them and trenches of Boer marksmen beyond. Artillery could not then provide covering fire so close and the fight reverted to a vicious firefight with small arms. The casualties of both sides were so great that a truce was arranged for 25 February to collect the wounded. The next day Pieters Hill, two summits westwards, was taken and then, again with close cover from artillery, Railway Hill was seized by the British. This left Hart's Hill, in the centre, untenable. The Boers streamed away northward and Ladysmith was entered by the British on the evening of 27 February.

East of Pretoria on 11–12 June Lord Roberts was held by a Transvaal force under Louis Botha before his Australians scaled Diamond Hill, enfilading the Boer line and forcing withdrawal. Advances in the north-eastern Orange Free State rounded up 4,000 Boers in the Brandwater basin (29 July). Buller, having advanced north from Natal by means of an unusually elegant seizure of Botha's Pass, west of Laing's Nek, on 8 June, demonstrated his skill as a field commander with the total defeat of Botha and the annihilation of the ZARP (police) force at Bergendal on 27 August. He followed this by pushing the rest of the Boer forces under Joos De la Rey and Jan Smuts out of the Mageliesberg mountains. President Paul Kruger left the country at Komati Poort on 11 September. Fourteen thousand Boers gave up their weapons. The British duly annexed the Boer republics, Buller and Roberts returned to England, and Kitchener assumed command of what most thought had now shrunk to a police action.

However, many Boers would not accept defeat. Hard fighting and the succession of defeats had removed old and inflexible leaders and brought to the fore enterprising and determined ones, notably Botha in eastern Transvaal, Christiaan De Wet in the Free State, and De la Rey in western Transvaal. Their aim was to harass their opponent into negotiations, and the British were more vulnerable than they seemed.

The British army was overstretched, trying to guard cities, gold mines, railway lines, and telegraph wires, escort convoys, and send out columns to pursue an elusive enemy.

Artillery moving up from Trichardt's Drift on the road that passes north of Spion Kop.

Its garrisons, baggage, and depots were exposed to raids, and many of its raw volunteers proved vulnerable when surprised or cornered. Even during Roberts's advance De Wet had pounced on isolated units at Sanna's Post, east of Bloemfontein (31 March 1900), when he was intending to destroy the waterworks and exacerbate the typhoid epidemic in the city. His mission was frustrated, but he took 428 prisoners. Four months later his brother Piet surrounded an Imperial Yeomanry battalion at Lindley (31 May 1900) and inflicted 80 casualties upon it before it gave in. Such feats grew common as the war progressed. Botha threatened Natal (7 September–2 October 1900), and De Wet broke into Cape Colony (10–28 February 1901). A few Boers even reached the sea at Lambert's Bay north of Cape Town (January 1901), exchanging shots with a British warship. Young Jan Smuts created confusion in the north-east Cape for many months (August 1901–April 1902). They did not always evade battle: De la Rey routed a British column at Tweebosch in western Transvaal and captured Lord Methuen on 25 February 1902.

But the Boers were hopelessly outnumbered and their movements were more often flights from pursuing columns than real offensives. Roberts had responded to Boer raids by burning farms and destroying livestock and stores to deprive commandos of supplies and shelter. Kitchener continued the policy, building lines of blockhouses linked by barbed wire. In an attempt to act humanely, women, children, surrendered Boers, and refugee blacks had been, during Roberts's time, housed in 'refugee' camps. Life in the camps was sometimes easier than subsistence on the war-torn veld, but malnutrition, disease, and neglect led to much suffering and many deaths, particularly of children. The evil was exposed by Emily Hobhouse, an Englishwoman who had been granted permission to visit the camps and deliver relief supplies. Her exposé was published in London in 1901, and liberal and international opinion was outraged. Patriotic opinion was unshaken, but the government was forced to appoint a commission of enquiry as a result of which administration of the camps passed to the civil authorities and conditions slowly improved. In all 27,927 white people, almost all women and children, died; records show 14,154 deaths, almost certainly fewer than in actuality, in the black camps. In considering these figures it is well to recall that most British deaths in the war resulted from disease; incompetence and ignorance injured everyone.

Originally devised to protect railways, the blockhouse lines were extended from mid-1901 into the countryside, dividing it into cul-de-sacs into which columns might sweep the commandos. Mounted regulars and volunteers, led by bright young commanders such as Colonel Michael Rimington, Brigadier General Herbert Plumer, and Colonel G. E. Benson, evolved into masterful horsemen adept at night marches and dawn attacks, often guided by some of the 5,000 or more Boers, mostly poor farmers, who abandoned the cause of their often wealthy leaders. By early 1902 British columns were methodically sweeping the countryside. Armoured trains mounted with artillery and searchlights patrolled railway lines. The inhabitants of burned farms were no longer taken into camps, but left to fend for themselves, which undermined Boer determination to resist. Boer leaders were faced with the choice of British rule or the destruction of their world.

Kitchener had proposed terms for peace as early as 7 March 1901, including voting rights as in Cape Colony for coloured people and a limited franchise for blacks. The 31 May 1902 peace agreement at Vereeniging led to a federated British South Africa. Boers and Britons shared power over non-white peoples, to whom the promises of votes were now forgotten by the British, and who outnumbered whites by four to one. It had taken nearly 500,000 soldiers from around the British empire, aided by the labour of 100,000 non-whites, to make British subjects of the Boers. Eight thousand blockhouses had been built and 6,000 km (3,730 miles) of barbed wire laid. In addition to those who died of disease and starvation, 8,000 British soldiers and 4,000 Boers had been killed in the fighting. Thirty thousand farms had been destroyed. Also destroyed were the hopes of non-whites who had expected land and citizenship after a British victory.

Further Reading

Chapter 1

Victor Davis Hanson started with *The Western Way of War: Infantry Battle in Classical Greece* (1989), and followed with other distinguished works. J. F. Lazenby, *The Spartan Army* (1985) and *The Defence of Greece* (1993), are masterly, and Donald Kagan's works, beginning with *The Outbreak of the Peloponnesian War* (1969), are invaluable. For the Romans at their peak see Adrian Goldsworthy, *The Roman Army at War* (1996) and in decline Hugh Elton, *Warfare in Roman Europe AD 350–425*. After *Rubicon*, his portrait of Caesar's age, Tom Holland wrote the sparkling *Persian Fire* (2005). For Alexander see A. B. Bosworth, *Conquest and Empire* (1988), and N. G. L. Hammond, *The Macedonian State* (1989) and *The Genius of Alexander the Great* (1989). Although there is no scholarly military history of ancient Egypt, Ian Shaw, *Egyptian Warfare and Weapons* (1991) is a well illustrated introduction. George Roux, *Ancient Iraq* (3rd edn. 1992) is useful for Mesopotamia, and Trevor Bryce, *The Kingdom of the Hittites* (1998) is strong on military aspects. Yigael Yadin's *The Art of Warfare in Biblical Lands* (1963) remains valuable.

Chapter 2

The newcomer might start with Brent D. Shaw, 'War and Violence', in Glen Bowerstock, Peter Brown, and Oleg Grabar, *Late Antiquity: A Guide to the Postclassical World* (1999), moving on to Guy Halsall (ed.), *Warfare and Society in the Barbarian West* (2002). The best guide to Byzantine warfare is John F. Haldon, *Warfare, State and Society in the Byzantine World* (1999). For the Anglo-Saxons see Richard P. Abels, *Lordship and Military Obligation in Anglo-Saxon England* (1988), and for the Franks, Paul Fouracre, 'The Frankish Empire to 814', in Rosamond McKitterick (ed.), *The New Cambridge Medieval History* (1995). Charles Oman, *History of the Art of War in the Middle Ages* (rev. 1923) and Hans Delbrück, *Medieval Warfare* (trans. 1982) were outclassed by R. C. Smail's *Crusading Warfare* (1956). Maurice Keen (ed.), *Medieval Warfare: A History* (1999) contains work by leading authorities. Matthew Strickland, *War and Chivalry* (1996), (as editor)

Anglo-Norman Warfare (1992), Michael Prestwich, *Armies and Warfare in the Middle Ages* (1996), John France, *Western Warfare in the Age of the Crusades* (1999), and Nicholas Hooper and Matthew Bennett, *Cambridge Illustrated History of Warfare: The Middle Ages* (1995) are all valuable. Jim Bradbury is a helpful guide to *The Medieval Archer* (1995) and *The Medieval Siege* (1992).

The best survey is Jonathan Riley-Smith, *The Crusades: A Short History* (1987). C. Marshal's *Warfare and the Latin East* (1992) takes Smail's story forward. John France discusses the First Crusade in *Victory in the East* (1994). David Nicolle, *Medieval Warfare Source Book* (1996) is invaluable. For specialist studies, see R. Rogers, *Latin Siege Warfare in the Twelfth Century* (1992), Helen Nicholson, *Templars, Hospitallers and Teutonic Knights* (1993), and Hugh Kennedy, *Crusader Castles* (1994).

For Crécy see Andrew Ayton, 'The English Army and the Normandy Campaign of 1346', in David Bates and Anne Curry (eds.), *England and Normandy in the Middle Ages* (1994), Matthew Bennett, 'The Development of Battle Tactics in the Hundred Years War', in Anne Curry and Michael Hughes (eds.), *Arms, Armies and Fortifications in the Hundred Years War* (1994), and Kelly DeVries, *Infantry Warfare in the Early Fourteenth Century* (1996). Jonathan Sumption, *The Hundred Years' War* (1991) is excellent, despite idiosyncratic assessment of Crécy. Robert Hardy offers wisdom in 'The Longbow', in Curry and Hughes (eds.), *Arms, Armies*. Matthew Bennett's popular *Agincourt 1415* (1991) is a sound starting point, and C. T. Allmand's *Henry V* (new edn. 1997) has lots to offer. Much earlier material has been outclassed by Anne Curry, *Agincourt: A New History* (2005) and Juliet Barker, *Agincourt: The King, the Campaign, the Battle* (2005).

For the Wars of the Roses see John Gillingham's popular *The Wars of the Roses* (1981) and Anthony Goodman's more academic *The Wars of the Roses* (1981).

Chapter 3

Michael Roberts's trail-blazing *The Military Revolu-*

tion 1560–1660 (1956) is worth reading, but Geoffrey Parker, *The Military Revolution* (2nd edn. 1996) and Jeremy Black, *A Military Revolution?* (1991) take the debate on.

Martyn Bennett offers a tautly stretched survey in *The Civil Wars in Britain and Ireland* (1997), and John Kenyon and Jane Ohlmeyer edited scholarly articles in *The Civil Wars* (1998). Ian Gentles, *The New Model Army* (1992) is comprehensive. Ronald Hutton, *The Royalist War Effort* has happily been reprinted (1999). See *Naseby: The Decisive Battle* (1996) where Glenn Foard sifts archaeological evidence, and P. R. Newman and P. R. Roberts, *Marston Moor 1644* (2003), based on detailed knowledge of terrain. Geoffrey Parker, *The Thirty Years War* (2nd edn. 1997) is the best history of that brutal conflict.

Christopher Duffy marches triumphantly across the eighteenth century. As well as *Fire and Stone* (1975) and *The Fortress in the Age of Vauban and Frederick the Great* (1985), he has painted portraits of the armies of Frederick the Great and Maria Theresa, written a cracking account of the rising of 1745, and his *The Military Experience in the Age of Reason* (1988) is wonderful. Jeremy Black, *European Warfare 1660–1815* (1994) is the standard survey, though John Childs, *Armies and Warfare in Europe* (1982) holds up well. Having dominated the Napoleonic period with *The Campaigns of Napoleon* (1966), David Chandler wrote *The Art of Warfare in the Age of Marlborough* (1976). There is no good comprehensive study of the Seven Years War: for its British background Alan Guy, *Oeconomy and Discipline* (1985) and J. A. Houlding's *Fit for Service* (1981) are essential.

Chapter 4

T. C. W. Blanning, *The French Revolutionary Wars* (1996) and John Lyn, *The Bayonets of the Republic* (1996) are excellent. Hew Strachan's *European Armies and the Conduct of War* (1983) is good on this period and much else. Charles Esdaile, *The Wars of Napoleon* (1995) and David Gates, *The Napoleonic Wars* (1997) are reliable guides. Adam Zamoyski, *1812: Napoleon's March on Moscow* (2004) is worth reading, as is Peter Hofschröer's controversial contribution to the Waterloo debate (1998 and 1999). A flotilla of books greeted the 200th anniversary of Trafalgar: a newcomer would do best to start with N. A. M. Rodger's incomparable *The Command of the Ocean* (2004).

Trevor Royle, *The Great Crimean War* (1999) is the best general history, although Ian Fletcher and Natalia Ischenko, *The Crimean War: A Clash of Empires* (2004) deserve credit for considering both sides. Andrew D. Lambert, *The Crimean War: British Grand Strategy against Russia* (1990) is a painstaking

study, while Mark Adkin, *The Charge: The Real Reason Why the Light Brigade Was Lost* (1996) comes as close as we can to assessing responsibility.

The 1859 Italian campaign remains a poorly tilled field: Arnold Blumberg, *A Carefully Planned Accident* (1990) is the best modern survey. The Austro-Prussian War of 1866 is better covered. Gordon Craig, *The Battle of Königgrätz* (1965) and Dennis E. Showalter, *Railroads and Rifles* (1975) are worth reading, but Geoffrey Wawro, *The Austro-Prussian War* (1996) is the best study. The magisterial Michael Howard, *The Franco-Prussian War* (1961) still astonishes.

Chapter 5

Hew Strachan, *The First World War* (2003) is the most accessible study, and volume one of his projected trilogy, *The First World War* (2001), is in a class of its own. Terence Zuber reappraises German strategy in *Inventing the Schlieffen Plan* (2002). Sewell Tyng, *The Campaign of the Marne 1914* (1935) is the best survey, and I remain devoted to Edward Spears, *Liaison 1914* (1930). Anthony Farrar-Hockley, *Death of an Army* (1967) is a good account of First Ypres. I disagree with Alan Clark, *The Donkeys* (1961), not least about the 'quote' on which its title is based, but it is a striking example of its school. There are now two useful books on Loos: Gordon Corrigan, *Loos 1915* (2005) and Niall Cherry, *Most Unfavourable Ground* (2005).

Alistair Horne, *The Price of Glory* (1962) is durable, although Malcolm Brown, *Verdun 1916* (1999) is the best account in English. Stéphane Audoine-Rousseau's book on the French soldier *Men at War 1914–18* (1992) is indispensable. For the Somme, see Gary Sheffield, *The Somme* (2003) and Peter Hart's anecdotal *The Somme* (2005). Peter H. Liddle, *Passchendaele in Perspective* (1997) contains essays, the best very useful. Martin Marix Evans provides a popular narrative in *Passchendaele* (2005), and in *Passchendaele* (2000) Nigel Steel and Peter Hart see the battle through the eyes of participants. J. P. Harris, *Men, Ideas and Tanks* (1995) has illuminating comments on Cambrai, and his *Amiens to Armistice* (2003) deals well with the last Hundred Days. Scholars like Tim Travers, Paddy Griffith, John Bourne, Robin Prior, and Trevor Wilson have all made notable contributions to our understanding of the evolution of armies and tactics on the Western Front.

Norman Stone, *The Eastern Front 1914–17* (1975) is the best survey, and Holger Herwig, *The First World War: Germany and Austria* (1997) paints the wider picture. For the Italian Front see John Gooch, 'Italy during the First World War', in Allan R. Millett and Williamson Murray, *The First World War* (1988). For

Mesopotamia, A. J. Barker, *The Neglected War* (1967) is illuminated by Bryan Cooper Busch, *Britain, India and the Arabs* (1971). Palestine is overshadowed by Allenby and Lawrence: David Bullock, *Allenby's War* (1988) and Matthew Hughes, *Allenby and British Strategy* (1999) are the best starting points. Robert Rhodes James, *Gallipoli* (1965) and Michael Hickey, *Gallipoli* (1995) are reliable surveys, and Tim Travers, *Gallipoli 1915* (2004) offers perceptive judgement. The best Australian history is L. A. Carlyon's towering *Gallipoli* (2002). Peter Chasseaud and Peter Doyle provide new evidence in *Grasping Gallipoli* (2005). For other 'sideshows' see Byron Farwell, *The Great War in Africa* (1986), Melvin Page, *Africa and the First World War* (1987), Charles Miller, *The Battle for the Bundu* (1974), and Alan Palmer, *The Gardeners of Salonika* (1965).

Andrew Gordon, *The Rules of the Game* (1996) is fundamental to understanding Jutland, and John Campbell, *Jutland* (1986) is excellent for technical detail. V. E. Tarrant considers the submarine threat in both world wars in *The U-Boat Offensive 1914–1945* (1989).

Chapter 6

R. J. Overy, *Why the Allies Won* (1995) and R. A. C. Parker, *The Study for Survival* (1989) are good introductions. For 1940 see Robert Doughty, *The Breaking Point* (1990) and Karl-Heinz Freiser's revealing *The Blitzkrieg Legend* (2005). Hugh Sebag-Montefiore, *Dunkirk* (2006) is the best recent study.

John Erikson's *The Road to Stalingrad* (1975) and *The Road to Berlin* (1983) pointed the way ahead. For Stalingrad see William Craig, *The Enemy at the Gates* (1973) and Antony Beevor, *Stalingrad* (1998). Mark Healy, *Kursk 1943* (1992) is a good survey, while David M. Glantz and Harold S. Orenstein, *The Battle for Kursk 1943* (1999) translated the Russian official history. Stephen J. Zaloga, *Bagration 1944* (1996) charts the destruction of Army Group Centre. Christopher Duffy, *Red Storm on the Reich* (1991) deals with the last campaign, and Antony Beevor, *Berlin: The Downfall* (2002) is suitably shocking. Max Hastings, *Armageddon* (2004) examines the final assault on Germany. Catherine Merridale, *Ivan's War* (2005) is an admirable account of the Red Army.

Niall Barr, *Pendulum of War* (2004) and John Bierman and Colin Smith, *Alamein* (2002) deal with El Alamein. Carlo d'Este, *Bitter Victory: The Battle for Sicily* (1988) and *Fatal Decision: Anzio and the Battle for Rome* (1991) are superb. John Ellis, *Cassino* (1984) and Matthew Powell, *Monte Cassino* (2003) stand ahead of the field. Carlo d'Este, *Decision in Normandy* (1983) is the wisest overview of Normandy. For Arnhem see A. D. Harvey, *Arnhem* (2001) and R. J. Kershaw, *It Never Snows in September* (1994).

Raymond Callahan, *The Worst Disaster* (1977) is a balanced account of the fall of Malaya and Singapore. For Pacific strategy see H. P. Willmott, *Empires in the Balance* (1982). Louis Allen, *Burma: The Longest War* (1984) is excellent, as are John Colvin's account of Kohima, *Not Ordinary Men* (2002) and, for the Kohima-Imphal campaign, David Rooney, *Burma Victory* (2002). Discussion of Pearl Harbor focuses on the debate over American foreknowledge: H. P. Willmott, *Pearl Harbor* (1990) is a good corrective. His *Battle of Leyte Gulf* (2005) and Hugh Bicheno, *Midway* (2001) are both helpful.

R. J. Overy, *The Battle of Britain* (2004) is the best introduction. A more controversial issue is examined by Charles Messenger in *'Bomber' Harris and the Strategic Bombing Offensive* (1973) and Alan J. Levine, *The Strategic Bombing of Germany* (1992). For specific operations see Martin Middlebrook, *The Nuremberg Raid* (1973), Frederick Taylor, *Dresden* (2004), and Paul Addison and Jeremy Crang (eds.), *Firestorm* (2004). Good recent studies of the submarine war are David F. White, *Bitter Ocean* (2006) and Bernard Ireland, *The Battle of the Atlantic* (2003).

Chapter 7

Ross Hassig, *War and Society in Ancient Mesoamerica* (1992) and *Mexico and the Spanish Conquest* (1994) are a good start, and John Hemming, *The Conquest of the Incas* (rev. 1983) is also useful.

Fred Anderson, *The Crucible of War* (2000) deals with 'The French and Indian War', and Ian. K. Steele offers novel analysis in *Warpaths* (1994). The War of Independence remains prey to popular historiography warped by nationality. Jeremy Black, *The War for America* is an excellent overview. Stanley Weintraub, *Iron Tears* (2005) puts the conflict in its international context, and Hugh Bicheno, *Rebels and Redcoats* (2003) is an acerbic corrective to many earlier works. Lawrence Babits's account of Cowpens, *A Devil of a Whipping* (1988), is the exemplar of a single-battle study. The War of 1812 is well covered in the updated J. Mackay Hitsman, *The Incredible War of 1812* (1999) and Donald R. Hickey, *The War of 1812* (1989). George E. F. Stanley, *The War of 1912: Land Operations* (1983) is a thorough account.

The American Civil War is a vast field. The best overviews are Peter J. Parish, *The American Civil War* (1975), Herman Hattaway and Archer Jones, *How the North Won* (1983), James M. McPherson, *The Battle Cry of Freedom* (1988), and Susan-Mary Grant and Brian Holden Reid (eds.), *The American Civil War* (2000). Michael Shaars's novel *The Killer Angels* says something that even the best historians cannot. But for the latter, see Edwin B. Codrington, *The*

Gettysburg Campaign (1997) and Hugh Bicheno, Gettysburg (2001).

For all the success of Dee Brown, Bury my Heart at Wounded Knee (1970), Robert M. Utley offers wiser comment on the nineteenth-century Indian Wars in Frontiersmen in Blue (1967) and subsequent books. The Spanish-American War is summarized in Joseph Smith, The Spanish American War (1994) and David Musicant, Empire by Default (1998).

The 1982 battle for the Falklands/Malvinas has a two-volume official history by Lawrence Freedman (2005), which might be read alongside Hugh Bicheno's very unofficial Razor's Edge (2006). The latter's political judgements are harsh, but its reconstruction of the war's battles will probably never be bettered.

Chapter 8

Frank A. Kierman Jr. and John K. Fairbank (eds.) have useful articles in Chinese Ways in Warfare (1974). Arthur Waldron, The Great Wall of China (1990) and Joseph Needham, The Gunpowder Epic (1989) are fascinating. Chung Tan, China and the Brave New World (1978) is the most comprehensive account of the Opium War of 1839–42.

Robert Marshall Storm from the East (1993) remains the best popular survey of the Mongols. See C. E. Boswell, 'The Saljuq and Mongol Periods', in J. A. Boyle (ed.), The Cambridge History of Iran (1968) and, for the Ottomans, Stanford J. Shaw, Empire of the Ghazis (The History of the Ottoman Empire and Modern Turkey, vol. i) (1975). V. J. Parry and M. E. Yapp, War, Technology and Society in the Middle East (1975) bursts with good sense, and Steven Runciman, The Fall of Constantinople (1965) remains a delight.

Stephen Turnbull, Samurai: The World of the Warrior (2003) is a sound introduction, taken further by Karl F. Friday, Hired Swords (1992) and Makoto Sugawa, The Ancient Samurai (1986). Richard Connaughton, The War of the Rising Sun and Tumbling Bear (1988) and J. N. Westwood, Russia against Japan (1986) are accessible accounts of 1904–5.

G. B. Malleson, The Decisive Battles of India (1885) and George Bruce, Six Battles for India (1969) remain helpful. For the Sikh Wars see Hugh Cook, The Sikh

Wars (1975) and the relevant chapters in Byron Farwell, Queen Victoria's Little Wars (1972). T. A. Heathcote offers the wisest summary of the Afghan Wars (1980). Patrick Macrory, Kabul Catastrophe (1986) is the best account of the First Afghan War, as is Brian Robson, The Road to Kabul (1986) of the Second. Saul David, The Indian Mutiny (2003) is a first-rate study.

Martin Windrow's book on Dien Bien Phu, The Last Valley (2004), has superseded Bernard Fall's account. George Herring, America's Longest War (3rd edn. 1996) is the standard military history of the Vietnam War, though it is thin on its latter period, for which Ronald H. Spector, After Tet (1993) partially compensates.

For the Arab–Israeli Wars see I. J. Bicketon and M. N. Pearson, The Arab–Israeli Conflict (1993) and A. H. Cordesman and A. R. Wagner, Lessons of Modern War (1991). Avigdor Kahalani, The Heights of Courage (1984) is a snapshot of the battle for the Golan.

The Gulf War of 1990–91 is well covered by Lawrence Freedman and Efraim Karsh, The Gulf Conflict (1993). The second war is admirably surveyed in Williamson Murray and Robert H. Scales Jr., The Iraq War (2003). My Dusty Warriors (2006) is a portrait of a British battalion in southern Iraq in 2004.

Chapter 9

For the French colonization of Algeria see Kenneth J. Perkins, Qaids, Captains and Colons (1980). For North Africa see Douglas Porch, The Conquest of Morocco (1982) and The Conquest of the Sahara (1984). Bruce Vandervort gives a reliable overview in Wars of Imperial Conquest in Africa (1998). Robin Neillands, The Dervish Wars is a readable survey of the events of 1880–98, and Winston Churchill's account, The River War, was last reprinted in 2002. The Anglo-Zulu war of 1879 remains popular and controversial. There are two good recent histories, Adrian Greaves, Crossing the Buffalo (2005) and Ian Knight, Brave Men's Blood (2003). Battles are regularly reappraised: see James Bancroft, Rorke's Drift (2003) and Mike Snook, How Can Man Die Better? (2005). Thomas Pakenham, The Boer War (1979) and Bill Nasson, The South African War (1999) remain the best general studies of this conflict.

Index

PICTURE ACKNOWLEDGEMENTS

Illustrations are © Topfoto with the following exceptions

6, 27, 48, 314 Topfoto/HIP
3 James Arnold
40 Topfoto/Woodmansterne
84, 113, 126 Topfoto/RV
58, 174, 354 Martin Marix Evans
286 Library of Congress, Prints & Photographs Division, Civil War Photographs, [reproduction number, LC-B811-2646.]